75p

THE THEORY AND PRACTICE
OF SOCIALISM

THE THEORY AND PRACTICE
OF SOCIALISM

by

JOHN STRACHEY

Author of

The Coming Struggle for Power, The Nature of Capitalist Crisis
and *The Menace of Fascism*

Emancipation of Labour is the only worthy object of
political warfare . . . that those who till the soil shall be its
first masters, that those who raise food shall be its first partakers, that those who build mansions shall live in them. . . .

GEORGE JULIAN HARNEY

Outside of Socialism there is no salvation for mankind from
war, hunger and the further destruction of millions and millions
of human beings.

LENIN

LONDON
VICTOR GOLLANCZ LTD
1936

First published November 1936
Second impression November 1936

Printed in Great Britain by
The Camelot Press Ltd., London and Southampton

CONTENTS

CONTENTS

PART III
SOCIALISM AND THE WORKING CLASS

PART IV
THE SCIENCE OF SOCIAL CHANGE

INTRODUCTION

THIS book attempts to say plainly what the working class movement of the world is striving for.

Such general re-statements of socialism and communism
become necessary from time to time. For socialism and communism are living, growing concepts. Moreover, there are to-day
special reasons for attempting to say exactly what socialism and
communism are, and are not. Socialism has now been established
in one of the major countries of the world. Hence a more positive,
descriptive, constructive, and a less analytical, negative, and
critical, approach to the subject is now possible. Formerly
socialism existed only as a doctrine, a critique of things as they
are, and an aspiration towards things as they might be. To-day
it exists as the institutions of a great state. Before this incarna-
tion the positive approach attempted in these pages was
impossible; it would have led to no more than fantasy-building
and dreaming. Then it was necessary to put almost all the
emphasis on the analysis of capitalism; now it is possible to shift
the emphasis to the elucidation of socialism.

But the capitalist five-sixths of the world also supply urgent
reasons for making an attempt to re-define the goal of socialists
and communists. In the highly developed capitalist empires, in
Britain for example and to a lesser extent in America, there exist
long-established movements, based upon the working class,
which have the abolition of capitalism and the establishment of
socialism as their objective. These movements possess an
enormous literature and a rich tradition of socialism. But some
of the events of the last two decades have tended to blur the
conception of socialism as the sole possible solution for the
world's present agony. By a tragic paradox, at the very moment
when socialism has been securely established on the face of the
earth for the first time in history, and when the conditions of
human life in the rest of the world cry aloud for the socialist
solution, some of the oldest and most powerful socialist movements, such as the British, have allowed themselves to become
confused, to lose direction and so to slacken their efforts to
produce a living realization of the necessity of social change
in the minds of men.

The causes of this extraordinary event will be discussed in the
concluding pages of this book. In the case of the British movement they are not far to seek. The British labour and socialist
movement has suffered severe defeats in the last fifteen years
because its comprehension of both the socialist objective and of
the methods necessary to social change was inadequate. This inadequacy resulted in an attempt to go forward towards socialism
along a road which could only lead, and which did lead, to temporary defeat. But already it is clear that the effect of the set backs
to the British labour movement which culminated in the political
defeat of 1931 could not, in contemporary conditions, last long.
In 1848 the defeat of Chartism, which was the first wave of
British working class revolt against capitalism, set our movement back by nearly fifty years; the equally severe defeats of
1926 and 1931 could delay the rising of the tide by a decade
at most. For the tide of British working class resistance to
capitalism is once more rising. But what is not yet decided is the
vital question of the degree of political and economic clarity to
which the British workers will attain in this new phase of their
century-old struggle. They can only win if this time not only the
leaders, but every active member of the British working class
movement, attains to a higher consciousness of the goal for
which he is struggling, and of the necessary methods of struggle.

There has appeared in the last five years in Britain a quite
unprecedented volume of literature, both in books and in
periodicals, aiming at the achievement of this higher level of
political consciousness and clarity in the working class movement. This literature is symptomatic of the fact that the events
of the last fifteen years have not been in vain. Now that once
again life itself is forcing the British workers to feel that socialism
is their only way out, they are coming to realize also the need for
the adoption of new methods and new principles of political
struggle. And this is doubly necessary. For not only did the old
methods prove totally inadequate but also the new wave of
working class activity is rising in conditions which are far more
complex and far more stormy than any which have ever before
faced our movment. The first aim of this book is to make a
contribution to the creation of that sharp, clear, passionate
realization both of what socialism is and of how it may be

established, without which the British working class movement cannot triumph in the struggles that lie before it.

In America the situation is very different. There the economic and social forces capable of creating a working class movement determined on the abolition of capitalism and the establishment of socialism only came to maturity with the 1929 crisis. But already such a movement is beginning to take shape. That America will possess, within the next decade, a powerful labour movement is not in doubt. Moreover, that movement will almost certainly be in some sense and degree anti-capitalist and pro-socialist. But what is not decided, and what is all-important, is the quality of the socialism of the coming American labour movement. Hence in America, even more than in Britain, though for different reasons, the need of the hour is the unceasing definition, re-statement and popularization of the basic principles of socialism and communism. The second, and equally important, purpose of this book is to make a contribution to this work.

In this connection it may be well to define at the outset how the words socialism and communism are used in these pages. For the history of both the working class movement and of the social science which that movement has evolved out of its struggles may be unfamiliar to some readers. Throughout the last century Marx and Engels used the words socialism and communism almost indifferently. Moreover, up till 1917 Lenin referred to himself as a Socialist or Social Democrat. It was not until the April of that year that he proposed to change the name of the Party which he led. He made his proposal in these words: " I am coming to the last point, the name of our party. We must call ourselves the Communist party—just as Marx and Engels called themselves Communists. . . . Mankind can pass directly from Capitalism only into Socialism, i.e. into social ownership of the means of production and the distribution of products according to the work of the individual. Our party looks farther ahead than that: Socialism is bound sooner or later to ripen into Communism, whose banner bears the motto, ' From each according to his ability, to each according to his needs.' " (The " April Theses.")

Socialism and communism are exactly defined in Chapter XI

of this book. But already the reader will see that Lenin states that communists are persons who work for the establishment of socialism and that they call themselves communists rather than socialists for certain historical reasons, and also because they look forward to a state of human society beyond socialism for which they reserve the word communism.

It is true, however, that there are important differences within the working class movement as to the proper methods, policies, and forms of organization by means of which capitalism may be replaced by socialism. These differences are discussed in the latter part of this book.

The problems with which this book attempts to grapple seem to me to be worthy of the attention not only of the British and American workers but also of those whose economic existence is relatively satisfactory. For some of this fortunate minority such questions as the comparative merits of economic systems, based respectively on production for profit and production for use, may seem remote from the daily business of their lives. But they are not. Those of us to whom fate has been comparatively kind would like to ignore these problems, for they put into question the very foundations of our contemporary society. We inevitably long to be allowed to lead our own personal lives against the background of a society which, however imperfect, is at any rate stable. But the society in which we live is not stable. We can no more escape its perturbations by refusing to take part in the social struggles of our times, than a frightened passenger can escape from a shipwreck by locking himself up in his cabin.

Thus ever-increasing numbers of relatively well-circumstanced men and women are now finding themselves impelled to examine the basis of contemporary society. A growing number of them are beginning to find that they cannot live lives which yield them an adequate degree of either mental or physical satisfaction in the existing world. Amongst the economically privileged there are, as there always have been, men and women who find it impossible to bear in silent complacency the sufferings, which they now see to be totally unnecessary, of by far the greater number of their fellow men. But it is the peculiar characteristic of our times that the property-owning members of society are themselves beginning to experience the effects of a contracting economic system.

In Britain and America the greater number of them have as yet maintained their incomes fairly well. But to an ever-increasing extent they find, and will find, that there are no constructive tasks left for them within the framework of capitalism. They will find that no longer can they, as did the fathers and grandfathers of the contemporary capitalist class, create both a fortune for themselves and some major productive enterprise (some new railway, some great plant, or the like) for the community. For the remaining roads to wealth lie increasingly through a mere manipulation of the ownership of existing enterprises, the merging of companies, the pushing of stocks, the shuffling and reshuffling of shares. Gambling, and the cheating which always goes with it, become more and more the essential occupations of the top layer of contemporary society. To such lengths has this prostitution of the older types of economic incentive now gone that the foremost theorists of the capitalist world are themselves profoundly disturbed by it. Mr. Maynard Keynes in his most recent book,[1] for example, complains that " the capital development of a country " has become the " by-product of the activities of a casino."

Morevoer, even in these purely financial fields, as well as in productive industry and in Imperial government, the positions of power tend more and more to become hereditary. The directors' sons, and sons-in-law, and nephews, fill the avenues to promotion. They sit in the Parliaments, the bank parlours, the managing directors' rooms, and in the headquarters staffs of the imperial apparatus of administration and coercion. Capitalist imperialism ossifies. With every decade the order of its hierarchy comes to have less and less relation to merit. The able serve the dull. The insensitive, the foolish, and the brutal command; the intelligent and the humane obey.

It is true that in the vast apparatus of the British and American systems many relatively important posts are still open to the claims of talent. Thousands of able architects, scientists, doctors, and civil servants are still employed on interesting and apparently constructive tasks by the great corporations and by

[1] *The General Theory of Employment, Interest and Money.*

the governmental agencies. And as yet many of these fortunate men and women feel satisfied with their work. But one by one even these workers will be unable to prevent themselves from realizing that the decay of the economic system within which they work is bringing to naught, or turning to vile uses, their most brilliant and devoted activities.

The frustration of the contemporary scientist, however well paid and well employed, is now a familiar theme. A notorious example is afforded by the chemist, bio-chemist, or physicist, who sees his work used more and more exclusively to perfect the technique of slaughter. But the technical inventor who produces a device which will enable a hundred men to produce the current supply of some article, where a thousand were required before, is in a similar case. For nothing is now more frequent than that the end result of his invention should be no net increase in the wealth of the world, and the ruin, by unemployment and destitution, of nine hundred of his fellow men. Or, again, the contemporary scientist, having developed some unquestionably useful device, may take it to market and may find a buyer; but his device is now often bought by some great Trust, not for use, but in order to prevent its use—so that existing plant and machinery may not be made obsolete.

The young doctor often finds that at the end of his training he must buy the right to attend to the medical needs of the small class of persons who can afford to pay him. If he (or she) cannot afford to buy a practice, he may well be forced into idleness, surrounded by men and women who suffer and die for lack of his services. For the invisible restraints of the economic system bar the way between his skill and their suffering. Slowly but surely the intolerable irrationality of such an arrangement must break through the formidable conditioning to an acceptance of the world as it is, which the young doctor (like every other young professional man) undergoes in the process of his training.

The situation of members of the other professions is in some ways less obviously affected by their social environment. At certain times and in certain places particular professions still enjoy periods of prosperity. In Britain, for example, the architectural profession, after some years of severe depression, is now (1936) well employed—just as were the architects of America before

1929. But even in these periods of intermittent, if intense, activity the modern architect must surely sometimes experience disgust at the use to which his talents are put? For example, the American architects in the boom period often derived the utmost satisfaction from solving the technical problems presented by new types of buildings, such as the skyscraper. But, after all, the ultimate purpose of a building is to serve, not as an exercise in statics, but as a place in which to live or work. Hence the architect must in the end be frustrated if his building remains for ever empty.

Again, modern architects can, and do, produce elaborate and technically excellent plans for the rehousing of the population on modern standards. And as yet the majority of British and American architects suppose that this is a technical problem. They cannot conceive what communists and socialists can mean when they say that the existing economic system makes the rehousing of the population economically and politically impossible. They believe that the fact that capitalism has never yet anywhere been able to undertake such an enterprise, and that the soviets, in spite of their inferior technical and material resources, actually are doing so, must be due to some peculiar accident. And yet in this field, too, the sheer force of experience will in the end drive one architect after another to look into the question of whether the frustration of the purpose of a growing proportion of his work is no accident, but an inherent and predicable effect of the existing social and economic system.

Another category of intellectual workers whose devotion to and enthusiasm for their work attest their earnest sense of its social importance are the teachers. And no doubt many British and American teachers still feel that they can constructively contribute to human welfare. This introduction is written soon after the series of teachers' conferences which are held in Britain during the Easter holidays. In the 1936 conferences teacher after teacher from the great distressed areas of Britain rose to report that their pupils were too undernourished to learn much.[1] (In America during recent years there have been states and cities—as, for instance, Chicago—where the teacher was as hungry as the pupil; for during many months they received no pay.) It must

[1] See p. 328 for figures upon this point.

surely begin to occur to the teaching profession that the first thing which it is necessary for us, and for them, to learn is how to arrange our economic life in such a way that we do not keep our children's minds in the numbness of semi-starvation.

In a very few, and relatively very small, fields of human activity (of which the book publishing trade is a good example) the able and enterprising, *if they are equipped with or can command the necessary capital*, can still find their way to success and independence in free competition with their fellows. How relatively narrow those remaining fields of genuinely competitive endeavour now are can only be envisaged by recalling that once the whole field was of this character. Once it was true that for those who had, or could obtain access to, a relatively moderate sum of capital (*but only for them*) there were great opportunities of independent success. But in one sphere after another the process of trustification and monopolization has gone forward.

It is true that the great privately owned corporations in banking, industry, commerce, and newspaper publication, which have now largely taken the place of the freely competing individual firms, offer young men attractive careers as their officers. But these are the careers of well-paid subordinates. The ownership and control remain in the hands of a more and more hereditary hierarchy of families. The broad purposes of these controlling families cannot be even questioned by the best paid employee. If they should be anti-social, he will be as powerless to affect them as the worker at the bench.

The higher officers of the state form another large group of relatively well-paid and secure workers. Such skilled civil servants may, and often do, feel that they are performing an invaluable function. A British civil servant may help to build up a system of unemployment insurance administration which undeniably saves whole districts from starvation. He may, and often does, derive great satisfaction from such work. But in the end the fact that the decay of the present economic system has alone produced the irrational problem of unemployment, which he spends his life in alleviating, should penetrate to his consciousness. Or, again, the imperial administrator may help to operate, often with devoted labours, the administrative machine which maintains peace and order in a sub-continent. Many Indian civil servants have up till now felt satisfied by such a life work. But can they ultimately fail to notice that the net effect of their work for the Indian people has been a steady, and now steep, decline in the Indian standard of life ?

The truth is that a contracting economic system brings to naught the best efforts of every type of intellectual worker. If society is confined within ever narrower limits; if the opportunities for constructive work grow more and more meagre, then the community must needs show those dreadful symptoms of decay which Shakespeare catalogued in his sixty-sixth sonnet :

And art made tongue-tied by authority,
And folly—doctor like—controlling skill,
And simple truth miscalled simplicity,
And captive good attending captain ill.

The frustrations of our epoch, although not yet universal, are growing. Of those who already experience them, communists and socialists ask only that they should not rest till they have satisfied themselves as to their cause. Of those who can still feel that their work is fruitful, we ask them only to notice the prediction that sooner or later their province, too, will be invaded by the symptoms of social decay. They may not believe us now. But we believe that experience can, and will, convince them.

Moreover, over us all, the employed and the unemployed, the prosperous and the destitute, there now hangs the prospect of war. This prospect as it advances must tend to prevent all constructive effort. For why should we build targets for the bombs, prevent the tubercle bacillus from destroying lungs destined for the poison gas, or administer with sterling probity the affairs of a city which may soon be uninhabited ? If men do not succeed in realizing that there is an alternative social order ready for their construction, they will despair when they realize the general frustration which is involved in the decay of the present order. If the best men and women of every class would save themselves from this despair, and from the personal degeneration which such despair brings with it, they must turn their attention to social science. For a science of society has now been evolved which can enable us to be rid of capitalism, and then to lay down social foundations upon which constructive work for the individual will once more be possible.

The best men and women of every class in Britain and America will come to the conclusion that they cannot find a worthy purpose for their lives except by participation in the organized movement to change the world.

Part I

THE ECONOMIC SYSTEM

Chapter I

Capitalist Production for Profit

THE economic and social system under which the British and American people now live is commonly called capitalism. By this word capitalism we mean an economic system under which the fields, factories and mines are owned by individuals and groups of individuals. These means of production, as they are called, are worked by those who do not own them, for the profit of those who do. Under capitalism it is profit making, not love, that makes the world go round. For it is the expectation of making a profit which induces those who own the above means of production to permit them to be used.

But profit making is not only the incentive, it is also the regulator of capitalist production. Under capitalism it is not only the object, it is the very *condition*, of production that a profit should result. Those things, that is to say, which will yield a profit can and will be produced, *but those things alone*. For anybody who produces things which do not, either directly or indirectly, yield a profit will sooner or later go bankrupt, lose his ownership of the means of production, and so cease to be an independent producer. Capitalism, in other words, uses profitability as the criterion, or test, of whether or not any given thing should be produced, and, if so, of how much of it should be produced.

Now the test of profitability ensures that those things, and only those things, for which there is demand shall be produced. Profit is, as it were, a magnet which draws production after demand. For it is profitable to produce those things for which there is a demand, and unprofitable to produce those things for which there is no demand.[1]

But things are not either in demand or not in demand. The demand for them varies in strength. Under capitalism it will be profitable to produce more and more of those things for which there is an increasing demand, and less and less of those things for which there is a decreasing demand. Thus our productive

[1] Whence demand comes, and whether it is not largely created by the producers themselves, is another matter, and one which the exponents of capitalism have somewhat neglected.

resources are continually being pulled by the magnet of profit towards the production of those things for which there is an increasing demand, and away from the production of those things for which there is a diminishing demand.

This is how the capitalist system works. The question is, Does it work well or badly? You would certainly suppose, would you not, that such a system as this would work exceedingly well? It seems to contain in this ingenious device of drawing production after demand by the magnet of profit a method of ensuring that all our productive resources should be used to the very best possible advantage. And this is just what admirers of the capitalist system claim for it. They claim that under it just those goods and services which most people most want, and no others, are bound to get produced. And they claim that no other economic system could possibly produce a more desirable result than this.

Why, then, do communists and socialists wish to abolish capitalism? We wish to do so because we have been unable to avoid noticing that capitalism does not give the above admirable result. The goods which most people most want are not produced. In contemporary Britain and America goods and services for the lack of which many millions of persons slowly perish[1] are not produced, and, instead, goods which only a few people want, and which they want only a little, are produced. For example, it is to-day unprofitable to produce the additional bread, meat, milk, clothes, and houses which millions of British and American citizens desperately need.[2] But it is profitable to produce the foolish luxuries desired by a handful of the very rich. Inevitably, then, so long as we continue to regulate our production by the principle of profitability, the luxuries are, and the necessaries are not, produced. We say that there must be something wrong with an economic system which gives results like that. We call this result of contemporary capitalism a gigantic, and very wicked, *misdirection* of production.

Moreover, capitalism now from time to time produces substantial quantities of things which the rich do not want and the poor cannot pay for, and which consequently have to be destroyed. This is a more extreme example of the misdirection of production.

[1] See p. 329.   See p. 327.

Such abominable absurdities as the deliberate destruction of food, when very many people are undernourished, to which it periodically leads, strike people very forcibly and have been responsible for making many people feel that something must be wrong with capitalism.

But, as a matter of fact, this dramatic type of breakdown is a less serious matter than is capitalism's now chronic inability to allow many of us to produce anything at all. The extent to which the British and American people are now unable to use their productive resources varies greatly from year to year and from place to place. In 1929, for example, the American people probably used their productive resources to the fullest extent that any people have ever been able to do under the capitalist system. But a careful survey[1] has since been made, by a number of conservatively minded American economists and statisticians, of what was the actual capacity of the American people to produce, both in that year and subsequently. They estimate that in 1929 the American people used their productive resources to 81 per cent of their capacity. *And in the immediately following years they used them to under 50 per cent of their capacity.* Now in these latter years (1930–31–32–33) the American capitalist system was working about as abnormally badly as it was working abnormally well in 1929. So we may say that the American people are nowadays never able to use somewhere between 19 and 50 *per cent* of their productive resources.

I do not know of any comparable figures for Britain. But the level of British unemployment gives us some idea of the extent of Britain's unused productive resources. Judging by this, and by some other indications, we may guess that the British people have never since the war been able to use as much (81 per cent) of their productive resources as the American people used in 1929, and have never been reduced to using so little of them (50 per cent) as the Americans used in 1931–32. Probably the average proportion of available productive resources actually used, calculated over a number of years, would not work out very differently for the two countries.

In any case, what is the exact percentage of our productive

[1] Undertaken by the Brookings Institution and published by that Institution under the title of *America's Capacity to Produce.*

resources which we cannot at present use at all is not the important question. The point is that this proportion has long been, and is now, substantial. For this means that we now lack all the goods and services which these idle resources could and would have produced, if we had used them. The British and American men and machines which have stood idle, and which now stand idle, could have produced those houses, that food, those clothes, those educational facilities, those medical services, etc., etc., for the lack of which either we, or the people whom we see around us, are at this moment suffering so bitterly.

Thus waste is to-day the most striking of all the characteristics of capitalism. The waste which has resulted from our failure to use at all many of our resources of production is cumulative and has now become almost immeasurable in both Britain and America. We are accustomed to think of it chiefly in terms of the waste of our available supply of labour, and to call it the problem of unemployment. And, truly, the waste which results from keeping between ten and twenty million British and American workers, many of them capable and industrious, in enforced idleness is the very worst part of the business. For this, waste results, not only in the loss of the goods which the unemployed would have produced had they been permitted to work; it also results in their own slow torture by destitution, frustration, and social humiliation.

These are the reasons why we say that although the British and American capitalist systems of production still work, yet they work in a way intolerable alike from its injustice and its waste. For under them not only do many hundreds of thousands of us British and American citizens work hard all day and every day to satisfy the foolish whims of the rich, while no one is allowed to work at producing the additional food, clothes, houses and the like which by far the greater number of us urgently need; but, worse still, some ten to twenty millions of us are prevented from working and producing at all.

It is this degree of failure in our economic system, and this alone, which keeps by far the larger number of us very poor. The extent of poverty varies greatly, it is true, between different capitalist states. The present destitution of the

inhabitants of many of the capitalist states of the world, such
as Poland, Italy, Austria, and many more, can hardly be exaggerated. A famous capitalist economist, John Stuart Mill, suggested
that the capitalist use of the marvellous inventions of science
had not lightened the toil of a single labourer by a single hour. In
the case of most contemporary states we may add that neither
has it put another yard of cloth on to the backs, nor a piece
of bread into the mouths, of the greater part of the population.
Moreover, even in Britain and America, the two richest capitalist
countries of the world, the mass of the population is much
poorer than we are accustomed to suppose. In Great Britain,
which is at the moment (1936) probably the richer and more
prosperous of the two, two-thirds of the population have incomes averaging £25 per head per year.[1] It will always remain
impossible for those of us whose incomes are of a different order
of magnitude to imagine what this degree of poverty means in
terms of the restriction, embitterment, and stunting of the
possibilities of human life. But at any rate we can all grasp this
essential fact: *the ocean of human suffering involved in such
poverty is now totally unnecessary.* It is a result, not of an inability to produce an adequate supply of goods and services,
but of the failure of our existing economic system. For that

[1] According to a calculation made by a well-known statistician and economist,
Mr. O. R. Hobson, and published in *Lloyds Bank Monthly Review* for July 1934.
This means, the reader will observe, that a family of four will have an income of
£100 a year or just under £2 a week. As Mr. Hobson's conclusion is startling,
it may be well to quote his calculation in full.

" The National Income of Great Britain and Northern Ireland is estimated
at about £3,400,000,000, equivalent to £74 per head of the population, a figure
which does not suggest that the danger of inconveniently large production is
very imminent. But of this £3,400,000,000, about £2,550,000,000 represents
income belonging to income tax payers—for this is the amount of ' actual
income ' assessed to income tax in 1932–33, and the ' actual income ' figure of
the Commissioners of Inland Revenue has been shown by Professor Bowley and
Sir Josiah Stamp to be very close to that part of the ' National Income which
accrues to the income tax paying class.' Thus the aggregate income of the class
below the income tax exemption limit (£100 assessable income, equivalent to
£125 earned income) was, say, £850,000,000. Now the total number of income
tax payers in 1932–33 was 3,500,000, and if we assume that each of these has, on
the average, two-and-a-half dependants, we arrive at the figure of 12,250,000 as
the number of persons in the ' income tax paying class.' Subtraction from the
total population of 46,000,000 therefore gives the number of persons whose
incomes are below the exemption limit as 33,750,000. Dividing this last figure
into the residual income of £850,000,000 we have a figure of approximately £25
as the average annual income per capital of the non-income tax paying classes."
But see Chapter XXVI for a more detailed discussion of the present standard of
life of the British people.

system does not allow us to use one part of our productive resources at all, and so misdirects the use of the other part that it largely fails to satisfy human needs.

The simple truth is that general plenty and security are now possible in both Britain and America. It is not, I think, possible to foretell with scientific accuracy exactly what standard of life the British and American people could provide themselves with if they used their productive resources continuously for the purpose of the satisfaction of their needs in the order of their urgency. We do now possess, however, in the case of America, an interesting estimate on just this point. In the year 1934 the Government of the United States of America appointed a Committee to enquire into the capacity of American industry and agriculture to produce goods and services. In February 1935 this Committee issued its report.[1] *It found that every family of four persons could provide itself with an income of $4,400 (about £915) a year, at 1929 prices, if America's productive resources were used to the full and their product equally divided between all families.*[2]

In the next chapter we shall discuss the extent to which this estimate is true—or rather, we shall discuss the conditions under which it is alone true. Speaking very broadly, however, this estimate is true. All sorts of circumstances, foreseeable and unforeseeable, might affect in one way or another the exact level of the standard of life with which the British and American people could provide themselves.[3] But what we are concerned with is not the exact figure arrived at—£915, or £1,000, or £700 a year—as the income now possible for all American families of four persons. What we are concerned with is the broad fact that the peoples of such highly developed countries as Britain and America could unquestionably now provide themselves with secure incomes of this order of magnitude—with the type of incomes now enjoyed by the middle sections of the professional

---

[1] This was the preliminary report issued under the title of *The Chart of Plenty* (Viking Press, New York City), issued by the National Survey of Potential Product Capacity.

[2] And *pro rata* for larger and smaller families.

[3] The above estimate is, however, the result of a detailed, thorough, and skilful investigation undertaken by a large team of able American statisticians working for many months. It cannot be brushed aside, as every capitalist apologist has attempted to brush it aside, except by critics who have undertaken a comparable enquiry.

classes. We are concerned with the fact that this conclusion cannot now be denied by anyone who takes the trouble to investigate the extent and nature of our available productive resources.

Let us pause a moment upon this question. General plenty, an average level of income for all families, of the order of magnitude of from £700 to £1,000 a year,[1] instead of from £75 to £200 a year, as at present, is now possible in all highly developed countries.[2] We cannot know what would be the effect of this abolition of poverty. But we do know that it would transform human life.

Unnecessary destitution is not the only disastrous effect produced upon us by the malfunctioning of capitalism. Almost more than plenty itself, the people of Britain and America desire security. Their lives are dominated even more by the fear of want than by want itself. The people of Britain and America, with the exception of the very small minority of the securely rich, and of the larger minority of the actually and presently destitute, live under the more or less imminent, and always awful, threat of destitution. The way in which we now organize our economic

[1] Again, less for families of under four persons, and more for families of over four persons.

[2] It may be suggested that the attainable level would be much lower in Great Britain than in America. In the absence of any statistical survey comparable to the above-mentioned American report it is impossible to do more than speculate as to what a British estimate would work out at. I am inclined to think, however, that net British productive capacity is nearer the American level than is often supposed. An experienced Cambridge economist makes the following estimate of the unused productive resources at present available to the British people :

" It seems hard to believe that the total reserves which could be speedily drawn upon could be *less* than between 30 and 40 per cent. It might even prove to be considerably more. Even if we take our very cautious minimum figure of 30 per cent, this would mean a potential increase of production equivalent to something in the neighbourhood of £1,000 millions, or an addition of something in the nature of 10s. per week to every working class man and woman and child, or an additional income of some £70 a year to every wage-earner and small-salary earner." (*Britain Without Capitalists*. Martin Lawrence.)

The reader will notice, however, that this calculation is not comparable with the American calculation, for it allows for no redistribution of income from the richer third of the British population. Moreover, as we shall discover in the next chapter, the two estimates proceed from fundamentally different premises. The British estimate is comparable with another American estimate made by the aforementioned Brookings Institution. It is incomparable with the National Survey of Potential Product Capacity, in that this later estimate alone allowed for the conscious reallotment of factors of production having alternative uses, i.e. planning. But see Chapter II.

life results in an extraordinary, and now ever-increasing, degree
of instability and insecurity for the whole population. Those
who live on the weekly wages paid by industry, the smaller,
independent, owner-producers, such as the farmers, and the
professional workers of all kinds, have this at least in common:
they all live under the fear of the disappearance of their livelihoods. And substantial numbers of them do continually suffer
this terrifying loss. For the violent and unpredictable fluctuations of trade which now more and more charaterize our economic
system fling about and capsize their little enterprises as row-
boats are tossed by the Atlantic.

The loss of a man's livelihood, although it does not in contemporary Britain and America usually involve his family in
actual starvation, does usually render it destitute. In Britain
and America the millions of the destitute are fed, and to some
extent clothed. But its amount, the uncertainty of its receipt,
and the onerous restrictions which it carries with it, prevent
the relief which is given them from effectively mitigating the
fate of those who lose their opportunity to work and earn.
They do not, for the most part, quickly die; but their lives
become so miserable that the dread of this fate is to-day the
haunting companion of almost everyone outside the small
class of the securely rich.

Our psychologists should, but do not, inform us of what is
the effect upon the psychological stability of our communities
of thus keeping the greater part of the population in anxiety
for their very livelihoods. The larger part of mankind is thereby
reduced to a condition of terrible, childish helplessness. Contemporary man fears, and has good reason to fear, social forces
which he does not comprehend, far less control. The mediæval
peasant, the savage huntsman even, knew no such helpless
insecurity. They had to contend with the drought, the flood, and
the storm; but the forces of nature were kinder than the forces of
man.

Whichever of the other ills of men are inevitable, this extraordinary economic insecurity is needless. The proposition that
we could all now provide ourselves with plenty is disputable (it
is, at any rate, sometimes disputed). Or, to put the matter more
precisely, the particular standard of life which our existing means

of production would make it possible for us all to enjoy, if we used them to the full, is disputable. But what is not disputable is that we could use our existing means of production to give us all *some* definite, stable, and secure standard of life. There *can* be no necessity for the sickening oscillations of our present economic system. There *can* be no necessity suddenly to leave great parts of our productive apparatus idle, and many millions of ourselves unemployed and destitute.

It is true, however, that the inability of capitalism to realize the dazzling possiblities of plenty and security which are now open to the British and American peoples is not, and never will be, an efficient cause for their abandonment of that economic system. We live in poverty and fear when we could live in plenty and security. But this is not in itself enough to make us act.

The true alternative which faces us, however, is not one of continuing in our present conditions, or achieving much superior ones. The truth is that we must attain security and plenty or suffer the rapid growth of every form of that fear and destitution which already ruin the lives of so many of us. For the existing evils of our societies are the result of certain features of the capitalist system which cannot be eradicated, but which must, on the contrary, grow more and more pronounced. Moreover, it is in the nature of capitalism to produce, not only unnecessary poverty and insecurity, but also certain other and far more rapidly disastrous consequences. It is of the nature of capitalism to produce civil conflict and international war. Communists and socialists propose, then, that we should rid ourselves of capitalism, not merely because it denies us a now plainly attainable plenty and security, but more especially because it is now visibly about to destroy us in the social and international violence which it generates.

But is there an alternative to capitalism ?

Chapter II

Socialist Production for Use

WE cannot reject capitalism unless we have some effective substitute to put in its place. Unless it can be shown that a workable alternative exists, denunciations of the evils of capitalism are vain and empty.

For every society must possess some way of organizing its economic life. If there were no practicable alternative we should have to put up with the existing way, no matter how unjust, how wasteful, and how finally catastrophic were its results. Hence before we go on to discuss the political and social systems, and the cultural and ethical values, associated respectively with capitalism and socialism, we must give a clear account of the economic ground plan of a socialist society. For " human beings must first of all eat, drink, shelter and clothe themselves before they can turn their attention to politics, science, art and religion."[1] Thus we shall have to plunge at once into questions of economics. For not until these questions have been given satisfactory and convincing answers can we go on to a description of the whole structure of socialist society.

The essential economic problem of socialism is this. If we are not to settle the question of what goods, and what quantities of goods, are to be produced, by producing only those which yield a profit, how are we to settle it ? For settled it must be.

If we reject the self-acting mechanism of profitability, as too unjust and too wasteful, we must find some other mechanism of regulation. The sole alternative method by which complex, highly developed, economic systems such as those of Britain and America can be regulated is by means of the deliberate decisions of some central body as to what goods, and how many of each of them, shall be produced.[2] The organization of produc-

[1] Friedrich Engels' speech beside the grave of Marx.

[2] A failure to realize that the provision of some regulating principle is a necessity for every productive system is the basic defect of all the various credit and currency reform schemes for abolishing the evils of capitalism without abolishing capitalism itself. Such schemes all in one way or another destroy, or gravely impair, the regulating principle that only what is profitable shall be produced, and fail to put any other regulator, such as that provided by the conscious planning of production, in its place. They ignore the fact that the imposition of the penalty of loss for making things that are not in effective demand is just as

tion by means of such conscious decisions is called a system of
" planned production for use." This is the type of economic
system now being built up in the Soviet Union. It is socialism.

The best way to define the principle upon which a socialist
economic system works is not to discuss socialism in the abstract,
but to describe a particular system of planned production for
use, worked out for Britain or America, or some other such
highly industrialized community.[1] In Britain and America we
still organize our economic life on the basis of the capitalist
system of production for profit. But this does not make it impossible to prepare a survey, or catalogue, of the productive
resources of either country and to estimate what results, in
terms of quantities of goods and services, these resources would
give us if they were used on the basis of planned production for
use. And in the case of America such a draft economic plan has
actually been made, *although unintentionally*. It was made by
the aforementioned authors of the National Survey of Potential
Product Capacity, who came to the conclusion that every American family of four might have an income of £915 a year.

This group of American statisticians and economists set out
with the limited purpose of discovering what was the real productive capacity of American industry and agriculture, without
reference to any particular economic system. Their enquiry was
to be, they imagined, strictly technical and statistical. Nothing,
surely, was farther from their thoughts, or from those of the
American government when it appointed and financed them,
than any idea of demonstrating how a planned economic system
—how, in other words, socialism—would work in the United
States of America ? And yet this is just what they did demonstrate. It will be worth our while to enquire how this misadven-
ture occurred; to observe how the N.S.P.P.C. investigators were

essential a part of the regulative mechanism of capitalism as is the provision of
profit for the producer of things for which there is a demand. These schemes, by
making all production profitable, would destroy the one governor which the
system possesses, and so would produce complete chaos.

[1] We shall of course have a great deal to say about the Soviet economic system.
But there is an objection to using it as our first example of a socialist economic
system. For we are seeking for an alternative economic system for two of the
most highly developed and industrialized countries in the world. It may be felt
therefore (though incorrectly) that any economic system which has been built
up in the very different conditions of the Soviet Union has only a remote relevance
for us.

led on, by one problem raising another, to elaborate the ground plan of a socialist America. For by so doing we shall stumble, as they did, upon one after another of the economic problems involved in the establishment of a socialist economic system. Moreover, we shall not only raise these problems, but we shall see how they can be solved in practice.

The authors of the N.S.P.P.C. report had been appointed by the American government in order to discover, we repeat, what was America's total productive capacity. They interpreted these terms of reference to mean what was the capacity of the American productive system to satisfy the needs of the American people. This naturally involved ascertaining what the needs of the American people were. But that did not seem difficult. In 1933, when the investigation was started, the American people seemed to be short of a great many prime necessaries, such as food, clothes, and shelter.

Let us take the example of shelter: 15½ million new dwellings were needed, it was estimated, to satisfy the American people's need for shelter. The building of this number of dwellings would, to be more precise, enable every American family of four to have a home of from five to six rooms, equipped with modern conveniences.[1] It would be reasonable to build them, the report estimated, under a ten-year building programme (involving the erection of 1,550,000 dwellings a year). But did there, or did there not, exist the productive resources necessary to enable the American people to build 1,550,000 dwellings a year? Was there enough labour, enough bricks, enough steel, enough power, enough of everything needed? This question clearly involved another. Of course there were enough of these productive resources if none of them were used for any other purpose. Clearly, however, some resources had to be used for other purposes. You cannot divert the whole of a community's available labour, for example, to building dwellings. You will starve if you do. Sufficient labour, sufficient steel, sufficient power, and sufficient everything else, has to be left to satisfy all the community's other equally urgent needs—such as the need for food and clothes—and for that matter, in practice, for transport, education, amusement and many other things as well.

[1] And *pro rata* for larger and smaller families.

So the question had to be restated thus: Would there be enough productive resources left over, *after the other equally urgent needs of the American people had bèen satisfied*, to enable them to build 1,550,000 dwellings a year for ten years? And this question, in its turn, clearly depended on what you meant by " equally urgent " needs. *How, in a word, was the question to be decided, as to what uses the American people's productive resources were to be put—and who was to decide it ?* For, when you come to think of it, most productive resources have alternative uses. You can use the labour of a given number of workers either to grow food or to build houses: you can use a given supply of copper either for domestic plumbing or for making locomotives. You can use so many units of electrical energy either to drive the machinery of a steel-mill or to light dwellings. *But you cannot use any of these things for both purposes simultaneously.*

Let us take a particular example. One of the productive resources needed for building 1,550,000 dwellings a year is structural steel. Would there be, the N.S.P.P.C. authors enquired, enough structural steel left over from other equally urgent work for the job ? At once we are led to ask whether all the uses which actually were made of the available structural steel were as urgent as building dwellings. Now in 1929 a very high proportion of America's output of structural steel was used to build skyscrapers, mainly intended for offices. And the authors of the N.S.P.P.C. report could not help noticing that what the American people seemed to need was not office skyscrapers, but dwellings. A substantial proportion of the American people were (and still are) housed in the most wretched kinds of run-down, tumble-down, insanitary and overcrowded slums and shacks. And on the other hand nothing was more notorious than that nobody needed more office accommodation. For a high proportion of the recently built skyscrapers stood empty, while those that had filled up with tenants had done so by emptying the surrounding office accommodation of theirs. Yet in 1929 most of America's structural steel was being used to build still more office skyscrapers. The authors of the report found this situation very peculiar because they, like the rest of us, had been brought up to believe that the fact that effective demand in 1929 had been for office skyscrapers, and not for dwellings, was proof that what the ill-housed and over-officed American people truly wanted and needed were office skyscrapers, and not homes And this they found incredible.

Their next discovery was that even in the boom year of 1929 the American people only used their steel plants to some 84 per cent of their capacity. (In 1932 they used them to under 20 per cent of their capacity.) If, in 1929, the Americans had chosen to use their capacity to produce steel to the full, they would have been able to turn out, amongst other forms of steel, another 8·7 million tons of structural steel. Hence this question arose for the authors of the N.S.P.P.C. report. In calculating how much structural steel could be made available for building dwellings, would you, or would you not, have to reckon that the American people would have allotted the same high proportion of this extra 8·7 million tons of the stuff, had they produced it, to building office skyscrapers ?

If you followed the guidance of demand you would have to assume just that. But if you did so, not enough structural steel would be left over to build the 1,550,000 dwellings a year. The authors of the report found it impossible to believe that the American people's real needs included a yearly output of *even more* towers than had been built in 1929. Surely these had been enough, and too many ? Why not, then, assume that if the 8·7 million tons extra of structural steel had been produced they could almost all have gone to building dwelling-houses ? Why not indeed ? The authors of the N.S.P.P.C. report made this assumption. It was one of the assumptions upon which they based their conclusion that every American family might have enjoyed that standard of life which was actually enjoyed by those families which had incomes of $4,400 (£915) in 1929. (For that is another way of putting their main conclusion.)

Now at first sight this action on the part of our ingenious authors may seem to have been innocent enough. But innocent it was not. For the assumption that almost all the extra structural steel which would have been produced by the capacity working of the American mills could have been used for building homes, involved the conscious and deliberate reallotment of resources of production between alternative uses. *And to do this is considered to be economic original sin. For it means breaking irrevocably with the capitalist system, the test of profitability, and the self-adjusting mechanism which this test provides.*

For see what our authors have taken upon themselves to do. They have decided that it would be better to use more of the available supply of steel for building dwellings, and less for building office skyscrapers. But the reputedly infallible indicator of demand showed that what the American people wanted was skyscrapers, not dwellings. Who made the authors of the N.S.P.P.C. report, the defenders of the capitalist system may object, into rulers and judges over us to say how we should or should not use our available supply of structural steel ?

Moreover, these authors did not content themselves with reallotting the available supply of structural steel as between skyscrapers and dwellings. *For as soon as the capacity of the American people to provide themselves with food, clothing, motor cars, and a hundred other kinds of goods and services was investigated, it became apparent that it was impossible to say to what extent their needs could be satisfied, unless the investigators could decide; not only the productive capacity of America's basic industries, but also what use was going to be made of the products of such basic industries.* Accordingly, they reallotted all the extra supplies of raw materials and semi-finished goods which the capacity working of America's basic industries would have produced: they allotted these extra supplies, not in proportion to the uses which actually were made of such goods in 1929, but to other uses which the authors of the report thought more desirable.

But how, we ask at once, did they decide what were the more, and what the less, desirable uses for these supplies ? They evidently worked on the assumption that it was more desirable to use available supplies in the way which best satisfied visible and urgent human needs—such as the need for decent dwellings to live in: that it was less desirable to use them in a way that satisfied less urgent human needs—such as the need to have towers to look at. But now we see that the authors of the report took upon themselves no less a task than to decide upon the relative urgency of human needs—in plain language to decide what people really wanted to have.

Before they had gone very far with their investigation they found themselves working out a comprehensive budget of the

Bs

needs of an American family. Then they worked back, through the productive system, and enquired whether or not there existed resources of production which could be used to supply the goods and services necessary to meet these needs. They came to the conclusion that such resources did exist. But some of these resources would have to be reallotted from their *existing uses, and used according to a plan. They would have to be used according to a plan which provided that the available raw materials and semi-finished products should be finally fabricated into the particular goods, and no others, which they had laid down in advance when they made out their family budget.*[1]

Now when our intrepid authors compiled this budget of human needs, they did something which almost every economist of almost every British and American University has declared to be impossible. It is quite impossible, say these authorities, to make any estimate of people's real needs. The multiplicity of human needs and the variety of human desires are so great, they continue, that it is quite impossible to *foretell* what people will want, and so consciously to plan production in advance. The only practicable procedure is our present one, namely, to allow people to express their wants by making money offers for particular goods and services, and then to allow production to adapt itself, by means of the pull of profit and the push of loss, to this ever-changing demand. If this method results in most of the community's structural steel being used to build useless skyscrapers, so that millions of its citizens must continue to live in slums; if it results in an important proportion of our productive resources not being used at all, so that we starve amidst potential plenty—well, this is unfortunate. But, say the economists, it cannot be helped. To cut across the free play of demand and supply involves attempting to dictate to people what they should buy: it involves forcing them to buy what you think they ought to have, instead of what they really want.

The reader will see that if we apply this argument to our wants in general, and not merely to the question of shelter, it

---

[1] As a matter of fact, they only reallotted the extra semi-finished products which would have come into being had America's basic industries been used to capacity. But once any conscious reallotment of factors is allowed, the principle is the same.

does not lack plausibility. It does seem a rather arbitrary proceeding to draw up a budget of food, clothing, housing, and everything else, for everybody, and say that these things, and consequently nothing else, shall be produced.

And yet this is just what the authors of the N.S.P.P.C. report found, greatly to their surprise, no difficulty in doing. Here is their description of how they did it :

" Strange as it may seem, it is easier to determine human needs than it is to determine the ability of society to extract raw materials. On the average, people of a given culture eat only so much food, wear out only so many clothes, live in only so many rooms. If ' scarcity values ' (of works of art, etc.) are excluded from consideration—and they naturally fall outside the scope of our study since our concern was with physical quantities—the amount of goods and services the population would like to consume can be calculated with an accuracy far greater than the accuracy with which we can determine the possible output of any industry.

In the case of food, for example, we employed the budget sponsored by the Department of Agriculture, adopting the preferred schedule, ' the liberal diet,' as a criterion of the desirable individual consumption in various foodstuffs.

In clothing, we based our budget on the actual expenditures of the professional classes in the San Francisco area.

In housing, we merely assumed that the American family would like to live in a modern five-or-six-room house or its equivalent (apartment, renovated old mansion, or the like), fully equipped with the best labour-saving devices, and that the single individual in the city would continue using smaller apartments.

For medical care, we took the advice of the medical authorities in regard to what we needed to care properly for the American people.

In education, our budget was set by authorities at Teachers' College, Columbia University; in recreation, we were governed by the existing taste of the people."

(*The Chart of Plenty*, pp. 9–10.)

And so on through the list of all the main classes of goods and services which human beings consume.

Now there seems nothing arbitrary about this procedure when we see it in practice. It does not seem as if the N.S.P.P.C. authors were ordering us to consume just those particular commodities which they thought we ought to consume, and no others. How has the arbitrary element been avoided, then? How were our authors able to make up a budget of needs the satisfaction of which would certainly mean a very decent civilized life for any family?

Two considerations made it possible for the authors of the N.S.P.P.C. report to show how the planning of the economic life of a great industrial nation could be accomplished. And these same considerations, after the abolition of capitalism, will make it possible for a British or American Planning Commission actually to do the job.

The first factor which makes possible the estimation in advance of consumers' real needs, is the fact that we know what people have consumed up till now. There is little difficulty in discovering how much food, medical attention, education, clothing, etc., etc., the population has consumed in the past year. We know that this standard of consumption was unsatisfactory. Still, it gives us a basis to go on. We shall be able to plan the production of additions to, or alterations of, the quantities of each commodity consumed last year. We shall budget for an increase of so many million tons of meat, and of so many million houses, and a decrease of so many hundred skyscrapers. We shall not, in other words, have to start from scratch and think up what a typical family ought to consume. We know already what they do consume, and we shall have to estimate merely what more they would have liked to have consumed.

The second factor is the existence of a certain number of families who can now buy the things which they need and want. The consumption of the immense majority of families is most unsatisfactory; but there do exist in our modern communities certain classes of people whose consumption is quite satisfactory. We are not thinking of the very rich, whose consumption is of a peculiar and fantastic nature, but of the professional classes in prosperous times. Thus, if we want to know what the mass of the population would consume, by way of food, clothes, transportation, or anything else, if only they were better off, we naturally look at what those families which *are* now better off actually do consume. Thus we notice that the N.S.P.P.C. authors have guessed that if the whole American people could buy all the clothes they need they would in fact buy the same amount and kind of clothes which the professional classes in and around San Francisco did in 1929 actually buy and consume. And we can, surely, agree that this is a reasonable assumption.

With the aid of these two guides it is possible to estimate what people would like to have produced for them, and then to allot the available resources of production in such a way that this quantity of goods and services will be produced. It is possible, that is to say, to satisfy people's needs by this method, instead of by the present method of allowing production to follow the pull of demand.

Let us envisage how the first budget, or plan of production, giving what is, in effect, a list of all the goods and services which are to be made available to the population, will be compiled in a socialist Britain or America. This first budget will be based upon the existing output of such goods with the additions indicated by what the better-off classes do now consume, and the realization of this production programme will be made possible by utilizing those productive resources at present grossly misdirected, or unused altogether, by capitalism. But only the first budget need be made up in this way. All subsequent budgets will be merely corrections of the miscalculations discovered in the first. For miscalculation there will certainly be. The planning authority will be sure to provide, say, too many new motor cars and not enough wireless sets, or too many transport facilities and not enough sports clothes, etc., etc. Such errors will show themselves in that at the end of the year some motor cars, for example, will be left over, while the stock of wireless sets will be exhausted before the end of the year.[1] But this error

[1] For clarity's sake we are oversimplifying the picture. In practice, of course, it would be a question of a continuous flow of production in each case—the flow being insufficient to meet the demand (at the prices fixed) in the case of wireless sets and over-sufficient in the case of motor cars. But the essential point is the same; the correction of this state of things will be made, in a planned economy, not by the price of wireless sets automatically rising and the price of motor cars automatically falling, but by the conscious decision of the planning authority.

will not be allowed to affect the respective prices of the two
goods, raising the price of wireless sets and lowering the price
of motor cars. Their respective prices which will be based upon
their respective costs of production will only be varied by the
conscious and deliberate decisions of the planning authority.

In the following year[1] the planning authority will arrange
for the production of more wireless sets and fewer motor cars.
In order to do so it will have to turn certain productive resources
(in this case metal, skilled labour, assembling-plants, etc., etc.),
which have been making motor cars, on to making wireless sets.
Year by year there will have to be corrections of this kind.

Such corrections will have to be made not only in order to
remedy errors and miscalculations upon the part of the planning
authority, but also in order to meet the development of new
methods of production and the changes in public taste which will
be associated with these developments. For we must not think
of the budget of human needs, which the planning authority
will draw up, as something fixed or permanent. On the contrary,
human needs develop *with* the capacity to satisfy them. The
planning authority will constantly have to allocate productive
resources to new purposes in order either to fulfil some new need
(e.g. for the widespread ownership of private aeroplanes) or
to fulfil an old need in some new, more efficient and economical
way (e.g. the production of one or other of the basic foodstuffs synthetically).

No planning authority will perfectly perform these functions.
But it is impossible to believe that even in the very first year,
and even if the planning authority is composed of the most
fallible of fallible human beings, it can fail to provide for human
needs to so gross an extent as does the capitalist principle of
regulating production by profitability. However serious were
the mistakes of the planning authority, it *could* not achieve
such grandiose misdirections of production as does capitalism.
It could not do anything so insane or so horrible as to produce a
plethora of yachts and beauty parlours while millions of men and
women lack for food and shelter: it could not succeed, as does
our present system, in *simultaneously* torturing the town workers
with a lack of bread and ruining the farmers by a glut of wheat.

[1] Again the adjustments will be in practice continual and therefore slight.

The authors of the N.S.P.P.C. report provided us with a demonstration of an exceedingly important economic principle. They did so when they decided that, in order to carry out their instructions to estimate America's capacity to produce wealth, they would have to make out a budget of the real needs of the American people, and to reallot resources of production to meet these needs. For by doing these two things they, in effect, made an outline One Year Plan for America. This was their great achievement.

Their detailed demonstration of how a One Year Plan of production for great industrial communities such as the United States and Britain could be, and will be, compiled is of unquestionable value. For it shows far better than could many pages of argumentation how socialist economic planning is done. It shows in particular and convincing detail how it will be possible to organize mighty and complex economic systems of production for use, and so establish general plenty and security. It shows what we could put in the place of the now grossly defective test of profitability as the regulating principle of production. We must certainly assume, however, that the N.S.P.P.C. authors' demonstration of the possibility of planned production for use was accidental. For if it were intentional they could be accused of using the money of the government of the United States in order to demonstrate the practicality, and the extreme desirability, of that system of production favoured by communists and socialists ! And I would not dream of bringing this serious allegation against Mr. Doan (the leader of the investigation) and his associates. No, let us assume that when they wrote the sketch of a One Year Plan of production for America, they did not know what they were doing. By the end of their report they had been talking pure socialism for 200 pages. But like M. Jourdain in Molière's play, they knew not what they did.

CHAPTER III

Planning

THIS, then, is how a socialist economic system works. This is
how a planning authority settles the relative proportions in
which consumers' goods (as they are called) shall be produced.
A planning authority has another task, however. There is
another proportion which must be decided upon, either by the
play of the market, as under capitalism, or by the conscious
decision of a planning authority. And this is the proportion
between the quantities of consumers' goods, on the one hand,
and of means of production, on the other, which shall be produced in any given year.

Consumers' goods are, as their name implies, the things which
we all consume, boots and shoes, milk and meat, and the like.
Means of production, on the other hand, are the things which
produce the consumers' goods, things like lathes and cranes,
machine tools and power stations, goods which no one can
consume, in the sense of satisfying their want directly from them.
Now every society must produce some consumers' goods, or it
will immediately starve to death, and some means of production,
or it will be unable to go on producing consumers' goods, and
will ultimately starve to death. We may put it like this: a
community must divert at least enough of its productive resources to making means of production to prevent its existing
stock from wearing out quicker than it is being replaced. But
a community *may* devote a much higher proportion of its resources than this to making means of production. And it may
be well worth its while to do so, if it can replace its present
stock of means of production with very much more efficient
ones.

But to do so inevitably involves, under either capitalism
or socialism, making do for the moment with a lower output of
consumers' goods than could have been produced, even with
the old outfit of means of production. For a community has only
a certain limited supply of labour, raw materials, organizing
skill, transport services, and the like, and these resources can
be used either for producing new consumers' goods, or for

producing new means of production, but not for both tasks simultaneously.

Here, then, is a very real choice which faces any community. We may express the choice like this. How much of its resources shall the community devote directly to satisfying its needs here and now, and how much shall it devote to building up means of production which will in the future, but only in the future, satisfy those needs far more plenteously? It is a case of how many birds in the bush of the future are worth the forgoing of one bird in the hand of the present. It is a question of balancing the forgoing of immediate satisfactions for the sake of being able to provide satisfactions more plenteously later on.

Every community in which the means of production are developed must take this choice, no matter what is its economic system. And its freedom of choice is wide. On the one hand a community may divert from the immediate production of consumers' goods and services only just enough resources to prevent its productive plant from falling into decay; or on the other hand it may leave only enough resources for the production of consumers' goods to provide itself with subsistence rations.

Let us now see how the two economic systems under discussion settle this question.

The capitalist system of production for profit claims to provide an automatic method of settling this question also. The proportion in which a capitalist community makes consumers' goods and means of production is settled by the proportion in which its citizens spend and save their money incomes. For when a man saves he does not throw the money down the drain; he invests it. And investing money means, if you think of it, buying means of production instead of buying consumers' goods. When, for example, an investor buys shares issued by a company which generates electrical power his money is used to buy a turbo-generator, or some transmitting cable, or means of production of some kind. But if he had spent his money he would have used it to buy units of electrical power or some other kind of consumers' goods. Hence the more people save, and the less they spend, the larger is the demand for means of production, and the smaller is the demand for consumers' goods (and vice versa). And productive resources, led by the magnet of profit, follow the pull of demand, and move, in this case, away from the making of consumers' goods, to the making of means of production.

Now this part of the self-regulating mechanism of capitalism is often criticized by the experts of that system themselves. The regulation of the proportionate output of consumers' goods and means of production by the proportion of saving to spending works most erratically. However it does, in a sense, work. The question is settled; but once again it is settled without the conscious decision of the community as a whole, or indeed of any individual or group of individuals. Once again the thing just happens. For the proportion in which the whole community spends and saves its income depends upon the decisions of innumerable individuals and corporations. Nobody decides upon this proportion. It is the blind result of the balancing of millions of different decisions. Under capitalism we make, and can make, no attempt to decide this vital question. We have to leave the matter to be settled for us by the play of forces which are outside our control.

A socialist economic system, however, must settle this question by the conscious, deliberate decision of a planning authority, set up and controlled, of course, by the whole community. If, in this matter also, we cease to rely on the pull and push of demand shifting our resources of production *from* the sphere in which their use is less profitable *to* the sphere in which it is more profitable, we must deliberately decide on where they are to be used.

A socialist planning authority will have, then, as one of its primary duties, to decide how much of the available labour supply, raw materials, transport facilities, and the like, are to be used for producing new plant and machinery and how much are to be used for directly satisfying the community's immediate wants. For example, a planning authority which had had control over America's productive resources in 1929 would have had to decide not only how much of the available supply of structural steel to use for building office skyscrapers, and how much to use for building dwellings, but also how much to use for providing these two kinds of consumers' goods taken together, and how much to use for building new steel-mills. For only by building new steel-mills could the total supply of steel available in future years be increased.

It at once occurs to us to ask how the authors of the N.S.P.P.C. report solved this question. They did so quite simply by providing for the production of the same amount of new means of production as actually were produced in 1929. They assumed, in other words, that the American people would go on replacing and developing their productive plant at the same rapid pace as they were doing in 1929. And they were able to show that the American people would still have enough productive resources left to provide every family of four with consumers' goods represented by an income of $4,400 (£915) a year at 1929 prices.

This was, for their illustrative purposes, a reasonable assumption. When, however, a real planning authority comes to allocate the American, or the British, people's productive resources to the best advantage it will not necessarily adopt this particular proportion. Such an authority might be instructed that the British or American people preferred to replace and develop their productive plant at a slower pace than they were doing in 1929. In that case the amount of consumers' goods and services which could be immediately provided would be increased—although the rate at which this figure could be still further raised in future years would be slower. Or the British and American people might decide to instruct their planning authority to devote a higher proportion of the community's productive resources to making means of production than was done in 1929. In this case the initial income with which they could provide themselves would be lower, but it could be raised more rapidly in future years. Their decision will depend, no doubt, on the circumstances of the time.

Now it will not matter very much which course the British and American people take (within the obvious limits of, on the one hand, providing themselves with enough consumers' goods to live on, and, on the other, of replacing their productive plant at least as rapidly as it wears out). What is vital is that they will have brought this decision under their conscious control. For one of the factors which makes our present system work so ruinously is that we leave this proportion to be determined by blind and violent fluctuations in the relative expectation of profit in the two spheres of production.[1]

What is to be the proportion between the output of means of production and consumers' goods will not, then, be a particularly difficult question for a British or American planning authority to decide. But this is only so because the British and American people are already well equipped with productive plant. No urgent need for new means of production will face a British or American planning authority. It may devote a high proportion of the productive resources which it finds available to the urgent task of satisfying at once the miserably unsatisfied need for consumers' goods of the mass of the British and American people. On the other hand, if for some reason the planning commission thought it advisable to devote a comparitively high proportion of our available productive resources to providing new plant and equipment, this could be done without any very grave sacrifice in the standard of life. It would involve at worst a postponement of any immediate increase in that standard above a level of health and decency.

But this enviable situation is not shared by a planning authority in an undeveloped or technically backward community. Such an authority faces a hard choice. It must either reconcile itself to a very slow rate of technical progress or it must call on the community to forgo for a time all but the most necessary consumers' goods and services. For only so can it free labour and factories, skill and equipment, for the production of new means of production.

As in so much else, so in the process of industrialization it is the beginning which is difficult. For then the productive equipment available, either for producing consumers' goods or means of production, is primitive and inefficient. Yet if this situation is to be remedied, better plant and equipment must be built up to replace this primitive equipment. Unskilled labour, obsolete machines, meagre transport facilities have to be diverted from the task of supplying the population with consumers' goods (and they are inadequate even for this task) on to the task of replacing

---

[1] We shall see in Chapter VII how the capitalist method of distributing income is to-day the controlling factor in the determination of this fundamental proportion. And we shall see how the present difficulties of capitalism are intimately related to this point.

themselves with modernized means of production. The obsolete steel-mills must make steel, not for houses or skyscrapers, or motor cars or railway trucks, but for building modernized steel-mills. Of the few available skilled engineers, many must be taken off production altogether and used to staff the colleges in which a really adequate number of engineers may be trained. Railways, already unable adequately to move the harvest and distribute the flow of consumers' goods from the existing means of production, must be used to carry huge quantities of constructional material for the building of new plants. The task of a planning authority in such conditions is really difficult—its choice must necessarily be to some extent a choice of evils. And these have been just the conditions faced by the only planning authority which has so far existed in the world—namely, the State Planning Commission of the Soviet Union.[1]

Again and again the soviets, acting through this commission, have had to face difficult decisions on exactly this point. How big a proportion of their existing productive resources could they deflect to the task of building up new and far superior means of production, while leaving enough resources to produce a supply of consumers' goods adequate to feed, clothe, and house the population? Political and military considerations imperatively demanded, upon pain of the destruction of the whole socialist system by foreign intervention, the utmost possible speed of industrialization. The resources initially available were tragically small. It was decided to apply an unparalleled proportion of them to the process of their own development. The first steps of such a process were bound to be painful. With every year that passed, however, the sum total of resources available grew. Hence what proportion of them should be used for making new means of production becomes a less acute question. It was only, however, last year (1935) that the Planning Commission found itself with margins of resources which it could turn at will in either direction.[2]

[1] The State Planning Commission is, of course, merely the executive instrument of the Soviet government, which is in turn the executive instrument of the federated peoples of the Soviet Union.

[2] Indeed, it is only this year (1936) that the first really sharp rise (30 per cent as against a previous annual increase of about 16 per cent) in the output of consumers' goods is being undertaken.

An extraordinary misapprehension exists in connection with this question. We have seen that the backward condition of Russian industry constituted a most formidable obstacle to the establishment of a planned economic system of production for use. It meant that a comparatively small increase in the output of consumer's goods could be immediately achieved by the Russian people, since every available productive resource had to be utilized for the creation of new means of production. Yet again and again we see it stated that this frightful difficulty was a great asset, that it alone made possible the establishment and successful working of a planned socialist system in the Soviet Union; that the absence of this obstacle in advanced communities such as Britain and America would make it impossible for them to establish such planned systems.

This notion appears to arise from the delusion that a planned economic system of production for use would or could have the same kind of difficulty in distributing the consumers' goods which it had produced as is experienced by capitalism. Writers who suffer from this delusion have noticed—indeed, who has not?—that capitalism cannot to-day distribute to the population those consumers' goods which it could so easily produce—that in times of crisis it cannot even distribute some of the consumers' goods which it has actually produced, and is forced to destroy them; to burn the wheat and the coffee, to plough in the cotton, and to slaughter the hogs.

"But," such writers conclude, "the same thing will happen in the Soviet Union, so soon as it has completed its task of industrialization, and begins to turn its attention to increasing its output of consumers' goods. A glut will surely follow; unemployment will reappear; then they will have to burn the wheat of the steppes as well as of the prairies; shirts will rot in Russian as well as Lancashire warehouses, while Russian as well as Lancashire backs are bare."[1]

[1] A foremost British economist, Mr. T. E. Gregory, was in 1933 writing, for example, along these lines. In his booklet, *Gold, Unemployment, and Capitalism*, he wrote: "... it is now quite clear that in the last few years Russia has been passing through a ' Construction boom ' analogous in every respect to that experienced in the Capitalistic world; and that, with the gradual slackening of the intensity of that boom, the phenomenon of unemployment is appearing." It is now 1936. Professor Gregory is still, I suppose, anxiously awaiting the appearance of unemployment in the Soviet Union.

Those who think in this way have failed to notice the reason why British and American capitalism cannot distribute anything approaching their possible output of consumers' goods. It is not, clearly, because we lack in Britain and America the physical means of transport necessary to take the goods from the warehouses and deliver them to the homes. It is, as every business man knows to his cost, simply and solely because an increased quantity of consumers' goods *cannot be sold at profitable prices*. In other words, our inability to distribute is a direct consequence of our system of production for profit. (In Chapter VII we shall describe how this inability arises.)

Such an inability to distribute could not conceivably arise in the case of a system of planned production for use. Truly, if some enormous error of planning had been committed, insufficient transport facilities might make it impossible to distribute, in this physical sense, the possible output of the factories in a given area. But this would be a hold-up due to a *shortage* of resources, not, as is the case under capitalism, a hold-up due to a *surplus* of resources. In no circumstances could a situation arise in which a socialist economic system possessed all the physical means for producing and distributing goods, and yet could not put the goods into people's hands. The capitalist system can get into this extraordinary predicament only because it must produce, if it is not to become utterly chaotic, *only those goods the production and distribution of which will yield a profit*.

A system of production—and consequently of distribution—for use has, as we have seen, its own difficulties to face. But it cannot conceivably encounter this particular difficulty. We may rely upon it that it will always be able to sell to its own people every single consumable food which it can get produced. This is already becoming apparent in the Soviet Union. The formidable initial difficulty of getting the process of industrialization into motion has been, to a large extent, overcome, and a now rapidly increasing flow of consumers' goods is appearing. Not the faintest difficulty in disposing of these goods to the population is being experienced. On the contrary, they disappear amongst the 170 million Russian consumers as disappear the rivers into the desert beyond Samarkand !

How has this state of things been achieved ? We shall discover the secret of it when we describe the socialist method of distribution (Chapter IX). Here we need only say that in a socialist system of planned production for use one of the essential, although one of the easiest, tasks of the planning authority is to arrange for the issue of just exactly the right amount of money to buy, at the prices fixed, all the goods and services which the community can produce in any given year. Thus the only limit to the market in a socialist society is the real need of the population for goods and services.

Every capitalist government is to-day faced with the urgent problem of finding an external market even for those goods which its half-stifled productive system has produced. The Soviet government alone is faced with the problem of how to satisfy the illimitable market provided by its own population. For it has taken good care to equip that population with the necessary purchasing power. Here is a description of the Soviet government's real problem.

" Who can compute the effect of the ever-widening desire for two or three rooms per family, instead of the one, or much less than one, with which nine-tenths of the population of tsarist Russia contented itself; of the never satisfied clamour for more clothing and better; of the ever-rising standards expected in public health and public education; of the demand for more hospitals and maternity centres, with an almost illimitable increase in the nurses and doctors serving all the villages between the Baltic and the Pacific; of the desire for more schools and libraries, with endlessly more teachers and professors and textbooks and scientific apparatus, over one-sixth of the entire land-surface of the globe ? Adapt and contrive as it may, the State Planning Commission is perpetually finding itself at a loss how best to allocate, among the constantly widening range and increasing magnitude of the consumers' effective demand, the always insufficient labour force, buildings and raw material by means of which alone this demand can be satisfied. Meanwhile no one can fail to recognize that, in 1935, there is vastly greater plenty, in the cities and in the villages, than there has been at any previous time in Russian history. The shops and stores are (1935) now abundantly supplied, ration cards have been one after another abolished, and the total retail sales are going up by leaps and bounds."

This passage is taken from Mr. and Mrs. Sidney Webb's *Soviet Communism: A New Civilization?* This is the definitive study of the political, economic and social life of the Soviet Union.[1]

It was worth while to discuss the delusion that developed means of production would be a difficulty for a socialist economic system, both because it is widespread, and also because of the light which it throws upon the mental confusion into which the economic confusion of our epoch has thrown us. How strange that anyone could imagine that it was an asset to a country to have to build up its basic productive equipment almost from the start; that it was a liability to possess splendidly developed means of production ! And yet this is just the delusion which is induced in our minds by the ever-growing confusion of capitalism. For, as we shall see, it *is* true that the only task for which capitalist production for profit is suited is the building up of a community's means of production. Hence, if we cannot imagine any other economic system, then, truly, it *is* a disaster when this task is accomplished. For then there remains nothing for the system to do, and it must necessarily fall into disorder.

But once we have realized that in capitalism " nature's copy's not eterne " we can realize also that the accomplishment of the process of industrialization is an epoch-making achievement. With toil and sacrifice man has built up a productive equipment which could give him plenty and security. Now, surely, he should enjoy the fruits of his achievement ? But it is becoming every day more clear that he cannot enjoy those fruits except under a socialist system of production for use. The

[1] As I shall necessarily make many references to the Soviet Union in subsequent chapters, it will be well to say here that my authority is, unless otherwise stated, my own personal observation in the Soviet Union or Mr. and Mrs. Webb's book. It seems to me better to use Mr. and Mrs. Webb's book as a single authority, of whose authenticity readers can readily judge for themselves, rather than to quote from a selection of the innumerable works on the Soviet Union, which are of varying degrees of accuracy and value. Moreover, Mr. and Mrs. Webb's book, besides being the culminating achievement of the two greatest social investigators of the English-speaking world, is a sort of epitome of the whole vast literature, in English, French and German, in this field; for almost every work in these three languages (and many in Russian) has been sifted and surveyed by Mr. and Mrs. Webb.

idea that developed means of production, which are in fact the pre-requisite for such a system, will prove a difficulty for it would be laughable, if it were not tragic.

Needless to say, the fact that the British and American people are the heirs apparent to incomparably better means of production than those which the State Planning Commission of the Soviet Union inherited from tsarism, will be a colossal advantage to them. It is not too much to say that a British and American system of planned production for use will start at a point which the Russian system, despite the extraordinary rapidity of its present progress, cannot hope to reach before the end of several five-year periods of planning.

As the N.S.P.P.C. report has demonstrated, there would be no question for us of the severe, although heroic, struggle for industrialization which has been waged by the Russian people. From the moment of their appointment British and American planning authorities could, and no doubt will, increase the output of consumers' goods and services, and so raise the general standard of life, to an extent which will transform the whole life of our communities.

CHAPTER IV

The Existing Socialist System of Production

THE report on America's productive resources which we have discussed could do no more than illuminate the principle upon which any socialist economic system must work. During the past eight years, however, 170 million human beings have in actual practice been organizing their economic life upon the basis of planned production for use. How have they done it?

The socialist economic system now at work in the Soviet Union is, surely, a most important, as it is certainly a most fascinating, object of study. For, if it is successful, it undeniably offers us all a way out of our thickening difficulties. Mr. and Mrs. Webb tell us that it was primarily this feature of Soviet life which challenged their attention. " Will this new system of economic relationships," they asked themselves, " and this new motivation of wealth production, prove permanently successful? "

" For if it does, it will not only show the rest of the world how to abolish technological, and indeed all other mass unemployment, together with the devastating alternation of commercial booms and slumps; but further, by opening the way to the maximum utilization of human enterprise and scientific discovery in the service of humanity, it will afford the prospect of increase beyond all computation, alike of national wealth and of individual well-being." (Ibid., p. 602.)

For a variety of reasons it did not prove possible to put the economic life of the Soviet Union on to anything which can be called a fully planned basis until the year 1928. The first step towards doing so was taken (some years earlier) when every type of organization within the Soviet Union was required to send to the State Planning Commission complete information as to its output of products, its consumption of raw materials, its employment of labour, etc., etc., etc., during the past year, and its proposed output, consumption, employment, etc., during the coming year. This collection at a single centre of comprehensive statistics of the entire economic system (a collection which is never possible to complete under capitalism) is the prerequisite of a planned economy.

But in order to use the immense flood of information which such a regulation must cause to pour in upon the planning authority, a very extensive and expert statistical and administrative machine must be evolved. The need to create such an institution was one of the reasons why planning could not be fully developed in the Soviet Union before 1928. By that year, however, an administrative machine capable of tackling the task of collecting, verifying, collating, arranging, and then making deductions from, this flood of information had been created. "Gozplan," as the State Planning Commission is called in Russia, had become by far the largest and most elaborate statistical centre in the world.

This brings us to the actual making of the plan, to the crucial question of what shall be produced and who shall produce it. Now most people suppose that this all-important question is decided, under a socialist system, by the arbitrary fiat of the planning authority. But this is not so. The first step in building the plan is not to coerce the productive organizations, but to consult them: to ask them what they propose to produce during the coming year, and what supplies of raw material, equipment, skilled and unskilled labour they estimate that they will need for the job. Their replies, when put together, make what is in a sense the very first draft of the plan. It is a plan which no one, and no single organization, has written. It is a plan which has emerged from the proposals for the coming year of the producers of the whole country, and it is based, of course, upon their experience during the past year. But this first, embryonic, draft may be, and indeed almost certainly will be, lacking in self-consistency. The building industry, for example, may be demanding 25 per cent more skilled bricklayers than exist. Or, again, the motor manufacturing enterprises, the shipbuilders, the builders, and all the other steel users, may be making a combined demand for steel which is 10 per cent above (or below) the total output proposed by the steel industry. Accordingly Gozplan must begin its complicated task of making the draft plan self-consistent. It must see to it that the total demand for, say, steel and coal, [put in by all steel and coal consuming industries, equals the proposed total output of steel and coal, minus the output used for domestic consumption. (This part of the task leads up to the decision as to the relative amount of the community's productive resources to be devoted to means of production and consumers' goods which we discussed in the last chapter. The collation and making self-consistent of the outputs proposed by the different consumers' goods industries is, on the other hand, the first step towards that meeting of the defined needs of the population which we discussed in Chapter II.) When this task is accomplished the planning authority will have before it some sort of self-consistent proposal, made by the productive organizations themselves, as to next year's production.[1]

We must notice the character of these productive organizations. For these are the basic units of a socialist economic system, the socialist analogues of the firms, farms, partnerships, joint stock companies, corporations, and trusts of the capitalist world. These organizations fall into three main categories. First, there are governmental agencies—state, regional, or municipal enterprises.[2] This form predominates in productive industry proper. It accounts for ninety-nine-hundredths of the output of new means of production, and of a smaller but still predominating percentage of the output of consumers' goods. Second, there are consumers' co-operative societies, constituted upon the same

[1] Although we are accustomed to speak of a Five Year Plan, the production programmes are apt to be revised so drastically each year that detailed planning is for one year ahead, with a much more general forecast for the following four, three, two and one years—as the plan progresses. Indeed, there is a sense in which planning must long remain predominantly on a one year basis. For the seasons, with their periodicity of crops, still dominated so important a section of man's productive activity that any detailed plan will naturally extend from harvest to harvest.

[2] These governmental productive agencies may be defined as organizations in which the means of production and the raw materials used are owned by the community as a whole, or by a regional government (as the government of one or other of the federated Republics of the Soviet Union such as the Ukraine, or the Karelian Republic), or by a municipality, and in which, consequently, the employees work for wages. But they are themselves of several different kinds, of which the " combine," consisting of a group of mines or factories is now the most important type. The history of the evolution of the combine as the predominant productive unit in Soviet industry is interesting, but is largely inaccessible to the English-speaking reader. It is one of the few aspects of Soviet life inadequately dealt with by Mr. and Mrs. Webb. An admirably clear account does exist in *Russia's Productive System*, by Mr. Emile Burns (Gollancz). But so rapidly do things move in the Soviet Union that this work (published 1930) is now to some extent out of date.

general lines as British or Western European consumers' co-operative societies, except that they do not pay cash dividends on the purchases of their members. This form of organization is important in what we call the distributive trades; in retail, and to a less extent in wholesale, selling. It has no monopoly of these spheres, however, since various governmental agencies carry on the wholesale and retail selling in the towns. On the other hand, consumers' co-operative societies (as in Britain) have penetrated into the field of the production of consumers' goods. Third, there are Producers' Co-operative Societies organized upon a basis which would have been more familiar to many British workers a hundred years ago than it is to-day. These are organizations of workers who, *as a group*, own and control their own means of production and raw materials, instead of working for wages with means of production and on raw materials owned by the community as a whole, as do the workers in state or municipal agencies. Moreover, these workers, since they themselves own their enterprises, receive, instead of wages, a dividend which represents their share[1] of the total price realized for the product of their enterprise. The essential sphere of these producers' co-operatives is agriculture. For the collective farms, which, to the extraordinary number of a quarter of a million, now cover the surface of the globe from the Baltic to the Pacific, are Producers' Co-operative Societies. But this form of organization is not confined to agriculture. It plays a subordinate but useful rôle in industrial production, where " artels," or Producers' Co-operatives of artizans with the substantial membership of three million, are at work producing goods (such as toys) or services (such as house repairs) and those types of maintenance and servicing which do not require large quantities of what we should call fixed capital. On the other hand, this form of organization has no monopoly of agricultural production. For there exist some 10,000 state farms which belong to the category of governmental agencies; for in them men work for wages exactly as in steel-works or print-shops.

These Producers' Co-operatives are a form of economic organization which has existed ever since the abolition of capitalism in Russia in 1917. But it is only in the last six years, with the estab-

[1] Usually calculated according to the amount of work which they have done.

lishment of 250,000 collective farms on the basis of producers' co-operation, that they have become a quantitatively important factor in the economic life of the country. That they have now done so is of the highest interest to students of the history of socialist thought and of the working class movement. For they represent the revival in new conditions of an early tendency which had become almost extinct. As we shall describe in Part III of this book, the concept of a group of workers, jointly owning their means of production and dividing amongst themselves the full proceeds of the sale of their products, was the form of organization originally aimed at by almost all the socialists of Western Europe. All through the nineteenth century repeated efforts to set up such organizations were made in Britain, France and America. They all failed, and, although with great reluctance, the working class and socialist movement gradually abandoned the hope of getting rid of the capitalist employer by this direct means of banding together to employ themselves. The experience of the Soviet Union has now shown that the ideal of co-operative production is an inherently sound one *if it is realized in a socialist environment*. We now know that the socialist pioneers who attempted to establish such co-operative enterprises were not mistaken in supposing that this was one of the forms which free men associating for productive purposes would adopt. Where they went wrong was to suppose that producers' co-operatives could co-exist with capitalist enterprise, and with the possession of political power by the capitalist class. It is not, we now know, until large-scale industry has been socialized, and until the capitalists have neither economic nor political power, that co-operative productive enterprises of this type can succeed.

These, then, are the economic organizations, the output and needs of which must be planned by the State Planning Commission. It is their proposals—rendered self-consistent—which must be compared by the State Planning Commission with the proposals for the development of the national economy formulated by the Soviet government. The Soviet government, for its part, will have many ends in view which we may think of as extra-economic. It will not be solely intent, that is to say, upon maximizing the total wealth production of the Soviet

Union. It will regard the plan as in one respect, at any rate, a plan for achieving certain given extra-economic purposes. One of these purposes must be for the present the defence of the Union from the return of the armies of those six capitalist states which were ravaging her just sixteen years ago. Another is the provision of an ever more adequate supply of all the goods and services needed for raising with unparalelled rapidity the whole cultural life of the community; the provision of schools and teachers, of textbooks and paper, of pens and ink, of pamphlets and newspapers—on a scale adequate to the needs of 170 million persons. A third purpose will be the supply of the elaborate equipment and highly trained staff needed to raise and maintain the whole physical level of that vast population: to provide hospitals and doctors, X-ray apparatuses and sanatoria, trained dentists with their apparatuses, and the thousand other things needful to an adequate health service. Finally, the Soviet government will have its view as to the general character of the coming year's plan, as to the degree of emphasis to be laid on the expansion of industries producing means of production relative to those producing consumers' goods, and so on.

When the Government's views have found expression in it, the Provisional Plan is ready. But this Provisional Plan is not now simply adopted by the Central Executive Committee of the U.S.S.R. Congress of Soviets and issued as an instruction. On the contrary, a second and extensive process of consultation is now undertaken. The Provisional Plan is now formally submitted to each of the commissariats or government departments, and is transmitted by them to each and all of the productive establishments the activities of which it will govern during the coming year. For this purpose the plan is in effect cut up into many thousands of separate pieces, each of which is concerned with the proposed activities of a particular establishment. And each establishment studies in minute detail its own piece of the plan. Moreover, it is not just the statistical office, or even the administrative staff of each enterprise, which undertakes this study. The plan is submitted to the whole body of workers by hand and brain attached to the establishment. Conferences of the whole staff are held at which proposals for the plan's revision are discussed and often adopted.

The plan, with all the emendations proposed by all the enterprises and institutions of the country, is then sent back to the State Planning Commission, where for a second time a process of comparison and collation must be gone through so that no suggestion which would contradict any other is adopted. The resultant document is the final or definitive plan. It is laid before the Council of People's Commissars and the Central Executive Committee of the U.S.S.R. (which roughly correspond to our Cabinet and Parliament, or Congress, respectively).[1] Upon its adoption by these bodies it becomes the law of the land. For when all the consultation, and comparison, and collation have been done a decision is necessary. As Mr. and Mrs. Webb write, " Once private ownership, with its profit-seeking motive of production for the competitive market is abandoned, specific directions must be given as to what each establishment has to produce." These specific directions are given and they have the force of law; but they are drawn up upon the basis of the information and the proposals of the productive establishments themselves.

It will not have escaped the reader's attention that the State Planning Commission will not be able to plan the activities of the Producers' Co-operatives in quite the same sense that it will be able to plan, as an instruction, the activities of the governmental agencies. The members of the Producers' Co-operatives, owning their own plant and some, at any rate, of their own raw materials, might in theory refuse to fall in with the instructions of the State Planning Commission. In the field of industry the Producers' Co-operatives are relatively so small, and so dependent upon the large governmental agencies, that the point is unimportant. In agriculture, however, they enormously predominate. And as they sell a great part of their produce upon the market, in which competing bidders exist, they might feel unwilling or unable to produce the quantities and types of produce required of them by the Commission. The Commission and the Government have, it is true, a number of methods of influencing them. They may vary the incidence of taxation; they may act upon the relative prices which governmental agencies will bid for different kinds of produce; and they may vary the prices

[1] See Chapter XIII.

and the quantities of the industrial products supplied to the villages, which are the ultimate inducement to the collective farmers to produce a surplus above their own needs (plus taxation and payments for the services, such as tractor ploughing, seed selection, etc., which governmental agencies perform for them).

All this, however, is something different from, and less than, direct control. Moreover, the existence of these numerous co-operative and individual producers for the market means that a large number of goods and services are distributed by means of exchanges between different producers, and not by allocation by the planning authority. It is important to make this distinction clear. We can imagine a socialist economic system in which every productive enterprise was directly owned by the state and in which, therefore, everyone was a wage-earning employee of one single employer, the State. (This, indeed, is the somewhat monotone picture of " the Socialist State " which is often drawn by those who favour the continuance of the capitalist system.) In such a society all the products would originally belong to the State and would be then sold by the State to its wage workers in return for their wages. The money paid out in such wages would be a mere ticket for goods up to a certain quantity. Unless the tendering of this ticket, in order to receive goods up to the value marked upon it, could be called an act of exchange, there would be no exchanging in such a community.

Now, whatever the merits or demerits of such a community might be, the existing socialist society bears little resemblance to it. Since an important proportion of the productive establishments are owned, not by the State, but by their own members, an important proportion of the total annual product comes on to a genuine market and is bought and sold, i.e. exchanged, between these organizations and between individuals. This system of socialist exchange, or trade, is not confined to the products of the producers' co-operative societies. State agencies of production often make contracts by which they buy a part of the product of either another state agency or a producers' co-operative society. Again, both forms of productive enterprise, in those cases in which they produce consumable goods, often set up direct retailing points (shops or stalls in an organized market or bazaar), in which they sell their products direct to the consuming public. Thus there exists a network of buying and selling (exchanging) of goods which never pass through the hands of the State as such, but move along a number of channels from their producers to their ultimate consumers.

The respects in which this form of socialist trade differs from capitalist trading are discussed in the last chapter of this Part, where we deal with the incentives by which the whole enormous economic mechanism of a socialist community is kept in motion. Here we need only say briefly that commodities are caused to circulate without two typical characteristics of capitalism appearing. At no point in the process is there the employment of wage labour for the purpose of making profit for any individual or group of individuals, and secondly no act of purchase is made with the object of re-selling the goods obtained, *at a profit* to a third individual or organization.[1]

The advantages of this decentralization of the distributive system are clearly very great. Indeed, Stalin has several times stated that without mutual trading or exchanging, of goods and services between state or co-operative organizations, the Soviet economic system could not work. " The expansion of Soviet trade is a very urgent problem," he said in the speech in which (in 1933) he summed up the results of the first Five Year Plan, " which if not solved will make further progress impossible." In fact, there has developed in subsequent years a complex network of trading amongst and between the State agencies, the Producers' Co-operatives and the Consumers' Co-operatives, the individual producers, and between all these and the consuming public. But it is, no doubt, also true that the existence of this system of socialist trading creates problems for the State Planning Commission. For example, it is clear that, so long as such exchanging exists, money is not a mere ticket entitling its recipient to such and such a quantity of goods to be drawn from

[1] This does not mean that a retailing organization, such as a consumers' co-operative society, may not buy an article from a factory and then re-sell it to its members. It may and does constantly do so, and is, of course, allowed to add to the article's price a sum sufficient to cover the cost of retailing. But what no organization must do is to buy an article on the market with the expectation and the intention of re-selling it, unchanged, at a profit. This is speculation and is one of the sins in the socialist calendar. The point is illustrated by the well-known story of the soviet child who was asked by his arithmetic teacher: " Now, Ivan, if a man bought a pound of apples for ten roubles and sold them again for twenty roubles, what would he get ? " " Three months in jail," answered Ivan.

a centralized state supply. It remains for this purpose a medium of circulation and standard of value, which are very different things. In general it will be more difficult to control and so plan in advance such decentralized economic activities.

Experience seems to indicate, however, that the State Planing Commission is in effective control of the situation. The amount of production which it can control by direct instruction is so great, and the influences which it can bring to bear upon the co-operative organizations and individuals which produce the remainder are so powerful, that it appears to be able to do the essential job of keeping any desired proportions between the different types of goods and services produced. It is certain that the socialist systems which their respective working classes will establish in Britain and America will include this kind of socialist trading. On the other hand, America and, still more, Britain are much more closely organized and integrated communities than is the Soviet Union. For this reason a greater degree of centralization, with the advantage that this will permit of more accurate and rapid planning, should at once be possible in a socialist Britain and a socialist America. Nor, as we shall see in Chapter XII, will this involve the least degree of regimentation for their populations.

This, then, is the character of the productive organizations, and the method of their regulation, developed by the first socialist economic system which has ever existed in the history of the world. What are the results? Controversy is endless upon this question. But one thing at any rate is certain: the first socialist economic system that the world has ever seen has now survived for eight years[1] and is rapidly developing. The statesmen and economists of the capitalist world continue to declare that socialism is a Utopian dream, that capitalism is not a particular economic system which might be succeeded by another, but is a sort of irreplaceable " natural order." But all the time a socialist system lives and grows before our eyes. This is by far the most important fact of our epoch.

[1] The establishment of socialism in the Soviet Union is usually, and in principle correctly, dated from the dispossession of the Russian capitalists in 1917. On this reckoning, socialism has been in existence for nineteen years. But it is only during the last eight years that a fully planned system of production for use has been in existence. Hence from a purely economic standpoint this period may be thought the more relevant.

Has the first socialist economic system not only survived, however, but proved itself superior to capitalism ? It would, of course, be possible to quote a flood of statistics upon the increases in production which have been, and are now being, achieved in the Soviet Union. The end of the second, and by far the larger, of the two Five Year Plans (the conclusions of which mark a time of general national stocktaking) has not yet arrived. But figures for the fulfilment of the First and smaller plan, which ended in 1932, are available :

" The gross output of industrial production increased from 15·7 billion roubles in 1928 to 34·3 billion roubles in 1932 (calculated at prices prevailing in 1926–27), which represents 218·5 per cent of 1928. The volume of industrial production in 1932 exceeded the pre-war level more than three-fold, and exceeded the level of 1928 more than two-fold. The First Five Year Plan as a whole was fulfilled (in four and a quarter years) to the extent of 93·7 per cent as far as the gross output of industry is concerned."[1]

These figures form a striking contrast to what was happening in the capitalist world, since during those particular years production was everywhere declining almost as rapidly as it was mounting in the Soviet Union. The figures of the Second Five Year Plan will show—it is easy to forecast on the basis of what has been achieved during the first three years—far larger increases in production. On the other hand, these have been years of some increases in production in most capitalist states. Hence the comparison may not be so striking.

In any event, such global statistics of production do not give us any very substantial idea of what has been achieved. It is when we pass from such statistical generalizations to particular instances of the power of a socialist economic system to furnish the population with goods and services that we begin to realize what has already been accomplished in the Soviet Union.

But is it not the case, the reader may ask, that many particular commodities are notoriously scarce in the Soviet Union ? And is not this scarcity a very bad advertisement for socialism ?

[1] *Summary of the Fulfilment of the First Five Year Plan.*

It is perfectly true that Soviet citizens feel that many commodities are scarce. Paradoxically enough, however, the creation of this feeling of scarcity (and it is undoubtedly a consquence of socialism) is one of the greatest achievements of the socialist economic system ! *For it co-exists with an enormous increase over pre-socialist levels in the production of just those commodities which the population feels to be scarce.*

For what is scarcity ? Scarcity is a situation in which the supply of any good or service does not equal the demand for it. Hence a good which has not previously been scarce can become so, either by the supply becoming smaller or the demand becoming larger. Indeed, it is clear that a good can, and will, become scarce even if the supply increases, if the demand for it increases more rapidly. *And this is just what has happened with good after good in the Soviet Union. Socialism has greatly increased the supply of these goods. But, at the same time, by distributing (in a manner to be described in subsequent chapters) adequate purchasing power to the entire population, it has increased the demand for these goods to a far greater extent. Hence the goods, in spite of a great increase in their production, have become scarce.*

Boots provide a typical example. In 1913, Russia produced between $\frac{1}{15}$ and $\frac{1}{20}$ pair of boots per person per year. In 1933 production was at the rate of half a pair a year per person. Thus boot production per head has gone up just about ten times.[1] Yet many Russians are inclined to feel that boots are scarcer than they were before the war ! For before the war " the average Russian " never dreamt that it was possible for him to possess boots. He wrapped his feet in canvas, flax, or straw " lapti." Socialism has both evoked in him the desire to possess boots and supplied him with the money to buy them. No wonder a ten-fold increase in production is still insufficient for such a market ! Far away indeed from even the possibility of that curse of the capitalist world, a " glut," are the producers of a socialist economic system ! Thus we may say that the towering achievement of the first socialist economic system has been the simultaneous abolition of glut and unemployment. This achievement has been made possible, we shall see, by the deliberate

---

[1] Figures from *Supply and Trade in the U.S.S.R.*, by W. Nodel. (These and other figures on boot production are quoted by the Webbs.)

and systematic distribution to the entire population of enough purchasing power to clear the market of all the goods produced.

It is now time to examine the view of those economists and experts of the capitalist world who deny that a socialist system of planned production for use can (or presumably, therefore, does) exist. Of these authorities Mr. and Mrs. Webb write with irony, that they " do not trouble to dispute the actual achievements of the planned economy of the U.S.S.R., because they claim to possess a science according to which these achievements are logically impossible." We might find this statement incredible had not a leading figure of this school of thought, Professor Ludwig von Mises, written a volume, the five hundred pages of which severally and collectively seek to disprove the possibility of the existence of a planned economic system of production for use, without once mentioning the existence of such a system in one-sixth of the world. Moreover, this school of capitalist economists are the essential leaders of the thought of their world. Other schools of their colleagues differ from them, that is to say, not so much in principle as by putting forward their views more cautiously.

We have already noticed (p. 20) that this school of economists claim that the capitalist system is inherently perfect and that any defects which may be noticeable in the capitalist world are the result of deviations from, and interference with, the essential principles upon which the system works. They represent our buying of commodities in a free market as a sort of permanent election in which the population as a whole chooses what commodities shall be produced for it. (And so, no doubt, it is. But it is an election in which some voters have approximately forty thousand times as many votes as others. For this, it is calculated, is about the difference between the size of the incomes of the richest and the poorest citizens of such capitalist communities as Britain and America.) Compared to capitalism, these economists suggest, a planned economic system is so crude as to be unworkable. If, however, we examine the statements of this school of thought we shall find that what they really amount to are declarations that planning would not achieve a perfect use of society's available productive resources. Thus Professor Robbins of London University tells us that:

" The requirement of a rational plan . . . is that the factors of production (the land, capital and labour) should be so distributed between the various alternatives of production that no commodity which is produced has less value than the commodities which might have been produced had the factors of production been free for other purposes."

(*The Great Depression*, by Lionel Robbins. Macmillan, 1934.)

By " value " Professor Robbins means, in this passage, " capacity to satisfy human needs." So the requirement of a rational plan is that no commodity should be produced which has less capacity to satisfy human needs than another commodity which might have been produced by a different use of the same means of production. In other words, the Professor asserts that the requirement of a rational plan is that the planning authority should never make a mistake.

There follow some passages which demonstrate that a planning authority would not be in a position to achieve this requirement. Therefore, Professor Robbins continues, half explicitly, half by implication, the results of planning must be inferior to those attained by the capitalist system: for that system can never make a mistake, or, at any rate, could not do so if it was left free from governmental interference.

The mechanism of the Professor's argument is visible to the naked eye. It is first demonstrated (quite irrefutably) that planning will not produce perfect results. Then this demonstration is treated as if it proved that planning would be, not merely imperfect, but impossible, and that the results of unplanned production are perfect. Therefore planned production is incomparably the inferior method ! How true it is that the results of socialist planning, in common with all other human activities without exception, are not perfect. And how wholly irrelevant is this conclusion to our desperately urgent task of devising an economic system which will not produce the tragic and preposterous catastrophes of capitalism.

Moreover, the mistakes which are made by a planning authority are not only of a different magnitude, but are also of a different kind, to the mistakes which arise from the breakdown of the self-regulating profits system. The mistakes of planning are mistakes incidental to bringing the adjustment of a complex productive system under conscious control. The huge misdirections of production which occur under capitalism should not perhaps be called " mistakes " at all. For they are not the errors of men consciously working towards the end of fitting production to human need. They are more analogous to natural catastrophes. Under the capitalist principle of production for profit, the adjustment of production to need takes place (in so far as it takes place at all) automatically and unconsciously. It is not something which anyone does: it is something which happens. Hence it is uncontrolled and uncontrollable.

Under capitalism the necessary regulation of the productive system is carried on unconsciously, independently of men's wills. Its regulatory principle asserts itself like a blind force of nature, leaving destruction and suffering in its wake. Things, not men, are in the saddle. We seem, and, under our present system, we actually are, the frightened dependents of those very machines which might be our tireless slaves. Under a planned economic system, on the other hand, men, working in association, tackle the job of consciously controlling, to suit themselves, their own productive system. The successful achievement of this control will mark a decisive step forward in human history.[1]

It may be objected that it is more difficult consciously to control production than to leave the matter to the violent self-regulation of the profits system. In a sense this is true. It is always more difficult to exercise conscious control than to allow things to take their own course. It is " more difficult " to drive a motor car than to take one's hands off the wheel and allow it to go into the ditch. It is, in this sense, more difficult to control our formidable methods of production than to let them control us. But since their control over us is proving ruinous, it is a difficulty which we must, and can, face. However inperfect our control may at first be, it cannot produce results one quarter so bad as does capitalism to-day. In fact such control will, in highly developed communities such as Britain

[1] In the case of the Soviet Union we can write " has marked."

Cs

and America, result from the beginning in general plenty and security and so transform human life. When men are in the saddle, and things have become the instruments of their will, but not before, we shall escape from the destitution, the insecurity, and the violence which are presently destroying us.

CHAPTER V

Incompatibility of the Two Productive Systems

IT is impossible to combine the capitalist and socialist systems of production. You cannot take *both* profitability *and* the deliberate decisions of a planning authority as the criterion of what goods, and of what quantities of goods, shall be produced. You cannot have it both ways. Either you must rely upon the supposedly self-regulating system of the market, drawing production after demand, by the magnet of profit, or you must scrap this mechanism and lay out your productive resources on a preconceived plan in order to meet a defined need for consumers' goods.

Imagine the confusion which would result from an effort to combine these two mutually exclusive systems. Let us say that a state planning commission was set up in Britain or America to-day, while our existing social and economic system was left otherwise unchanged. The commission would have no difficulty, it is true, in finding both unused productive resources and unsatisfied human needs. It would find men and women who lacked clothes, for example, existing together with idle textile mills, unemployed weavers and dyers, and a surplus of raw cotton. Let us suppose, therefore, that the commission ordered the owners of the closed-down textile mills to open them and begin producing shirts and dresses and underclothes for the millions who are ragged to-day.

Now at that moment the state of the market for textiles might be in one of two conditions. It might be such that production from the closed mills would be profitable, or it might be such that production would be unprofitable. And the market would necessarily be in one condition or the other. Let us see what must happen in either case. If production were profitable, the owners of the idle textile mills would readily obey the instructions of the planning commission. Indeed, unless the commission acted promptly, it would find that the owners had opened their mills already without waiting for any instructions. In short, the instructions would be quiet unnecessary.

But what would happen in the case of production being

unprofitable ? Let us suppose that the planning commission is armed with all the powers of the State and that it forces the owners to open their mills and produce. Week by week the operations of the mills will show a loss. Moreover, it will be a growing loss. For the appearance on the market of the additional supplies of textiles will, other things being equal, depress their prices to new and still more unprofitable levels. This cannot go on. The owners of the textile mills must either disobey the planning commission's instructions or they must cease to be the owners of the textile mills. For they will go bankrupt. Thus in one case the instructions of the commission will be totally unnecessary, and in the other they will be impossible to comply with. *Hence, so long as our present economic system remains in existence it is quite impossible to organize production on the basis of a conscious, predetermined plan.*

We have discovered here the reason for a phenomenon which everybody must have noticed. Every capitalist government is nowadays confronted with the problem of trying to find a use for resources of production which it has become unprofitable to use, and which, consequently, are standing idle. In particular, pressure is always exerted on such governments to find a use for the human factor in production; in plain words, to find work for the unemployed. Now, when large-scale unemployment exists in a community, a mass of unsatisfied needs always exist also. On the face of it, then, one would not expect that capitalist governments would have any difficulty in deciding what work to give the unemployed to do. Surely they will put them on to the obvious, urgent work of producing food and clothing and fuel and housing for the destitute ?[1] But, we observe, our governments never do anything of the sort.

Instead, they begin an elaborate search for what are called " work schemes." At a time when millions of the population lack for necessities the unemployed are put on to such tasks as making redundant roads, levelling pit dumps, planting forests, improving parks, and in America, for some unknown reason, above all, to building post offices.[2]

[1] Who are largely, but not exclusively, the unemployed themselves.
[2] The alarmed British traveller in the United States sometimes fears that in a few years' time the whole land surface of the United States will be covered by post offices.

It seems as if some magic circle had been drawn round the ordinary, urgent work of satisfying elementary human needs, forbidding the unemployed from making a single really useful or sensible thing, condemning the government to rack its brains to discover some outlandish or unlikely task on which they can be set. And this, we now see, is just about what has happened. For under capitalism the satisfaction of all the main human needs is the exclusive prerogative of profit-making, and must necessarily be so if the system is not to fall into chaos.

Hence the government must hunt round for work which will not in any case yield a profit, within a time attractive to private enterprise, such as afforestation, or work which is, by long-standing convention, outside the profit-making sphere, such as the collection and delivery of mails. For the government cannot seriously invade the profit-making sphere without throwing the system into disorder. We have already shown what would happen if the government ordered the owners of the means for the production of necessities to employ the unemployed on unprofitable production. They would simply go bankrupt. Nor can a capitalist government (even if it would) build up, and man with the unemployed, new means for the production of these necessities.[1]

For just as soon as these new government-built, owned, and operated means of production began putting an additional supply of food, clothes, fuel, and consumers' goods in general on to the market, they would come into the sharpest competition with the goods from the privately owned means of production which could still be operated profitably. Down would go the price of every one of these goods. Soon even those private means of production which it had hitherto been profitable to operate would begin to show losses. As these losses accumulated it would be necessary to close down these private plants and to discharge their workers. For every worker, in short, which the government re-employed in its own factories, it would throw out another from private industry.

No, the two systems of production will not mix. All talk, and the whole English-speaking world is deluged with such talk, of the planning of production under capitalism is nonsense. The very essence of capitalism, the great advantage which is claimed

[1] As Mr. Upton Sinclair proposed to do in California.

for it, is that under it production can be left unplanned, free to adapt itself to the changing pull of demand.

But, it may be objected, capitalist governments are nowadays continually intervening in the economic field, and increasingly they do so in the name of planning. Surely this proves that in practice a certain degree of planning, at any rate, is compatible with capitalism ? No one would deny the frequency of these governmental interventions. Hardly a month passes without the British or American government announcing a new tariff, a new scheme for the restriction of this or that crop, a " quota " of coal, set as a maximum above which the coal mines of the country must not produce, a devaluation of the currency, an imposition of " cuts " in the amount of money paid out in social service, or a direct reduction in such wage rates as the government can control or influence. Such measures are undoubtedly interventions in the economic life of the country. If we call them planning, then, beyond doubt, contemporary capitalist governments never cease to plan.

There is, however, a distinction between such measures and the kind of planned production for use defined above. Planned production for use means the deliberate allotment of the resources of production to making certain particular goods, and this, as we have seen, inevitably involves the planning of almost all the community's available resources. For it must soon make impossible (as every capitalist spokesman correctly insists when he is objecting to " socialist experiments ") the allotment of the rest according to profitability.

But the kind of economic measures which our governments now indulge in, and which they call planning, are of a different kind. They are measures designed to restore to production the condition of profitability, which has for some reason been lost, and without which capitalist production cannot be carried on. If we examine these measures we shall find that they all have one or other of two purposes. They are all designed either to raise prices or to reduce costs of production by cutting wages. The purpose of the group of measures designed to restrict production is, avowedly, to raise the price of the products of that portion of the means of production which is still permitted to operate. If cotton and wheat acreage is legally restricted as in America;

if fishing is often restricted to every other day; if the amount of coal which each mine may produce is laid down by law; if the amount of milk and potatoes which each farmer may grow is fixed by a " scheme " having the force of law, as in Britain (to take examples from each country),—then such measures may succeed in creating a relative scarcity of these products, and so to raise their prices to a profitable level. They are a sort of economic contraception, a process of birth-control applied to the means of production, by which a certain proportion of these means of production are rendered sterile, in order that the price realized for the products of the remaining, and still fertile, means of production may be raised. If this elaborate creation of shortage is planning, then, again, capitalist governments never cease to plan.

The reduction of the gold content of the money of the community and the consequential issue of credits on a large scale is designed to have the same effect, viz. the raising of prices. Tariffs and imports-quotas also fall into this price-raising category.

The second group of economic measures taken by capitalist governments are more direct in their action. They are designed to reduce the costs of production by reducing the amounts paid out for labour—either by way of wages or (where, as in Great Britain, these exist) by way of other payments made to the workers, such as insurances, pensions, etc. The purpose of both these groups of measures is to restore profitability to production and so get the self-regulating mechanism of capitalism into motion again. For profits *are* the difference between costs and prices, and they can only be restored either by raising prices or by cutting costs.

Now the government measures which we have listed may or may not be effective for the purpose for which they are designed: that purpose itself may or may not be self-contradictory in any degree. This does not concern us here. We are solely intent to establish the difference between such measures and anything which can be called planning in the sense proper to that word. The measures taken by our capitalist governments constitute, if you will, plans for the better making of profit; they are plans to restore the profit-making system to working order. But that system is itself the antithesis of a system of planned production for use. The planning of our available resources of production, so that they can be used to the best advantage to provide us with the maximum possible quantity of consumers' goods and services, is a process, then, which cannot even begin till after capitalism has ended.

The two systems are, moreover, mutually incompatible for another and more obvious reason. For capitalist production for profit can only be carried on if the means of production are privately and separately owned, while planned production for use can only be carried on if the means of production are pooled under public ownership. The two systems of production are, in a word, each indissolubly associated with a particular *ownership* of the means of production.

For a planning authority cannot begin to plan until it has effective and permanent control over a predominating part of the means of production. Unless it can allot labour, plant, raw materials, and other productive resources in such a way as to produce its pre-defined output of consumers' goods, it will be powerless. But so long as these resources are left in private hands their owners will not, and for that matter cannot, allow their use to be dictated to them by any outside authority. For so long as the means of production are in private hands they must, of necessity, be operated for profit, and not in accordance with any central plan. But this is obvious and amounts merely to saying that you must first get hold of your means of production before you can begin to plan their use.

CHAPTER VI

The Capitalist Method of Distribution

THE only rational purpose of production is consumption. The proper object of digging up coal, growing wheat, and fabricating motor cars, is the consumption of the resultant goods. Hence the economic life of any community cannot consist in its productive system alone. For in order to consume goods and services you must not only produce but distribute them.

The word " distribute " can, however, be used in two different senses. It can be used to mean the process of transporting goods or services from the point of their production to the point of their consumption. And it can also be used to mean the process of sharing out the available supply between the individual citizens of the community. In this chapter we are concerned exclusively with this second use of the term, with the question of sharing out.[1]

Here, then, we shall enquire, not how goods and services are to be sent into people's homes, but how we are to decide which homes they are to be sent into. We shall enquire how we are to share out the available supply amongst us all. For, so long as the supply is limited, this question has got to be settled. It is second only in importance to the question of what goods and services shall be produced.

Now the most convenient way (under any system of production) of sharing out a limited supply of goods and services is not to send everybody a certain mixed ration, whether equal or unequal, of the actual goods and services, but to give people a certain amount of money which they can then use to buy the particular goods and services which they prefer, *up to the amount of the money which they have received*. In other words, the question of how the supply of goods and services is to be shared out is the same question as that of how money incomes are to be distributed. For the distribution of money incomes will command the distribution of goods and services. When we discuss the

[1] The physical transportation of goods to the point of consumption is best regarded as part of the process of their production—and has been so regarded in the above account of the Productive System. All the estimates of productive capacity cited allow, that is to say, for the necessary resources of production being used for this purpose.

question of distribution, what we are really discussing, then, is the question of how incomes are to be allotted. The question is: *What are people to get paid for, and how much is each of them to be paid.*[1]

Under the capitalist system we pay people for two distinct and different functions. In the first place, we pay people according to the quantity and the quality of the work which they do. We call these payments wages, salaries and fees. In the case of wages it is mainly a question of the quantity of work. The worker is paid so much per week of, say, forty-eight hours of work. But the quality of the work—whether it is intense, like the work of a man on a conveyer belt, or comparatively leisurely, like that of an agricultural labourer, and whether it is skilled, like that of an engineer, or unskilled, like that of a general labourer—also determines the amount of the wage. In the case of the larger payments for work done, which we call salaries or fees, it is this factor of skill, of the quality of the work, which predominantly determines the rate of pay.[2]

This is the first method of distributing incomes. But capitalist societies have also a second method. We pay people, not for anything they do, but for what they own. People are paid annual incomes if they own certain kinds of goods. This is not true, we observe, of all kinds of goods. No one is paid anything because he owns a motor car, for example. But a person is paid an income if he or she owns a motor-car-making factory—or a share in such a factory. This reveals to us the distinction. Persons are paid an income if they own property in the means of production. They are paid an income if they own, that is to say, anything which has to be used in order to produce a supply of consumers' goods and services. They are paid an income, for example, if they own land on which crops are grown or stock is raised; if they own a mine from which coal is dug, or a factory in which goods are manufactured.

[1] In investigating the capitalist method of distribution we shall come upon the reason why our present economic system produces those lamentable results which we noted, but did not try to explain, in Chapter I. We shall discover *why* an economic system founded upon the apparently excellent principle of allowing production to be adjusted to demand by the magnet of profit produces, instead of the promised perfection, poverty in the midst of potential plenty, illimitable injustice and waste.

[2] The best worker does not always get the best pay. But no doubt, on the long-run average, superior skill does tend to command superior pay.

If we ask why persons should be paid incomes in respect of such ownership, we shall be told that this is done in order to induce them to allow their property to be used for productive purposes. And, indeed, such owners could legally refuse to allow their property to be so used. For the means of production are just as much their private property as are their shirts or their shoes. The landowner could (and occasionally does) refuse to allow his estate to be ploughed, and could keep it as a pleasure park or a deer forest. The man who owns, say, a two-thirds share in a mine or factory can perfectly legally prevent production from being carried on there. Hence, under the existing system, it is necessary to pay these owners rent on their land, or interest on their shares in a factory, in order to induce them to hire out these indispensable means to people who want to use them for production. And it is clear that these owners will, in fact, hire out their means of production to the persons who agree to pay them the most rent or interest.

But whence comes this rent or interest which is paid by the people who hire and use these means of production ? It has to come out of the profits which the actual users of the means of production can make.[1]

This raises the question of why the aforesaid owners of the means of production should not use them for productive purposes themselves, instead of hiring them out to others. The answer is that they often do so use them. In that case the owners get no *interest* or *rent*, but they do get all the *profit* which they can make out of using their means of production. They get, we see, more profit than would someone who had to hire these means of production before he could use them. For they do not have to pay, as he would, any rent or interest. Or, as it is often reckoned, they pay rent and interest to themselves, and so get the rent, the interest and the profit.

The profit made out of the use of the means of production is, then, the essential sum which is paid to people in respect of ownership. For rent and interest turn out to be, as it were, subdivisions into which profit is split up when their owners hire

[1] By the " actual users " of the means of production I do not here mean the manual and technical workers who do the job of production, but the " entrepreneur " who first hires these means from their owners (if these owners do not choose to use them themselves) and then hires the actual workers to operate them.

out the means of production, instead of using them themselves.[1] Where, then, does profit come from? There is no doubt or mystery about it. The owners of the means of production are paid a profit by the rest of us, because unless we do pay them this profit they will not allow us access to those indispensable means of production, without which we cannot feed, shelter or house ourselves. It is their ownership of the only available land, the workable minerals, and the essential means of fabricating such raw materials into finished goods, which forces all the rest of the population to pay money to these persons. Moreover, so powerful is the bargaining power which these people derive from the fact that the rest of the population simply cannot get on at all without their means of production, that they are able to appropriate pretty well everything over and above what the rest of the population must keep in order to live and work.

To put it in terms of goods and services, instead of money, the owners of the means of production are able to appropriate for themselves nearly all the goods and services produced over and above what are needed to keep the non-owners going. For if ever, and whenever, the non-owners try to pay them less, and so keep some more for themselves, the owners refuse to allow the use of their mines, land, or factories; they " lock out," as the phrase goes, those who wish to use their property for productive purposes. And this nearly always forces the non-owners to come to terms with them; for the non-owners must starve unless they can get the use of these indispensable means of production.

Thus, the owners, or capitalists, get the difference between the value of all the goods which are produced in the whole productive system and the value of the goods which have to be given to the non-capitalists to live on. Clearly, then, the capitalists would get nothing if the non-capitalists could produce no more than was necessary to keep themselves alive. But nowadays the non-capitalists can produce much more than this amount; and almost the whole surplus above this amount goes to the capitalists.

This is where profit comes from. The effective, legally

---

[1] We need here, the reader will see, some new comprehensive term to cover rent, interest and profit; to cover, that is to say, all income derived from ownership in the means of production. Marx coined such a term :surplus value.

protected, ownership of the means of production by private persons necessitates the payment to these persons of incomes (and of very large incomes) in respect of this ownership. Moreover, as we saw in the previous chapters, the payment of these incomes by way of profits is not only necessary in order to induce the owners to allow their property to be used for production; it is also necessary as the regulator of the system. We saw that any system, such as capitalism, which relies upon production adapting itself to the pull of demand must use profitability as a test of what is, and what is not, to be produced. Only those things which it is profitable to produce can, under such a system, be allowed to come into existence. We see, then, that our present method of distributing our supply of products is a necessary part of our whole economic system. Under capitalism it is entirely necessary that men and women should be paid not only for the work they do, but also for the property they own. If you tried to run capitalism without paying the owners of property in the means of production their rent, interest and profit you would destroy both the incentive and the regulator of the system.

This necessity of paying large incomes to the relatively small group of the owners of the means of production is, however, the cause of those disastrous characteristics of capitalism which we noted in Chapter I. For it is this necessity which forces capitalism to distribute money incomes with little regard to the real needs of their recipients. This is what has caused money demand to diverge so disastrously from human need. This is what has brought about that supremely evil state of affairs in which it is profitable to produce the silly luxuries of the rich, and unprofitable to produce the urgent necessaries of many millions of the population.

Moreover, although this is by no means so obvious, it is this gross *maldistribution* of income which is at length making it impossible for capitalism to allow some 20 per cent of us to produce anything at all.

CHAPTER VII

The Changing Shape of Capitalism

THE necessity of paying very large incomes to the owners of the means of production is making capitalism so lopsided as to be unworkable.

This only becomes apparent if we think in terms of goods instead of money. So long as we think in terms of money there seems nothing impracticable about giving one man, say, a thousand times as high an income as another. It is often done. We may or may not think such a procedure just, but there does not seem to be anything about it likely to disorganize the productive system. The payment of such disproportionately large money incomes does not, after all, mean any decrease in the total amount of purchasing power distributed. The net amount of purchasing power distributed remains the same, for example, if you give 1,000 men £1 a week each as if you give one man £1,000 a week. Hence the maldistribution of money incomes cannot in itself cause any net deficiency in demand. And capitalism is obviously suffering from precisely such a deficiency.

But now think of the matter in terms of goods. To give one man a thousand times as many goods and services as another is impracticable. For one man cannot possibly use a thousand times as many goods and services as another. Why, one man can scarcely eat twice as much food as another, let alone a thousand times as much; and no matter how rich a man may be, we defy him to sleep in more than one bed or wear more than one suit of clothes at a time. The contemporary rich have, it is true, developed great ingenuity in the matter of wasteful and useless expenditure. But they do not manage to consume anything like the number of goods and services by the value of which their incomes exceed the average incomes of the wage earners.

It is important to trace the economic consequence of this situation. The capitalist system (contrary to the opinion of some of its less informed critics) does distribute, by way of wages, salaries, rent, interest, and profit, enough purchasing power to buy all the goods and services which it produces. But it distributes this purchasing power so unevenly that in fact by no means all the *consumable* goods and services which are produced, far less all that could be produced, can find a market. So much of the available purchasing power is given to so few people, and so little is given to so many people, that the many poor cannot buy the goods and services which they need, and the few rich do not need the goods and services which they can buy.[1]

As the rich will not buy these, to them, useless goods and services, and the poor cannot buy them, no one buys them. They do not find a market, and so cannot be profitably produced. The familiar demonstration that nothing much can be wrong with capitalism because it can be shown to distribute enough purchasing power to buy all the commodities which it produces is a case of the fallacy of averages. It can be shown, for instance, that in the production of 100 £5 beds £500 are distributed. But this will not necessarily mean that all the beds can be sold. If £400 is given to one man and £2 each to 50 men, the 50 men may not each buy two-fifths of a bed, and the one man may not buy 80 beds. Some of the 50 men may not be able to afford to buy even one bed and the one man will almost certainly have no use for 80 beds. An important proportion of the beds will in these circumstances remain unsold. The maldistribution of purchasing power can have the same effect upon the productive system as an insufficient distribution of purchasing power. Here, then, we have an explanation of why we cannot under capitalism use an important part of our means of production to satisfy our wants: of how poverty and plenty, destitution and unemployment, can co-exist.

At this point the reader will surely be feeling that we have proved too much. " If all this were really true," he may object, " capitalism must have broken down long ago. For if the incomes of the rich are so large as to be unspendable, their recipients must simply hoard them. This must cause a continually

---

[1] The proposals of the Douglasites and other currency reformers are based on the view that capitalism does not distribute enough money to sell its products at profitable prices. We noticed (p. 28) that their proposals for dealing with this supposed difficulty broke down because they provided no regulator for the productive system. We now see that this analysis of our troubles is itself faulty. For the real trouble is that capitalism distributes so much money to so few people that this money is not available for buying consumers' goods. And this characteristic of capitalist distribution is, as we have seen, an inevitable consequence of the private ownership of the means of production. All currency reform schemes leave this ownership intact. Hence they cannot help us.

increasing deficiency in money demand, a chronic and never
alleviated inability to sell a large proportion of the output of
industry. But no system which produced results as bad as that
could have survived until now. The mere continued existence of
capitalism proves that some way of getting over this difficulty
of maldistributed purchasing power must have been found."

The objecting reader is perfectly in the right. There must
obviously be something which the rich can buy with their
enormous incomes, so that they do not simply have to hoard the
money. There is. The owners of the means of production do not
spend upon consumers' goods or services the vast sums which
have to be paid them so long as we maintain the capitalist
system. But they can, and do, spend those incomes on buying
new means of production. *With the money derived from their
ownership of the means of production they buy further means of
production, so that their ownership of this particular kind of
property is continually increased.*

To go back to our example; the man who is paid £400 for the
use of his property in making 100 beds will not buy 80 beds; but
he very likely will use this money to build a new bed-making
factory. To repeat the point in general terms, the large blocks of
purchasing power distributed by way of rent, interest and profit
to a few individuals cannot be used to buy consumers' goods,
but they can be, and are, used to buy means of production.[1]
And the productive system, obedient as ever to the pull of money
demand, swings away from the production of consumers' goods to
the production of means of production. Those resources of production which the extremely unequal distribution of income makes
it impossible to use for one purpose can be used for the other.

---

[1] To put the point into our familiar financial terminology, the rich neither
spend nor hoard their incomes, but reinvest them. We have implied above that
the rich simply cannot spend their incomes on consumers' goods, and this is
literally true of the richest member of the contemporary capitalist class. But as
a matter of fact, the owners of the means of production have always saved a
great deal of income which they could have used for buying luxury consumers'
goods and services. For the historical tradition of capitalism is accumulative. It
was accumulation, rather than cleanliness, which stood next to godliness in
the hierarchy of nineteenth century virtues. Nor, as we shall see immediately,
was this an inappropriate point of view for the then existing economic situation.
Hence the reader must not suppose that the owners of the means of production
save nothing until their powers of spending are exhausted. On the contrary,
many of them live relatively frugal lives and save as much as 90 per cent of their
incomes, thereby considerably accelerating the general development of the
system outlined in this chapter.

At first sight this seems to be a complete solution of the difficulty. It seems to disprove our former allegation that a sufficient maldistribution of income will make it impossible to use all of a community's productive resources. All that need happen, we now see, is that, as the distribution of income becomes more and more unequal, more and more of the community's resources must be used for producing means of production, and less and less for producing consumers' goods.[1]

What, then, is the difficulty ? The difficulty is that the reinvestment of their property-derived incomes by the rich—the purchase, that is to say, of further means of production—while undoubtedly enabling the system to function for a definite historical period, is a solution which steadily makes the problem more acute. For the only ultimate rational purpose of production is, we repeat, consumption. The only rational purpose of building up new means of production is to use them to produce consumers' goods. But now we have discovered that, as, under capitalism, these new means of production will also be privately owned, the income which their use will create will be so unequally distributed that it will be impossible to use the larger part of it to buy the consumers' goods which these new means will turn out. Therefore it can only be used to buy still further means. But when this third series of means has come into existence, they, too, will be privately owned, and the larger part of the income created by their use will be distributed to a few persons by way of rent, interest, and profit, and so will not be available for purchasing consumers' goods.

And so on and so on. This process is usually called " the

[1] This proportion is determined by the proportion in which the community saves and spends its income. We now see that the proportion of saving to spending is, under capitalism, itself determined by the degree to which income is unequally distributed. For the rich will clearly have to save, and the poor to spend, a high proportion of their incomes.

There is another point in this connection. A great part (in Britain a predominant part) of the total income derived from ownership in the means of production is not now distributed to the individual capitalists at all. It is retained in the hands of the capitalist class, as a class. For it is accumulated and reinvested (used, that is to say, to buy new means of production) by the great organizations of the capitalist class, the large-scale industrial Joint Stock Companies, Trusts, and Banks. For a variety of reasons these great organizations now prefer to " plough back " a large part of their profits directly into their own industries instead of distributing these profits to their individual shareholders and then raising the money again from them. The reader will see that this method of accumulation makes no fundamental difference to the way the system works.

accumulation of capital." For capital consists of resources of production used in a particular way: used, that is to say, in *this* particular way; used to create, to accumulate, new resources of production in a never ending series.[1] In Chapter I we saw that the object of capitalist production was profit. Now we see that the object of profit making is, in its turn, the accumulation of capital. We see that the accumulation of capital, looked at in terms of real goods, instead of money, is the piling up in the hands of the makers of the profit of a store of a particular type of goods, namely, means of production.

Now it is often said by critics of the system that the object of capitalist production is to make money, not to make goods. It is pointed out that a capitalist motor car factory is operated in order to create so many million pounds of profit, not so many thousand motor cars. The creation of the motor cars is merely a necessary means to the essential end of creating the pounds of profit. When people say this they are really saying that the essential object of the capitalist system is the accumulation of capital. And the accumulation of capital is itself only a financial way of describing the development of the means of production. For the lump of profit in which any successful act of capitalist production must result is but the financial reckoning up of the resources of production freed for the development of new means of production. The total profit of the capitalist class is, then, merely the financial symbol of the new means of production which it is the object of capitalism to create. Thus in the last analysis the object of capitalism is to produce new means of production.

The process of the accumulation of capital is, moreover, self-accelerating. The new means of production which are created by the savings of the rich are now usually of a different kind to the means of production which they replace. They are more efficient, or more highly mechanized, as we say. But what do such words as " mechanized " and " efficient " mean? They mean that the

[1] We are using the terms means of production and resources of production almost synonymously. But the term resources of production seems to me to carry a wider connotation. I use it in passages where it is important to emphasize that what is referred to are not merely machines, etc., but also such things as available electric power and, above all, the command of skilled and unskilled labour. Another term often used synonymously is factors of production.

production to which they refer is carried on less by means of human labour, and more by means of all kinds of plant and machinery. And, as we saw just now, income is, under capitalism, distributed both in respect of work done and in respect of plant and machinery owned. Hence, if for the production of a particular batch of goods—say our 100 beds again—less work, and more plant and machinery, are now needed, it must mean that more income will be distributed by way of rent, interest, and profit to the *owners*, and that less income will be distributed by way of wages and salaries to the now less numerous *earners*.

Yet, as we saw, the earners will spend their incomes predominantly on consumers' goods, while the owners will spend theirs predominantly on new means of production. And this third lot of means of production, when it comes into existence, will be still more efficient and mechanized. Its creation will result, therefore, in a still more unequal distribution of income. More will go to the owners by way of rent, interest and profit for the use of their ever more essential means of production, and less will go to the earners to pay them for their now less necessary work. A capitalist community must, then, not only use an ever higher and higher proportion of its resources for building up new, and ever newer, means of production; but the pace at which this change of proportion takes place must be an accelerating one.

Another development of capitalism is closely associated with this progressive transformation in the nature of the means of production from small and simple to large and complex. For, both as a cause and as an effect of the worse and worse distribution of income necessitated by the growth of the means of production, ownership of the means of production becomes less and less scattered, individual and competitive and more and more concentrated, corporate and monopolistic. It is almost always the owners of the old means of production who are able to buy the new, with the income derived from their original ownership. Moreover, within the class of owners it is above all the large owners who are able, with their large profits, to buy a predominant part of the new means which are continually coming into existence. We have only to think of the typical capitalist enterprise of the middle of the last century, the Lancashire or New England cotton mill, usually owned by a partnership, and compare it with the typical capitalist enterprise of to-day, the Imperial Chemical Industries or the General Motor Corporation, to see how fast and how far the process has gone.

This process of concentration has had vitally important consequences. It has made the owners of the means of production fewer and richer. It has meant that purchasing power is more and more distributed without regard to human need. It has meant that the remaining tens of thousands of capitalists who in Britain or America receive the really substantial blocks of purchasing power only spend a small proportion of their incomes on consumers' goods, while the great mass of the population cannot anything like satisfy their normal needs.

The process of the concentration of ownership has another and still more striking effect, however. It progressively modifies and qualifies one of capitalism's leading characteristics, namely, free competition between the producers. Such free competition alone enables the system to be regulated by the pull of profit and the push of loss in the way which we noticed in Chapter I. It is clear that in so far as whole spheres of production become complete or even partial monopolies this mechanism is gravely impaired. The laws of capitalist development begin to be modified.

This monopolistic stage of capitalism is necessarily reached by each capitalist state in the course of its development. At this point the impossibility of disposing of its products to its own population beings to stare it in the face. It is indissolubly associated with, it is indeed the very basis of, a vital feature of latter day capitalism which is now universally known as imperialism. What happens is that each national capitalism, as it reaches a given point in the development of its means of production, in the concentration of ownership, in the elimination of competition between its capitalists, and in the relative impoverishment of the immense majority of its population, *turns outwards in search of the markets which its own development has destroyed at home.* This necessity to turn towards economic (and consequently political) expansion is experienced by all capitalist states at a certain point in their development. This necessity makes war recurrent and inevitable under capitalism. But this fatal aspect of the development of capitalism is of such transcendent importance in the world to-day that we shall reserve it for separate and detailed discussion in Chapters XX, XXI and XXII. Here we are merely concerned to give a general picture of the line of development inevitably followed by capitalism.

These are the objections to the solution of the rich finding a use for their now huge incomes by buying new means of production with them. If they do so they progressively accentuate the maldistribution of wealth, the concentration of ownership and the elimination of competition, until a point is reached when each capitalist community taken in isolation can no longer exist. We observe that this is a difficulty which only arises with the passage of time, and the gradual creation of more, and more highly developed, means of production.

Indeed, this characteristic of capitalism was once its great advantage. It was a sort of automatic self-denying ordinance which made it possible for society to go through that early and painful stage of industrialization, which we discussed in Chapter III, without there being any necessity for anyone consciously to face up to the job. It is only as and when a community's means of production become highly developed that this characteristic of the capitalist system becomes the curse and the monstrosity which it is to-day. It is only when we already have means of production which could (without stinting their further development) give us all plenty and security, that it becomes a criminal absurdity to keep the mass of the population in destitution, and devote ourselves to creating still further means of production, which in their turn can never be used for anything but giving birth to still more such means, in an infinite series.

I have written so far as if it were *possible*, though very odd, to go on using an ever increasing proportion of our productive resources for the further development of these resources, and an ever decreasing proportion for satisfying our present wants. But beyond a certain point this is not even possible. Beyond a certain point (and it is a point which we in America and Britain have reached), it becomes periodically impossible, because unprofitable, even to go on developing our resources of production.

The picture we have drawn of a system using all its means of production, but using an unreasonably high proportion of them for creating new means, is now only approximated to by capitalism at the very height of a boom. (And even then, as in America in 1929, which was the greatest boom in the history of capitalism, 19 per cent of these means, we saw, remained idle.) To-day the normal, characteristic, situation of capitalism is, on the contrary, one in which it is as impossible to use a substantial proportion of our means of production for their own further development as it is to use them to produce consumers' goods. For it becomes less and less profitable to develop new means of production which can never be used, or at best can be used only to produce still further means of production, which in turn can be used only—and so on and so on. In fine, the hard fact that the only ultimate use of means of production is not to create a pyramid of ever newer means of production, but actually to produce an increased supply of consumers' goods, is beginning to assert itself.

This, then, is the contradiction in capitalism to which communists and socialists often—and often none too explicitly—refer. Capitalist methods of production and distribution (and they are indissolubly linked together) provide an effective (if ruthless) method of industrializing the world; but they cannot perform any other function. When once the primary process of industrialization has been accomplished, the difficulties of the system thicken upon it. The very characteristics which were its principal advantages become its fatal defects. The frugality which it forced upon the greater part of the population once enabled it to free resources of production for industrialization. But in the last resort the only purpose of industrialization is to enable the population to enjoy a more copious supply of goods and services. Hence the very feature of capitalism which once made industrialization possible now makes it impossible for nine-tenths of us ever to enjoy the fruits of industrialization.

It is important to notice this fact of the *ever changing* character of capitalism in relation to the technical and social environment which it creates and within which it operates. For this is the crux of the matter. Without a realization of this dynamic, changing factor, debate as to the nature of capitalism inevitably becomes barren. The contradiction between capitalism's ability to produce and its inability to sell its products is not a simple, flat, unchanging arithmetical factor, such as it would be if the system did not distribute enough purchasing power to buy all the goods and services which it produces. It does distribute enough purchasing power, but it distributes it so unevenly that a large proportion of it cannot be used to buy consumers' goods and services. There *was* a solution, and, in a sense, a socially advantageous solution, for this difficulty. This solution was provided by the allocation of a very high proportion of the community's resources of production to the further development of these resources.

It is only now that this solution is *becoming* unworkable. As our productive resources become adequate, *both* to give us plenty of consumers' goods and services and to continue their own further development at at least the existing pace, it becomes impossible within the limits of capitalism to use them for either task. The contradiction between the *heaping up* of new means of production and the *holding down* of the purchasing power of the mass of the population becomes ever more insoluble.

The capitalist economists are themselves beginning to notice that there is something queer about the fact that in a depression it is necessary, in order to make the production of new means of production profitable again, to cut down the population's power to purchase consumers' goods. For they cannot fail to realize that in so doing they are making impossible the use of the new means of production when they come into being —or at best are making it inevitable that these new means of production shall be used for the self-perpetuating task of producing still further means of production, alone. When they strike on this difficulty they are very near to a consciousness of the basic contradiction of the system; namely, the unceasing growth of the disproportion between every capitalist society's means of production and the purchasing power which it can distribute to the mass of the population.

It is the disproportion between these two factors that matters. It is true that at certain times and places the purchasing power of the population of particular capitalist communities has grown fairly considerably. Capitalist economists calculate that the *per capita* purchasing power of the British population has grown four-fold in the last hundred and fifty years.[1] A good deal could be said as to the basis of this calculation, but even if we were to accept it, we should be immediately confronted with the fact that the power of the British people to produce has admittedly grown at an incomparably more rapid rate during the same period. Thus there has been a continuous growth in the above disproportion during the whole period.

During the earlier part of the period this growing disproportion created no insuperable difficulties for the system. Indeed, society's powers of production could not have grown nearly so rapidly if this disproportion had not arisen; if, that is to say, the consuming power of the population had not been rigorously curtailed. For there did not exist sufficient means of production, both rapidly to increase the output of consumers' goods and rapidly to develop new means of production. It is only to-day that this holding down of the population's purchasing power has become both the parent of the monstrous poverty-in-the-midst-of-plenty paradox, and also a barrier to the further development of the means of production themselves. For now the restriction of the population's power to consume, although it still frees productive resources for the production of new means of production, makes their use, even for this purpose, impossible. For new means of production which will obviously find no market for their products cannot be profitably produced.

Something has turned into its opposite. What was a prerequisite for the development of new means of production has become an impassable barrier to their further development. In order to understand economic and social phenomena we must observe them, not as they are at any one given moment, but as they develop and change. And until we understand them we cannot hope to shape them to our ends.

[1] See Chapter XXVI for some discussion of this question.

Chapter VIII

The Two Classes

THE capitalist method of distribution has important social consequences. It is clear that such a method of distribution must create two groups, or classes, of persons, the first of which derives its income from payments for its work, and the second of which derives its income from payments in respect of its ownership of property in the means of production.[1] The first of these two groups or classes of persons are commonly called workers, and the second capitalists. Those who deny the existence of these two groups or classes either do not understand the question at issue or are intent to confuse it.

It is sometimes argued, however, that income derived from the ownership of the means of production is not really distinct from income derived from work. For, we are told, those persons who own the means of production only do so by virtue of the fact that in the past they saved up a part of incomes which they derived from work. It was with these work-derived savings that they bought their means of production. Hence they are now just as entitled to derive income from such ownership as are those who derive their incomes from work. Income paid for ownership is justified, in other words, as merely a postponed form of income derived from work. In the phrase of the man who first advanced this view (W. N. Senior), it is " the wage of abstinence "; it is the reward which a man gets for saving up a part of his work-derived income.

Now this argument had at one time a small measure of truth, but to-day it has become a laughable error. It *was* once true

---

[1] It has already been strongly emphasized that the capitalist method of distribution is itself but a necessary consequence of the capitalist method of production, i.e. of the ownership of the means of production by private persons and their operation for profit. Hence socialists usually, and with scientific correctness, speak of the creation of classes as the result of the capitalist system of production. This avoids the possibility of giving the wholly erroneous impression that capitalist methods of distribution can be abolished without abolishing capitalist production. (And this is a common illusion.) But since we have expressly explained that this is impossible we may perhaps write that it is the method of distribution which gives rise to antagonistic social classes. For this is the observable, verifiable fact. But it must be clearly recognized that methods of distribution are always consequential on methods of production.

that the means of production were partly developed out of the
savings made by the better-paid workers and small independent
producers. (In Britain, however, even a hundred years ago,
they were predominantly developed out of the savings of the
landlords, who already derived their income from ownership,
and out of the colonial plunder of the merchant adventurers.
Indeed even in the case of America it is an historical illusion
to suppose that the American industrial system was substantially built up out of the savings of American workers and
farmers. The real primary sources of American capital were
imports of capital from Britain—themselves accumulated as
above—and the profits derived from the slave labour of the
negroes of the South.) But it is absurd to suggest that any
appreciable part of contemporary property owners' incomes
comes from means of production which were originally bought
out of savings which these property owners had made out of
incomes derived from work. To a predominating extent in
Britain, and to a rapidly increasing extent in America, the
capitalist class has become a hereditary caste. Its members
derive their incomes from their parents, and from their own
success in increasing the size of their ownership in the means
of production. They have not bought their factories, their
mines, their ships or their fields by saving up wages paid to
them as frugal and industrious youths.

Even our prominent, but relatively rare, examples of self-made
men invariably owe their present large ownership in the means of
production, not to saving pennies out of their wages as newspaper
boys or half-time cotton operatives, but to their luck or skill in
taking some sudden opportunity to hire on credit particular
means of production from their owner. With these hired means
of production they have made a large initial profit, and thus got
started on the process of accumulation. Thus there is no longer
any appreciable measure of truth in the view that income from
property in the means of production is a postponed form of
income derived from work.

It is important to notice that what places a particular individual in one or other class is not the size, but the *source*, of his
income. For example, some workers have larger incomes than
some capitalists. There are highly specialized, technical workers

who derive incomes of £500 a year[1] from their work (not to take the individual cases of intellectual workers with much higher incomes). There are capitalists who own so small a portion of the means of production that they only derive, say, £400 a year by way of rent, interest, or profit. But such incomes do not make the first man a capitalist or the second a worker. (Though they sometimes give such individuals the attitudes of mind more usually associated with the members of the class to which they do not belong.) The rarity of these exceptions illustrate, however, the general rule that the capitalists' incomes are large and the workers' incomes small. The categories, capitalists and workers, however, are clearly defined, according to the source from which income is derived, and are by no means synonymous with rich and poor.[2]

The political consequences of this division of the community into two great groups or classes are extremely important.[3] It will have become clear that the economic interests of these two groups are by no means identical; that the more of the available supply of goods and services is allotted to the workers by way of wages and salaries, the less will be left to be allotted to the capitalists by way of rent, interest and profit, and vice versa. Moreover, we saw that in general the incomes allotted to the workers could not much exceed what was necessary to maintain them in a condition fit to do their work, while the incomes allotted to the capitalists would in general be very large. Thus one class is enabled, by incomes derived from ownership, to live a life of plenteous security, whilst the other class can, by working long and hard, obtain incomes which suffice to maintain no more than scant, narrow, and, above all, insecure existences. This arrangement is considered by some members of the second class to be unjust.

[1] e.g. compositors on daily newspapers.
[2] There are other social groups and numerous distinguishable subdivisions of the two main groups.
[3] It is quite possible for a particular individual to derive some of his income from one source and some from the other. And such an individual is undoubtedly half capitalist, half worker. There are a fair number of such individuals to be found, particularly amongst brain workers, in Britain and America. But their relative number is so small that they do not perceptibly blur the distinction. Moreover, they usually serve to illustrate the view that men's opinions are, on the average, determined by the source of their incomes. For it can almost always be observed that such persons share some of the opinions appropriate to workers, and some of the opinions appropriate to capitalists.

Indeed, the historical developments of the last three hundred years have established in most men's minds an ill-defined but strong opinion that this type of inequality between man and man is in some sense wrong. Hence the spokesmen of the capitalist class usually slur over, rather than defend, this feature of their system. When they do refer to it they often treat it as a necessary evil. They agree that this type of inequality is itself undesirable, but they assert that it is none the less defensible as the necessary price which must be paid for the extreme economic efficiency and stability exhibited, they say, by the capitalist system. If, we are told, this type of inequality were even modified, all incentive for human endeavour would be removed, and civilization could no longer be sustained.

The claim that capitalism is either efficient or stable is a curious one; nor shall we be willing to admit the view that it is necessary to pay one class of persons very large sums of money in order to induce another class of persons to work. We must, on the contrary, conclude that the social consequences of the capitalist method of distribution are disastrous. Our communities are split up into two classes, sundered both by the fact that they draw their incomes from antithetical sources, and by the fact that the lives which these differently derived and grossly unequal incomes enable them to lead are extremely dissimilar. The inevitable antagonism, now open, now veiled, now conscious, now unconscious, between these two classes, poisons the life of our communities at its source.

Chapter IX

The Socialist Method of Distribution

The capitalist method of distribution has become one of the main factors disorganizing the productive system. Moreover, it produces injustices compared to which all other injustices are merely secondary and consequential.

What, then, is the alternative socialist method of distribution? It would not be possible, even if we desired to do so, to pay persons rent, interest or profit under a socialist economic system of planned production for use. For rent, interest and profit are paid in respect of their recipients' ownership of property in the means of production. But, as we have seen, a system of planned production for use necessitates the abolition of private individual property in the means of production. You can no more stick the capitalist method of distribution on to the socialist method of production that you can stick (as is more often suggested) the socialist method of distribution on to the capitalist method of production.

A method must, then, be developed of distributing amongst the different members of the community the supply of goods and services which a socialist system of planned production for use provides. How much shall this man get—how much the other? Who shall provide for these children? What shall this woman earn? No questions pose themselves more urgently than these.

The simplest principle of distribution compatible with a system of planned production for use would be to give everyone an equal share of the available consumers' goods and services. We have discussed an estimate of what each family in America could be provided with, using the American productive system to the full, on this basis of equality. Each family of four persons could earn, it was estimated, a mixed bag of all the types of goods and services which American families (when they get the chance) are accustomed to consume, to the value of $4,400 (£915) a year at 1929 prices.

Many people suppose that this arrangement is what the communists and socialists propose; but this is not so. They do not propose, either as an immediate or as an ultimate aim, the provision of equal incomes to all members of the community. Marx and Engels, the founders of the modern communist and socialist movements, proposed a quite different method of distribution; and Lenin and Stalin have established this method of distribution in the Soviet Union.

Some non-Marxist socialists, notably Mr. George Bernard Shaw, have, it is true, proposed equality of income as the method of distribution appropriate to a planned system of production for use. Mr. Shaw, in fact, makes this demand for equality of income the centre of his whole programme, and goes so far as to write, in his *Intelligent Woman's Guide to Socialism and Capitalism*, that socialism consists in equality of income; that none who do not demand that incomes shall be made equal are socialists. On this basis neither Marx, Engels, nor Lenin were socialists. Now it would, of course, have been open to Mr. Shaw to explain to us why Engels, for example, was wrong in saying that any demand for equality of income which " goes beyond the demand for the abolition of classes, passes into absurdity." It would have been equally open to Mr. Shaw to show us why he considered that Lenin and Stalin were wrong in not attempting to establish equality of income in the Soviet Union.

But Mr. Shaw gives his readers no indication that this question of economic equality has ever been raised before, either in practice or in theory. He blandly ignores the thinking and experience of all the greatest minds who have ever concerned themselves with the problem, and lays it down *ex-cathedra* that socialism means equality of income. Can it be that Mr. Shaw simply does not know that the question of equality under socialism has been exhaustively discussed by all the important leaders of the working class movement? Such invincible ignorance is perfectly credible.

The matter has been, however, the subject of repeated, detailed and specific statements by leaders of socialist thinking and doing. Stalin, for example, speaking to the 17th Congress of the Communist Party of the Soviet Union said that " Marxism starts out with the assumption that people's abilities and requirements are not, and cannot be, equal." Again two British socialist thinkers, Mr. and Mrs. Webb, have recently pronounced upon the point. Their evidence is important for, although far from sharing Mr. Shaw's ignorance, Mr. and Mrs. Webb are non-Marxists, and in the past have been strongly anti-Marxist, writers who cannot possibly be accused of twisting Marxist doctrine to fit Soviet practice. " At this point," they write severely,

> " we may observe that it is a false assumption, current among the uninstructed, and even among persons who think themselves educated, that the Communist Party in the U.S.S.R. began its task of building the socialist state upon the basis of identical incomes for all workers by hand and brain, on the ground that all men are born equal, with an inherent right to equal shares in the commodities and services produced by the community in which they live and move and have their being. There has never been any such idea among the Marxists. Quite the contrary. Karl Marx and, after him, Lenin were always denouncing the conception of an abstract equality between man and man, whether in the new-born babe, or in the adults as moulded by circumstances. In so far as individual communists have indulged in ideals as to how the wealth of the community should be distributed among its members, the slogan has always been one of inequality." (*Soviet Communism: A New Civilization ?* pp. 701–2.)

On what principle, then, is it proposed to distribute the goods and services produced by a socialist system of planned production for use, and why is the proposal to distribute them equally rejected ? Two methods of distribution are proposed, the one as an immediate, the other as an ultimate, aim. It is proposed, as the immediate alternative to capitalism, to distribute the goods and services produced by a system of planned production for use in accordance with the quantity and the quality of the work done. It is proposed, that is to say, to continue (for a time) to distribute goods and services along the first of the channels used to-day, but to close the second of these channels (namely, distribution by way of rent, interest and profit to persons in respect of their ownership of property in the means of production).

It is proposed, to put the same point in a different way, to abolish unearned income, leaving earned income as the sole method of obtaining a livelihood. Under such a system the one thing that a man can get paid for is his work.[1]

This definition of the principle upon which purchasing power, and consequently goods and services themselves, are distributed in a socialist society covers, we notice, both the payments made to the wage workers in Soviet state-owned industry and the payments made to the owner-producers in the producers' co-operatives, such as the collective farmers, in payment for their produce. For these latter persons, although they do own their means of production, are paid not in virtue of that fact, but in virtue of the fact that they themselves work with these means of production.

Although this change in the method of distribution is consequential upon the change in the system of production, its economic and social effects are far-reaching.

Let us first consider the economic effects. The principal thing to notice is that such a method of distribution allows of the use of the community's productive resources either for producing consumers' goods and services or for producing means of production in any desired proportion. (That proportion will be settled, as we have seen, by the conscious decisions of the planning authority, acting, of course, under the instructions of the community.) There can be no quesion of a distribution of income so unequal that there is no effective demand for the full attainable output of consumers' goods. For it is the gigantic inequalities caused by the existence of unearned incomes which make it impossible under capitalism for an important proportion of

---

1 If we put the point in this way, however, we must immediately qualify it. For it will at once occur to the reader that there are large sections of the population, namely, children and adolescents up till the end of their education, and the aged and invalids, who cannot work. A number of such persons are provided for under this first socialist method of distribution just as they are to-day. They remain dependants of one or more of the working population. (This arrangement is inextricably bound up with the family.) There remains, however, an important number of the aged, of invalids, and of adolescents during education, for whom a socialist system of distribution must provide. Accordingly, old age pensions, insurance benefits for accidents or invalidity, and bursaries for all higher educational work are provided, in the existing socialist community, far more widely than in any capitalist state. But these payments do not modify the principle that income is distributed uniquely as a payment for work. For old age pensions are clearly merely postponed payments for work which has already been done, scholarships and bursaries are payments in order to enable their recipients to qualify themselves for work, and payments for accidents and invalidity are insurances against the risks of work.

the total purchasing power distributed to be used for buying consumers' goods and services. The relatively modest differences between what workers earn, in a socialist society, according to the quantity and quality of the work which they do, enable some workers to buy more consumers' goods and services than others. But they cannot possibly result in a worker being unable to spend his income.

This method of distribution guarantees a socialist society against that torturing, paradoxical tragedy of our epoch, simultaneous glut and unemployment. This is the simple secret of the Soviet Union's freedom from glut and unemployment. For if the entire national income (other than what is consciously reserved for the further development of the means of production) is distributed to the population in payment for work, it can never be impossible to sell the entire attainable output of consumers' goods and services. For exactly the same reason the compulsory unemployment of either men or machines can never occur.

The other economic consequences of the establishment of such a system of distribution are somewhat dwarfed by this tremendous fact. Here is an economic system which, whatever its other disadvantages and difficulties may be, is able to abolish want and unemployment and establish plenty and security.

We observe, however, that the level of income which American and British families might reasonably expect to enjoy under such a system would not be what the N.S.P.P.C. report estimated, namely, $4,400 (£915) a year for a family of four. That estimate was based upon the hypothesis of equality of income. This was a useful hypothesis for statistical purposes, but it must now be abandoned, since we see that it is not proposed to distribute income equally, but, on the contrary, in proportion to the quantity and quality of work done. Hence some families, having, say, several skilled wage-earners, would undoubtedly receive more than this amount, and others, having, say, only one unskilled wage-earner, would receive less. Thus under such a system there will be (and there are in the Soviet Union) inequalities in the economic fortunes of families, due not only to differing rates of pay for different kinds of work, but also to the differing number of wage-earners per family.

Ds

It is important, however, to observe the limits of these inequalities as compared to the inequalities which exist in present-day capitalist Britain and America. First, since the productive resources of Britain and America are adequate immediately to provide even the worst-off families with sufficient goods and services to enable them to lead decent, healthy, and secure lives, the worst-off family will still have an income adequate for this purpose. This is the cardinal fact. For inequalities *above* such a minimum level of health and decency for all are qualitatively different from the inequality which exists between those who are destitute and those who are secure.

Second, the actual quantitative degree of inequality between different earned incomes is always small as compared with the inequality between earned and unearned incomes. It is reasonable to suppose (on the basis of Soviet experience) that the inequalities between different earned incomes in socialist societies are normally of the order of magnitude of 1 as compared to 15. It has been calculated, however, that the " spread " of incomes in contemporary Britain and America, between the unskilled labourer and the millionaire owner of the means of production, is as 1 to 40,000.

This great diminution in inequality is, as we have seen, of economic as well as social significance. For while an income of fifteen times the minimum level can easily be spent on consumers' goods and services, an income of 40,000 times the minimum level cannot be so spent, and must be in a large measure accumulated. But this means that it must be used to buy further income-bearing property in the means of production and so to pile up at compound interest.

This brings us to the general question of private accumulation under socialism. Such a system is clearly incompatible with private accumulation, for private accumulation is merely the financial phrase for the continued purchase of the means of production by individuals. How, then, is private accumulation to be prevented? In the first place, we have seen that the enormous diminution in the inequality of incomes, which is effected by the abolition of unearned income, makes private accumulation unnecessary. It will be natural for the individual to spend his income on consumption goods and services. But what, it may be insisted, is there to prevent one of the recipients of the higher earned incomes—a highly skilled technical worker, for example—from saving up a large proportion of his income, and with it purchasing means of production ?

The answer is that in a socialist system no means of production are for sale. No stocks or shares, representing the ownership of portions of particular means of production, are on the market. For example, it is no more possible for a man, no matter how much of his income he saves, to buy a share in a Soviet factory or railway than it is for an American or British subject to buy a battleship or a post office. In fine, the legal code of any state using a system of planned production for use prevents absolutely the passage into private, individual hands of any portion of the means of production.[1]

Thus the possibility of private *investment* does not exist under such a system. The recipients of high earned incomes can indeed save a proportion of their incomes; but when they have done so they will find nothing to do with their savings except to hoard them—presumably in the form of currency.[2] And in a society in which there is no need for the individual to provide himself with security against accident or old age they will soon tire of such sterile hoarding.

[1] Except the tools used by independently working artisans and the remaining peasants. That important part of the means of production represented by the lands of the collective farmers cannot, I think, be said to be in private, and are certainly not in individual, hands. On the other hand, *access* to the means of production is restored to the whole population, which has almost completely lost such access to-day, by community and group ownership.

[2] At present in the U.S.S.R. they can buy interest-bearing Government bonds with them. It is probable that this will prove a temporary and transitional feature of a system of planned production for use. It is not, moreover, a quantitatively important feature and its origin in the early and difficult period of Soviet accumulation can readily be understood. I hazard the forecast that it will be ultimately eliminated. It will disappear as and when Soviet industry finds it possible itself to provide all the funds necessary for accumulation and as and when the motive for the individual to provide for his or her future has been eliminated, as it will be, both by sufficiently comprehensive social services and, still more, by the general plenty of the community. It may, no doubt, be many years before this is wholly accomplished. And until then individual savings by way of purchase of Government bonds, which do not of course carry any ownership of means of production with them, are undoubtedly a useful and necessary feature of the Soviet economic system. The Soviet Government has also sold some £2 million of bonds to foreigners. These bonds are all due to be paid off during the nineteen-forties and there seems no reason why the Soviet Government should borrow again in this particular way. In any case the amount of these bonds is quite trivial. They are a feature of the present transitional world situation and could not, obviously, exist in a socialist, or predominantly socialist, world.

We can now make another definition of a socialist system of planned production for use. *Such a system is one in which consumers' goods, but not means of production, pass into private hands.*

This definition illuminates the nature of some of the confusions current on the question of private property under socialism. An essential pre-requisite for such a system is the abolition of private property in the means of production. But this does not mean that it is necessary or desirable to abolish private property in consumers' goods. On the contrary, a socialist system will enormously increase the quantities of such private property in the hands of the immense majority of the population. It is one of the ironies of the capitalist " system of private property " that it leaves some seven-tenths of the population almost destitute of private property.

The object of a socialist system of planned production for use may, in one sense, be defined as the equipment of the mass of the population with the maximum possible quantities of private property in consumers' goods. The British and American people will have, under such a system, incomparably more private property than they have to-day—they will have incomparably more food, more clothes, more house room, more gardens, more motor cars, more of every type of consumers' goods.

Yet so utterly have we been confused by the vociferous spokesmen of capitalism, whose business it is to confuse us, that the now rapid increase in the standard of life in the Soviet Union, involving the passage into private hands of more and more consumers' goods, such as food and clothing and motor cars, is described as the abandonment of socialism ! What would mark the abandonment of socialism in the Soviet Union would be the appearance of a Soviet citizen who owned, not a motor car, but a motor-car-building factory, the appearance of a Soviet Ford, or Nuffield, or Citroën. But of such an apparition there is not, and never will be, any sign. The ownership of motor cars by Soviet citizens does not mark the abandonment of socialism. On the contrary, the first task of a socialist economic system— namely, the attainment of general plenty—will not have been fully accomplished till every Soviet citizen who wants one owns a motor car.

Chapter X

The Abolition of Classes

THE social effects of the socialist method of distribution are at least as important as its economic effects. For the payment of income in respect of work done, and for that alone, abolishes classes.

As we have seen, the two great social classes into which our existing communities are split are distinguished by the antithetical sources of their members' incomes. The less of any given total of production goes to the capitalists, the more goes to the workers, and vice versa. This flat opposition of interest is the basis upon which is built up the whole fatal dichotomy of modern society. It is impossible to exaggerate the benefit of the merging of these opposed social classes into a homogeneous community, all the members of which derive their livelihoods from the same source and whose interests are, therefore, genuinely compatible with each other.

Equality of opportunity, unattainable for a hundred reasons in any society dominated by a small class drawing its income from ownership of the means of production, can at once become a reality in such an environment. It is true that in a socialist society the children of the higher paid workers enjoy advantages as against the children of the lower paid. But such advantages can be almost completely offset by a sufficiently comprehensive system of social services, state education, with maintenance allowances, etc. The more subtle social inequalities, the hidden but enormous advantages of being " well connected," correctly spoken, well nurtured and the like, which make absurd all talk of equality of opportunity in capitalist society, do not exist.

Again, the level of intelligence of the leaders of such homogenous communities will rise sharply.[1] For our contemporary capitalist societies draw nine-tenths of their leaders from a now largely hereditary ruling class, from, say, 15 to 20 per cent of the population.[2]

---

[1] For, needless to say, the abolition of classes will not even modify society's need for leadership in every field of human endeavour.

[2] The capitalist class has solidified into a rigid hereditary caste to a greater extent in Britain than in America, and to a greater extent in Eastern than in Western

Homogeneous, classless societies, on the other hand, draw their leaders from the whole 100 per cent of the population. Thus the chance of the appearance and utilization of such rare, but invaluable, human types as geniuses, whether in science, the technique of production, literature, art, administration, political leadership, or any other field of human activity, is very substantially increased. No Milton need be either mute or inglorious once the essential condition of genuine equality of opportunity— namely, a society free from social classes—has been established.[1] Above all, the abolition of social classes is the pre-requisite of social peace. So long as one small group of citizens derives very large incomes from the ownership of the means of production, and another large group derives very small incomes from being permitted to work with these privately owned means, there is no possibility of social peace. The proof of this assertion is written into the whole history of human civilization. For until now there never has existed a civilized society which was not divided into a ruling and a subjected class. And never, since the dawn of civilization, has there been a period of voluntarily maintained social peace.

America. But the process has gone much further than is supposed and pretended even in Western America. The second generation of the great American entrepreneurs are at the moment just entering into their heritage. It may be permissible to paraphrase the famous passage from *Henry IV* and write:

> *This is the Western not the Turkish Court,*
> *Not Amurath an Amurath succeeds,*
> *But Edsel Henry.*

[1] There is a further point in this connection, which Mr. Bernard Shaw is fond of making. The two main classes in capitalist societies intermarry to but a negligible degree. Hence the area of sexual selection for the comparatively small capitalist class is very restricted and the class probably suffers from inbreeding. (The well-known degeneracy of small, exclusive aristocracies is an example of whither such a tendency leads.) It is reasonable to expect that the far wider area of sexual choice open to every citizen of a homogeneous, classless society will, over a few generations, have a markedly eugenic effect, and so increase the mental and physical powers of the race.

It would, I fancy, be dangerous in the present state of our ignorance of the science of eugenics to regard this as more than a reasonable expectation. But it is, at any rate, an incomparably more rational hypothesis than is the monstrous nonsense of " eugenics " as that infant science is taught in capitalist states to-day. I say nothing of the delirium of fascist " race theories." But in England and America a bastard eugenics is current in which the fact that the working class which is permanently ill-nourished, ill-housed, ill-clad, and deprived of adequate medical attention, or the knowledge of modern hygienic principles, necessarily suffers in physique, is used, not as an argument for improving the workers' conditions, but in order to prove that the workers are of " inferior stock " to the capitalists ! Of all the nauseating perversions which science undergoes under latter-day capitalism, this is at once the meanest and the most idiotic.

The communist and socialist theory of the part which the division of society into antagonistic classes has played in both the rise and the fall of the successive phases of human civilization is both elaborate and important.[1] The essential historical discovery is that the rise of every one of the civilizations which have hitherto existed was associated with, and was dependent upon, the splitting up of an originally homogeneous, primitive society into a ruling and a subjected class. For it was not possible, until the contemporary leap forward in man's capacity to produce wealth took place, to create a classless civilization. All of the civilizations which arose were civilizations *of* a ruling class *imposed upon* a subjected class. For the ruling class appropriated to itself most of the advantages of civilization over barbarism, and imposed almost all of the burdens of maintaining civilization upon the subjected class.

This arrangement represented an advance in human development, but it was an advance paid for at a high price. For such a class civilization necessarily involved a perpetual coercion of the ruled by the ruling, and a perpetual resistance to the ruling on the part of the ruled. It was not to be supposed that the subjected class would voluntarily carry the burden of a civilization in the benefits of which it hardly shared. Hence civilization has up till now been something imposed upon the mass of the population by a small ruling, and enjoying, minority. Until a way of abolishing classes was found, there could never be anything which could be called a voluntary civilization. The need for the ceaseless coercion of the majority of the population has so maimed, perverted, and poisoned all existing and past civilizations that many of the noblest and most generous minds of all ages have doubted whether civilization did in fact represent an advance over barbarism.

But now the possibility of a classless, homogeneous, and so voluntary, civilization has arisen. Men can now produce so much wealth that the apparatus of civilization, with an ever growing staff of administrators, research scientists, artists, etc., can easily be maintained while setting aside ample wealth to provide free and civilized lives for the whole population. The establishment of a civilization in the benefits of which the whole

[1] We discuss it in Chapters XVII and XXX.

population can genuinely and substantially share, is at last practicable.

Limitless possibilities of development are opened to mankind by this fact. For no social form has been more artificial or unstable than class civilization. In the latter stages of such communities especially, every activity, whether practical or theoretical, of the ruling class is to a lesser or greater extent modified by the overmastering necessity of remaining a ruling class. A time comes in the development of every class-divided society when nothing can be done, nothing attempted, no thought even can be conceived, which may endanger the precarious stability of the social pyramid. By an all-pervasive system, which is the more potent for being only semi-conscious, the ruling class comes to repress, not only the subjected class, but also every free, lively, and creative impulse from within itself. For creative thinking would endanger its own regnant position. In such societies, in their stages of decay, the artist must not see, the poet hear, or the scientist investigate anything which may disturb the social equilibrium. And by degrees this mandate comes to mean that they must not see, hear, or investigate the most striking phenomena around them.

For example, a man need not have the eye of an artist, the ear of a poet, or the brain of a scientist to see, to hear, or to understand the tragic conflicts of our epoch. He need only be neither blind nor deaf, nor mentally defective. Yet so pervasive is the power of class interest that the greater number of the most gifted artists and thinkers of our existing ruling class see almost nothing of the real world around them. It is not, in the main, that the ruling class has to prevent them. They are themselves a part of the ruling class, and they perform, with it, the act of self-mutilation which is now necessary to the preservation of their class in power.

This stultification of the creative powers of a ruling class, together with an intensification of the coercion of the subjected class, develops as and when the historic function of each ruling class is accomplished. One hundred years ago, for example, when the capitalist class of Britain and America certainly had a function, when their economic system of production for profit was the indispensable method of developing the community's means of production, nothing approaching the present degree of either characteristic existed.

Men could still see and hear and think with comparative freedom, for the reality which they apprehended when they did so was not, as it is to-day, one sustained challenge to the existing social order. Nor was it necessary to devise new and elaborate methods of coercion for the subjected classes, methods which to-day are tending to turn the capitalist world into one vast prison house or barrack. For then the workers, however meagrely they shared in the benefits of civilization, felt instinctively that the capitalists were the natural and inevitable leaders of society, who were performing a real function in industrializing the world.

The justification for the existence of our ruling class has, however, disappeared. The ruling class of to-day, far from performing a function for society, must necessarily strive to shackle, thwart, or pervert every creative or progressive development, whether in the economic, the æsthetic or the scientific field. Those of the rich who elect to be idle have become demoralized and demoralizing parasites upon our communities, spoiling and soiling everything which they touch, degrading every value, their art turned to futility, their lives to waste, emptiness and decay. But those of the rich who choose to work do us far more harm. By their financial manipulations, their grandiose gambling in human necessities, they disrupt the economic life of the world. Huge blocks of capital are thrown from one financial centre to another, from London to New York, from Paris to London, and back again, either in pursuit of the possibility of profiting by a carefully created shortage in some necessity of life, or in flight from the political risks which they themselves have helped to create. The whole world becomes a gigantic casino; the pledges are ten million bushels of wheat, the rubber supply of a continent, or cotton enough to clothe the naked backs of Asia. One group of players wins, another loses. But the men, women, and children whose still unalleviated toil has produced this mountain of wealth are not even admitted to the tables.

Moreover, the dice are loaded. Some groups of the gamblers have won for themselves positions of world power so strong that they can hardly lose, while others have been put to such disadvantages that they cannot hope to win without a change of place. These dissatisfied players arm, therefore, the producing millions under their command, for an attempt to reverse the verdict of the last slaughter; and whole generations must prepare to die in order that one group of gamblers rather than another may hold the loaded dice.

To such fantastic tragedies does the continuance of class rule beyond its natural term condemn our world. It is from these enormous evils that the abolition of social classes can deliver us. The abolition of classes is the supreme social consequence of a socialist system of planned production for use, distributing its products according to the quality and quantity of work done.

CHAPTER XI

Socialism and Communism Distinguished

THE socialist system of distribution will, then, abolish social classes. But it will not create equality of income. Why, then, is this system of distribution preferred to, for example, Mr. Shaw's suggestion of paying every worker an equal wage ?

Now communists and socialists have quite as clear and realistic a view of what is called human nature as have the capitalists. In fact they have a much more accurate grasp of human nature, for they have discovered what determines human nature within wide limits. They are not only able to see, as shrewdly as anyone else, what human beings are like to-day; they are also free from the peculiar illusion that human beings have always been the same as they are at present, and will always remain the same in the future.

Having a science of history, they are able, for example, to observe, and to account for, the fact that the human nature of both the slaves and the patricians of classical antiquity was markedly different from that of either the serfs or the lords of the Middle Ages, and that the human nature of these latter feudal personages was different again from that of contemporary industrial wage workers and capitalists. In a word, they are convinced that there is no such thing as abstract human nature, independent of time and place. The nature of human beings is, on the contrary, invariably modified by any major change in the social system under which they live. Undoubtedly, however, the immediately important consideration for the establishment of a new economic system is what human beings are like to-day. And to-day we have all been moulded by nearly two centuries of capitalism, and before that by many centuries of feudalism and of the slow and confused transition from feudalism to capitalism.

Now one of the characteristics of contemporary human beings, who have been modified in this specific way, is that they are accustomed to work for an individual reward. This is a characteristic which, although it may now seem a fixed feature of eternal human nature, in historical fact dates only from recent centuries, and has been built up only as a result of the economic conditions of the modern epoch. For example, such an idea simply could not occur to a slave—since he is not individually remunerated for his labour at all, but is maintained as an instrument of production, in the same way that an engine is fuelled or a draft animal fed. Thus the conception that men will work only inasmuch as they are encouraged to work by increased rewards is a product of the developing economic system of the last five hundred years.

During this period the main political task before humanity has been to break feudal fetters on ever rising powers of production. The developing capitalist class did this job by raising in men's minds the hope of individual enrichment by way of increased work. The individual enrichment was presumed to follow inevitably, by the laws of nature, as discovered by the political economists, from increased industry and thrift. But this presumption was true within very strict limits alone. In general it held good only for those who were able to acquire, or command, some of the means of production; in a word, it held good for the capitalists, but not for the workers. Indeed, the conception that individual *profit* is the only thing for which anyone will work necessarily remains a strictly capitalist conception, which cannot have penetrated the working class, for, if it had, the workers would never, on this theory, work; for they have no hope of making a profit.

But the wider conception that increased individual reward is appropriate and necessary to increased work has undoubtedly become a strongly established conviction of all of us. It *is* human nature, during and immediately after the capitalist epoch, to expect and demand such increased individual reward, although this has not always been the human nature of past epochs and will not be the human nature of future epochs.

This particular aspect of contemporary human nature is a factor which cannot be neglected in the development of any new system of distribution. If to-day we attempted to give equal pay for unequal work, we should flout one of our most strongly held conceptions of justice. If the skilled worker got no more than the unskilled, if the highly qualified technician received, after years of training, no more than the boy or girl whose first job it was to sweep out the factory, we should nearly all feel that an important and natural incentive to better work had been removed, and a grave injustice done.

And for our times and for our circumstances we should be right. Enormously as man's powers of production have developed, they have not yet developed to the point at which we can dispense with varying rewards to those who make varying contributions to society. Any attempt to impose to-day a flat equality of wages on all workers would show a misunderstanding of the real circumstances in which we live. For undoubtedly such a flat equality would check and thwart the further development of production. Men and women, as they are to-day, would not always work well or hard unless they knew that harder and better work would bring them individual rewards.[1]

This is the first, practical, reason why communists and socialists reject the principle of equality of wages and salaries. To attempt to impose such an equality of pay to-day would show a failure to grasp the nature of our particular phase of historical development, both of the means of production and, correspondingly, of human personality. It would be to attempt the impossible. Moreover, and this brings us to the second reason for its rejection, a flat equality of pay would not only be impossible; it would also be undesirable. Such an arrangement, as we noticed above, is not proposed even as the ultimate goal of society.

Complete equality of economic status, in which nobody is any " better off " than anyone else, is probably the vaguely defined ideal of those who feel intensely the monstrous injustices of capitalist society but have not devoted much attention to the question of what form of distribution would be " just." Perfect justice, they feel, would only be achieved by no one being any better off than anyone else. It is clear that this conception of what would be just conflicts with the former equally widely held conception that it would be unjust to pay as much for less intense and less skilled work as for more intense and more skilled work— more especially in communities which had established genuine equality of opportunity.

---

[1] We shall elucidate in the next chapter the difference between this fact and the illusion that men and women would not work unless they had the legal, though not the practical, possibility of private accumulation, of acquiring a part of the means of production—in a word, of becoming capitalists.

Apart from this contradiction, however, it is important to notice how impossible it would be in practice to ensure that nobody should be any better off than anyone else. As we could not avoid noticing in our discussion of the various statistical estimates of possible production, the family income, "the amount of money coming into the house," is what matters most to a majority of the population. This family income depends, we saw, not only, and in some cases not even principally, on the rates of pay received by the workers, but on the number of workers in the family. Thus equal rates of pay for all workers would still leave a family of four which contained three earners thrice as well off as a family of four which contained only one earner. Short, then, of ceasing to pay workers in respect of their work at all, even at equal rates of pay, and giving each family an income in proportion to its numbers, equality of economic status could not be achieved.

And even then there would be no equality. For every human being differs from every other, not only in their physical and intellectual powers, so that they can contribute different quotas of service to society, but also in their needs and tastes. One man's health forces him to live a long way from his work; one family must have, because it contains several young children, much more house room than another; one woman is, and another is not, naturally ascetic, and so on and so on. The distribution of equal incomes either per family or, still less, per individual worker would not then put people on an equal economic status. It would not answer that vaguely defined demand for justice which we noticed above; it would flout our feeling that better work should receive better pay, and in so doing it would, at our present level of economic development, hamper most seriously the working of a system of planned production for use.

For these reasons the proposal to pay everyone an equal wage was decisively rejected as a matter of theory by Marx and Engels,[1] and was rejected in practice by Lenin and Stalin when they came to the actual job of devising an appropriate method of distribution for a socialist society. Marx and Engels advocated, and Lenin and Stalin have established, the system of

[1] See Marx's *Critique of the Gotha Programme* and Engels's *Anti-Dühring*, especially.

distribution in accordance with the quality and quantity of work done which we have described.

This method of distribution is appropriate and necessary both to our present stage in the development of the means of production, and to contemporary human nature as it has emerged from its prolonged moulding by the capitalist system. But just because it necessarily bears many traces of capitalism within it, it has marked limitations and imperfections. We saw that it abolished the fatal and preposterous injustices which arise from the payment of incomes derived from ownership in the means of production. But it leaves in existence substantial inequalities, not all of which can, in practice, be perfectly adjusted to ability, between man and man. These inequalities are large enough to require careful offsetting by educational assistance, etc., to the poorer families, if they are not to qualify effective equality of opportunity.

Moreover, this method of distribution inevitably produces sharp competition between different workers for the better paid posts. (From one point of view this is one of its advantages.) Economic competition is eliminated, but what we may call personal competition continues. It is clear that in such a society there is still need for the " keeping of order," if only to see that the limits within which this personal competition may take place are not transgressed. And the " keeping of order " necessarily and always involves coercion. Such a method of distribution is, in a word, by no means ideal. It makes possible an immense advance on our class-riven societies of to-day. But it leaves in existence substantial possibilities of social discord.

Is it suggested, then, that this is the best that can be done, that humanity must reconcile itself to this state of things as the furthest point to which social progress can attain ? This is not so. The above defined method of distribution is no more than a more or less prolonged transitional stage to a society in which the distribution of products will be based on a different principle. And the word communism is reserved to describe this second and ultimate form of society.[1] Under communism

---

[1] Ultimate only in the sense that it is as far ahead as we can see. But time will not stand still on the full attainment of communism. Human society will, on the contrary, continue to change and develop, and, we may be sure, to change and develop very much more rapidly than it has ever done before. It is quite impossible

consumable goods and services will be distributed according to need, and work will be performed according to ability. Do we mean by that, the reader will at once ask, that everybody is to be allowed to have as much of everything as he likes, and, more extraordinary proposal still, that nobody is to be compelled to do more work than he wants to ? Yes, this is just what is meant. But is this not an utterly impossible form of social organization—unworkable both because there would never be enough of everything to go round and because most people would not work at all, unless they had to do so in order to earn their livings ? Yes, such a system of society is unworkable to-day and will be unworkable to-morrow, when the workers of Britain and America are facing the job of building up a new economic system. That is why it is not proposed as the immediate successor to capitalism.

This principle of distribution has been defined in a well-known phrase, " from each according to his ability and to each according to his needs." Men will be expected to contribute service to society according to their abilities and to take from the social store of wealth according to their needs. We shall find on examination that this principle of distribution (and not equality), however impracticable its early adoption may be, is the only one which can satisfy our vague and at present conflicting feelings as to what would be just. It alone will permit of the full development of human beings, and will eliminate altogether coercion from human affairs. Nor, when certain essential conditions have been fulfilled, will it be impracticable to adopt it.

We have now outlined two distinct forms of social organization. First we described a system of planned production for use in which the products are distributed in accordance with

for us, however, to more than guess at the character of these developments. It seems reasonable to suppose that the solution of men's economic problems by the conscious organization of the community's economic life will seem to future generations an extremely elementary step in human development. The socialist system of production and distribution, in particular, is surely but the A B C of community living. When that A B C has been learnt, men will pass on to attack far more complex problems—of which some of the most important may be of a psychological nature. It may even be that there are fairly strict limits to the increase in human happiness which can be achieved until some of these psychological problems have been solved. It is certainly useless, and it may be actually harmful, to devote primary attention to these problems to-day, however. For the establishment of a reasonable economic system is the sole possible foundation for their solution.

the quantity and quality of the work done. This is socialism. Now we have outlined a social system which is also based upon planned production for use, but in which the products are distributed according to need, and work is done according to ability. This is communism.

We also saw that it is impossible to establish communism as the immediate successor to capitalism. It is accordingly proposed to establish socialism as something which we can put in the place of our present decaying capitalism. Hence communists work for the establishment of socialism as a necessary transition stage on the road to communism.

This is how Lenin used, and Stalin uses, the two words socialism and communism. Marx, on the other hand, called a system of planned production for use, which distributed its products in accordance with the quality and quantity of work done, the first stage of communism, rather than socialism.[1] The usage adopted by Lenin and Stalin seems well established, however, and it is convenient. So in this book we shall use the word socialism to describe the one system and communism to describe the other. This, then, is the difference between communism and socialism.

It remains to enquire whether communism, as distinct from socialism, is not a mere dream. It is not. It will be possible to base society upon this principle, as soon as certain psychological and material pre-requisites have been established.[2] It is the function of the socialist system of planned production for use, and distribution according to work done, to establish the pre-requisites of this higher form of society, which is communism.

[1] Marx did so in the principal work in which he is intent on distinguishing the two systems, namely, *The Critique of the Gotha Programme*; but in other places he often uses the word socialism to describe the system of society which must succeed capitalism. The reader will notice that what we have here defined is the difference between communism and socialism. This is an entirely different thing from the political questions involved in the difference between various British and American political parties, such as the British Labour Party and the Communist Party of Great Britain, or the American Socialist Party and the Communist Party of the U.S.A. These political questions are discussed in the last Part of this book.

[2] Moreover, as usual when a hard and fast definition has been made, it is necessary to qualify it. A given society, while it will always no doubt be predominantly either socialist or communist, may have features of both systems. Thus in the Soviet Union to-day it is usually calculated that about one quarter of the purchasing power received by the population comes to it, not in the form of wages for work done, but by way of all kinds of social and free public services. And these services are distributed on the basis of needs. Here, then, the communist principle of distribution is already making its appearance.

Two things must be accomplished before there can be any possibility of basing society upon the principle of from each according to his ability and to each according to his needs. First we must have the technical ability to create super-abundance. The means of production must be developed to a much higher point than they have yet reached, even in Britain and America. We must have equipped ourselves with machines and productive plant of every kind by means of which we can satisfy all our wants with a minimum of labour, and especially of toilsome, painful, or degrading labour. Science must have discovered ways of eliminating all of that huge amount of dreary, monotonous, primitive and heavy labour which is performed, and some of which is necessary, to-day.

This technical pre-requisite to communism may be very much nearer the possibility of accomplishment than we are accustomed to suppose. The mere application to productive processes of the scientific knowledge which has already been attained, but which, because of the decay of our present economic system, is not used, would, we are told by the younger scientists, vastly increase our capacity to produce.[1] To this must be added the fact, which we may already deduce from soviet experience, that science, freed from its present enslavement to profit, bounds forward.

The rate at which, living under a socialist system of planned production for use, men can bring their environment under their command (for this is the broadest possible way of putting the point) is very rapid indeed. It would be futile to guess how long it will be, after the abolition of capitalism in Britain and America, before the technical basis necessary to give everyone as much of everything as they liked to have can be established. It may be that a hundred years would be too short an estimate; it may be that it would be much too long.[2] Moreover, it is not particularly worth while even to attempt such a guess, for the

[1] It is worth pointing out that no allowance was made for this factor in the estimates of productive capacity discussed above.

[2] Let us remember the technical progress of the last hundred years—from the general application of the steam engine to the general electrification of production and its automatic control by the photo-electric cell; and let us remember that technical progress can take place at a rapidly accelerating speed, at something like geometric progression. One achievement always opens up the possibility of many more.

second condition necessary for the appearance of communism will almost certainly take the longer to achieve.

Before there can be any possibility of society giving everyone as much of everything as they like to have, and asking from them only what work they desire to give, human beings must be given time to adapt themselves to the extreme reversal in the nature of their environment which any approximation to such a society will constitute. Up till now the condition of existence for nine-tenths of the human race has been unremitting and all-absorbing toil. To this toil everything else has had to be sacrificed. Nor has the extraordinary development of our productive powers during the last hundred and fifty years done much to alter this apparently eternal condition of human life. For, as we have seen, under the peculiar economic arrangement which we call capitalism, almost the whole of this increase in our power to produce has been automatically reserved for the still further increase of those powers.[1]

For a race accustomed from its appearance on the earth to scarcity and toil to be suddenly plunged into an environment in which a very moderate amount of pleasant work will suffice to provide plenty of everything for everybody, will be a reversal of fortune without parallel. It would be unreasonable to expect an even approximate adaptation to such a change in less than two or three generations. But this adaptation, too, will begin just so soon as the relative plenty and security of a socialist system is established.

It may be that we should waste and spoil the social store of wealth if we had free access to it. It may be that we should idle all our days away in meaningless leisure if we were not compelled to work for our livings. It may be, in a word, that if we suddenly strayed into the garden of universal plenty we should barbarously misuse and destroy it. But we have no right to suppose that our descendants will be as churlish or as childish as we are.[2]

[1] And, of course, for providing an abundance of goods and services to the capitalist class; but that also has made little difference to the lives lived by everyone else.

[2] Even such immature creatures as we are would not be likely, however, to make impossible demands for goods if we were told that we could have everything we wanted without restriction. Even to-day, if we were told that we could have all we wanted, we should not demand ten motors, two steam yachts, three

Men and women who have never had the opportunity to possess the goods and services necessary to more than a wretched existence might gorge starved appetites. But to the inhabitants of a land in which want and insecurity were unknown, the idea of a man taking more of any particular good than he needed might well seem unaccountably odd. Again, we should be able to understand how work could become the main delight of life—a delight which men would not dream of forgoing. For already those fortunate few amongst us whose work is pleasant and interesting find in it one of the most enduring satisfactions of their lives.

In any case it is always rash to declare that such and such a development in the way of life of mankind is impossible. To-day we smile indulgently at our great-grandfathers for declaring the railway an absurdity, applaud Icarus, and scoff at the generations of practical men who invented the myth in order to warn us of the folly of attempting to fly. Nothing is easier than such retrospective enlightenment. What is not so easy is to avoid committing the same mistakes as to the possibilities open to future generations. In this matter we run the risk of cutting very sorry figures for posterity. For as Engels remarks, the generations which will put us right are likely to be far more numerous than those which we so patronizingly correct. The world itself is very young. Life is in its childhood. The human race has only just been born.

hundred suits of clothes, six houses, and the like. For in conditions of universally accessible plenty there would be no one but ourselves to look after these possessions. There would be no one but ourselves to drive, and wash and clean and oil the ten motor cars—no one but ourselves to man the steam yachts, wear the three hundred suits of clothes, or do the work of the six houses. The sole reason why the contemporary rich can, and sometimes do, demand goods on this sort of ludicrous scale is because they are able to force dozens of the rest of us to work for them. But, given universal plenty and security, no one could be forced into the service of any other individual. In such conditions none of us would demand more goods than we were prepared to look after ourselves. This condition would not, under communism, it is true, put nearly so straight a limit upon the amount of our possessions as it would to-day, for we are postulating a level of technique in which machines and mechanized devices would be almost self-maintaining, and easily replaceable when they became worn, and in which these devices had eliminated most of the drudgery which the maintenance of possessions involves to-day.

Moreover, some of the citizens of such a community would, no doubt, work some of their time on the job of maintaining society's stock of possessions instead of on production. Still, the amount of consumable goods of a durable character which any individual would wish to acquire would be a good deal limited by these considerations. And the amount of non-durable goods which an individual can consume is narrowly controlled by physiological limits.

Chapter XII

Incentives to Work

MEN must have an incentive to produce. Unless it provides such an incentive, the best organised economic system will not create a single good or service. Moreover, an economic system should be able not only to induce men to work, but to work steadily, effectively, and willingly, and to prepare themselves for more skilled and responsible work. What incentives to work do socialism and capitalism respectively provide ?

Now capitalism undoubtedly makes some workers work very hard indeed. In order to do so, it uses both rewards and punishments. The rewards are of two kinds. In the first place, capitalism rewards without stint those members of the capitalist class who work at the task of using the means of production which they own. A capitalist, if he owns the whole, or the controlling part, of some particular productive plant, can manage the plant himself; or, if he owns shares in a number of such plants, he can devote himself to buying and selling those shares. The individual rewards obtainable by such work are often enormous. Again, the more successful members of the professional classes, e.g. lawyers, doctors, actors, accountants, authors, engineers, are often highly rewarded for their work. They are sometimes so well paid as to be enabled to acquire, by one means or another (often by marriage, for example), property in the means of production and so to merge with the capitalist class.

Now many people sincerely suppose that capitalism gets the work of the world done by offering this type of reward. They suppose that the mass of the manual and clerical workers are induced to work by the prospect of being rewarded with a share in the ownership of the means of production, carrying with it a right to unearned income. They honestly believe that the great advantage of the capitalist system is that it induces the workers to go to work in the morning without any need for compulsion, by offering them the glittering prospect of making their pile. Moreover, it is asserted that this prospect is no illusion; that the workers will become rich owners of the means of production if only they will work hard enough. A picture of the world is drawn for us in which everyone starts out equal, and the clever, thrifty, and industrious emerge, by a process of economic natural selection, rich and happy, while the foolish, thriftless, and idle remain in poverty.

In Britain the social scene never bore much resemblance to this picture. For in Britain a semi-feudal hereditary governing class was established before the rise of modern capitalism. In the Western America of the last century, however, capitalism did bear some recognizable resemblance to this, its ideal representation. There really did exist at that time and in that place a certain degree of genuine equality of opportunity. The process of economic natural selection did operate, and selected Mr. Rockefeller Senior as the fittest to survive.[1] An important proportion of the population really were stimulated to work their hardest by a non-illusory hope of becoming rich owners of the means of production.

In contemporary Britain and America, however, the chance of the worker becoming through his own efforts an owner of the means of production is statistically negligible. This does not mean that, especially in America, the recollection of the epoch has disappeared, in which this transformation was frequent enough to be worth struggling for, or that, consequently, the hope of becoming rich capitalists does not play a rôle as an incentive to work amongst present-day American workers.

But this is a hang over from social conditions which have largely ceased to exist—an example of the considerable time which it takes for men and women to adapt themselves to rapid changes in their environment. Moreover, the hope of becoming rich capitalists is not now the most important incentive to work, even amongst American workers, and it is hardly present amongst British workers.[2]

Capitalism, however, uses, though to a slowly diminishing degree, another and limited, but real instead of illusory, system

[1] From the analysis of preceding chapters we can see why. Mr. Rockefeller is acquisition personified. The acquisition of private wealth is the method by which capitalist society performs its historical function of developing the means of production. Hence acquisitiveness is the essential capitalist virtue.

[2] The illusory hope of becoming a rich capitalist is still, however, especially in America, an extremely important factor in preventing the worker from becoming consciously hostile to capitalism; it still conditions much of his political thinking, that is to say.

of rewards. Capitalism has seldom given an appreciable number of workers an opportunity to acquire property in the means of production. But it has often given many of them, if they worked especially well and hard, an increase of pay sufficient to enable them appreciably to better their standard of life. An elaborate system, both of differential wage rates, which encourage the worker to become skilled, and of payment by result (piece-work), which encourages him to produce rapidly, has been developed. It is important to distinguish clearly between such limited, but real, rewards, and the illusory reward of an opportunity to acquire property in the means of production, and thus to secure an unearned income in perpetuity. For, as we shall see, these two forms of reward are constantly confused, and one of them can, while the other cannot, be used in a socialist society.

This second system of rewards by differential wage rates for skilled and unskilled, and for fast and slow, workers is being used by capitalism to a diminishing extent, however. In Britain especially (I am informed that the same process has begun in America) the gap between the wages obtainable by the skilled and the unskilled is tending to decrease in many industries (notably coal mining). Thus, while the prospect of becoming an owner of the means of production has become increasingly illusory, capitalism to-day relies less than it once did upon this second type of limited, but real, reward in order to induce men to work, and to work hard.

And yet it cannot be denied that contemporary capitalism knows some way of making many workers toil, in many cases to the very limit of their physical and nervous capacity. The men on the conveyer belts of Detroit, the miners lying on their sides working in the narrow, twisting coal seams of the South Wales Valleys, are clearly under some very effective incentive to work. For they often work themselves to the point of disease and premature death. What is the incentive ? The incentive by which contemporary capitalism succeeds in wringing the last ounce of work out of those workers whom it still consents to employ is predominantly not the promise of any reward, but the threat of extreme punishment if the worker relaxes his efforts. That punishment takes the form of a refusal to allow the worker access to the means of production. He is shut out of the factory gates so that he cannot earn his living. Moreover, by the bitterest irony, the capitalists' inability to employ by any means all of the workers greatly increases their power over those whom they do employ. For there are always a hundred unemployed men forced to stand ready to take a dismissed worker's place.

This, then, is the incentive to work, and to an extreme intensity of work, which capitalism predominantly uses to-day. It cannot be denied that it is an effective incentive. But it is based on a system of punishment and compulsion, not of rewards. The seldom recognized truth is that capitalism uses a system of forced labour, all the more rigorous because its compulsions are concealed.[1] The slave owner is directly and obviously responsible (and may suffer pecuniary loss) if he works his slaves to premature death. But the contemporary factory worker appears to consent to a speed and intensity of work which often in the end destroys him. He is a free man; no legal coercion will be applied to him if he refuses to time his movements to the ever accelerating conveyer belts of modern industry. He is perfectly free to refuse the terms upon which alone his employer will allow him to enter the factory gates. But if he does so he loses his capacity to earn his living. Thus the capitalists do not now in the main induce men to work by holding any reward, either limited and real, or unlimited and illusory, before their eyes. In the main they compel men to work, and to work at any pace which they decree, by imposing starvation upon them if they do not.

So far we have considered the incentives operating upon those workers to whom capitalism still offers employment. But capitalism to-day denies employment to some 15 per cent to 30 per cent of all workers. To speak of capitalism providing any incentive to work in their case would be paradoxical in the extreme.

It is worth envisaging what this degree of inability to use our productive resources means to the contemporary young men and women just finishing their period of education. We can all remember the fund of creative energy which we possessed at that moment. The motives which powerfully impel a young man

---

[1] " As a producer of diligence in others . . . capitalism, in its energy, remorselessness, and efficiency, has outsoared all the earlier systems of production." (Marx, *Capital*, Vol. I, p. 320.)

or woman towards work at this time in their lives are no doubt mixed. They are made up partly of a natural desire to do, to make, to create—to play a part in the exciting drama of life. And they are partly composed of the equally natural desire to achieve individual success, to rise, to shine, to acquire wealth and power and prestige.

In his biennial report for 1932–34 President Coffman, President of the University of Minnesota, stated that of the twenty-one and a half million American young men and women between sixteen and twenty-five years of age, one million were in college, two millions were in secondary schools, two millions were at work, while sixteen and a half millions were out of school and out of work.[1]

These sixteen and a half million young Americans may typify the other uncounted millions of young men and women of every capitalist nation who have found that the world of to-day has no use for them. It is horrible to imagine the sense of frustration which these millions of idle young men and women must experience. To be twenty years old, and to have nothing to do; to discover that nowhere in the whole gigantic, complex, dazzling panorama of modern life is there a single task with which one can be entrusted; to find that no man needs one for anything, anywhere—what could be worse than this ?

To-day, capitalism imposes a torture of frustration by compulsory idleness upon a substantial proportion of the youth of the world. And yet capitalism is said to possess the transcendent advantage of providing an incomparably efficient incentive to work ! We must not touch it, we are told, for if we did we should destroy men's freedom to make money, and if this right were taken away no one would go to work again ! Moreover, so extraordinary is the hold on us of such doctrines as these that many of the very men and women who, far from being given an incentive to work, are actually prevented by capitalism from working at all, believe and repeat this argument !

Many a boy or girl leaving school or college to face the prospect of years of unemployment bases his or her view of capitalism, not on the facts of their own experience, but upon the pretty fictions

[1] *Youth and To-morrow's Education*, President Coffman's Biennial Message to the People of Minnesota. Published by the University of Minnesota, 1934.

about freedom of opportunity and enterprise which their professors, their books, and their newspapers have taught them. Suffering themselves, in many cases, an extreme degree of frustration and destitution because capitalism imposes idleness upon them, they solemnly protest that private enterprise and iniative must be preserved at all costs—or no one will ever go to work again ! It sometimes seems as if the word was stronger than the fact; that whatever is written in newspaper or textbook must be true; that if experience presumes to contradict, then so much the worse for experience ! But such extraordinary social hypnoses as these cannot be maintained indefinitely. Sooner or later the fact asserts itself. And the longer its recognition is avoided the more brutally it asserts itself.

Let us sum up the incentives provided by present-day capitalism. The only people whom it predominantly induces to work by the promise of increased reward are the members of the capitalist class, and the result of their work is as often pernicious as beneficial. Capitalism, however, uses to some extent the reward of higher pay as an incentive to harder work on the part of the working class. But to an increasing extent it forces, rather than induces, the workers to spend themselves in toil. Its basic incentive is negative instead of positive; it is based on the fear of punishment, not the hope of reward. It uses a compulsion differing chiefly in its invisibility and its efficacy from the palpable lash of the slave owner. Finally, for that 15 to 30 per cent of the working population which is to-day unemployed, capitalism provides no incentive to work. On the contrary, it denies them all opportunity to work.

We shall not, then, be willing to admit the contention that capitalism provides such perfect incentives to work that on this ground alone it is irreplaceable. But this does not absolve any social system, which claims to be able to take capitalism's place, from itself providing effective incentives. What incentives does socialism provide ?

In the first place, a socialist society (as distinct from a communist society) retains, though in a greatly modified form, the ultimate compulsion that able-bodied men and women shall not receive a livelihood unless they work. Indeed, in one respect, it applies this compulsion more rigorously than does capitalism. For capitalism applies it only to the working class, while providing the amplest livelihoods to persons who do no work at all. For example, many of the very largest contemporary incomes go to young ladies and gentlemen who have had the foresight to be born into families which possess important means of production, and none of whom have ever been suspected of working. Under socialism they would not be so fortunate.[1] They would find it necessary to work if they desired to receive an income. Thus socialism applies a strong motive to work to one group of persons to whom capitalism supplies no such motive. On the other hand, socialism does not first compel men and women to work by cutting off their livelihoods if they do not, and then make it impossible for them to work by refusing them access to the means of production. In everyday language, socialism makes it necessary for everyone able to work to do so, and simultaneously, by abolishing unemployment, makes it possible for everyone to work.

Moreover, it is worth while noticing that socialism applies this negative incentive to work to the whole population by the same type of mechanism by which capitalism applies it to the non-property-owning section of the population. Just as in present-day capitalist Britain and America economic, as distinct from legal, compulsion forces all those who do not possess property-derived incomes to work, so in the socialist society of the Soviet Union a man is quite entitled to refuse to work, if he can find some other legitimate means of existence. This aspect of socialism, namely, its universal application of that economic obligation to work which is confined under capitalism to the non-property-owning class, will never, it is to be feared, do anything to recommend it to many members of the capitalist class. Indeed, it may be that it is this feature of the system which causes those heartfelt lamentations as to the slavish nature of socialism with which we have all been made familiar. For the re-imposition upon persons long exempt from it of that obligation to labour, if they would eat, which nature imposed upon us all at the

[1] Or rather, so unfortunate. For the endowment of some young girl or boy with fantastic wealth is as unfair to them as it is socially monstrous.

beginning, may well seem slavery to the contemporary rich. But for that vast majority of the population who already live by their labour, the fact that socialism gives every man the opportunity to work and earn will seem to far outbalance the disadvantage—and they will not see it as a disadvantage—that it takes away the privilege of highly remunerated idleness from a few.

It may be objected, however, that socialism does produce a servile state of things in that under it there is but one employer of labour, namely, the state, and that therefore no man can have a choice of employment. This accusation is based on a simple misunderstanding of the structure of a socialist economic system. As we saw in Chapter IV, in the existing socialist economy there are three different types of employers of labour, namely, state or municipal agencies, producers' co-operative societies, and consumers' co-operative societies. And within each of these types there are a great variety and an enormous number of employing organizations. Mr. and Mrs. Webb thus describe the multiformity of socialist employing agencies:

" There are several hundred U.S.S.R. trusts and combines, and no one of them is exactly like the others. More diverse still are the thousands of separate enterprises, whether factories or institutes, mines or farms, oil-fields or power stations, which are independently conducted for their peculiar purposes, unassociated with any trust or combine, and responsible to one or other higher authority. There are also village enterprises, oblast (provincial) enterprises, enterprises of the several constituent or autonomous republics, none of them identical in management or organization with the corresponding enterprises directly subject to the People's Commissars or Sovnarkom of the U.S.S.R. The trade unions and factory managements themselves now conduct quite extensive productive enterprises outside their primary occupations, in the shape of farms, dairies, piggeries, etc., for ' self-supply.' So also do many of the forty odd thousand co-operative societies, whose business now far exceeds mere distribution, and those productive undertakings differ markedly in system and organization one from another. It is among these different employments, all of them separately taking on additional staff, that the individual worker, and notably the boy or girl leaving school, has the utmost possible freedom of choice." (Ibid., pp. 771-2.)

We may add that if anyone has a distaste for working for wages he can join one of the 250,000 collective farms, or other producers' co-operatives. Or again, if he has the necessary abilities, he can start out offering on the market some good or service which he himself produces. He can, for instance, become a freelance journalist and author, or a house repairer, or a painter, or a musician, or a craftsman producing artistic goods of one kind or another. He can, if he likes, join a producers' co-operative organization for these purposes, or he can work as an isolated individual. The one thing which he must not do is to hire someone to work for him at a wage and pocket the proceeds of this hired man's work over and above what he pays him.

Socialism retains the ultimate, negative incentive of paying income only to those who work, in order to prevent the possibility of particular individuals exploiting the community by receiving all its benefits while rendering it no services. But a socialist society does not principally rely on this negative incentive in order to get its work done—and done well. It uses a well developed system of rewards in order to secure not only work, but efficient work, from every available member of the community. We saw in the last chapter that the proposal to distribute incomes equally was rejected partly in order to retain the possibility of rewarding more intense and more skilled work. Hence the first and simplest way in which a socialist society gets men to work hard and efficiently is by paying them better when they do so. A socialist society not only retains, but enormously develops, the incentive of giving better pay for better work which capitalism uses, but now uses decreasingly.

This enables us to disentangle one of the most curious of the confusions current on this subject. Not only do many people sincerely believe that more money is the one thing for which people will work, but they conceive of more money in the exclusively capitalist form of the acquisition of capital, the right of private accumulation. We have seen that this involves the private ownership of the means of production, and, consequently, is impossible in a socialist society. But how strange is it to conclude from this that it is impossible under socialism to induce men to work hard and well by offering them more money ! Even under capitalism the offer of higher pay, without any opportunity to acquire property in the means of production, is used for this purpose. One, though of course, only one, of the motives which induces, say, an army officer, a salaried official of a great corporation, a bank clerk, or a manual worker, to work well is the knowledge that, if he does so, he may expect promotion and better pay. In most cases he cannot expect to become a capitalist; he will not be given any part of the means of production. Nevertheless, he strongly desires to get the increase of pay. For such an increase will enable him to buy more consumers' goods and services—to raise his standard of life. Nothing is more certain, even from the experience of capitalism, than that increased pay, without the acquisition of means of production, is a most effective incentive to work.

In a socialist society this incentive can, however, be much more effectively applied. For the genuine equality of opportunity which socialism establishes opens up the higher paid posts to every worker. To-day, barriers of education, of class connection, of family nepotism, effectively close a great many of the better paid posts to the workers, thus rendering their existence useless as an incentive, since the worker knows perfectly well that nothing he can do will ever get him one. Socialism effectively destroys such barriers, and in so doing provides an important stimulus to the whole working population.

The existing socialist society in the Soviet Union has developed this system of individual rewards for better work to a very striking extent. Not only, and not merely, has piecework or payment by result been applied wherever and whenever it is practicable throughout Soviet industry, but an extensive system of grading the basic wage rates of all the workers according to the demand for work of a particular character has been adopted. Thus the workers in any given trade will be divided by the trade union concerned into anything from eight to seventeen separate categories, ranging from the least to the most skilled operation required in the trade. Then a basic wage rate of so much an hour is fixed for each category, with the maximum practicable difference between the hourly rates of the more and the less skilled. But how, it may be asked, are the workers placed in one or other category? The answer is at their own request. A worker in the lowest category can demand to be placed in the highest. And his demand must be acceded to, on the one condition that he can show himself capable of doing the much more skilled work involved. He demands, that is to say, a trial on the work of some category above him, and if he makes good at his new job he at once receives the higher rate of pay.

The reader will see that socialism, with its limitless market, and consequently its insatiable demand for more and more, and for more and more skilled, workers can thus develop the old incentive of better pay for better work to a degree quite unknown under capitalism. Mr. and Mrs. Webb give it as their opinion that in the Soviet Union " the upward march, from grade to grade, of the more ambitious, the more able, the more industrious, and the more zealous workers in industrial occupations is widespread and continuous. In no other country, not even in the United States, is it so general. . . . The capitalist employers in every other country, whilst complacent about their own superior efficiency in profit-making, must now and then envy the industrial directors of the U.S.S.R. the extraordinary increases of output obtained by the incentives that Soviet Communism supplies to its labour force ! " (pp. 712 and 719).

Again, promotion from grade to grade within the factory is, naturally, but the first step in the broad and open stairway of personal progress open to the citizens of a socialist community such as the Soviet Union. Every ambitious soviet youth means to pass on and up from the top rank of the skilled workers into positions of ever growing managerial or technical responsibility. And each of these positions will, of course, carry better pay with it.

The prospect of better pay is, however, only one of the incentives which makes a man work and hope for promotion. Many men (and women) are as much, or more, allured by the increased power which promotion nearly always brings with it. Associated with power is prestige. Promotion is a public recognition of worth—and what will men and women not do for such recognition ? Nor is there any reason why a socialist society should not use those badges of public esteem, those medals and orders which, from their abuse, have become ridiculous in our societies, but which are in themselves a reasonable and sensible device. And, in fact, the existing socialist society does reward its outstanding workers with such orders and medals,[1] and they are highly coveted.

Again, promotion almost always means pleasanter and more interesting work. It means the opportunity to develop and use all the mental and physical powers which we possess. It allows a man " to show what he is worth ": it " gives a man a chance." These colloquial phrases show how promotion in itself provides a very sweet reward. The lack of promotion has always been considered one of the worst fates which can befall a man. Shakespeare, for example, made his dissembling Hamlet find ample reason for his melancholy with the phrase, " Why, sir, I lack advancement." In the stagnant societies of contemporary capitalism millions of capable men and women lack not only advancement but all hope of advancement. All possibility of using their skill and knowledge has been taken away from large sections of the population. Almost every mine in Britain to-day contains men holding mine managers' certificates, who are used to fill the coal tubs. Almost every foc'sle contains seamen who not only hold masters' certificates, but who have actually captained vessels. With what splendid incentives to efficient work has capitalism provided such men as these! Nothing is more tragic or more monstrous than the enormous waste of human skill and diligence represented by these facts. It is one of the major claims of socialism upon the support of every capable man and woman that it can, and does, present unlimited opportunities for the exercise of every ounce of skill, knowledge, and efficiency which they possess.

The above are the personal incentives which act upon the wage workers in socialist industry. Another group of incentives comes into play, however, in the case of those producers' co-operatives which, as we saw, play some part in the industrial production, and a predominant part in the agricultural

[1] For example, the Order of Lenin, the Order of the Red Banner of Toil, the Order of the Red Star.

production, of the existing socialist society. These organizations, since they own their means of production, also own the product when they have made it. Thus the soviet collective farmers own their crop (although, like other farmers, they have to pay taxation to the state) and divide amongst themselves either the actual wheat, milk, meat, or other agricultural produce which they raise, or the money which its sale on the market yields them. In the same way, the co-operative societies which produce handicrafts, or some speciality needed by large-scale industry, or which perform some service, such as house repairing, all enjoy the proceeds of their labour sold on the market. It is clear that in their case the familiar, traditional incentive to good and hard work provided by sale in a competitive market operates to the full. (And the same consideration applies to those individual workers, artists, craftsmen, intellectual workers, journalists, laundresses, and many others who continue to exist and to sell the products of their labour on the market.)

In what respect, then, it may be asked, does the position of these workers in a socialist society differ from that of a capitalist employer who sells the products of his firm on the market for what they will fetch? The answer is that the members of a producers' co-operative society, or an individual self-employing craftsman, in a socialist society sell the products of their own labour. A capitalist employer, on the contrary, sells the products of his workers' labour. No soviet collective farm employs, or will ever be allowed to employ, workers who have no part or lot in the enterprise, and whose labour, remunerated by a fixed wage, would yield a profit to the members of the collective farm. In the same way, no individual craftsman must employ other persons to work at wages for him with his tools, on his raw materials, producing commodities for his profit. This would be, clearly, to re-introduce that exploitation for profit of the labour of others, by the owners of the means of production, which is the essence of capitalism. But so long as this is strictly avoided there is nothing in socialism which forbids the free sale of the product of a man's labour on the market for what it will fetch. And there is, as we have seen, an enormous and increasing amount of such selling in the Soviet Union to-day.

In the case of the members of the 250,000 collective farms,

Es

which, of course, constitute by far the largest class of such sellers
of the products of their labour, a complex combination of
incentives to work has been developed. In the first place, all the
members know that the total sum to be divided amongst them
depends upon how hard they all work. But in a co-operative
organization containing several hundred workers this is considered to be too diffused an incentive to be effective. Hence each
individual collective farmer shares in the total product of the
enterprise in accordance with the amount of work which he does,
this amount being calculated either on a piecework or a time-
work basis. To this ingenious combination of two different
incentives is added a third. In the typical collective farm the
members also engage in individual agricultural production either
for the needs of their own families or for sale on the market.
Thus the Soviet government strongly encourages the collective
farmer to own a cow, or pigs, or poultry, and to cultivate a plot
of land of anything up to three acres in extent round his house.
It is often only the production of the main agricultural staple
of the district, be it wheat, or sugar beet, or stock raising, which
is co-operatively undertaken. But again, of course, no collective
farmer must in the course of his individual productive operations hire the labour of some other persons for wages.

These, then, are the incentives to hard work, capable of
appealing to the most severely self-seeking types, which a
socialist society provides. These are the reasons which impel
even those citizens of socialist societies who cannot be touched
in the slightest by considerations which do not benefit them
individually and immediately, to go to work, and to work hard
and well. Nothing is more certain than that the Soviet Union has
been able to secure a high output of work from its citizens. And
it has done so partly by the provision of this type of incentive.

It would be quite unrealistic to suggest, however, that men
and women were responsive to nothing but considerations of
immediate, individual self-interest. The fact is that men often
respond powerfully to the most various, the most idealistic,
and the most impersonal appeals. Indeed, what tragedies have
not been caused by the fact that they respond to such appeals
as hastily and as uncritically as they do ! Again and again it has

been found possible to make men, not only work, but die for ideals and causes good, bad and indifferent. Men have always been only too ready to fling themselves into every kind of impersonal enterprise or combat—and have helped to wreck civilization by so doing. Gibbon in a famous passage tells us how whole generations of the men of antiquity died for a diphthong.[1] Century after century, men have been willing to throw away their most substantial concerns and to devote themselves body and soul to some cause which they believed to be sacred. The more we read history the less we shall doubt men's idealism and the more we shall doubt their perspicacity.

If, then, almost every government has been able to enlist men's all-too-ready idealism for causes which could bring those who worked or fought for them no benefit, how much more should a socialist government be able to enlist that idealism for the cause of acquiring for themselves all the material and moral benefits of a new civilization? And, in fact, we find that the existing socialist government has been able to tap an immense fund of constructive idealism amongst its citizens. It has done so partly by devising a system of rewards and punishments, which, while they directly affect the individual, do not affect his or her material interests. We might call it a system of public praising for good work and public blaming for bad work. It is applied informally and variously in nearly all Soviet establishments by such methods as writing up the names and performances of especially good workers on lists of honour hung in some public place, and writing the names of especially bad workers and their performances on corresponding rolls of dishonour. There are a dozen ways of applying this system of praising and blaming, but they all depend upon the existence of a genuine desire upon the part of the population as a whole to

[1] The orthodox doctrine of the Trinity was expressed by the word Homoousion; the doctrines of the Semi-Arians by the word Homoiousion. As Gibbon remarks, the resemblance of the words is in itself a mere coincidence. But the resemblance of the doctrines is fully as close as the resemblance of the words. Yet for several centuries hundreds of thousands of men sacrificed their lives in wars waged between the two factions of the Church which respectively held these doctrines. (It may be, however, that adequate historical research could unearth the real, substantial causes of these wars. For no doubt there were real causes, which merely came into the consciousness of the combatants in the fantastically distorted forms of theological controversy. What a field is presented by the first ten centuries A.D. for an historian equipped with the materialist conception of history!)

improve the productive system. For unless that desire exists there will be no genuine pressure from public opinion acting upon the individual and influencing him to give his best. Nor (except during a still popular war) can such a public opinion very well arise in a capitalist community. For in such a community increased efficiency of production primarily benefits the capitalists. Their monopolistic hold on the means necessary to wealth production enables them to appropriate almost the whole of society's ever growing surplus over and above the necessities of the rest of the population. In a socialist society, however, in which there is no such privileged class, any increase in production will undeniably benefit the entire community. Hence a vigorous and genuine public demand for efficiency and diligence can arise.

The first socialist society has also devised a whole series of methods by which the more generalized, and more definitely idealistic, impulses which certainly influence the conduct of many persons to a significant degree, can be made use of for the benefit of society. There is, for example, the device of socialist competition by which a particular works challenges another to achieve the highest output, or by which this same principle is applied within a given establishment, one group of workers, or one individual, challenging another group or another individual. Again, there have been occasions on which almost the whole populations of particular cities have turned out on their weekly free days to help complete some especially urgent or especially desirable job (for example, a perceptible part of the immense amount of unskilled clearing work necessary to the construction of the Moscow underground was done in this way). Or, again, there is a system of patronage, by which one organization, a Red army battalion, or a scientific institute, or a factory, will take a permanent interest in, and assume a measure of responsibility for, some other organization, say, a disorganized collective farm, or a struggling elementary school, and give it sustained technical, moral and material support.

These and many other methods have been devised for utilizing the great reservoir of willing social service which exists in a socialist community. It is true that the desire to render social service exists in capitalist communities such as Britain and

America, and a great deal of unpaid work is done both by members of the working class in their characteristic organizations and by the capitalist class in various administrative and governmental fields. But a socialist society which has rid itself both of class divisions and of the monopoly-hold of individuals upon the means of production can utilize this social idealism far more simply and directly than any capitalist society can ever do.

When once the purpose of work has become undeniably the improvement of the conditions of life for all, much of it is done without regard to, and without hope of, personal, individual reward. It is done simply and directly in order to develop, to improve, to embellish the way of life led by the whole community. Such work foreshadows the attainment of communism itself, when, as we saw, a technical and psychological basis will have been laid which will make it possible for all work to be done from this incentive. But already in a socialist society men's attitude to their ordinary work, for which they are paid individually and by results, is profoundly modified by these non-personal incentives.

Stalin, in a speech at a conference of specially efficient Russian workers named after the miner Stakhanov, in November 1935, said:

" Under capitalism, labour has a private, personal character. If you have worked more, you receive more and live for yourself as you know best. Nobody knows you or wants to know you. You work for capitalists, you enrich them. And how otherwise ? It is for that you were hired, to enrich the exploiters. You do not agree with this—then join the ranks of the unemployed and eke out an existence as best you can—we shall find others more tractable. It is for this reason that the labour of people is not highly valued under capitalism. . . . It is a different matter in the conditions of the Soviet system. Here the man of labour is held in honour. Here he works not for the exploiters but for himself, for his class, for society. Here the man of labour cannot feel himself neglected and alone. On the contrary, the man of labour feels himself in our country to be a free citizen of his country, a sort of public figure. And if he works well and gives to society what he is able to give—he is a hero of labour, he is surrounded with glory."

In another speech, Stalin defined the kind of help and encouragement which must be given to the workers in a socialist society in order that he should not feel " neglected and alone." " Men must be grown as carefully and attentively as a gardener grows a favourite fruit tree. To educate, to help to grow, to offer a prospect, to promote in time, to transfer in time to another position if a man does not manage his work, without waiting for him to fail completely; carefully to grow and train people . . . " this, said Stalin, was the job of a socialist society.

To sum up: any economic system which is to get the best out of such beings as we are to-day must know how to provide incentives appropriate for the varying natures of different men and women, and of the same men and women at different times. Present-day men and women respond to the most diverse incentives. Our contemporary human nature is very variable. Sometimes men seem incapable of anything but narrow and grubbing self-interest; at others they dazzle us with the flame of their idealism. The socialist system of distribution of income in accordance with the quality and quantity of work done, combined with socialism's power to evoke our constructive impulses in the cause of direct production for use, is well adapted to the needs of such beings as ourselves.

In the Soviet Union the incentives to work provided by socialism have proved very powerful. Mr. and Mrs. Webb write : " The Bolshevik experiment has, in the course of the past decade, demonstrated beyond all denial that neither the incentive of profit-making nor the existence of a capitalist class as the leaders and directors of industry is indispensable to wealth production on a colossal scale, or to its continuous increase."

Thus there is not the slightest fear of the socialist form of economic organization failing because of an inability to get men and women to work the machines. On the contrary, the incentives to work which come into play in a socialist society are not only incomparably more just and humane, but are also much more varied and powerful, than are those provided by capitalism.

PART II
THE POLITICAL SYSTEM

CHAPTER XIII

A New Kind of Democracy

IF we change our economic system from capitalism to socialism we must make a corresponding change in our political institutions. For our existing political institutions are inseparably associated with our existing economic system.

Does this mean that the establishment of a socialist economic system involves the abolition of democracy ? It is often alleged that it does. We are told that the establishment of socialism or communism (the words are used indiscriminately in this connection) involves the destruction of democracy, civil and religious liberty, and the establishment of the irresponsible dictatorship of a single individual or group of individuals. And this, it is felt, is too high a price to pay even for general plenty and security.

If these were the political conditions for the abolition of capitalism, then certainly the price of plenty would be high indeed. But they are not. It is not proposed that we should destroy democracy, nor abolish civil and religious liberty, nor set up the irresponsible dictatorship of an individual or group of individuals as the means of obtaining socialism. It is proposed, on the contrary, that we should enormously extend the principle and practice of democracy.

But how so, it may be objected ? Have we not democracy already in Britain and America ? If, then, it is admitted that it is proposed to abolish our existing political system, how can it be claimed that democracy will not be destroyed ? But what we now possess is only one particular form of democracy. Our existing political institutions constitute the characteristic capitalist form of democracy. They were established, that is to say, by the ancestors of the present owners of the means of production, and they were established for the express purpose of providing the appropriate political framework for the capitalist economic system. The early merchants and manufacturers found a political system in existence which made impossible the full development of capitalist production for profit. They felt that they must have freedom from laws which were throttling and stunting their commercial and productive operations. Hence they endeavoured to establish the principle that the government should be elected by and should be responsible to the capitalist class. The establishment of this control over governments was absolutely necessary to the capitalists if they were to be able to devote themselves to their historic mission, namely the development of the community's productive resources with the maximum rapidity, or, to put the matter personally instead of socially, to profit-making. For otherwise (and bitter experience had taught them this truth) they had no safeguard against being plundered by irresponsible monarchies for the benefit of clouds of courtiers, aristocrats, and other drone-like parasites.

But the capitalists found that they were not able to win their struggle for power without the support of the mass of the population. They succeeded in obtaining that support, but in doing so their struggle for self-government for themselves inevitably became, to some extent, a struggle for self-government for everyone. The demand for democracy for the capitalists was widened into the demand for democracy for the whole population. Certain democratic rights, such as the vote, were in the end extended, not only to the capitalists, but to the whole population. (Increasingly, however, democratic rights were won by a struggle carried on not by the capitalists, but by the working class and lower middle class, which the capitalists had previously set in motion. Indeed in its later stages the struggle was often carried on *against* the capitalist class. Thus, for example, that essential, liberal principle of the freedom of the Press was in Britian won much more by the courageous struggle of the working class, Chartist, movement than by the arguments of the Liberal theorists of capitalism. This and many other of our existing democratic rights are the fruits of long and gallant working class struggles.)

But, despite this gradual, and reluctant, extension of democractic rights, effective political power remains to this day in such States as Britain and America in the hands of the capitalist class. The mass of the population did not, however, commit an error when it joined with the capitalists in establishing the basis of our present form of democracy Even though the capitalists have obtained nine-tenths of the benefits, even though they repeatedly attempted to bilk the rest of the population after their successes in the joint struggle, the workers were on the whole right to aid the capitalists to set up the kind of democracies under which we now live. For our present form of democracy, with its characteristic institutions, namely responsible government, freedom of the Press from direct governmental interference, guarantees of personal liberty, periodic general elections, parliaments or congresses, and constitutional monarchies or republics, is the political system appropriate to capitalism. And capitalism was the only possible economic system to establish upon the gradual break-up of feudalism. It suited the stage of development of both the productive powers and the state of consciousness which the human race had reached. There was no alternative to it. Such are the historical origins and present character of our democracies. Hence we may also define them, from a rather different point of view, as the main method by which the British and American capitalist classes originally got, and now maintain, their power over society. The capitalists have, naturally, ruled in their own interests. But their interests coincided, for a time, with the interest of society. Hence parliamentary democracy, as we know it, was the proper method of government for the particular stage in the development of human civilization through which we have just passed. For our contemporary needs, however, our present capitalist form of democracy is narrow and imperfect. It amounts to little more than democracy for the capitalist class alone. For it leaves that pre-requisite of freedom, independent access to the means of production, exclusively in the hands of the capitalists. So long as a limited class owns society's very means of life, that class will rule; and the most perfectly democratic constitution in the world can do no more than mask, and a little mitigate, its dictatorship. This is why socialists and communists propose that we should abolish our existing political institutions and substitute for them others which will constitute a very much broader, deeper, and more highly developed form of democracy.

But where, it may be asked, are these new democratic institutions to come from ? Must they be thought out in the heads of political scientists? On the contrary, they can only be deduced from a study of certain special and peculiar democratic institutions which have grown up within capitalism. These institutions can be developed and pushed to the front so that, with the change of economic system, they may become the new forms under which we organize our self-government.

For certain peculiar democratic institutions already exist under capitalism, which can be retained, developed and made predominant under socialism. These institutions are of a different kind from the characteristic institutions of capitalist democracies, such as parliaments, congresses, general elections, and the like. They were not established by the capitalist class, and that class has never shown any love for them. The most familiar example of such institutions is afforded by the Trade Unions.

Now, on the one hand, Trade Unions exist in all well-developed capitalist democracies, while, on the other, capitalist political science has not, or has most unwillingly, recognized their existence. And, what is more, capitalist governing practice, as expressed by the rulings of the courts and the actions of employers, has continually attempted to prevent their effective operation. In America especially, the right of association is still, in practice, although not on paper, resisted with force and violence by the American capitalists. Except in a few exceptional industries, American workers associate for the purpose of collective bargaining always at the peril of their jobs, and often at the peril of their lives.

Trade Unions are, therefore, democratic institutions which can and do exist under capitalism, but which cannot possibly be said to be capitalist democratic institutions. They were not established by the capitalists; their existence is still frequently disputed by the capitalists[1]; and they tend to impair, by maintaining wages at unnecessarily high levels,[2] the efficient working of capitalism. They are, in a word, institutions which have extra-capitalist implications.

[1] The subtler British capitalists have chosen to pervert rather than to resist. In Britain, the right of existence of Trade Unions is usually (though not always) undisputed; but it is only not disputed after Trade Union leaders have been brought over, by one means or another, to a " reasonable " (i.e. a capitalist) frame of mind.

[2] At levels above the rates which will serve to produce and reproduce workers of the required strength, skill, education, and intelligence, that is to say.

Here, then, is the first example of those peculiar democratic institutions which, although they exist to-day under capitalism, can be not only retained but greatly developed under a new economic system: which can become an important part of the organization of our self-government in socialist society. The Trade Unions, enormously enlarged and improved, enabled to become genuinely inclusive of all workers, will undoubtedly play an important part in organizing the new economic system of production for use in Britain and America.

We already know, from soviet experience, the general rôle which Trade Unions are destined to play in a socialist society. They protect the interests of the workers as workers, against, for example, over-enthusiastic " planners." They take the leading part in the determination of the relative size of wages paid in each industry, and for each job within an industry. And this is an essential part of the whole comprehensive task of economic planning which we outlined in Part I. For the relative levels of wages will predominantly determine and direct the supply of labour offering itself in each particular branch of production. Second, the Trade Unions are the appropriate bodies for the administration of that comprehensive system of social services, i.e. old age pensions, insurances (but not unemployment insurance, for unemployment can be, and has been, eliminated by socialist planning), and the like, which, as we saw, are still necessary in a socialist, as distinct from a communist, society. Third, they can and do play a leading part in building up the whole community life of the population, in ensuring that every factory, or mine, is not merely a place where production is carried on, but is also, through its clubs, its educational institutions, its crèches, its restaurants, and the like, a many-sided centre enabling what we might well call its " members " (i.e. the workers employed there) to live the good life.

The Trade Unions will not, however, play a more decisively governing rôle than this in a socialist society. It has been some-times suggested (by a now almost extinct[1] sect of workers, called the Syndicalists) that the Trade Unions should be the institutions which should take over the government of the

[1] Except in Spain.

country from the capitalists; that the workers should exercise their rule through the Trade Unions in the same way as the capitalists exercise their rule through parliament and congress. The Trade Unions are not, however, and cannot be made, sufficiently wide and all-inclusive to be able adequately to fulfil this supreme function. They are inevitably to some extent sectional organizations. They represent the worker as carpenter, or miner, or transport worker, or engineer, rather than as worker. Hence they are not appropriate organs for the supreme function of exercising the political rule of the working class. Moreover, the Trade Unions are only half extra-capitalist institutions. Although they are often injurious to capitalism they can and do function within capitalism. They do not, in themselves, adequately express the workers' need to break through the basic premises of capitalist production, if they are ever to lead tolerable lives.

What democratic institutions, then, should be established for the organization of our self-government in a socialist economic system? What, in a word, is the political counterpart of an economic system of planned production for use? It would be useless to try to answer this question also by sitting down and " thinking up " some new type of political organization. What must be done is to seize upon every scrap of experience of what the workers have done, in actual practice, when they have, even temporarily, held the power of the State in their hands.

Before the Russian workers got power in 1917 there were two important examples from which we might learn what the workers in fact did when power was, even though temporarily and partially, in their hands. There was, first, the Paris Commune of 1870, during which the French workers held in their hands the power of the French State in Paris for some two months. Now on that occasion the French workers did not attempt to elect an ordinary type of parliament. It is true that they preserved the ordinary methods of election by geographical district. But the Parliament or Commune which they elected was both a legislative and executive body. Moreover, it was predominantly composed (for the first time in the history of representative institutions) of working men. The delegates elected to it were entrusted with the task, not only of making the laws, but of carrying on the whole administration of the common life of the community. Although the Commune lasted for only two months, and although most of its own members were unaware of what they were doing, it is now possible to see in their work the first vague outlines of a new form of democracy, of a workers' State, of which we now have a well-developed example before our eyes.[1]

The second important piece of historical evidence bearing on the point arose from the Russian revolution of 1905. Then it was found that as the workers got near to possessing power (though on this occasion they never achieved it), they threw up a network of councils. The Russian word for these bodies is soviets. Everywhere in Russia these soviets sprang up as the workers found an urgent need of some sort of organization both to fight for their interests and to defend those interests wherever they had been in any degree satisfied. It became evident that these councils, or soviets, were the natural form of organization which the workers threw up both for attempting to take power, and for using that power when they had got it.

Indeed, it may be observed, that it did not, and does not, take a revolutionary crisis to make the workers turn to the creation of councils for the promotion of their interests. In many strikes, especially when the workers concerned are not already organized into long established Trade Unions, such committees or councils come into being. And, if the strike is sufficiently extensive for a number of councils to be formed, they at once show a tendency to get into touch with each other, to federate, by the interchange of delegates.

This tendency was very marked in the case of the largest strike in which a working class has ever been engaged, the British General Strike of 1926. It is not too much to say that in the short space of the nine days which the strike lasted the whole of Great Britain was covered by a network of these councils. Such an extremely rapid formation of workers' councils was only possible because there existed, and exists, in Britain,[2] a permanent nucleus of such bodies in the Trades Councils. In almost

---

[1] The astounding thing is that Marx was able to see this at the time. See his pamphlet *The Civil War in France*, published within two days of the fall of the Commune.

[2] Similar institutions exist in many parts of America.

every town in Britain the different Trade Unions have long been accustomed to send delegates to a periodical meeting of a " Trades and Labour Council," which considers all matters affecting the workers in general, rather than any particular trade in that locality. Moreover, not only the Trade Unions, but also the working class political parties, send delegates to these bodies (delegates from the Independent Labour Party and the Communist Party are now excluded). It was round the nuclei of these bodies that the strike committees of the British General Strike were formed. Hence it is true to say that for a few days many British Trades Councils functioned almost as soviets.

But this is not to say that Trades Councils are embryonic soviets. Their composition, which is based essentially upon the Trade Union branch is too narrow for that. The type of political organization which suddenly and spontaneously covered the face of Russia upon the fall of the Tsar, which played a great part in the abolition of Russian capitalism seven months later, and which has provided the political framework within which the first socialist economic system has been built up, was of a far wider character than that of any existing British or American Trades Council. It directly represented all the workers, whether or not they were members of Trade Unions or political parties, in its own area. And it secured their representation by basing itself upon the actual places of work, the factories, mines and offices of those workers.

It seems clear, then, that a network of councils, representing not only every type of worker, but the whole adult population, male and female, is the specific form of democracy by means of which the workers may organize their self-government in a socialist economic system. Of such a kind, experience appears to indicate, are the political institutions which correspond to a socialist economic system of planned production for use.

Communists and socialists advocate, then, the replacement of the extremely cramped and limited kind of democracy which is alone possible under capitalism by a wider, broader, and more effective kind of democracy. These new democratic institutions are capable of making genuine self-government possible for the whole population; they open the gates of democracy to excluded millions. They will go far to make democracy all inclusive, for the workers in Britain and America form so high a proportion of the population that once they are in a position to play a controlling part in affairs we really shall approach, for the first time, the ideal of a self-governing community.

We must now describe the way in which this new kind of democracy works. The network of directly elected councils is so constituted that every worker is eligible for one or other of them. But they are not elected on the territorial basis of the present franchise in Britain and America. For in modern life we are often much more intimately related with our place of work, our office, or our factory, than with the particular area in which we live. An office or a factory, and not a block of streets, is the centre of most workers' lives: this is where they are in contact with their fellows: this is where questions are discussed: this is where working class opinion is formed. Hence the collective will of the working class, as distinct from the other classes of the community, is more readily expressed by this type of semi-occupational representation than by our more familiar geographically defined constituencies.

Again, certain workers must temporarily cut themselves off from their homes altogether. Serving soldiers, sailors, and airmen (or, for that matter, merchant seamen) are examples. How painfully elaborate and artificial is the attempt made in Britain to give such serving soldiers a vote by post in the constituency in which their parents live! The soviet form of democracy provides that the units of the armed forces themselves elect councils (in itself a significant fact); that each merchant ship has its council; that, in a word, representation is given, not to the abstract individual " voter," but to the real units in which men and women actually live and work. At the same time, some workers (especially married women) do their work at home, and for them councils elected upon a territorial basis are established.

The function of these directly elected councils is a double one. In the first place, they deal with all matters exclusively affecting the particular unit which elects them. For instance, a ship's, or a factory's, or an office's council deals with the question of the quality of the food served, with disputes over discipline, with leave—with, in a word, matters which may sound trivial, but which, as everyone who has ever worked in a ship, office, or factory knows, are questions which matter intensely to people in their daily lives.

Again, there is a whole range of questions which these primary councils will not be able to settle for themselves, but on which they will make very strong representations to the higher authorities which they themselves establish. A factory may be inadequately served by trains and buses. " Why," its council will demand to know, " were additional buses put on to route 2 which passes other factories, while none was put on to route 1 which passes our factory ? " This is the sort of question which the primary councils must continually take up.

Their other function is to elect delegates to what we may call secondary councils which federate a group of primary councils. These secondary councils, naturally, have a wider jurisdiction. They usually cover a whole town or region. They do work analogous to that of our municipalities or county councils.

These secondary councils in turn elect delegates to a supreme central council in which sovereignty resides. This central council, elected by the regional councils, is analagous to the British Parliament and the American Congress. It cannot make, and is not intended to make, any attempt to carry on the actual work of governing the country. For this purpose it elects a smaller, but still large, executive committee which reviews legislative and administrative work in some detail. But this executive committee is itself too large for actual administration.[1] Accordingly, it selects certain individuals who form a body analogous to the British and American cabinets. Each member of this governing executive has charge of a department of State. Some of these departments are the same as those existing in capitalist States, e.g. Foreign Affairs, Justice, Education, Post and Telegraphs, Defence; others are different. For in a socialist economic system there must be departments responsible for particular groups of industries.

[1] In many ways this executive committee is more analogous to Congress or Parliament. But actual sovereignty resides in the larger Congress.

There is no doubt that these new democratic institutions produce a far wider measure of democracy than do Parliaments or Congresses. They enable large numbers of the population actually to participate in the making of the innumerable day-to-day decisions which concern the primary local councils. They enable a miner, for example, to have an effective say in whether available funds should be spent on new pithead baths or on a new housing scheme, as well as enabling him to help to choose the men who are to fill the highest posts in the central government. They provide a method of permeating society from top to bottom with democratically made decisions. The difference between existing capitalist democracy and this new kind of working class, or " soviet," democracy, as it is often called from the Russian example, has been put this way. The former enables the workers to decided which of two nominees of the capitalist class should govern them. The latter enables the workers to govern themselves. Such is the outline of that form of democracy which the working class has evolved for the purposes of its struggle to abolish capitalism and to establish socialism.

It is now becoming clear, however, that as and when that task is, in its main essentials, accomplished, the type of democratic structure corresponding to a socialist economic system of planned production for use undergoes further development. It is becoming clear that such features of the soviet system, as an occupational instead of a geographical electoral basis, and the indirect election of the higher organs of government by the lower, are essential parts of the rule of the working class as such. As and when socialism is achieved and a society free from class divisions appears, they become unnecessary.

As these chapters are being written (summer 1936) the whole vast population of the Soviet Union is engaged in high debate upon the draft of a new constitution, which has been prepared for the consideration of a new Congress of Soviets to be summoned in the latter months of 1936. The present draft does not, as it has been ignorantly alleged, abolish the system of workers' soviets or councils as the essential political organs of a socialist economic system. On the contrary, Articles 2 and 3 of the draft

declare that " the political foundation of the U.S.S.R. is formed
by the soviets of toilers deputies. . . . All power in the U.S.S.R.
belongs to the toilers of the town and village in the form of
soviets of toilers deputies." The whole elaborate structure of
these soviets, or councils, is preserved. What is altered is the
method by which these bodies are to be elected. In future all
of them, including the Supreme Council of the U.S.S.R., are to
be elected by direct, universal and secret ballot, upon the basis
of geographically defined constituencies.

Thus two features of the present system are abandoned,
viz. the occupational franchise and the election of the higher
councils by the lower ones instead of by the electorate as a
whole. This latter change is obviously a general extension of
democratic rights, made practicable by the growing experience
and political activity of the soviet population. The former
change, from an occupational to a geographical franchise, is
more interesting. That it has been proposed in the draft constitution indicates that in the opinion of the leaders of soviet
thought a classless society is, for the first time in the history
of human civilization, actually coming into being. For, once
classes have actually been abolished, the objections to the
geographical constituency, and the advantages of the occupational constituency, disappear. In a classless society the presuppositions of liberal political theory, upon which we have all
been brought up—in particular the postulate that each citizen
can be given his or her exact share in the government by giving
him or her one, and only one, vote—become true. These presuppositions are disastrously false in any society in which the
means of production are owned by a limited class. For in such
societies this limited class of owners will inevitably dominate
the whole community, whatever the constitution may say.
These liberal presuppositions are still false during the transitional period when the working class has captured political
power, is taking over the means of production, and is building
them up into a system of planned production for use. But these
presuppositions become true when such an economic system
has begun to function, and when, accordingly, class differences
have largely disappeared. Then, but not till then, a system of
formal democracy can fulfil its promise of giving all its citizens,

when it gives them the vote, a real share in the government of the community. Hence, paradoxically enough, a socialist society re-adopts some of the democratic forms with which we are familiar. But it does not do so until, by its complete transformation of the economic and social system, it has laid down the indispensable foundation without which these democratic institutions can be only a little better than empty forms.

To put the matter in another way: during the transitional stage between capitalism and socialism there is no possibility of an all-inclusive democracy. For, during this stage, classes still exist. And there can be no democracy *between* classes: there can be no democracy between those who own and those who do not own the means of production. During this stage, if socialism is to be built up, the working class must dominate the community just as completely as does the capitalist class in a capitalist society. But this consideration takes us to the next stage in our description of that political structure which corresponds to a socialist economic system.

CHAPTER XIV

The Dictatorship of the Working Class

THE political objective of communists and socialists is, then, the establishment of a broader and more highly developed form of democracy. What, then, is meant by the famous phrase, " the dictatorship of the proletariat " ?

Now most people when they use the word dictatorship have in mind the absolute, irresponsible, and uncontrolled rule of one man over the whole of the rest of the community. The régime of the Roman Emperors from Augustus to Augustulus (27 B.C. to A.D. 475) is the classical example of this type of government. The Fascist régimes of Hitler and Mussolini are its contemporary prototypes.[1] The undesirability of this type of government is so well established that we need not discuss it. Is this the kind of government which we should have in a socialist Britain and America ? It is not. When we speak of the necessity of establishing " the dictatorship of the proletariat," as a condition for the achievement of socialism, we mean something totally different.

We saw in Chapter VIII that the capitalist economic system inevitably produced two classes, or groups, of citizens, namely the capitalists, drawing their incomes from their ownership of the means of production, and the workers, drawing their incomes in respect of work. *Now so long as these two classes exist, one is going to rule the other.* Either the capitalists will be on top ruling the workers, or the workers will be on top ruling the capitalists. Nor can there be, except for very brief and unstable periods, any intermediate position: there cannot be, for long, any balance of power between these two classes. One class or the other is bound to be in effective control of the State machinery for making and unmaking the laws and enforcing them upon the rest of the community. There can be little or no reality in any political theory which ignores this division of our existing

[1] It will be found on examination, however, that the dictator is never anything like so absolute or uncontrolled as he appears to be. He is always, in fact, ruling on behalf of some class or, possibly, coalition of classes.

societies into two classes, living different lives and drawing their incomes from different sources.[1]

The original form of capitalist or parliamentary democracy did not ignore class division. During most of the last century in Britain democracy was frankly and openly democracy for the capitalist class alone. The property qualification for the franchise debarred anyone who did not have a certain minimum amount of property from voting. But since the establishment of a universal franchise this has been changed. We seem to have established in Britain and America a democracy for all, whether they are capitalists or workers. Each has one vote, and only one. Each seems to take an equal part in governing the country.

But communists and socialists (and almost everyone else, for that matter) are convinced that this is an illusion. In spite of the establishment of universal franchise, the capitalist class is almost, though not quite, as exclusively the ruling class, dictating to the workers, as ever it was. The methods by which the capitalist class has maintained, in all essentials, its exclusive power to make and unmake the laws, in spite of the grant of the franchise to the workers, are also well known to most people. They are based upon the fact that their ownership of the means of production gives the capitalists control over men's whole lives. In particular, the capitalists own the essential means for the production of political opinion, the newspapers, the wireless, the schools, and the cinemas, in exactly the same way that they own the means for the production of steel and of concrete.

Moreover, they have set up, in both England and America, extremely elaborate political organizations, in the form of capitalist political parties (viz. the Republican and Democratic parties in America and the Conservative party in Britain). These vast political organizations are themselves very powerful means for the production of political opinions—for inducing men to vote in any desired manner. And these organizations are again the almost exclusive possession of the capitalist class. For the cost of their establishment and maintenance is extremely high (some millions of pounds per annum all told), so that the workers

---

[1] And, be it observed, orthodox political theory, as it is taught in British and American Universities, does almost wholly ignore the division of modern society into these two classes. Hence its notorious futility.

cannot effectively maintain such organizations. By these means the capitalists have, in Britain and America, been able to induce a majority of the population to vote for a continuance of capitalist rule. They can claim to have thus obtained the workers' assent to the capitalists' dictatorship. But that fact does not mean that their rule is not still in fact a dictatorship.

But, it may be objected, a régime which has to use all these elaborate methods to induce members of the subjected classes to assent to it, has evidently become modified. Has it not been modified so much that it can no longer be called a dictatorship? Does not the development of the last fifty years in Britain, for example, mark the gradual emergence of a genuine democracy independent of, and above, either class? It is true that the need of the British and American capitalists to win the assent of the workers in one sense weakens their dictatorship. But it is not true that it causes it to cease to be a dictatorship. The test arises if, and whenever, the above means for the production of political opinion fail of their effect. If ever and whenever the workers, despite all the suasion and all the pressure which can be put upon them, vote for something which seriously infringes upon the dictatorship of the capitalist class, then a way is always found by which their democractic decision is discounted and the rule of the capitalists is maintained substantially intact. Capitalist democracies always turn out to be truly democratic so long as the workers vote for the capitalists, and not for one moment longer. For if the workers persist in voting for measures incompatible with the proper functioning of capitalism, the capitalists unhesitatingly scrap democracy and carry on their dictatorship without the assent of the workers.

This has actually happened in a series of European States. And the situation in which it happened will sooner or later occur in both Britain and America. For even our existing imperfect democratic institutions are becoming more and more incompatible with capitalism. In spite of all their highly perfected methods for the formation of opinion, the capitalists are finding it more and more difficult to induce the workers to give their assent to the measures which are now necessary to the preservation of capitalism. For these measures are becoming ever more disastrous to the workers: they involve ever more serious "sacrifices" (as they are called) from the whole non-capitalist population. The ever-growing economic difficulties in which the system is becoming involved necessitate taking their employment, and so their livelihoods, from more and more workers, and reducing drastically the incomes of many others. The propaganda technique needed to induce men to give their own consent to such measures taxes more and more the resources of the capitalist spokesmen.

Moreover, under the conditions of capitalist democracy, the capitalist's monopoly of the means of propaganda is never perfect. As formally, legalistically, the workers are free to publish a few very small newspapers, if they can ever command sufficient resources, to hold meetings out of doors or in inexpensive halls, and to organize, though with great difficulty and by means of heavy self-sacrifice, their own political parties —they are able to make themselves articulate to some extent. These means of counter-propaganda, puny as they are compared to the means possessed by the capitalists, serve to make it still more difficult to induce the workers to vote for their own destitution.

Accordingly, the capitalists find themselves forced, so long as they preserve democracy, to make some concessions. In order to give their vast propaganda apparatus something plausible to say, they sometimes (especially in Britain) have made concessions, or, more often, have refrained from imposing cuts, which were really necessary to the proper functioning of capitalism. Thus the necessity under democracy of winning the workers' consent becomes a more and more intolerable limitation on that freedom of action which, as the economic crisis gets worse, becomes more and more necessary to the capitalists.

It is at this point that the fact of capitalist class dictatorship, underlying all democratic forms, reveals itself unmistakably. For experience proves that if the workers now try to use the existing democratic institutions to supersede capitalism itself, then those institutions are abolished by the capitalists.

The only way in which the workers can rid themselves of capitalism and organize a socialist economic system is rapidly to push to the front the specifically working class democratic institutions, such as trade unions and workers' councils, which exist in an embryonic form under capitalism and which, we saw, become the main political institutions of a socialist society.

Now these institutions, when they have been developed into institutions of government, will constitute a democracy for the workers. *But at the same time these institutions will constitute a workers' dictatorship over the capitalist class.* This is what we mean when we say that in order to get rid of capitalism it is necessary to establish a workers' dictatorship.[1] In order to establish a socialist economic system it is necessary, that is to say, for the working class to assume exactly that political relationship to the capitalist class which the capitalist class now assumes to the working class. Within the working class there will be effective democracy, just as to-day there is effective democracy within the capitalist class. Over the capitalist class there will be dictatorship, just as to-day there is dictatorship over the working class.

For the existence of social classes cannot, unfortunately, be abolished overnight with the accession to power of the working class. Separate classes will be abolished as and when a socialist economic system of production for use is built up. For, as we saw in Part I, such a system distributes income, not from two antithetical sources, but uniquely in respect of work done. But the building up of such a system takes time. The workers will not be able to take all the means of production out of the hands of the capitalists on the day after their accession to power. And even after that has been done experience indicates that the former capitalists constitute for some time a well-defined and aggressively hostile class which has to be ruled.

The rule of the working class, coming to their decisions democratically amongst themselves, but dictating to the capitalist class, is, then, what is meant by a workers' dictatorship.

Mr. and Mrs. Sidney Webb's *Soviet Communism* contains a passage in which they admit with characteristic candour their

---

[1] For the sake of simplicity I use the phrase " workers' dictatorship " or " the dictatorship of the working class " instead of the correct scientific term, " the dictatorship of the proletariat."

inability to understand the political concept represented by the phrase, " the dictatorship of the proletariat." They write:

" This high-sounding phrase, used more than once by Karl Marx, and repeatedly and vehemently endorsed by Lenin, has been accepted by those in authority as an official designation of the constitution of the U.S.S.R., in preference to any reference to the leadership of the Communist party or the early slogan of ' All Power to the Soviets.' We frankly confess that we do not understand what was or is meant by this phrase. As rendered in English it seems to mean a dictatorship exercised by the proletariat over the community as a whole. But if terms are to be taken literally this is a union of two terms which contradict each other. Dictatorship, as government by the will of a single person, cannot be government by the will of an immense class of persons. Moreover, if by the proletariat is meant the immense mass of the population dependent upon their daily earnings, or as Marx frequently meant, the whole of the workers engaged in industrial production for wages, the dictatorship of proletariat would, in highly developed capitalist societies like Great Britain, where three-quarters of all men of working age are wage earners, mean no more than the rule of the immense majority of the population. Why, then, should it be termed a dictatorship ? "

This passage contains a number of separate misapprehensions. Dictatorship, in the sense of that word habitually used by communists, does not mean the rule of one individual. The dictatorship of the working class does mean precisely what Mr. and Mrs. Webb say it would mean in Great Britain (or America)—" the rule of an immense majority over a minority." Why, then, do not communists claim that the political system which they advocate is a complete democracy ? They do not make this claim because they see that such a system does imply the non-democratic, coercive, and, in that precise sense, dictatorial, rule of the immense majority of the population over the minority of remaining capitalists. And, as communists are political scientists before they are propagandists, they give such a system a name which correctly characterizes it—namely the dictatorship of one class, the workers, over another class, the capitalists. For, they repeat, it is not until neither of these classes any longer exists, and both have been fused into a homogeneous society, that a true all-inclusive democracy, free from dictatorial elements, can be established.

It has been necessary for communists to stress the necessity of the establishment of a working class dictatorship. For it has been, and still is, continually alleged by those labour leaders who at present control the British and American working class movements that our existing democratic institutions have nothing specifically capitalist about them; that they can be used by the workers as readily as by the capitalists, that they can in particular be used to replace capitalism by socialism. There exists, we are told, an abstract democracy, independent of economic systems or class relations. And this abstract democracy the workers can use and must not dare to abolish.

No view has been more fatal than this to any hope of success for the workers in the task of ridding themselves of capitalism and establishing socialism. For it has served to lull them into the false security of believing that they had nothing to do to get socialism but to vote against the capitalists in sufficient numbers. The consequences of the acceptance by the workers of this false view of the nature of democracy have proved very terrible. For this was an important factor in making it possible for the Italian and German capitalists to set up their Fascist régimes. Hence we must insist upon the necessity of that transformation of our political institutions which is best described as the establishment of a workers' dictatorship, if there is to be any hope of socialism.

But this necessity has, unavoidably, enabled the capitalist spokesmen to confuse our minds with their clamour about the communists' and socialists' intention to destroy democracy and establish a dictatorship. Communists and socialists propose, on the contrary, that the workers should destroy one dictatorship, that of the capitalists, and replace it with another, their own. But a workers' dictatorship will establish democracy for by far the greater part of the population while destroying democracy for the small capitalist class alone. For it will be the comparatively small capitalist class alone over which the new dictatorship will be exercised.

Moreover, the capitalist class, having had its ownership of the means of production taken from it, will be gradually absorbed into the working class, which will thus become co-extensive with society itself. Then, and not till then, will the establishment of true, all-inclusive democracy become possible. (The extraordinary historical importance of the new Soviet Constitution is that it shows that the Soviet Union is now reaching this point.) Thus what the spokesmen of capitalism call democracy means the effective subjection of the mass of the population to a small minority, whilst what communists and socialists call dictatorship means the subjection of a small and ever-dwindling minority to the great majority of the population—which is itself democratically organized.

democracy for the small . . . . too . . . . For it will be
the comparatively small capitalist class alone over which the
new dictatorship will be exercised.

CHAPTER XV

A Party of the Working Class

WE have not yet described one of the most important of the
political institutions of working class democracy. This institution
plays an essential part both in the workers' rule over society
as a whole during the period of the transition from capitalism
to socialism and in the mobilization of the whole population for
the continuous economic, social and cultural development of
the community, once the foundations of socialism have been laid.

This intrument is a new type of political party. The working
class, both in its struggles against capitalism and during its
struggle to maintain and secure its own rule after the abolition
of capitalism, is forced by the very conditions of these struggles
to evolve a new type of political organization, known as a working
class party.   We say advisedly that this is a new type of political
organization, for although it is described by the old term
" party," it has in reality very little resemblance to the familiar
political parties of such countries as Britain and America.
(It may, indeed, be a pity that some new term has not been
devised to describe this new political entity. For to English
and American ears the term party has come almost to imply
the existence of another party, to carry with it the suggestion
of electoral competition between organizations designed to
catch the maximum number of votes in elections; and nothing
could be much further than this from the conception of " the
party," as that conception has been developed in the international working class movement.)

The working class conception of a party, is on the contrary,
that of an organization which comprises all the most active,
intelligent, conscientious and politically conscious members of
the working class. It is the essential political organization of the
workers as a class, just as the Trade Unions are, as we saw, the
essential economic and sectional organizations of the workers, as
engineers, miners, spinners, weavers, or dockers. This form of
organization has been found to be just as important an instrument for the exercise of working class rule as the above-described
structure of workers' councils.

But these two instruments of government, the workers'

councils and the workers' party, are not mutually exclusive; they inter-penetrate each other. The workers' party does not work separately from, or in rivalry with, the councils. It works *in* the councils. It brings together the keenest, most efficient, intelligent and hard-working members of these councils and gives them the opportunity to lead and guide the work. Above all, it permeates every institution of a workers' State with common methods of work and with a common will and purpose. It will be seen how meaningless those who hold this conception of the party as an essential instrument of working class rule must find the familiar accusation that what has actually been established in the Soviet Union is not the rule of the working class, but the rule of a particular party, in this case the Russian Communist party, *over* the working class.

We are entirely unable to separate such a party from the working class out of which it has sprung. The Russian Communist party has been slowly and painfully built up, over the decades, by the enormous struggles of the Russian workers. It now comprises, with its auxiliary organizations, nearly ten million persons, the great majority of whom are still actively engaged in productive work. How such an organization could separate itself off from the class of which it forms an indissoluble part, we are unable to understand. We are far from denying the dominating part which the workers' party takes in every sphere of soviet life. But we are convinced that this very fact is itself a demonstration that in the socialist society of the Soviet Union the working class, in actual practice, and having found the appropriate forms of organization to enable it to do so, rules and directs the whole life of the community.

A working class political party, of which the Russian Communist party is the first fully developed example, is naturally not wholly different from the political organizations which the capitalist class has always formed for the exercise of its rule. For the capitalist class habitually rules by means of one or more political parties, even though these capitalist parties are far less fully and consciously developed organizations for making effective the will of a given class than is a workers' party. The British governing class, for example, has always maintained and still maintains its rule quite as much by means of its political parties, or party, as by means of its king, law courts, parliaments and state apparatus.

The British capitalists have now, to all intents and purposes, followed the example of the Russian workers in creating one unified party for the expression of the will of their class. In the past in Britain, and even now in America, the capitalists have organized two or more political parties, usually representing sub-divisions of their class, with differing interests on particular points, to carry on their rule in alternating periods of office (e.g. the Conservative and Liberal parties in Great Britain, the Republican and Democratic parties in America).

But such a division of its forces is only possible to any class when its rule is virtually unchallenged. Whenever the right and ability of the class as a whole to rule the community is seriously challenged, either by a new class aspiring to power, or by an old class but lately dethroned, and determined to regain its position, differing interests within the ruling class become relatively insignificant. In such circumstances a ruling class invariably consolidates its political organizations; it forges a unique instrument for the expression of its will.

This doctrine may seem strange to some readers; but if it does so, that is merely because the capitalist class does not think, or at any rate does not speak, self-consciously. Capitalist spokesmen sometimes talk, it is true, of their particular political party ruling the country.[1] But they do not notice, or, at any rate, they do not say, that the real position is that the capitalist class rules the country *through or by means of* a particular political party. Hence there is nothing peculiar or exceptional about the fact that the working class, when it gets power, organizes a political party as the instrument of carrying out its will. What is peculiar to the working class is that its parties are much more developed **types** of political organization. Hence they are even more firmly, and **far more** frankly, rooted in the class which has given them birth than are the capitalist parties.

---

[1] One of the last of the philosopher statesmen of the British capitalists (Lord Balfour) once told an audience that they must see to it that " the Great Unionist Party should still control, whether in power or in opposition, the destinies of this great Empire." (Quoted in *The State in Theory and Practice*, by Harold J. Laski. This valuable volume is an exception to the assertion made on p. 151 that political theory as taught in British and American universities ignores the existence of classes.)

We are now in a position to see the main features of a working class state such as can alone provide the necessary political framework for the building up of a socialist economic system. The workers in their struggles with capitalism slowly become conscious of themselves as a separate class in society. Out of that consciousness comes the impulse to build up a political party, a higher type of organization, that is to say, than a Trade Union. They are impelled to evolve an organization which can represent them as workers, instead of sectionally. This organization, this party, must always be the main and essential instrument by which the workers acquire political power, take the means of production from the capitalists and maintain themselves in power during the period of the construction of a socialist economic system. But as soon as the workers have acquired political power they abolish the existing political system of parliamentary democracy and put in its place the system of workers' political institutions which we have described above. The conjunction of these two things, viz. a dominant workers' party, working in and through the institutions of working class democracy, constitutes a working class state.

There is still, however, one more essential element in a working class state. Just as the class is evolved out of the social and economic relations of capitalist society, and just as the party is evolved out of the struggles of the class, so a group of leaders, and often one predominant leader, are evolved out of the struggles of the party. The Russian Communist party was fortunate in throwing up (or rather it is to be admired for having thrown up, for no doubt parties have the leaders which they deserve) two men as its leaders who proved themselves to be built upon a scale adequate to the gigantic events of the period through which they lived. Lenin and Stalin showed themselves men capable of piloting a working class through the successive stages of the capture of the power of the state from the capitalists, the acquisition of the means of production, and the organization of a socialist economic system. Men have never accomplished larger tasks. It is a profoundly encouraging fact that such leaders were evolved by the working class. Far from seeking to minimize or to apologize for the vital part

Fs

which they have played, and which Stalin still plays, in the life of the soviet state, we take very great pride in their work. Their work is the highest example of all the enormous mass of devoted work which has been necessary for the first successful attempt at consciously willed social change which the world has ever seen.

Thus in this case also we can find no meaning in the allegation that first Lenin and now Stalin made themselves personal dictators. Stalin is the culminating figure in a whole group of men, which includes the several million members of the Communist party, and in the last analysis includes the whole Russian working class, who exercises power in the Soviet Union. After more than a decade of startlingly successful leadership Stalin's authority is now immense. But this is not to suggest for a moment that Stalin is able to rule according to his own whim or fancy. If we can imagine Stalin losing his reason and ordering the Russian Communist party and the soviets to restore their property in the means of production to the former Russian capitalists we should soon see whether or not he was a " personal dictator." Stalin leads and rules because he has proved (and not merely since he became the leading figure in the Russian Communist party, but during his whole life) that he can show the Russian workers the way forward to the establishment of the first socialist system in the history of the world. If he were to lose that ability he would give way to some other leader. Again there is nothing peculiar to the working class in a necessity to rule through and by means of chosen leaders. All other classes which have ever ruled society, including the capitalist class, have had to do so by means of leaders. They have ruled not only by setting up their characteristic political institutions (monarchies, empires, parliaments, republics and the like); they have done so not only by organizing their most active members into political parties; they have also been compelled by the necessities of government to select appropriate individuals as leaders, and to give these leaders a great measure of power. This is how all classes have had to rule: there is no other way. For classes, consisting of hundreds of thousands, or millions of men, have never been able to exercise their rule directly. They have had to delegate the task to a group of specialists. The working class is no exception to this rule. The fact that it, like every other class, governs through, and by means of, particular individuals or leaders as well as through and by means of a political party, no more means that it is not the governing class in the Soviet Union than a similar necessity means that the capitalists are not the governing class in Britain or America. The Russian workers rule through Stalin, Kalinin, Kaganovich, Voroshilov, and their other leaders, just as at the moment of writing (1936) the British capitalists rule through Baldwin, Chamberlain, MacDonald, etc., and the American capitalists through Roosevelt, Hull, Farley, etc. What is, however, unique about the working class rule is that the workers choose their leaders far more carefully, through the long and searching apprenticeship of work in the party, and control them far more closely, than do the capitalists.

The necessity which all former governing classes have had, to exercise their rule through a party, and ultimately through a group of leaders, or even predominantly through an individual leader, has often given rise to enormous abuses. Political parties frequently become demagogic and corrupt. They may cease adequately to serve even the interests of the class which has organized them: they may attempt to turn themselves into independent parasitical oligarchies, living off a sort of tribute. This tribute may be out of all proportion to the services which they render to the ruling class. (The capitalist class invariably has trouble of this sort with its Fascist parties.)

Again, groups of leaders, or individual leaders, have often proved unwilling or unable effectively to safeguard the interest of the class which they serve. They may (as did the later Roman emperors, for example) make themselves almost intolerable even to the governing class by means of their arbitrary exactions, their favouritism, and their power of life and death over individuals. For they often trade on the fact of their indispensability to the governing class, more especially when that class is in decline. They know that in such a period a governing class must often put up with every injustice and infamy rather than attempt to change its executive officers, and thus cause a disunity and confusion which may be fatal to its rule.

The working class, so long as capitalism exists (and it is, therefore, surrounded by a capitalist environment), has no perfect guarantee against the same type of difficulty. But after capitalism has been overthrown, or at any rate after the remains of capitalism have substantially disappeared, this kind of thing becomes practically impossible. We are not suggesting of course that the working class, after the full establishment of socialism, will secure perfect leaders. Its leaders will continue to have all sorts of human imperfections and inadequacies. But it will be, in a fully socialist environment, increasingly impossible for working class leaders (and still more for a working class party) to separate themselves off from the working class and divert or pervert the power with which they have been entrusted to personal or base uses.

For it is only so long as substantial elements of capitalism are in existence (as they were, for example, until very recently in the Soviet Union) that a mercenary or corrupt leader will find scope for his tastes. As and when socialist forms of economic life and the cultural and ethical values which go with them, come into existence, it will become more and more out of the question for considerable troubles to arise from the personal defects of leaders.

It is not claimed that the Soviet Union has yet reached a point of development at which the safeguarding of the highest level of character amongst the leading figures in every sphere of national life has ceased to be necessary. And in fact the Russian workers have evolved a highly developed and very effective method for maintaining this standard. Every member of the Russian Communist party has to undergo a periodical re-examination of his whole record, and he is unhesitatingly dropped from membership of the party, and thus ceases to be eligible for the higher fields of leadership, if he cannot demonstrate from his whole life's record his suitability for positions of trust.

Finally we must notice the views of those who complain that the Russian workers have been slow in building up effective democratic institutions. " It may be," such critics say, " that full democracy, even for the workers, could not be introduced at the time of the revolution. It may be that democracy for all cannot be achieved until social classes have disappeared. But has the Soviet Union yet established the most ordinary democratic practices ? Why, one of the most elementary of democratic institutions, viz. voting by secret ballot instead of by open show of hands, was only proposed in 1936—nineteen years after the revolution."

But progress in the establishment, and practice in the use, of democratic institutions must be measured whence you start. The Russian workers started out without the most elementary experience in self-government. Five centuries of unbroken autocracy had deprived the Russian masses of that useful experience in self-government which the workers of the Western world, with their Trade Unions, their co-operative societies, their access to elected local authorities, and their experience of universal suffrage, have enjoyed.

Moreover, the question is in fact broader than this. The great development of our productive resources which British and American capitalism has achieved, has at once enabled and necessitated a substantial improvement in the cultural level of the masses. For example, literate workers are necessary to the effective conduct of modern methods of production. In order to meet that need, extensive, and in some respects efficient, educational systems have been created. Little of this development took place in Tsarist Russia. In particular the vast majority of the population remained illiterate. (In this fact alone we have a sufficient explanation of why the ballot was not introduced before 1936; for voting by secret ballot is impossible for an illiterate population; and it was only by 1936 that the soviets had accomplished, even in the main, the colossal task of teaching a hundred and sixty million Russians to read and write.)

The irony of history dictated that the extreme backwardness of Tsarism, which led to its overthrow, and which thus gave the Russian workers their opportunity to build a socialist society, has at the same time made the building of a socialist society much more difficult than it will be elsewhere. For every socialist society must necessarily start at the point of cultural, as well as economic, development reached by the particular capitalism which it supersedes.[1]

---

[1] Marx foresaw clearly that this must inevitably be so. Indeed, he could hardly have expressed himself more forcibly on the point. " A communist society emerges from capitalist society," he wrote, " in every respect tainted economically, morally and intellectually with the hereditary diseases of the old society from whose womb it is emerging." (*The Critique of the Gotha Programme*, p. 29 of the Martin Lawrence edition.) As we noted on p. 113, Marx is here using the concept of the lower stage of communism in the sense which we are using the word socialism.

This fact is becoming recognized in the economic sphere. It is becoming clear to many people that the Russians have had to make such heroic and painful efforts in order to achieve industrialization because of the extremely backward state of the productive apparatus which they inherited. Many people are coming to realize that the British and American people would start out upon the building up of socialism with imcomparably better productive equipment. But it is still almost invariably overlooked that a similar consideration applies, with equal force, in the case of cultural development.

It is true that from the moment of their accession to power in 1917 the Russian workers established democratic institutions far superior, for the immense majority of the population, than any which the world had hitherto known. But they had to learn to *use* these institutions: to learn to *use* their Trade Unions, their Co-operative Societies, their elaborate and all-pervasive system of councils, and their party. (One of the things which the new Constitution implies is that the Russian people have passed on to a new and far higher stage in their political self-education.) The heritage of Tsardom made it necessary for the Russian people to educate themselves, both in the literal sense of teaching themselves to read and to write, and more generally in the sense of learning by experience how to work democratic machinery. Thus when the British and American peoples establish institutions as democratic as those of the Soviet Union, their peoples should be able to develop an all-pervasive system of genuine self-government even more rapidly than have the Russians. For the British and American peoples will start out on the process of building up their socialist societies with advantages almost as important for the organization of a free political as of a free economic life. The advantages which general literacy, a widely diffused capacity to do arithmetic, to keep straightforward accounts, and the habits of regularity, disciplined work and punctuality, engendered by modern mechanical methods of production, will all be invaluable for the task of organizing the new kind of democracy.

The British and American peoples will inevitably reach that critical point at which any form of democracy becomes incompatible with capitalism and the choice presents itself of going forward into a workers' democracy, capable of laying the foundations of socialism, or backwards into a capitalist autocracy. If at that point they go forward, they will possess certain striking advantages which were altogether lacking to the Russian people. But if they turn back and allow a capitalist autocracy on the Fascist model to be established, they will begin to lose these advantages. The habits and experience of democracy will begin to be lost. Every year of fascist despotism serves to destroy those qualities in a people which are most useful for the building of socialism. Hitler and Mussolini, for example, have devoted their not inconsiderable energies to stamping out the independence, the self-reliance, the initiative, and power of self-government of the German and Italian peoples. Fascist régimes gradually reduce the whole cultural level of a people. They begin by the destruction of its art and literature. Then the educational system is drastically curtailed, and what is left perverted to narrowly military ends. Next, the whole of the community's economic and political life falls under the blight. The abilities of a people to build socialism are reduced. Finally fascism, by precipitating war, leads to the physical destruction of our modern means of production. Thus any people which allows its capitalists to establish a fascist tyranny over it, and which long endures such a tyranny, may well find that in the end, when as in sheer self-preservation it must, it overthrows its capitalists and begins the task of building up socialism, it will be no better equipped, either materially or culturally, than were the Russian people. Such a people will know, however, from the example of the Russian soviets, that even in such circumstances it is possible to build a socialist society. Let us trust, however, that the British and American people have no such terrible experiences in front of them. They certainly have the opportunity to carry over with them into socialism, from their relatively advanced capitalist democracies, economic and cultural assets of great value.

But there is a counteracting factor. The main difficulty which faces the British and American workers in organizing themselves first for taking command of the State, and then for building up socialism, is undoubtedly the tenacious grip which the whole point of view of capitalism has upon their minds. The strength of " capitalist ideology," as communists call it, is very great, not only amongst the British and American property owning classes, but also amongst the British and American workers themselves. Inevitably so. For capitalism has unquestionably been more successful in Britain and America than anywhere else. For four generations the British and American workers have seen their respective capitalist classes go from triumph to triumph. The British capitalists made their island into the workshop of the world and the mistress of the seven seas. The American capitalists industrialized a virgin continent and have carried the technique of production to the highest point ever reached in human history. The British and American workers have always had a scanty share in the fruits of these triumphs. But this has not prevented them from feeling that these were their triumphs also.

For subjected classes, as Engels points out (vide *Anti-Dühring* p. 170), will always support a governing class so long as that governing class succeeds in performing its historical function. So long as our capitalists really were developing our powers of production at the utmost speed, they might give the workers most of the work of this development and little of its fruits, and yet be assured of no unsurmountable opposition. It is only when, as now, a governing class begins to fail in its essential task, that the subjected classes turn towards opposition. Accordingly, it is extraordinarily difficult for the British and American peoples, even in the face of high piled and conclusive evidence, to believe that their capitalists have celebrated their last triumphs. With a very pathetic faith, the workers of Great Britain (encouraged by their leaders in the official positions of the Labour Party and Trade Union movement) have every year since the war believed that " recovery " was coming. In America it is still easier to account for the hold of capitalist ideology. For there capitalism only passed its highest point of achievement in 1929, and faith in it is still widespread amongst the American masses.

The faith of the British and American peoples in capitalism forms a serious obstacle to its abolition, and it will form a serious obstacle to the construction of a socialist society. For we must face the fact that habituation to the whole point of view of capitalism will persist even after the abolition of that system. There will undoubtedly be many British and American citizens who, although they will possess the technical training and ability to take an effective part in socialist construction, will find it difficult to do so because their whole habit of mind is cast in the mould of a production-for-profit system.

To borrow a phrase of that remarkable American writer, Thorstein Veblen, they will possess a " trained incapacity " for working in a society based upon production for use. Moreover, they already have a trained incapacity even to imagine an economic system based on any principle other than that of profitability. It is this incapacity which makes it so hard for many a sincerely perplexed British or American citizen to see any way out of the world's present plight. The extent to which we have been " conditioned," as the psychologists would say, by the powerful influence of a century and a half of triumphant capitalism, can hardly be exaggerated. Perhaps we may envisage it by instancing a complete example of conditioning. The erudite American critic, Mr. Kenneth Burke, in his book, *Permanence and Change*, instances the following experiment:

" Pavlov's dog had acquired a meaning for bells when conditioned to salivate at the sound of one. Other experiments have shown that such meanings can be made still more accurate: chickens can be taught that only one specific pitch is a food-signal, and they will allow bells of other pitches to ring unheeded. But people never tremble enough at the thought of how flimsy such interpreting of characters is. If one rings the bell next time, not to feed the chickens, but to assemble them for chopping off their heads, they come faithfully running, on the strength of the character which a ringing bell possesses for them. Chickens not so well educated would have acted more wisely." (pp. 13-14.)

The chickens which had their heads cut off, Mr. Burke implies, possessed a " trained incapacity " to avoid this fate by running away, instead of assembling, when the bell rang. In exactly the same way, he indicates, the peoples of the Western world assemble for mutual extermination whenever their present, capitalist, leaders blow the trumpet of imperialist war. They have a highly trained incapacity to realize that they are being summoned to a torturing death in order to attempt to keep the profits system going in their particular part of the world, by subjecting another area to the rule of their profiteers.

Thus when we compare the enormous advantages in economic resources, and technical and cultural capacities, which the American and British people could bring to the construction of a socialist society, we must not forget the one great asset possessed, on the contrary, by the Russians. The Russian people were not trained for anything, either for capitalism or for socialism. So they had, at any rate, nothing much to unlearn. Their ignorance has proved a frightful handicap, but we must not overlook the liability which our trained incapacity for anything but a capitalist way of thinking and acting imposes, and will impose, upon us. We can only overcome this handicap by becoming aware of it. We can only prove that we are not like the highly conditioned chickens, unable to distinguish form from substance, unable to differentiate between a summons to food and a summons to death, if we use the one characteristic which sharply distinguishes us from chickens, namely our capacity for conscious rational, deliberate reflection.

CHAPTER XVI

The State

THE three preceding chapters have given a description of the political framework which the working class must establish in order to make possible the building up of a socialist economic system. But what is a " political framework " ? Have we not some word to express both that structure of institutions which we have described above as corresponding to a socialist economic system, and that other structure of institutions with which we are familiar in Britain and America, and which corresponds to a capitalist economic system ? There is such a word. It is the State.

What we have been comparing are two forms of the State. We have been comparing what is called the capitalist State and the very different form of State which the workers set up when they acquire the power to do so. This introduces one of the most important of the political conceptions of communists and socialists, namely our theory of the State. It is important to master this conception. For without it it is impossible to understand one of the most interesting of the predictions made by socialists and communists as to the way in which human society will develop when the basis of a socialist economic system has been laid down. This is the well-known prediction that in such conditions the State will gradually disappear. This claim must seem extremely paradoxical. For not only do people habitually refer to a " socialist State," but it is often alleged that socialism involves an immense enlargement of the functions of the State. How, then, can it possibly be said that socialism will eliminate the State altogether?

The nature of the State has been extensively discussed by the political scientists of the capitalist epoch. Its leading philosophers have almost all had their say on the subject. On the whole, what is called the idealist conception of the State, as enunciated by such philosophers as Hegel and Bosanquet, has predominated. The State, said Hegel, " is the divine Idea as it exists on earth," and he added, it is the individual's " highest duty to be a member of the State." Bosanquet wrote that the State " has the function of maintaining the external conditions necessary to the best life."[1]

An alternative to an acceptance of this very favourable view of the State is, however, to examine some existing States and see what they look like. How, for example, do we most frequently encounter the State in our daily lives ? We encounter the State dressed in blue, whenever we walk or drive in the streets of a city. We meet a policeman, and that State official is engaged in the task of enforcing the law. Nor will this familiar embodiment of the State and its powers lead us astray. The more closely we examine the State the more we shall become convinced that it is an apparatus for enforcing the will, as declared in a system of laws, of those who at any given moment control society.

The State is an apparatus designed for the purpose of coercing people to do certain things, and to refrain from doing certain other things. It is an apparatus for the application of force, or, as it is more usual to say, for enforcing law and order. For behind the policeman is the police force. Behind the police force is the police station, the jail and the condemned cell. And behind all these are the armed forces of the State, the Army, Navy and Air Force. These latter forces are ready either to assist the police in imposing the will of those who have made the laws upon other citizens of their own State, or to attempt to enforce their will upon other States in international war.

Now the view that the State is essentially an apparatus of coercion is to many minds both novel and distasteful. For we are accustomed to think of all sorts of other activities as characteristic of the State. And it is true that in contemporary capitalist society the State does undertake all sorts of other activities as well as the enforcement of the law. (This was not true of the earlier stages of capitalist society, and is still regarded by the strictest capitalist political scientists as something exceptional and regrettable.) Moreover, many of these activities are in themselves beneficent. The contemporary State contributes, for example, to unemployment insurance benefit; organizes a health and sanitation service; provides various forms of pensions, and generally appears in the rôle of a distributor of income.

[1] For a critical review of these theories of the State see the first chapter of *The State in Theory and Practice*, by Harold J. Laski.

How, then, can it be said that the State is essentially an apparatus of coercion ? This view can only be established by tracing the historical origins of the State. Human societies only threw up those social organisms which we call States (we shall describe the process in the next chapter) when they split up into distinct social classes, such as we defined in Part I. And the reason why the early tribal societies were stateless was because they were classless. All civilized societies take the form of States because they contain antagonistic social classes. For the function of the State is to resolve the conflicts of these classes in favour of the dominant or governing class which wields the State's apparatus of coercion.

This hypothesis is able to account for the existence of those other beneficent activities which the capitalist State has lately undertaken. For when we examine these activities we find that the need for them also, to a predominant degree, arises from the fact that our contemporary societies are split up into the separate classes of capitalists and workers. For example, unemployment, and so the need for the distribution of unemployment insurance benefit, arises, as we saw in Part I, out of the extreme inequality in the distribution of income inevitable to capitalism. The need for pensions, health insurance, and other social services springs also, to a great extent, from the same general cause, viz. the relative destitution of the mass of the population in a class-divided community. Hence these novel functions of the State also arise from the division of society into classes.[1] Moreover, they are by no means unrelated to the State's essential and original function of coercion. As every contemporary capitalist statesman knows, there are two ways of dealing with unemployed workers. You can send for the police, and after the police for the military, or you can pay the unemployed a dole. Either type of State action is necessitated by the existence of the social stress which the destitution, and consequent desperation, of the unemployed has created.

We can now define both the character and the function of the State more fully. The State is an apparatus of coercion, capable

[1] Some of these social services form a necessary part of a socialist system. But this is only because a socialist economic system can only gradually achieve its economic ends. They will be indispensable only until complete and universal plenty has been attained.

of enforcing the will of that class which has acquired the power
to make the laws. The function of the State is to deal with the
conflicts and crises which the divisions of society into distinct
classes with opposed interests is bound to create. It will deal
with these conflicts principally, although not exclusively, by
employing force, or the threat of force, in order to ensure that
the will of the dominant or ruling class shall prevail.

This conception of the State seems especially strange to those
who have forgotten that the present high development of the
State apparatus of coercion is a very recent one. It is difficult for
the contemporary Englishman to remember, for example, that
when he summons " a bobby " he is commemorating the fact
that a State police force was instituted by Sir Robert Peel only
just over a hundred years ago. Nor do his newspapers, his
schools, or his wireless service ever remind him, as they describe
some review, or tattoo, that his forebears waged some of their
sternest political struggles against the creation of a standing
army by which those who wielded the power of the State might
coerce the rest of the nation. Indeed, it is true to say that before
1688, a principal date in the struggle for the acquisition of the
power of the State waged by the present British governing class,
the main modern apparatus of State coercion did not exist.

The permanent existence amongst us of a very large and complex apparatus of force, though it now seems to most people a
matter of course, is in fact a recent innovation. In the past, men
lived together without anything like the means of coercion
which are evidently essential to the existence of our contemporary form of society. This suggests that something has happened which has produced internecine conflicts within society of
a much more formidable character than any which occurred
previously. Those who rule society now seem to need much more
powerful means for enforcing their will upon those whom they
rule than heretofore. (And this in spite of the growth of the
democratic institutions which we noticed above.) It is true that
there were class conflicts in Britain before 1688. There were many
such conflicts, and there was a State whose function it was to
solve those conflicts in the interests of the governing class. But
the instruments of force (such as *ad hoc* levies and temporary
armies raised for special occasions, and the like), which the State

used for this purpose, were puny and embryonic when compared to the instruments of State coercion which are now maintained in permanency. Hence it is difficult to avoid the conclusion that those conflicts were relatively mild and infrequent. The opposing classes into which society is now split up have evidently become more solidly and fixedly ranked against each other than ever before. The extraordinary growth in the State apparatus of coercion indicates that the conflicts between these classes have become little less than " wars," now latent, now open, which can be resolved in favour of the ruling class by the employment of a formidable and permanently maintained apparatus of force alone.

While these lines are being written a flaming exemplification of the class character of the State is being enacted in Spain. There a Liberal Government was hesitatingly moving towards the use of the State's power to modify the property rights of some sections of the governing class. In particular it had begun the dispossession of some of the still feudal landlords, in favour, not indeed of any form of collective or associated ownership, but for the benefit of individual, landless peasants. Immediately the ruling class, outraged by the very idea that *their* State could be used against them, rose in armed rebellion against the legally constituted Government. They are at the moment of writing making a ruthless war, conducted by means of mercenary levies, upon the people of Spain, and they are doing so to the applause of every governing class in Europe. Alphonso, true to the traditions of his house, has declared himself ready to return to the throne in order to serve the Spanish people once more. He adds, however, that the parties of the Left, which comprise some three-quarters of the Spanish people, must first be " exterminated." (This was the word used by the last of the Bourbons.) As in Paris in 1871, in every city of the Russian Empire between 1917 and 1921, and in Vienna in 1934, so now in Spain in 1936, it is demonstrated that those who own the means of production have no other conception of the State than that of an instrument of coercion designed to protect their property.

They are correct in this opinion. A State is, to reach a full definition, an apparatus for the employment of force on behalf of the governing class of any community which has split up into antagonistic social classes. Its function is to resolve according to the will of the governing class the social conflicts inevitable to such societies.

What the workers have to do, then, is to set up *their* State: to set up an apparatus of coercion by means of which they may exercise their rule over the other classes of society, just as to-day the capitalists, through their State apparatus, exercise their rule over society. The State is not, as the philosophers have supposed or pretended, an independent, or God-given, institution suspended over the heads of the various classes of society, and dealing down an even-handed justice upon worker and capitalist, landlord and peasant alike. It is, on the contrary, always and everywhere the weapon of a class (or exceptionally of a coalition of classes) which has established its dominance over the rest of society. Moreover, the whole character of the State apparatus, the type of structure which is built up and the way it works, is indissolubly associated with the particular class which reigns.

Thus the slave owners of antiquity made their own particular type of State, the feudal overlords of the Middle Ages made another kind, and the capitalists have made yet a third kind of State. In the same way the workers when they come to power have to build up for themselves their own peculiar type of State. They cannot just take over the capitalist State, the very purpose of which has been to keep them in order, and use it to keep the capitalists, and former capitalists, in order. They have, as we have seen, to abolish the characteristic capitalist organs of State, its monarchies or republics, its present type of parliaments, its law courts, State Churches, and capitalist-class-dominated armed forces and police forces. Then they have to build up those characteristic working class State institutions which we have just described. (Naturally in practice the processes of abolition and reconstruction are simultaneous.)

Moreover, there is a far greater difference between the working class State of a socialist society and a capitalist State, than there was between the capitalist State and the older feudal State. For a working class State is a State wielded by the immense majority of the population and used to coerce a small (though at first very powerful) and rapidly dwindling minority of the population. This is a characteristic unique in the history of States, which have all hitherto been the instruments of small minorities used to coerce the great majority of the population. This difference is so important that Lenin often referred to the working class State as only a " semi-State." He meant that the element of coercion in human society diminishes so sharply, after the workers get power, that one can only to some extent compare the institutions which the workers set up, for controlling the former ruling class, with the old forms of the State. And, above all, he meant that the workers' State is only a temporary structure: that as and when a truly classless society appears it can be done away with.

It will then be possible to return, though on an incomparably higher level of culture, to the stateless, because classless, condition of human society which existed before the dawn of civilization. In order to understand this idea it is necessary to outline the history of the State. It is necessary, above all, to see that the State has a history: to realize that there was a time before the State existed and that, therefore, there can be a time when it shall have disappeared.

CHAPTER XVII

Origin and Future of the State

CERTAIN human societies have existed which no one thinks of calling States. No one, for example, talks of the States of the North American Indians. We talk of their tribes. And the same thing is true of all primitive communities.

Were, then, these tribal communities without social classes? For, if these stateless communities possessed social classes, the view that the State is essentially an instrument of class domination will evidently not hold water. These early tribal communities were, however, classless. In fact, classless societies have existed whenever mankind has been passing through one particular stage of development. They have existed in that early stage in which men live by hunting and by gardening; the stage of the bow, the arrow, and the spade. This is the stage of human development which immediately precedes the one in which the means and methods of production have developed sufficiently to allow of field agriculture, or the general domestication of animals. This was the stage through which the American Indians of the eastern half of the continent were passing at the time of the white conquest: this was the stage out of which the Homeric Greeks had lately emerged: this is the stage of development of many races of Africa and the Southern Pacific to-day.

The societies formed by peoples at this stage of development must necessarily be classless. For in this stage of human development the subjection of their fellow men, even if it had been possible, would have done a conquering group or class no good. For a man was on the average able to produce no more than he and his dependants could live on. He could produce no surplus over and above his own and his dependants' needs. Hence there existed no surplus which could be taken from him. In these conditions any form of the subjection of one class of men to another simply would not have paid—it was an economic impossibility. In these conditions there could be no such thing as slavery, for example, for it would have cost just as much to keep a slave alive and fit for hunting and digging as he would have been able to bring in. The master would have got nothing. Accordingly, in this stage of human development, slavery is unknown.

Now, we repeat, the political institutions of these early classless societies do not constitute anything which anyone has ever thought of calling a State. Men in this stage of development aggregate into quite large communities. But they organize themselves not into States, but into tribes, and within these tribes into an extremely interesting institution for which every race has had a different name, but which is usually known to us under its Latin title of the *gens*. We shall discuss this basic social unit in a moment. Upon it tribesmen organize their political life by appointing chiefs, or executive officers, for particular purposes, very often, for example, appointing a different officer for peaceful and for warlike purposes. All the tribesmen and women meet together in general assemblies (both of the *gens* and of the whole tribe) to decide democratically every important question. These tribal political institutions show a considerable variation from one part of the world to another, and even more variation according to whether the people concerned is entering or leaving this tribal stage of development.[1] But a similar social pattern is invariably thrown up by mankind as it passes through this stage of development.

These early, tribal, classless forms of society neither needed nor possessed an organized, standing apparatus for the coercion of one group of their citizens by another. They were organized upon what was in the last analysis a sexual basis. They were organized, that is to say, by families and groups of families. But the families of early society were of a very different character from the family of to-day.

The fundamental social unit, the *gens,* as the Romans called

[1] For example, chiefs are usually elective and temporary, and have very limited powers, at the beginning of such periods, and are hereditary and have wider powers at the close of such periods. Again, recent anthropological research has shown that this basic institutional pattern has been much modified by contact between races existing in the tribal, or gentile, stage and races which have passed on into higher stages of development. For example, it is now known that the tribal, gentile institutions which can be discerned as the starting-point of both Greek and Roman history were modified, and finally supplanted, not merely by the spontaneous development of these peoples, but also, and perhaps above all, by their contact with earlier civilized States, viz. the Etruscan in the case of Rome and the Asiatic monarchies in the case of Greece.

it, or the clan as the tribes of Scotland called it (and as their descendants call it to this day), was only an extremely large family. For many years this fact was not realized because the existing *gentes* amongst the primitive tribes then known were not families. Their members were not, that is to say, related to each other. It has now been discovered, however, that the original form of the *gens* (which still persists amongst certain very primitive peoples) was a family, but a family of a very special type, known as the matrilinear family. This form of the family was based upon the principle that descent and relationship passed through the female line alone. Thus a man considered that he was a close blood relation of his mother's sister's son, but no relation at all to his own father. And he did so for the very good reason that he very often did not know who his father was. For the monogamous, patriarchal family, such as we know to-day, had not come into existence. Originally the essential, because only continuing, social unit appears to have consisted of a group of mothers. These mothers may sometimes have been the wives of one dominant male ; but such an embryo patriarch was apt to be a transitory phenomenon, since he ran the risks of war, hunting, and domestic revolt from his sons. At other times, according to some authorities, a form of group marriage existed. Under this arrangement all the women of one particular social group were lawfully accessible to all the men of another group.

In any case it is clear that in early society paternity was so difficult to determine that it was discounted as a blood relationship. The only possible type of family and the only ascertainable blood relationship were matrilinear. Each of these matrilinear families, which naturally became very large, since all cousins on the mother's side were considered to be members of the same family, was called a *gens*. And the *gens* became the fundamental social unit, so that the tribe was only a coalition of these matrilinear families, or *gentes*.

At one stage of development the most stringent of all tribal regulations was that which prohibited a man from cohabiting with a woman of his own *gens*. For this was incest, and horror and reprobation were felt over the mere possibility of its occurrence. The *gens*, however, proved so stable a social unit that it everywhere long survived the matrilinear family. It continued to exist

as the basic self-governing unit of the community long after
blood relationship had come to be counted as it is to-day. The
appearance of the patrilinear family was itself closely associated
with economic changes in the community's way of life. Property
began to become a significant factor in life. Ornaments were
fashioned. Above all, individual huts inhabited by a man and
wife and their children, or by only two such families, began to
appear alongside of the long huts in which the large matrilinear
groups, or *gentes*, lived. These economic developments tended to
make the mating relationships between individual men and
women more stable. The gradual appearance of the patrilinear
type of family in turn greatly accelerated economic development. Yet throughout this series of social changes the *gens* continued to exist as a group of people who felt themselves to be
closely associated with each other and to command men's strong
allegiance. *But its origin in a blood relationship, reckoned on a
matrilinear basis, was forgotten.*

Or rather, the original family basis of the *gens* was remembered,
but it was remembered only unconsciously, or symbolically. For
all the members of the *gens* traced their descent to a common,
and mythical, divine ancestor. By this characteristically devious
device of the human unconscious, men were able to explain to
themselves why they were behaving as if their fellow gentiles
were their blood relations, though they knew that they were not.
Many of the original customs, such as the cast-iron command
to marry only outside the *gens*, which had been based upon the
real existence of a blood relationship, and for which the whole
rational basis had consequently now disappeared, nevertheless
continued to exist for a long time.[1]

The gentile form of social organization was not, then, immediately destroyed by the change in family relationship from
a matrilinear to a patrilinear basis. On the contrary, most of the
gentile forms of society with which we are familiar have been
studied after the patrilinear family had become predominant.[2]

[1] At a still later stage, during the process of the disintegration of the gentile
system of society (before, as we shall see, the force of private ownership), this
command was in certain cases changed into its opposite. Marriage for heiresses
was only permitted within the *gens*, in order that the property of the *gens* (still
partly held in common) might not be dissipated !

[2] The *gens* was so deeply imprinted upon men's minds by its centuries
upon centuries of existence as *the* fundamental social unit that even after its

We have a considerable knowledge of what men's lives were like at this stage of social development, both from the earlier historical records of the classical world and from the reports and description of men of our epoch who have come into close contact with tribes still living in this way.

For example, we have much evidence of the kind of life led by the North American aborigines, who were in the gentile stage of development at the time of their conquest by the white man. Now there is no need to accept the sentimental, Fenimore Cooper, view of the Red Indian or other " noble savage "; but neither is there any reason to accept the extreme contemporary reaction against that view. For it is an indisputable fact that wherever civilized men have come into contact with tribesmen in the higher stages of gentile culture they have been impressed by their whole moral and physical development. It has invariably been reported that the gentiles lived in a primitive manner, that their command over natural forces was very limited. But equally invariably it has been reported that they evidently possessed advantages which partly compensated for this. For they seemed to be at least as creditable specimens of humanity as are the inhabitants of modern civilizations.

Most investigators have been at a loss to account for this fact. There is no doubt, however, that the main compensating advantage possessed by tribesmen in the gentile stage of development consists in the fact that their form of social organization is classless, and so permits of freedom and equality. Their communities, however much they may be at the mercy of nature, are not riven by class antagonisms nor burdened and poisoned by an overshadowing apparatus of coercion. Engels has an eloquent passage

supersession by the State, for all practical purposes it continued to exist simply from use and wont. Thus, all through the period of the Roman Republic, men were acutely conscious of what *gens* they belonged to, and felt intense loyalty and solidarity to other members of the same *gens* (for instance, a wealthy *gens* would undertake to ransom any of its members taken prisoner in war). Julius Cæsar, for example, was a member of the great Julian *gens* and was well aware of the fact.

Indeed, as suggested above, faint traces of this gentile order remain in British society to this day in the shape of the Scottish clans, which were the *gentes* of the long unconquered Celts of North Britain. A faint echo of the primal solidarity felt for the *gens* can be heard in our use of the word " clannish." Again, the Chinese family is a lineal descendant of the Chinese *gens*, and retains, or rather is only now losing, much of the primal vitality of this tremendously enduring institution.

in his book, *The Origin of the Family, Private Property, and the State*, in which he describes the attraction of the old gentile constitution:

"How wonderful this gentile constitution is in all its natural simplicity ! No soldiers, gendarmes and policemen, no nobility, kings, regents, prefects or judges, no prisons, no law-suits, and still affairs run smoothly. All quarrels and disputes are settled by the entire community involved in them, either the *gens* or the tribe or the various *gentes* among themselves. Only in very rare cases the blood revenge is threatened as an extreme measure. Our capital punishment is simply a civilized form of it, afflicted with all the advantages and drawbacks of civilization. Not a vestige of our cumbersome and intricate system of administration is needed, although there are more public affairs to be settled than nowadays: the communistic household is shared by a number of families, the land belongs to the tribe, only the gardens are temporarily assigned to the households. The parties involved in a question settle it and in most cases the hundred-year-old traditions have settled every-thing beforehand. There cannot be any poor and destitute—the communistic households and the *gentes* know their duties towards the aged, sick and disabled. All are free and equal—the women included. There is no room yet for slaves, nor for the subjugation of foreign tribes. When about 1651 the Iroquois had vanquished the Eries and the ' Neutral Nation,' they offered to adopt them into the league on equal terms. Only when the vanquished declined this offer they were driven out of their territory.

"What splendid men and women were produced by such a society ! All the white men who came into contact with unspoiled Indians admired the personal dignity, straight-forwardness, strength of character and bravery of these barbarians.

"We lately received proofs of such bravery in Africa. A few years ago the Zulus, and some months ago the Nubians, both of which tribes still retain the gentile organization, did what no European army can do. Armed only with lances and spears, without any firearms, they advanced under a hail of bullets

from breechloaders up to the bayonets of the English infantry
—the best in the world for fighting in closed ranks—and threw
them into confusion more than once, yes, even forced them to
retreat in spite of the immense disparity of weapons, and in
spite of the fact that they have no military service and don't
know anything about drill. How enduring and able they are, is
proved by the complaints of the English, who admit that a
Kaffir can cover a longer distance in twenty-four hours than
a horse. The smallest muscle springs forth, hard and tough like
a whip-lash, says an English painter.

" Such was human society and its members before the
division into classes had taken place. And a comparison of that
social condition with the condition of the overwhelming
majority of present-day society shows the enormous chasm
that separates our proletarian and small farmer from the free
gentile of old."

What was it, then, which destroyed this ancient, immensely
long-enduring and, in spite of its narrow limitations, attractive
form of human society ? The disappearance of the matrilinear
family, out of which the *gens* had arisen, did not in itself do so;
for the *gens* adapted itself to the new conditions. It was a change,
not in the sexual, but in the economic, life of man which destroyed
the gentile order and created the State.[1] What destroyed the
gens was a gradual development of new means of production;
for this development necessitated the appearance of private
property in the means of production, and the class division of
society which is associated with such property.

These new methods of production were field agriculture, using
the plough; the domestication of cattle and sheep; the working
of some metals; and new methods of transport, by coasting ships,
and by pack animals, making possible the exchange in trade of
the products of the new methods of production. But these
technical innovations could not be developed without the institution of private property, both in the products themselves and
in the means (viz. the land or the ships) used in producing and
exchanging them, plus a method of mediating exchanges, such
as money.

[1] Or rather the sexual and the economic changes were interdependent.

In the gardening-hunting communities of the gentile stage, private property was too meagre to be of much importance. Every man owned his hunting weapons and his gardening tools, and there was very little else to own. But no sooner had men learnt how to make useful and attractive objects, and, above all, to create the means for the production of such objects, than the question arose as to who was to own them. For these objects, an iron sword, a sailing ship, flocks and herds, a wooden plough, or a fertile field, were highly desirable. Their use enabled a family to emerge from that extreme and painful dependence upon the forces of nature which, as Engels does not fail to point out, was the other and dark side of the gentile order of society.

But no sooner had desirable objects such as these made their appearance than the idea arose of obtaining them, not by producing them oneself, but by producing something else and then exchanging it for the desired object. Trade was born. It was born between, rather than amidst, the gentile communities.[1] Or, again, it arose between a community still in the gentile stage and one which had already become a city and a State. It was trade, for example, which, growing up with the city States of Asia, disintegrated the gentile order of Attica. This was the Trojan horse by which the countrymen of Troy avenged (before it happened) the stratagem of Odysseus, and set in motion that swift development which was to give Socrates and Aristotle, Pericles and Phidias, and the slavery which supported them, to the world.

We know something about the dissolution of the gentile order in Attica, for the Greeks became literate soon afterwards. Thus certain records of the transition were preserved. We know that

[1] Modern anthropological research has suggested how trade, or the habit of exchange, may grow up within a gentile community. The first half of an exchange is a gift. And anthropologists (for instance, Prof. Malinowski amongst the Trobrianders of the Southern Pacific) have found that the giving of gifts plays an important part in the economic life of primitive peoples. At marriages, funerals and other feasts very substantial gifts are made according to a precise ritual. But, it has been discovered, the recipients of these gifts have an obligation to make counter-gifts to the donors at subsequent feasts. An elaborate system of gifts and counter-gifts is thus built up.

It is easy to see that we have here the basis of a system of exchange. Even ratios of exchange will tend to establish themselves. For if a man gives 12 pigs on the occasion of the marriage of his sister's son, the happy pair will be expected to provide, say, 200 mangoes on the occasion of the funeral of their maternal uncle. Hence 12 pigs = 200 mangoes. A ratio of exchange is established.

when the Greeks learnt to plough, to trade, and to possess, their gentile form of social organization became more and more unworkable. The Greeks of the Homeric epoch were passing through the critical stage of the development of production in which private property first becomes important; and were simultaneously learning how to acquire property by means of trade and plunder (*vide* the Iliad). At this point in the development of every human community a new social order, based upon the acquisition and retention of private property, becomes essential. Moreover, it becomes essential to create political institutions appropriate to this new social order. And the chief of these is the State. This is Engels' account of the social problem as it presented itself to the Greeks of the Homeric epoch:

" In the Grecian constitution of heroic times, then, we still find the old gentilism fully alive, but we also perceive the beginnings of the elements that undermine it; paternal law and inheritance of property by the father's children, favouring accumulation of wealth in the family and giving to the latter a power apart from the *gens*; influence of the difference of wealth on the constitution by the formation of the first rudiments of hereditary nobility and monarchy, slavery, first limited to prisoners of war, but already paving the way to the enslavement of tribal and gentile associates; degeneration of the old feuds into a regular mode of existing by systematic plundering on land and sea for the purpose of acquiring cattle, slaves, and treasures. In short, wealth is praised and respected as the highest treasure, and the old gentile institutions are abused in order to justify the forcible robbery of wealth. Only one thing was missing; an institution that not only secured the newly acquired property of private individuals against the communistic traditions of the *gens*, that not only declared as sacred the formerly so despised private property and represented the protection of this sacred property as the highest purpose of human society, but that also stamped the gradually developing new forms of acquiring property, of constantly increasing wealth, with the universal sanction of society. An institution that lent the character of perpetuity not only to the newly rising division into classes, but also to the right of the possessing classes to exploit and rule the non-possessing classes. " And this institution was found. The State arose."

(The Origin of the Family, pp. 129–30.)

Engels in this passage explains the need for a State which a people reaching this stage of development must experience. But how, in fact, did the gentile institutions decay and give place to those new political institutions which constitute a State ?

We may define a gentile, as compared to a State, order of society by saying that in the former men were originally classified *sexually*, according, that is to say, to the matrilinear family to which they belonged, while in the latter they are classified *economically*, according, that is to say, either to the amount of property which they own or to the trade which they practise. Moreover, it was, we have just seen, the ever-growing necessity to recognize these new, *economic*, classifications of property and trade which made it essential to found the State and to destroy the power of the *gens* and the tribe. For a man's wealth and his occupation gradually became the most important things about him; became far more important than his membership of this or that *gens*. For example, the rich men belonging to different *gentes* found that they had much more in common with each other than with their fellow gentiles. Or, again, sailors found themselves associating with sailors, carpenters with carpenters, masons with masons, farmers with farmers, rather than with the members of the particular *gens* to which they belonged.

The *gens*, in fact, was a social unit exclusively suitable to a society in which not only was everybody approximately as well off as everyone else, but in which, also, everybody did much the same sort of work; in a word, to a classless society in which the division of labour had not yet been extensively developed. For the growth of the division of labour, involving as it must the growth of trade, has a particularly disintegrating effect upon the gentile order.

We know something of the way in which the State arose in Attica.[1] The growth of trade brought men flocking into the

---

[1] It must be emphasized, however, that the growth of the Attic State was by no means an original or spontaneous process. Attica lay close to the States of Asia Minor and its development from gentilism to statehood was profoundly influenced and accelerated by these powerful neighbours. In general, modern

trading centre, in this case Athens. Soon the members of different *gentes* began to be inextricably intermingled. Hitherto each *gens* had lived in a particular area (more precisely a group of *gentes* forming a tribe—for Attica was a federation of tribes— had each lived in its own territory). Moreover, not only did trade soon pick out individuals from every *gens* and tribe and bring them down to Athens, but strangers from outside of Attica altogether were brought to Athens by the same attraction. They were members of no *gens*. What was to be done with them? They nowhere fitted into the body politic.

And then slaves appeared. The improved methods of production had made it profitable to keep a man (say a prisoner of war) on condition that he worked for you. He could now produce a surplus above his own needs, and this surplus his master could, and did, take from him, for that master's own use and enjoyment. Thus an ever-growing number of slaves, who, of course, could not possibly be admitted to any *gens*, appeared. What was to be done with them? In particular, how were they to be kept in order? Gentile society knew no need for police or standing army: it presumed that every citizen was free and a warrior. Law and order, and there was very strict law and order, were self-preserved by a force which was co-extensive with the community itself. The appearance of slavery destroyed, however, all possibility of this. A class which had to be kept down had appeared. Moreover, society was soon confronted with a second class in need of subjection. No sooner had the aforementioned technical and economic developments taken place than there appeared not only slaves and masters, but also rich and poor, landowners and tenants, debtors and creditors. For the general growth of private property included the growth of private property in land. The new agricultural methods were

research tends to emphasize the extent to which the example of the earlier States, or civilizations as they are often called, affected the development out of gentilism of all subsequent peoples. (The extreme form of this view is afforded by the " diffusionist " school of anthropologists who assert that all the institutions of the State, and the advantages and disadvantages of civilization which go with them, came from one original centre.) It is clear, indeed, that some peoples or groups of peoples must have been the first to pass on from gentilism. Unfortunately, however, we know nothing of this original transit of human society, which is thought to have occurred in Asia Minor, Persia or on the banks of the Indus. For the earliest records which we possess show these peoples to be already living in well-developed civilized States. Hence we can only study the transition in later examples such as that afforded by Attica.

unsuitable, it was found, to the old system by which the *gens* itself held the land, temporarily parcelling out particular garden plots to individuals. More elaborate agricultural methods led to the permanent " freehold " ownership of land by individuals.

Or rather their freehold ownership seemed permanent to these first Attic peasants: but it did not prove so. For not only did these peasants begin cultivating by new and improved methods; they also began to cultivate not merely for their own needs, but also for the market; they began to cultivate in order to sell or exchange their produce for the slave-produced commodities of the city. On the top of the technical change there was superimposed an economic change.

In a word, the Attic farmers, like many farmers since, " went into business ": and naturally some of them succeeded, and succeeded splendidly, while many more of them failed. These unsuccessfully trading farmers soon ran into debt. And so hard upon the heels of the ditches that demarcated the new private holdings of the peasants there appeared " mortgage poles " which told that such and such a plot was mortgaged to the " Eupatrides " (well born) of Athens ! For with fatal ingenuity the Greeks had learnt from their neighbours, or invented for themselves, not only agriculture, trade, private property, and money, but also the debt, the mortgage, the foreclosure and the distraint. Soon not only the farms, but the farmers themselves and their children, were being sold up to pay the mortgages.

The simple gentile order could do nothing to protect men from the consequences of all these formidable new economic and social forces. A new social order which could recognize and sanction the new class divisions of society into rich and poor, master and slave, and at the same time could regulate the ferocity of the conflicts engendered by these relationships, was imperatively necessary. The only political institution which could do this job was the State. The State was born. Gradually power was taken out of the hands of the gentile and tribal assemblies and centralized in the hands of a national assembly and its executive officers meeting in Athens.

The definitive founding of the Athenian State is usually reckoned from the constitution of Solon. In this constitution we see clearly that the new State served *both* to stereotype and

enforce the new class divisions, and to mitigate the impossibly
ferocious oppression of the subjected classes which would have
resulted from a free play of the economic forces let loose by the
establishment of private property in land and the other means
of production, and by trade.[1] Solon is said to have divided the
citizens of the new State into four classes *according to the amount
of property which they owned*, thus entirely superseding the
political functions of the *gentes*. Only members of the three top
classes could hold office, though the fourth class could speak and
vote in the national assembly. But at the same time he cancelled
the creditors' claims on the land of the debtors, restricted the
contraction of new mortgages by fixing a maximum amount of
land which any citizen might own, and made it illegal for a debtor
to pledge his own person or that of his children as security.

Such measures for the protection of men against the appalling
social consequences of the particular step in economic development which the Greeks had just taken have been continually
forced upon governments. Private property, the division of
labour, and trade, are both caused by, and make possible, we
repeat, the critically important technical advances of field
agriculture, the handicraft production of metals, and the transport of goods by sea-going ships and pack animals. These associated social and technical changes constitute a leap forward in
human development. They amount to the transit of society from
barbarism to civilization. But men have achieved the advantages
of civilization at the cost of social disaster alone. On the one
hand, the attainment of civilization enables man to take a long
step towards the command over nature; but, on the other hand,
it involves not only the subjection of man to man, but also the
subjugation of man to economic forces which have proved as
cruel, as uncontrolled, and as destructive as the forces of nature.

The primitive form of production carried on by men in the gentile stage of development yielded no more than a bare living. But,
unless natural catastrophe intervened, it did yield a living. Man
was far from dominating nature, but there was no danger whatever of his simple economic system getting out of order. The gentile

---

[1] The capitalist ideal of " *laissez-faire, laissez-aller*," was apparently no more
attainable in the Attica of 600 B.C. than in the France of A.D. 1789 or the
Britain and America of 1936.

knew that, if he fished, hunted and dug, and if nature did not ruin him by drought or storm, he and his would certainly eat.

And this certainty men have never enjoyed again. The invention of private property, the division of labour, trade, classes, and the State have destroyed it.[1] *For these institutions have created so complicated a form of economic organization that it is continually getting out of control and ruining us. Men have lost control of both the productive process and of the product.* Their misfortunes flow from the fact that it was necessary, in order to enjoy the advantages of the division of labour, for men to produce, not for their own use, *but for exchange on the market.* And when men launch their products, and consequently their economic destinies, upon the market, they set sail upon a sea more stormy than ever long-suffering Odysseus encountered. The result has been that, while our ever-improving methods of production have given us civilization, they have also created insecurity, subjection and destitution for the greater part of mankind.

The extraordinary interest of early Greek history consists in the fact that this double development can be studied as it took place in the tiny social laboratory of Attica before the year 600 B.C.[2] Greek civilization was born, the Greek peasants were ruined. The ship and the plough, the slave and the eviction made their interdependent appearance. And finally Solon made a name for himself (which still echoes in American newspapers) by giving its earliest form to the Greek State.

By imposing the restraining hand of the State upon the ravages of the new economic relationships, Solon made possible a breathing space between the birth and the decay of the Greek agricultural, trading, slave-owning, economic system. And in that breathing space there flowered the lovely blossom of Hellas. But neither Solon nor all his epigones have been able to do more. All the lawgivers of all the communities based upon private property in the means of production, and the satisfaction of human needs indirectly by means of exchanges mediated by

---

[1] Men have approached most nearly to it in those historical interludes of peasant proprietorship which have sometimes intervened between the abolition of feudal relations and the rise of capitalism, viz. the Britain of 1450, or the France of 1800.

[2] Although, as noted above, it did not take place in a pure form. There were numerous and powerful extraneous factors.

money, have never been able to do more than postpone sufficiently to allow of a few centuries of civilization the inevitable
disintegration to which such communities are subject.

We may describe the purpose of the establishment of socialism
and communism as being to restore at last the stability, security,
social freedom, and equality enjoyed by the old free men of the
gentile order, while retaining the immense gains in economic
power made during the epoch of private property, trade, class
divisions, and the State. But this can only be done by doing
away not only with capitalism, the specific system of the last
hundred and fifty years, but with what we call " commodity
production " also. By " commodity production " we mean the
satisfaction of men's wants by means of exchanges between
individuals of goods individually owned and produced. (For the
word commodity means a product made to be exchanged for
another product.) Capitalism is, then, only one sub-division of
this general category of an economic system of commodity production. The other sub-divisions are the servile system (such as
grew up in ancient Attica) and feudalism (although in feudalism
the exchange of commodities plays a much more modest part
than in the other two sub-divisions; hence both the relatively
low level to which feudal civilization can attain and its relatively
great stability). Thus the task before us is to abolish capitalism
and to replace it, not with any of the alternative forms of commodity production, but with a new economic system which does
not involve private property in the means of production, or
exchanges between individuals mediated by money. This can
be done by the organization of that system of planned production
for use which we described in Part I.[1]

The purpose of this excursion into primitive history has been
to explain the grounds upon which we based the assertion that
in a socialist society the State is destined to disappear once
more. For this is a necessary deduction from the view just
expressed of how and why the State arose. The State arose
because the community had split up into classes which could

---

[1] As the reader will recall, the existing socialist society has not by any means
completely eliminated exchange between individuals mediated by money. But
it has almost certainly already reduced their importance in the economic life of
the community to a point at which they cannot get out of hand and cause social
dislocation.

only solve their conflicts by the dominant class possessing an apparatus of force with which to hold down its class opponent. An economic system of planned production for use will re-create a homogeneous society free from class divisions. Hence it will also eliminate the need for the State. The State with its characteristic institutions for the coercion of one social group by another will atrophy—just as parts of the human organism which have become functionless become vestiginal and finally disappear altogether. As in the past when there were no classes the State did not exist, so in the future, when again there will be no classes, the State will not exist. For there will be no social group or class which it will be necessary to coerce.

It must not be supposed, however, that the State can be abolished on the morrow of the workers becoming the ruling class and abolishing the capitalist form of the State. At that moment, and for some years afterwards, it will not, unfortunately, be the case that there will be no class which it is necessary to coerce. The dispossessed capitalists and their adherents will, on the contrary, form a compact and formidable class, which will, experience demonstrates, attempt everything to win back its former position of dominance. Towards it the young workers' State must be, and will be, very firm. It will have to build up, and that quickly, its own instruments of coercion (for, it cannot simply take over the capitalists' instruments) in order to maintain itself against strong, able, and resolute antagonists.

The simple nonsense of the anarchists consists in the view that the workers could, and so should, abolish all institutions of State coercion immediately upon their accession to power. No proposal could more surely result in the re-establishment, after a ferocious white terror, of the capitalists in power. Still, the anarchists have at any rate grasped the fact that it is the ultimate object and possibility of the workers to abolish the State. They have merely overlooked all the practical conditions which must be fulfilled before this can be done.

The resistance of the dispossessed capitalists to the workers' State, though intense, cannot be long continued. Once the means of production have become public property, the capitalists have been dispossessed; unless, therefore, they can quickly regain possession of the means of production they begin to disappear as a class.

Gs

But the disappearance of the capitalists will not in itself render a workers' State unnecessary. The individual members of the capitalist class will be absorbed into the mass of the population, but their attitude of mind will, unfortunately, survive them. Especially in such communities as Britain and America, which are soaked through and through with capitalist ideology, many people will for a long time find it difficult to adapt themselves to the new society. Indeed, it is probably not too much to say that anything approaching perfect adaptation is not to be expected till a new generation, bred and educated in the new social conditions, has come of age. Our trained incapacities for living in any but a capitalist society are unfortunately certain to hamper us for some time after the foundations of socialism in Britain and America have been laid down. And so long as they do so, some elements of the State apparatus will be necessary.[1] On the other hand, we cannot doubt that adaptation to the new environment will gradually occur. The habits necessary to an economic system of planned production for use will gradually become the innate characteristics of men. The idea of refusing to play their part, to the best of their ability, in the social and productive life of the community will no more occur to those citizens of the future than the idea of refusing to dig, to hunt or to come to the general assembly of the tribe occurred to an Iroquois or a pre-Homeric Achæan gentile. As and when this adaptation takes place, the need for any special apparatus of coercion will disappear. And as soon as that has happened the State will be no more.[2]

[1] The Soviet Union faces another and most important necessity for the maintenance and development of the apparatus of coercion of the workers' State, namely, the ceaseless menace of foreign intervention from the remaining capitalist States. The Russian capitalists within Russia have almost completely ceased to exist as a class. But they exist amongst, and act through, their still ruling fellow capitalists in the rest of the world. This is a situation which will not confront subsequent workers' States in the same large degree, and will hardly confront, say, the fourth or fifth workers' States to be established, at all.

[2] This does not necessarily mean that communities which have reached this, to us, extremely high point of development will not formulate rules or laws for the guidance of their members. Nor does it even mean that such communities will lack means of enforcing these rules upon their members. They will possess all those very effective means by which a club, or any other voluntary association, to-day enforces conformity to its rules. Such suasion, based upon the strength of public opinion, will no doubt prove an extremely efficient means of providing against vagaries which, if indulged in, would in the opinion of its citizens injure the community. But the creation and maintenance of a special apparatus of coercion, such as the State, will have become wholly unnecessary.

CHAPTER XVIII

Socialism and Liberty

" WE built a socialist society," said Joseph Stalin in a recent (1936) interview. " We built this society in order that the human personality might feel really free. We built it for the sake of real personal liberty."

Stalin's designation of liberty as the essential goal of communists and socialists may be unfamiliar. The reader of the last two chapters will have seen, however, that the theory of the State contained in them leads to a particular, precise and comprehensive conception of human liberty. Those who accept it will have as their goal a liberty more complete than any which non-socialists have envisaged. But, at the same time, they will be aware that basic changes in our social and economic system are necessary, not only to attain to such ideal liberty, but even to achieve an elementary degree of freedom for the greater part of mankind. For it is evident that our conception of liberty differs from all previous conceptions in that it traces a decisive connection between the type of economic organization which a society possesses and the degree of liberty which its citizens may hope to enjoy. It conceives that the whole coercive, anti-libertarian apparatus which we call the State is an outgrowth of a particular set of economic and social relations and can be dispensed with when those relations are superseded, but not before.

The achievement of the maximum degree of human liberty is then one way of stating the proper goal of all human endeavour. But we must reckon into the determination of how much liberty a man or a community enjoys many factors which are often wholly neglected. We must reckon, for example, such things as the number of hours which a man works, whether he is sure of being able to work and earn at all, and the degree of access to the culture of his age with which he is provided. These are clearly liberties of a different kind from the traditional liberties for which our forefathers struggled. We must disentangle these two kinds of liberties. In what, then, do the liberties which we possess, or claim to possess, in contemporary

Britain and America, and those liberties which, as Stalin declares, it is a principal object of socialism to achieve, respectively consist ?

Those civil liberties which exist, either in practice or in theory, in Britain and America to-day consist, primarily, of a series of provisions, built upon the foundation of a bill of rights, by which the State limits its own freedom of action in the coercion of its citizens. For example, the British and American States[1] guarantee that a man shall be tried for a criminal offence by a jury of his peers and that he shall not be imprisoned without such trial. They further guarantee that citizens shall be free to meet for the discussion of any problem, that they shall be free to form associations for the promotion of any object not specifically declared illegal by statute, or by common law decision, and that they may print and publish any views and opinions not so declared illegal. These are extremely valuable liberties. They have, it is true, been perceptibly infringed upon both in Britain and America during recent years. Moreover, our now extreme class inequalities have served to change the character of some of the most important of them. They are a heritage imperfect and incomplete; nevertheless, they are precious.

How can their existence be explained on the basis of the theory of the State which we have outlined above ? For if the State is essentially the coercive instrument of the dominant capitalist class, why should that class have thus blunted the edge of its weapon ? The answer to this question is, in part, that many of these liberties date from an epoch in which the capitalists were not the governing class in society. They date from an epoch in which, on the contrary, the capitalist class was often itself the victim of the State's apparatus of force. Hence it was to be expected that the young and struggling capitalists should attempt to limit the power of the State.

In a word, the establishment of our civil liberties was due to

[1] I am neglecting the complication introduced by the existence of the forty-eight separate and nominally sovereign States in America. The degree of civil liberty enjoyed by the citizen in each of these States varies appreciably in theory and widely in practice.

the same general causes as the establishment of democracy—
of which they are in a sense a part. We instanced the obstinate
resistance which Parliament, then as now the essential mouth-
piece of the capitalists as a class, offered to the creation of a
standing army as an example of the capitalists' efforts to prevent
the creation of too effective an apparatus of coercion, so long
as that apparatus might be used against them.[1]

It was in the course of this same struggle that our original
civil liberties were established. They were established in the
interests of the rising capitalist class. But this does not mean
that they were not, and are not now, of genuine value to the
rest of the population. For the interests of a young, vigorous
class, cleaving its way upward for the fulfilment of its historic
mission, always coincide, on the whole, with the interests of the
community. This is the explanation of how our existing civil
liberties originally came into being in the seventeenth and
eighteenth centuries. But it will not cover the considerable
development of these liberties which took place in the nineteenth
century. From 1832 onwards the British capitalists were in
ever greater control of the State. How, then, do we account
for the fact that for some decades the restrictions with
which coercive State action was hedged about were increased ?
The explanation lies in the fact that the capitalists in their
long and arduous struggle with the feudalists and semi-feudalists
had had to call into political activity the classes lying below
them. They had to set in motion both the lower middle class
of petty traders and, in the early nineteenth century, the new
class of industrial workers. It was these popular forces which
won—usually in conflict with the capitalists, who were already
becoming more and more conservative—our more recent civil
liberties.

[1] This determination led to curious contradictions and confusions during the
seventeenth and early eighteenth centuries, when the British capitalists had a
precarious hold on State power. For, while they had to use the State power to
fight their battles against their commercial rivals (principally the Dutch and the
French), and to strengthen it for this purpose, yet they still feared that the State
power might be used against them, and therefore desired to limit and curb it.
Hence the recruitment of *ad hoc* armies for each war and the insistence on their
immediate disbandment at each peace. Our history books give no even plausible
explanation of this phenomenon, contenting themselves with talking about " the
jealousy of Parliament " or some such meaningless phrase—much to the bewilder-
ment of the unfortunate student.

To-day the capitalists have become wholly conservative. For their power is quite unchallenged from the now completely absorbed feudalists above them, and is increasingly challenged from the ever-growing working class below them. Naturally, therefore, they have come to have less and less use for liberties which have grown quite unnecessary to them for curbing the power of non-existent feudalists, and which hamper them before the growing menace of the workers. This is the explanation of why both the British and American capitalists are becoming more and more anti-libertarian. This is why they are making efforts to revoke those civil liberties which their ancestors played the leading part in establishing. In Britain and America these efforts have only recently begun. In Germany and Italy they have been disastrously successful.

It will be evident that those who take this view of the origin of our present liberties will not hesitate to fight for their retention by every possible means. For a knowledge of their origin and nature serves but to make us aware that these liberties are not only good in themselves but are also a vital asset to the workers in their struggle to abolish the more and more intolerably defective capitalist economic system. This is why communists and socialists are always ready to stand and to fight side by side with everyone, no matter what his other opinions may be, who is ready to defend our civil liberties.

Now let us look at the other side of the picture. Our existing civil liberties, however necessary it may be to prevent even them from being taken away from us, are, for the workers, poor, thin, and half-illusory things.

Stalin, in the interview just quoted, remarks that it is difficult for him to imagine " what personal liberty can be held by an unemployed man who goes hungry and cannot find a means of using his labour. Real liberty exists only where exploitation has been annihilated, where no oppression of some peoples by others exists, where there is no unemployment, no poverty, where a person does not tremble because to-morrow he may lose his job, his home, his food."[1]

[1] The interview was with Mr. Roy Howard of the Scripps–Howard newspapers.

This incomparably more substantial conception of liberty is genuinely incomprehensible to most of those who set the tone of public discussion in Britain and America. Having never trembled because to-morrow they may lose their jobs, their homes or their food, they cannot conceive what such questions have to do with liberty. For them liberty is almost exclusively a matter of the absence of legal prohibitions against saying, writing or, more rarely, doing, things displeasing to the Government. But for by far the greater part of the population such liberty of prophesying is not, and cannot be, by any means the most important or valued liberty. As Stalin implied, the liberty for which by far the greater part of the world's population is still fighting desperately is not the liberty to speak, but the liberty to eat.

The denial by their owners of access to those means of production without which a man cannot earn his livelihood is an incomparable oppression. Every other form of tyranny is but consequential to it. Nor is this oppression confined to those millions of the population to whom access to the means of production is wholly forbidden. The whole body of the employed workers are to a varying degree subjected to the irresponsible, invisible, and so partly unrealized, dictation of the owners of the means of production. For they are allowed to work and earn only upon conditions laid down by the wholly unchecked decision of the owners. Nor are these conditions confined to matters of wages and hours of work. They often extend, openly or tacitly, to the words and deeds of every employee. In many establishments to refrain from the expression of views, or the commission of acts, displeasing to the management is made into a condition of employment. No statute, bill of rights, or legal enactment whatsoever, can prevent those who neither own nor have independent access to the means of production from dependence upon those who have this ownership and access. Only a fortunate minority of those who have ever earned their living by selling their ability to work are likely to be unaware of this fact. For the great majority of workers have to adapt their actions, and in many cases their words, to the wishes of those who employ them.

But the spell cast by the ideas of the owners of the means of production (and *they* really do enjoy an admirable degree of liberty under capitalism) is so strong that only a minority of the workers ever reach a clear consciousness of the fact that the greater part of the liberty which the British and American Constitutions guarantee them has now been invisibly withdrawn from them by their ever more perfect exclusion from all independent opportunity to work and earn. The idea that this is why their actual situation does not correspond at all to the picture of a community of free citizens which is painted for them, by school textbook, newspaper and political leader, is only slowly and confusedly dawning upon them.

Another aspect of the communist and socialist conception of liberty is almost always incomprehensible to minds steeped in the ways of thinking developed in the epoch of capitalism. Liberty in the capitalist epoch has been conceived of almost exclusively as the absence of restraints; it is seldom thought of as the presence of opportunity.[1] And yet for the mass of the population of any highly organized community the question of the provision of effective opportunity to speak and write, and to act, is the more important consideration. For example, the liberty which chiefly matters to the studious and ambitious is the availabilty of education, of books, of apparatus. A liberty which matters intensely, to take a simpler but only less important case, to the citizens of any great city is not merely that there should be no legal prohibitions against them amusing themselves, but that there should be enough playing-fields, enough, and cheap enough, transport to the country, enough, and cheap enough, cinema and theatre seats and the like. But the provision of these positive liberties to think, to learn, to speak, to play, and to do is not a matter of paper laws or decrees. It is a matter of the allocation of important economic resources. The provision of the educational opportunities now open to the children of the governing class in Britain to all children would necessitate, for example, the allocation, for this purpose, of substantial resources of production. The same thing is true of the

---

[1] See J. S. Mill's famous essay, for example. It is true that great emphasis has been laid by many defenders of capitalism on one opportunity with which capitalism is said to provide the workers—the opportunity of becoming capitalists by acquiring means of production themselves. We have noticed how little reality is left in this claim to-day. But almost no attention has been given to the opportunities which society provides to workers while they remain workers.

provision, to all, of the opportunities for sport, amusement and travel now monopolized by about 10 per cent of the population.

The supply of economic resources is limited. Hence those who engross for themselves the whole supply available for the effective enjoyment of such fundamental liberties as those of self-improvement and recreation, deny these liberties to the rest of the population. No one who fails not merely to accept, but imaginatively to realize, the full implications of this truth has begun to understand the problem of the provision of liberty, not to a fortunate class, but to a whole community. Unless they really do see that an economic arrangement which reserves all, for example, of the available facilities for foreign travel to the governing class is almost (although, no doubt, never quite) as real a denial of liberty to the rest of the population as if men were legally forbidden to go more than so many miles from their homes, they are still under the capitalist hypnosis. Mr. and Mrs. Webb put the point thus:

" There is, in any given place, at any given time, only a certain amount of opportunity open to the population in the aggregate. Anyone who takes to himself more than the appropriate amount and kind of opportunity that falls properly to his share, not only robs another of some or all of the opportunity that he might otherwise have enjoyed, but also, by increasing inequality, inevitably lessens the aggregate amount of individual freedoms within the community. The social organization which allows the British shipowner to treat himself and his family to a long and expensive holiday in Switzerland and Italy, whilst the hundreds of dock labourers who are unloading his ships, together with their families, get nothing more like a holiday than their wageless days of involuntary unemployment, not only injures them, but also diminishes the total aggregate of freedom within the community. Lenin is said once to have observed in his epigrammatic way: ' It is true that liberty is precious—so precious that it must be rationed.' " (pp. 1035-6.)

The rationing of liberty must necessarily seem a most deplorable thing to the unreflecting members of the capitalist class of

Britain and America. For they now enjoy the almost unlimited supply of liberty, both in the sense of freedom from restraint and provision of opportunity, which their money can buy; nor have they cared to reflect that their present almost perfect liberty is only achieved by the almost equally perfect servitude to them of the rest of the population. They are careful never to become conscious of the fact (to return to Mr. and Mrs. Webb's example) that they can have unlimited holidays only because their workers can have no holidays at all. But the rationing, in the sense of the sharing out upon a just basis, of those opportunities without which liberty is little more than a name, will seem to every worker one of the most necessary and elementary acts of any socialist society.

An essential part of the communist and socialist conception of liberty is, then, the positive provision for the entire population of effective opportunity to work, to earn, and so to live, and also to improve and develop themselves by study, and to enjoy themselves. Until this has been done, liberty will remain for the greater part of men an aspiration, glorious but insubstantial. In fine, liberty cannot be effectively enjoyed, outside the ranks of the capitalist class, without that general plenty and security which socialism alone can provide.

Once this cardinal fact is realized, however, it is of importance to examine the question of that liberty of expression on which the attention of capitalist opinion is exclusively concentrated. For this is undoubtedly a very precious liberty. The question is, To what extent does the mass of the population possess this liberty under capitalism and socialism respectively?

Now the capitalists' ownership of the means of production includes the ownership of the means of production of opinion: it includes the ownership, that is to say, of the Press, the wireless, the cinema, and the control of the educational system. Yet to-day liberty of expression, if it is not to be illusory, must mean liberty of access to the Press, the wireless, and the cinema. It cannot become a reality for the mass of the population so long as those three methods of effective expression are in the exclusive possession of a limited ruling class. It is hardly too much to say that the worker under capitalism has the right of free speech—so long as there is no possibility of his making himself heard. In a socialist society the workers are not only free to speak; they are free to speak into the microphone, free to use the great printing presses, free to use the incomparable instrument of the cinema, to make articulate and visible their whole view of the world. In a word, it becomes apparent upon examination that effective liberty of expression is almost as closely bound up with the question of who is to own the means of production as is the basic question of the liberty to work and eat. If the means of production of opinion are in the hands of the capitalist class, they and they alone will enjoy effective liberty of expression; if they are in the hands of the workers, it is they who will enjoy this liberty.

This is the short answer to those who feel that the educational system, the Press, the cinema, and the wireless, in the existing socialist community, are in some sense unfree in which they are free in Britain and America. In order to get any significance out of this allegation we must at once ask the counter-question—free to whom ? For it is perfectly true that the Press of a socialist Britain and America will be as unfree to Messrs. Hearst and Howard, to Lords Rothermere and Beaverbrook, as it is now unfree to the mass of the population. The mass of the population can only own the means of expression, to coin a generic term for Press, cinema, and wireless, through their own organizations —their Government, their Trade Unions, their political parties, their Co-operative Societies and the like. These are the organizations which own and control the Press of the Soviet Union, for example. Is it not remarkable that many quite sincere persons feel that such ownership constitutes a denial of the freedom of the Press, while the ownership of chains of newspapers by individual millionaires such as Mr. Hearst and Lord Rothermere constitutes the freedom of the Press ? No doubt the fact which weighs with those who feel like this is that formally, legally, there is nothing to prevent any British citizen from establishing, say, a London daily newspaper in competition with Lord Rothermere's *Daily Mail*, or Lord Beaverbrook's *Daily Express*, or Mr. Elias' *Daily Herald*—nothing, that is to say, except the need to command at least one million pounds sterling. But this is an economic obstacle. And an economic obstacle seems to many people in some way not to count. Monopoly is not for them monopoly unless it is legally recognized. So long as our Press lords are content with the *fact* of monopolizing the effective expression of news and opinion, and do not lay claim to a legal title to this monopoly, they will not, it seems, be accused of even infringing the freedom of the Press. They will remain free to drench us with the news and the views, and those alone, which suit their interests: to select, to suppress, to distort, to harangue; to deafen and to madden the world with their campaigns and their crusades; to prevent us even from noticing, far less resenting, their exploitations; and finally to drive us into mutual slaughter to settle their accounts. And they will do all this in the sacred name of the freedom of the Press.

But let the democratically established organizations of the Russian working class put before the readers of the newspapers which they own the view of the world which the most responsible leaders of the community consider, after decades of reflection and of social experiment, to be the truth, so far as the human mind has yet apprehended it, and they are accused of using a kept Press for propaganda purposes ! Certainly the workers' Press of the Soviet Union is full of propaganda. As Mr. and Mrs. Webb quietly remark, it is so full of propaganda that " it would be hard to decide whether there is, in the aggregate, more or less of it than in Great Britain and the United States." The difference is that in a socialist community the propaganda emanates from definite and democratically elected public bodies, which can be replaced at any time, from bodies which can scarcely have interests different from those of the mass of the population, from which they emanate; whilst in capitalist countries the propaganda emanates from some half a dozen totally irresponsible multi-millionaires, whose interests are often in deadly contradiction to those of the remainder of the community.

So much for the question of the liberty of expression respectively provided for the mass of the population by a capitalist and a socialist Press. The same considerations apply to such vital means of expression as the educational system, the wireless, and the cinema. To suppose that any of these means of expression can be free from propaganda—can fail, that is to say, to influence powerfully the minds of men—is a delusion. But if the capitalists own them, the propaganda which they will emit will be capitalist propaganda; if the workers own them, it will be socialist propaganda. And this is a very important difference.

Finally, we may notice a more subtle ground for the allegation that socialism will fail to maximize the liberty of expression of the individual man. We are sometimes told that, even if there will be no tyranny of legal coercion in a socialist community, there will be a tyranny of public opinion, an overmastering and all-pervading conformity which will stifle all idiosyncrasy or even individuality. In this case also it is necessary, in order to retain a sense of proportion, to envisage the degree of freedom for non-conformity which exists in capitalist communities. Just one hundred years ago the first great socialist which the English-speaking world ever produced wrote with insight and force on this point:

> " Some nations such as the British and their descendants, the population of the United States of North America, imagine that they now possess what they term civil and religious liberty; while both nations are in the very bondage of mental slavery, both civil and religious. Their civil and religious liberty consists in expressing within a small circle such thoughts and feelings as they know by experience will pass current within that circle. If they infringe these bounds they are likely to have lynch law in one country, and fine and imprisonment in the other."

(Robert Owen, *The Book of the New Moral World.*)

Neither self-satisfaction as an ingrained national characteristic, nor their differing methods of repression, seem to have changed much in Britain and America since Owen's day. Owen may be thought to have overstated his case somewhat. But it remains true that a united, identically educated and carefully trained governing class (such as the British, for example), which controls almost all access to the means of effective expression and employment, can and does impose its point of view upon a community to an extent which makes non-conformity difficult and usually dangerous.

The question is this: are the citizens of a socialist community likely to impose upon themselves an even more severe pressure towards conformity? Nothing would seem more unlikely. A community in which a genuine identity of interest between all citizens has been established will be able to afford to tolerate far more idiosyncrasy, salty variety, and even plain eccentricity, in its citizens than can a community which is maintaining the precarious eminence of a governing class. Again, the mere achievement of general plenty and security, the elimination of the fear that at any moment a man may be shut out from the opportunity to work and earn, will in itself foster an individuality which is totally impossible to the wage earning population to-day; an individuality which to-day can only exist amongst that tiny handful of the securely rich who have no such fears.

To sum up: nothing can prevent the capitalists from using the immense powers of coercion given them by their ownership of the means of production drastically to curtail every one of the liberties of the workers. The right of the capitalists to allow or to refuse the workers the possibility of earning their living is a power which, so long as it exists, transcends and overrides every constitution in the world. The initial act of dispossessing the capitalists creates at a stroke more liberty than has ever, or can ever, exist under capitalism, except for the capitalists. Neither constitutions nor bills of right, republics nor constitutional monarchies, can ever make men free so long as their livelihoods are at the mercy of a small class which holds sway over the means of life. In a socialist society alone those liberties, of which the workers of Britain and America possess little more than the shadow, can assume form and substance. In a socialist society the workers get, not merely the theoretical right, but also the practical, daily opportunity to use their liberties. They are enabled to live, and not merely to work. Under socialism work becomes a means to a free and good life. Under capitalism the life of the worker is preserved as a necessary means to the extraction of the maximum possible amount of work from him.

Let us now apply our argument to the existing socialist community. It is frequently alleged that British and American socialists and, more particularly, communists have no right to defend our liberties against the growing attacks of the capitalists. For their colleagues, it is said, have destroyed civil liberty in the Soviet Union. Preceding chapters will have explained why all those who approach political problems historically find such an appeal to an abstract and ideal liberty, independent of time and place, devoid of meaning. We are unable to agree that it is inconsistent to defend those liberties which can be used by the workers in Britain and America to protect themselves against their capitalists, while denying to the remaining capitalists in the Soviet Union the liberty to attack the workers.

Apart altogether from this basic consideration, the allegation that the Russian communists have destroyed the civil liberties of the Russian people is untrue. For the Russian people never possessed, and had little conception of, the civil liberties of the Western world. The Russian capitalists only secured their first substantial step towards acquiring the power of the State in 1905. And they only acquired predominant power, for six months, in February 1917. That period was far too short for there to be any possibility of the emergence of a period of liberal capitalism such as the West has known. Thus the Russian communists certainly did not destroy the non-existent civil liberties of Russia.

The complaint may be made, however, that the Russian communists have not themselves developed libertarian institutions sufficiently rapidly. This complaint (if it is not, as it usually is, a mere cover for the desire for a capitalist restoration) is founded on ignorance of the conditions which the soviet régime has faced.

We described in Chapter XIII the problems faced by the Russian communists in the establishment of democracy for the Russian workers. In general the same problems have arisen in regard to the task of building up, not indeed the same civil liberties which exist in Britain and America (for that is not the intention), but those incomparably more substantial liberties which become possible in a socialist society.

Not only have the dispossessed Russian capitalists formed an irreconcilably hostile group; not only have they up till now invariably used any liberties granted to them for the purpose of attempting to win back their lost dominance; not only does the presence round every Russian frontier of avid and hostile capitalist powers make a quasi-military discipline a necessity of existence for the soviets; but also the Russian people have to establish, slowly and painfully, the customs, habits, and traditions of a free existence. If, as in the case of democracy, we are told that they are making but slow progress in the building up of a free life for themselves, we must reply that when we remember whence they started, their progress has been, on the contrary, incomparably more rapid than that made by any other people in history.

It is true that the Russian workers are only now in a position to modify the use of those secret police methods which we in Britain and America suppose (erroneously, as a matter of fact) that we have long outgrown. It is true that some of the technical methods employed by one secret police resemble those of another. But to leap from this fact to the conclusion that the secret police force used by the Russian Soviets from 1918 to 1935, namely the G.P.U., was nothing more nor less than the old Tsarist Okrana under a new name is to evince incorrigible political illiteracy. The class which the Okrana held down wielded the weapon of the G.P.U., while the class which used the Okrana was held down by the G.P.U. Thus even if the methods of the two organizations had been identical, which they were not, they would have served precisely opposite social purposes.[1] And, of course, nobody in practice does confuse the two. Did the capitalists of Europe raise up their hands in horror at the methods of the Okrana ? They did not. On the contrary, they arranged a series of loans to the Tsarist Government which controlled the Okrana. In the same way, the workers of Europe feel no horror over the severity which the G.P.U. has shown to the irreconcilable enemies of the soviets. Confusion between the two bodies is only possible for those whose intention it is to be confused themselves and to confuse others.

[1] How quaint the officials of the Okrana would have found the suggestion that they should maintain an institution such as the Bolschevo settlement long maintained by the G.P.U. (and now maintained by the Commissariat of Internal Affairs): an institution which all British and American penalogists who are acquainted with it unite in describing as one of the finest social experiments in the world.

It is interesting to speculate upon the problems which will face the British and American workers when they come to the job of building up a free life for themselves. In this matter also they possess great advantages which the Russian workers lacked. The measure of liberty which they have enjoyed under capitalism will undoubtedly help them rapidly to create the basis of a free life. The existence of a tradition of relative self-government, self-reliance, and independence will be of great assistance to them in building up a socialist society. In this respect also they will start out from a point of development to which the Russians had laboriously to climb.

But here, too, the British and American people will face a special difficulty. Our traditions of relative civil liberty will no doubt be used by the dispossessed British and American capitalists to demand their " right " to combine for the overthrow of the workers' State and the re-acquisition of the means of production. They will, no doubt, make both night and day hideous with their outcry at the " monstrous, outrageous violation of liberty " of which the workers' government will be guilty when it protects itself against their implacable hostility. Their complaints will seem to themselves perfectly justified, for *they* really did enjoy liberty under capitalism; and *they* really will have that liberty severely curtailed under socialism.

Moreover, their specious agitation is only too likely to take in a number of quite sincere and disinterested people. For the level of political education is so low in Britain and America that some people will be quite unable to detect the fallacy of their plea. Our minds have been so bemused with centuries of talk about liberty in the abstract, without any rational attempt to discover what this great word means, or to ascertain the conditions under which alone effective liberty for the greater part of the population can be achieved, that a considerable amount of confusion is only too likely to occur.

And this confusion will, paradoxically enough, necessitate a more considerable temporary curtailment of the liberty of some sections of the population than would otherwise be necessary. If everyone could be relied upon to see clearly that when the dispossessed capitalists cried out that they were the champions of the immortal cause of human freedom, they were merely crying for their lost dividends, then there would be little need to restrict their liberty to cry out; for they would be crying for the moon. But if certain sections of the population are still confused enough to take them at their word, then it will become necessary to restrain the outcry.

Thus we must face the fact that, for a period, the British and American workers will almost certainly be compelled to restrict the civil liberties of the dispossessed classes to an extent that these classes will consider outrageous. But even during that period the degree of liberty enjoyed by incomparably the greater part of the population will have been enormously extended. It will still be restricted and imperfect compared to the liberty which will be possible when a truly classless society will have emerged. But it will be incomparably fuller and richer than are those partial, if precious, liberties which we possess in Britain and America to-day.

CHAPTER XIX

Socialism and Religion

RELIGIOUS as well as civil liberty is a hard-won right in the possession of which the British and American peoples take much pride. It is a common allegation that socialists and communists propose to destroy this right, to persecute religion, burn down the churches, lock out their congregations, and punish everyone who dares to hold a prayer meeting or to confess their faith in God.

But this allegation is not true. In a well-known passage in the *Anti-Dühring*[1] Friedrich Engels both defines our attitude to religion and describes the practical policy which should result from such an attitude. Engels' book is a sustained polemic against the views of a certain Herr Dühring. Dühring was a German university professor of the eighties of the last century who, on becoming a socialist, considered it his task and privilege to revise socialist theory from top to bottom.

This he did in several extensive volumes. As his views were almost totally erroneous and at the same time sufficiently specious and pretentious to have a considerable influence amongst the German socialists of the time, it became necessary for the unfortunate Engels to refute them in detail. Much to his chagrin, Engels had to devote many months, first to reading, and then to answering, Herr Dühring's whole case. Engels' loss was, however, our gain. For Dühring had written nonsense on almost every subject under the sun. Hence in answering him Engels had to state his position on every subject also. The result is a book which, if one disregards the now dead and buried controversy with Dühring, is of the greatest use in that it gives a concise statement of almost every aspect of the communist and socialist position.[2]

Herr Dühring had announced that a socialist society will "abolish all the paraphernalia of religious magic, and herewith all the essential elements of religious cults." Engels at once

[1] See Bibliography, p. 468.

[2] English and American readers usually find an initial difficulty in the fact that the book begins in the philosophical field. Not a bad plan is to read Part II, "Political Economy," and Part III, "Socialism," first. The full title of the book is *Herr Eugen Dühring's Revolution in Science*.

denies this. Dühring proposes, he says, to incite " his gendarmes of the future to attack religion and thereby help it to martyrdom and a prolonged lease of life." Nothing, he continues, could be more contrary, either to what socialists[1] propose that we should do, or to the view of the nature of religion which they hold. This leads Engels to a statement of theory and practice in this field which we cannot do better than epitomize.

Our approach to the study of religious belief must be historical. Just as when we wish to discover what the State is we investigate the question of how the State arose, so when we wish to find out what religion is we study how religion arose. All religion, Engels writes,

" is nothing but the fantastic reflection in men's minds of those external forces which control their daily life, a reflection in which terrestrial forces assume the form of supernatural forces. In the beginning of history it was the forces of nature that were at first so reflected, and, in the course of further evolution, they underwent the most manifold and varied personifications amongst the various peoples. Comparative mythology has traced back this first process, at least in the case of the Indo-European nations, to its origin in the Indian Vedas, and has shown its detailed evolution among the Indians, Persians, Greeks, Romans, Germans, and, so far as material is available, also amongst the Celts, Lithuanians and Slavs. But it is not long before, side by side with the forces of nature, social forces begin to be active; forces which present themselves to man as equally extraneous and at first equally inexplicable, dominating them with the same apparent necessity as the forces of nature themselves. The fantastic personifications, which at first only reflected the mysterious forces of nature, at this point acquire social attributes, become representative of the forces of history."
(*Anti-Dühring*, pp. 353–4).

When Engels calls religion " a fantastic reflection in men's minds of external forces," he is simply alluding to the well-known

[1] The words communists and socialists were used almost interchangeably during most of the nineteenth century. Engels as a matter of fact speaks of socialism and socialists in the *Anti-Dühring*.

fact that the early gods and goddesses were personifications of natural forces—of the thunder, the rain, the sun, the
moon, and the like. There is no difficulty in understanding
why men made gods and goddesses out of these natural forces.
They were by far the most important things in their lives.
For until men had developed an adequate technique of production their livelihoods depended upon the favour of the elements.
And the elements were violent and capricious. The lightning
struck, the flood or the drought came, and the best-laid schemes
were destroyed. Nor had men any but puny and ineffective
means of guiding or controlling these forces.

Naturally, therefore, men stood in wonder and fear before
them. Wonder and fear are the parents of the desire to propitiate
and to influence. But how were men to influence the lightning
or the rain ? Such questions lead to thinking about these natural
forces, to theories as to their nature and origin. Once such
thinking had begun it was natural to suppose that these forces
were the effects of mighty beings, comparable, though infinitely
superior, to men themselves; that the sunshine came from the
happy countenance of a god, that the lightning was the javelin
of an angry deity, that the rain beat down from a third celestial.

Moreover, if natural forces were but the effects of the great
inhabitants of the sky, they might be to some extent controlled.
For their authors might be propitiated and cajoled. If this
theory of the universe were true, a method of influencing natural
forces had been found. Prayer and sacrifice might be made to
the gods, and perhaps they would grant the fertilizing rain
and withhold the lightning and the flood. We cannot doubt that
such is the explanation of why all primitive races have invented
polytheistic religions which personify the main natural forces.
We cannot doubt that this is how religion arose. Religion is,
then, a theory of the nature of the universe in general, and of
the origin and character of natural forces in particular. It is a
kind of statement, all the more impressive for being indirect
and symbolical, as to what things in general are like.

Moreover, every religion has naturally drawn positive deductions from its theory of the universe. If things are so and so,
then we should do such and such. If the thunder, the rain, and
the sunshine are the expression of the wills of certain formidable

beings, then we must propitiate and persuade those beings in
every possible way. We may do this both by direct efforts at
suasion, by prayer and sacrifice, and also by behaving in such
a way as we suppose pleasing to these beings. Precept is added
to doctrine, ethics to theology.

But, Engels continues, the reflection of natural forces by
their personification as gods and goddesses is only the first
stage of religion. " It is not long before, side by side with the
forces of nature, social forces begin to be active; forces which
present themselves to man as equally extraneous, and at first
equally inexplicable, dominating them with the same apparent
necessity as the forces of nature themselves." What Engels
means by these dominating and inexplicable social forces is
clear if we recollect what happened to the Attic peasants when
their means of production developed to that point which is
inevitably associated with the birth of private property in the
means of production and trade. Up till then, we saw the sons
of the Achæans had lived a simple, unchanging life, subject
to the natural ills of drought and flood, but enjoying, under
their gentile social system, not only a considerable degree of
freedom and equality, but a measure of economic security.

So long as no natural catastrophes intervened, they knew
that their digging and hunting and fishing would produce them
a sufficiency of food: that their women would weave them
covering against the winter: that they would not lack for a
house to sleep in. But, by the cruellest paradox, no sooner had
they developed new powers over nature, than this measure of
economic security disappeared. The peasant farmer, who had
nominally been given his plot of land, free from the old control
by the *gens*, soon found it mortgaged to the hilt; then the
mortgage was foreclosed, and he himself, his farm, and his
children were sold into slavery ! Nor had the peasant any idea
of how these frightful disasters had come upon him. They had
just happened. No one had willed them. No one had deliberately
changed the old conditions of society or instituted the new.
It was merely that trade and money (themselves based on
private property in the means of production) had silently disintegrated the old security; had at length pitchforked the
wretched farmers into destitution or slavery. Such are the social

forces, fully as dominating, as inexplicable, and as terrifying as the forces of nature, with which civilized men have had to contend. With the birth of civilization a new function for religion arises. Not only, and soon not even principally, is religion any longer needed to provide men with a method, objectively ineffective but enormously reassuring, of dealing with those natural forces which they are steadily learning to comprehend and to control. With the emergence of civilization, religion becomes increasingly the explanation of, and the only available, if insubstantial, shield against, the new terrors and disasters with which social and economic forces afflict the greater part of mankind. And this is what religion has ever since remained. For during all the long centuries since first men ate of the tree of technical and economic knowledge, revolutionized their methods of production and established private property, commerce, class divisions, and the State, social and economic forces have remained devastating, uncomprehended and uncontrolled. " In existing bourgeois society, men are dominated by the economic conditions created by themselves," Engels continues, " by the means of production which they themselves have produced, as if by an extraneous force."

" The actual basis of religious reflex action therefore continues to exist, and with it the religious reflex itself. And although bourgeois political economy has given a certain insight into the causal basis of this domination by extraneous forces, this makes no essential difference. Bourgeois economics can neither prevent crises in general, nor protect the individual capitalist from losses, bad debts and bankruptcy, nor secure the individual workers against unemployment and destitution. It is still true that man proposes and God (that is, the extraneous forces of the Capitalist mode of production) disposes." (p. 354.)

In the year A.D. 1929, as in the year 590 B.C., men were almost helpless before the unexpected and uncomprehended consequences of the economic relationships into which they had entered. The uncontrolled forces of our runaway economic system have replaced the now bridled forces of nature as our oppressors. To the tyranny of flood and storm has succeeded the tyranny of slump, of currency crash, of the enslavement of man by man, of the fratricide of nation by nation.

We now know that the steps which we can take for our own sustenance will seldom be frustrated by natural forces. We can defy the elements: we can be assured of being able to produce enough food and clothing and shelter for our needs. We can be assured of being able to produce these things: but we cannot be assured of receiving them ! The formidable social forces which havè been generated by the economic system which we have built up snatch the food from our mouths and the clothes from our backs. The operation of these social forces is at least as mysterious to most men to-day as was the operation of natural forces to the savage. So long as this is the case we need religion to offer to us some explanation (however fantastic) of these social forces, just as the savage needed religion to offer him some explanation of natural forces. We need a God to whom we can pray for protection against the starvation which comes (we have seen how and why) from growing too much wheat, as the savage needed a god to protect him from the starvation which came when hail destroyed his wheat.

It is suggested, then, that the incomprehensible disasters with which our now more and more uncontrollable economic system afflicts us are a sufficient explanation of the continuance of religious belief, after the subjugation of natural forces. Engels foretold that when the terrifying economic insecurity of modern life was abolished religious belief would begin to fade out of man's consciousness. " When Society," he concludes,

" by taking possession of all means of production and using them on a planned basis, has freed itself and all its members from the bondage in which they are now held by the means of production, which they themselves have produced but which now confront them as an irresistible extraneous force; when therefore man no longer merely proposes but also disposes—only then will the last extraneous force which is still reflected in religion vanish; and with it will also vanish the religious reflection itself, for the simple reason that then there will be nothing left to reflect."

It is clear that no one holding this view of the origin and nature of religious belief will favour a policy of suppressing religion. Engels believed that religious belief would disappear when the cause which engendered it had been removed. He believed, therefore, that, while it was impossible to suppress religious belief before social security had been established, it would be as unnecessary as it would be pernicious to attempt to do so after that event.

I personally believe that the above view of the cause of the persistence of religious belief after man's conquest of external forces is in itself correct—but that it is incomplete. The psycho-analytical school of psychologists trace another strain in the genesis of religion. They call attention to the fact that in many well-developed religions the principal deity is called " the father." And they deduce from this, and from much further, evidence that religious belief is primarily an adult generalization of the child's attitude to its parents. They suggest that the feeling of helplessness, the need for propitiation, the fear, the need to love and to evoke love, which the religious adult feels towards his heavenly father, are but an altered expression of the feelings which he experienced as a child in regard to his terrestrial father.

That this generalization of an originally infantile attitude is an important element in religious belief appears to me to be established. But that it was the main element in the genesis of religion may be questioned. For religion everywhere appears as polytheism, with numerous gods personifying natural forces, and only turns to monotheism at a much later stage. The concept of God the Father, even before he becomes the sole occupant of the heavens, is one of the later developments of religion. But if a prolongation into adult life of the child's attitude to its terrestrial father had been a primary element in the genesis of religious belief, we should expect religion to have been originally monotheistic.[1]

It seems necessary to make another qualification to Engels' statement. For, after all, by no means all natural forces have yet been fully comprehended. For example, man's main antagonist, his own still inevitable death after seventy or eighty brief years

---

[1] Unless, indeed, the primacy of polytheism can be explained by the primacy of the matrilinear family.

of life, is as yet, if not as mysterious, almost as invincible, as ever. Until and unless that last enemy is defeated or, at any rate, driven back, so that his empire does not descend upon us till we have had perhaps double our present span[1] of life, a powerful generator of religious belief will remain in existence. We may expect, however, that the enormous growth of social consciousness which is produced by the achievement of socialism will do something to take away the sting of death. When men really feel part of an ever-continuing social organism, instead of isolated and transitory individuals, they will find, as many men already do, that consolation which religious mythology can no longer give.

I believe that it is important to recognize these additional factors in the generation of religious belief if over-simplification is to be avoided. When full weight has been given to them, however, the view, that the main and substantial cause of the continuance of religious belief is the appalling insecurity of life under capitalism, remains incontestable.[2] (The only deduction of practical importance which we need make from the above qualifications is that the fading out of religious belief in conditions of general security and plenty will be a very slow process.)

It should now be clear that any attempt to suppress religious belief, or to curtail freedom of worship, is totally out of accord with the views of communists and socialists. This does not mean, however, that disputes may not arise between workers' governments in Britain and America and certain of the religious denominations. Such disputes are, no doubt, especially likely in Britain, where the Church is a State institution, with special rights of compulsory taxation over the rest of the community, and owning substantial means of production, such as much excellent land. No workers' government will be able to recognize any such rights or privileges, and the disestablishment and disendowment of the Church of England will be a necessary part of the general acquisition of the means of production by the

---

[1] This, we are informed, is a very possible achievement of science, but not for some centuries. Already, however, human life has been greatly prolonged. For instance, according to Prof. Jameson, the expectation of life at birth in Britain has risen from 44 years in the eighteen-seventies to 60 years to-day.

[2] Moreover, as that security is now ever increasing we shall expect to see some signs of an increase in religious belief. And, at any rate amongst the intelligentsia, such signs have appeared. The present state of the world has produced a noticeable increase of conversions to that catholicism of despair which has always been one of the refuges of discouragement.

British workers. No doubt this act will be represented in some circles as an outrageous attack upon religion. But we may hope that the more enlightened clergy and devout laymen will recognize that a religion which is compelled to use the power of the State in order to force the population to pay special taxes for its maintenance is one of the strangest of our remaining anachronisms.[1]

No such problem as this will arise in America, where religious belief has no overt connection with the State. But we must not slur over the fact that serious disputes will still be possible, and are unfortunately even likely, between particular religious organizations and any workers' State. For religious institutions, whether State supported or not, can be used for purposes of which socialists and communists cannot but actively disapprove. If religious belief is to-day predominantly sustained by the social and economic insecurity of life in the capitalist world, religion itself, as organized by many of the Churches, plays no inconsiderable part in maintaining this condition of its own existence. Religious belief has predominantly arisen from men's need to explain and influence terrifying natural or social forces; but religious institutions can be used to justify and to perpetuate attitudes of submission to, and resignation before, these forces. For those very social institutions, such as private property in the means of production, which create frightful insecurity for the majority of mankind, are also conditions of existence for the ruling class. Accordingly, the Churches have been used as instruments by the governing class for the intellectual and emotional subjection of the rest of the population. Many of the more odious tyrannies of both the ancient and the modern world have supported themselves upon the mitre and the cross.

Moreover, if some Churches have played a part in movements of social protest, others have not been content to remain the apologists of lay tyrants. They have themselves become the active instruments of oppression: they have identified, and largely

---

[1] It was one of the better-known clerics of the Anglican Church, Dr. Jowett, who said the final word on such compulsory religion. Dr. Jowett, then Master of Balliol College, Oxford, favoured the abolition of the compulsory attendance of undergraduates at chapel. It was objected by the Professor of Theology that this would mean an end to the religious life of the college. " It's compulsory religion or no religion at all," exclaimed the theologian. " Unfortunately," replied Dr. Jowett, " my mind is not of sufficient subtlety to distinguish between the two."

merged, themselves with the State apparatus of coercion. The
rôles of priest and policeman have become indistinguishable or
interchangeable. Sovereign pontiffs and prince-bishops have
eclipsed kings and emperors in the extent of their power, and
their extortions. For these reasons it cannot be denied that
acute conflicts between the claims of particular religious organizations and workers' States may occur. For no workers' State
will tolerate the use of religious organizations for political ends.
But these conflicts will never be provoked by any attempt on the
part of the workers' States to suppress religious belief or deny the
freedom of worship.

Workers' States will not only exercise, however, their right to
deny the political pretensions of Churches which still make either
direct or indirect attempts at temporal sovereignty. They will
also actively combat the hold of religious mythology over men's
minds. For religious mythology is profoundly inimical to the
specifically scientific attitude to the universe which must be the
mental climate of a free, socialist society. This is attested by the
fact that all the shrewdest leaders of each successive ruling class
of Europe, from the Emperor Constantine to Napoleon Bonaparte, have highly valued, for their purposes of subjugation, the
hold of religion over the minds of the people. The Church's
promise of future bliss was, in the opinion of Bonaparte, for
example, a most important factor in obtaining the acquiescence
of the masses in the manifest injustice of their present lot.
Accordingly he re-established the religious institutions of
France, convinced that they were indispensable to the maintenance of any class-divided society.

Religious institutions have served the purposes of the governors
of society by giving the mass of the population sufficient hope
in the possibility of recompense after death to enable them to
endure the unendurable in life. It was this which made Marx call
religion the opium of the people.[1] And it is this consideration

---

[1] But Marx's words are seldom given in full, and they deserve to be.
" Of this world, religion is the general theory, its encyclopædic compendium,
its logic in popular form, its spiritual *point d'honneur*, its enthusiasm, its moral
sanction, its solemn complement, its general consolation and justification. . . .
Religion is the sigh of the hard-pressed creature, the heart of a heartless world,
as it is the soul of soulless circumstances. It is the opium of the people." (On
Hegel's *Philosophy of Law*. Available to English readers in *The Jewish Question*;
Lawrence & Wishart.)

which makes it necessary for all those who care for human progress to carry on an unceasing protest against the deception of the poor by means of the promise of celestial remedies for terrestrial ills. Hence, communists and socialists, although understanding both the impossibility of the disappearance of religious belief while the social and economic conditions which give rise to it still exist, and the harmfulness of attempting to destroy religion by force, yet carry on an active campaign of enlightenment as to the part which religious belief has played in making class oppression possible throughout the centuries.

Such rationalist propaganda will, no doubt, always be keenly resented by some of the Churches. They will represent it as an attack upon religious liberty. But in fact it is no more than an assertion of the same liberty for anti-religious as for religious preaching. For surely citizens of such highly developed communities as Britain and America are now ready to face the need to give up the profoundly immature way of thinking and feeling which is represented by religion ? Is it not time that we grew up and faced, as adults, the universe as it is, and not as the fancies of the childhood of our race have pictured it ?

One of the principal examples of the direct participation of a Church in the rule of a corrupt and tyrannous governing class is afforded by the Greek Orthodox Church of the Russian Empire. The Russian Church was fused with the State apparatus of coercion to an extent unknown, or long extinct, in the rest of Christendom.[1] The head of the Church was a lay minister of the State appointed by, and responsible to, the Tsar. His status, and indeed his functions, hardly differed from those of the other Ministers of State, such as the Minister of the Interior. The whole vast ecclesiastical apparatus was supported either out of State funds raised by the taxation of the masses or by the Church's ownership of extensive tracts of land. Religion was imposed on the Russian people by the Government.

Moreover, this State-imposed religion was a mediæval, Byzantine form of Christianity—a religion more akin to primitive magic than to modern Protestant doctrine. The grossest superstitions, the most primitive conceptions of the universe, were

[1] Except Spain.

preached to, and the most odious deceptions were practised upon, the Russian people. The Russian hierarchy, stretching down from the Procurator of the Holy Synod to the humblest, the most illiterate, and the most barbarous parish " pope," was composed of State officials charged with the special function of the policing of men's minds. Nor did these ecclesiastical policemen fail to work in the closest association with the civil police.

Thus the Orthodox Church of the Tsarist Empire was an organization as different in its doctrines, its rights, its practices, and its endowments, from one of the free Protestant Churches of contemporary Britain or America as can well be imagined. It was quite inevitable that the Russian Orthodox Church should fall with the Tsarist State of which it had become an integral part. Nor, as events proved, could it be expected that the Russian Church would not use all its formidable resources both to maintain that State when it was threatened and to attempt its restoration when it had been overthrown.[1]

Between such an organization and the party of the Russian working class decisive struggle was inevitable. It was no less necessary for the Russian communists to break the political power of the Russian Church than it was necessary for them to break the power of the other organs of the Tsarist State. And when that initial task had been accomplished it was necessary to dispel quickly, and if need be by summary means, the frightful pall of superstition which the Orthodox Church had hung over the Russian land.

These are the historical facts which explain " the attack upon religious liberty " which the Russian communists are said to have undertaken. The Russian communists certainly did attack, and did destroy, both the political power of the Russian Church and the right of that Church to prevent the Russian people from hearing any theory of the universe more rational than that current in the Byzantium of A.D. 1000. If to do these things is to destroy religious liberty, then the Russian communists are guilty

[1] The reader interested in the story of the relations between the Soviet Government and the Russian Orthodox Church in the early years of the Revolution should consult *Religion and Communism*, by Julius Hecker. By so doing he will be enabled to judge for himself, with the help of the original documents, of the one-sided character of the allegation of the persecution of that Church by the soviets. He will see that, during the earlier years of the Revolution, the soviets were protecting themselves against determined attacks from the Church.

of that crime. Those, however, who are genuinely concerned to preserve the freedom of worship of the voluntary Churches of Britain and America will hardly care to denounce the termination of the religious monopoly of the Orthodox Church of Russia—of a Church, that is to say, which obstinately denied them any freedom of worship.

In any event, the communist and socialist parties of Britain and America advocate, in strict conformity with their basic theory, full freedom of worship to every denomination, and they will establish such freedom. As evidence of good faith, they can point to the fact that, even in the extreme case of the Russian Orthodox Church, the Russian communists have in fact preserved that freedom. The churches have remained open in Russia throughout the eighteen years which the working class has been in power. Anyone can walk into a church in any city in the Soviet Union and hear divine service being conducted according to the elaborate and, to some tastes, exceedingly superstitious ritual of the Orthodox Church. (I myself have done so in cities as far apart as Moscow, Kiev, and Rostov on Don, for example.)[1] It is perfectly true that many, and no doubt very burdensome, restrictions have been, and still are, placed upon the priests and their regular congregations. But these restrictions are an inevitable feature of the struggle by means of which alone the political power and the intellectual (if one can use such a word in this connection) monopoly of the Russian Church were abolished.

Nor was this struggle an easy one. The Russian Church had held a jealous and exclusive power for many centuries. It was not willing to abdicate that power and to become one of a number of voluntary associations able to persuade, if it could, but not to coerce, and having to tolerate the equal right of other religious and lay organizations to existence. In the course of the struggle to dethrone so deeply entrenched a religious monopoly, it was inevitable that harsh blows should be struck. The activities of so formidable and so aggressive an organization had to be curbed

[1] Incidentally, this freedom, both for religious and anti-religious propaganda, is written into the draft of the New Soviet Constitution. Article 124 reads: " To ensure to citizens freedom of conscience the Church in the U.S.S.R. is separated from the State, and the school from the Church. Freedom to perform religious rites and freedom of anti-religious propaganda is recognized for all citizens."

to an extent which will be both unnecessary and undesirable in the case of such very different organizations as the free Churches of Britain and America. Just as the Russian Orthodox Church enjoyed monstrously unfair privileges under the Tsar, so now it has had to submit to a degree of restriction which will be unnecessary, and would be inequitable, in the case of Churches which have never had, or have long relinquished, these pernicious privileges.

It is true that in addition to this struggle with the Church there has been in the Soviet Union a far more open and vigorous repudiation of religious doctrine by those who have ceased to believe than has occurred anywhere else. We have been made familiar by the capitalist Press, although always in a distorted form, with the anti-religious campaigns of the League of the Godless. Many people of genuine goodwill, even though they have recognized that our accounts of the activities of this organization have been exceedingly biased, have felt that much of the anti-religious propaganda which has gone on in the Soviet Union has been offensively crude. Why, many British and American Liberals have been inclined to ask, have the Russian communists adopted this dogmatic, aggressive atheism—this rasping denial of all those traditions of fidelity and worship which form so beautiful a heritage of the race ? Why cannot they silently assent, as we do, to religious ceremonies and institutions in which we have long ceased to believe, but to which we are sentimentally attached ?

It is, I think, seldom realized that communists and socialists find such a view as this even more shocking than their own teaching appears to the religious. The claim of religion to divine revelation is not, and never can be, a matter of indifference. It is a matter of the highest moment for men to decide whether they are in possession of an infallible, because divinely inspired, code of conduct and theory of the universe, or whether, on the contrary, they have to build up such a code and such a theory for themselves.[1] It seems to us that those who have come to the latter conclusion have a positive duty to inform their fellow men of it, and to ask them to put away the intellectually stunting, if

[1] Many sincere Churchmen must surely find the communist and socialist attitude to religion, with its intense realization of the importance of the issues involved, far preferable to the condescending lip service with which their beliefs are at once accepted and dismissed by many liberals of the Western world.

comfortable, beliefs of the childhood of the race. A hypocritical pretence upon the part of the leaders of the community that they believe in the objective, historical truth of mythologies which are manifestly part of the world of fantasy is a betrayal of trust. Mr. and Mrs. Webb, in the work from which we have repeatedly quoted, thus austerely arraign the hypocrisy of many of the religious observances of the Western world:

" It is not with impunity that nations or individuals, outgrowing any genuine faith in a personal deity who hears their prayers and governs alike the ocean and the earthquake, the harvest and the hearts of men, can continue to practise rites and accept religious institutions as if they were still believers. No code of conduct professedly based on the supposed commands of an all-powerful ruler will outlast the discovery that it has, in fact, no such foundation. One result of this widely spread equivocation is seen in the practical abandonment at the present time by millions of young persons in Europe and America, not only of Christianity, but also, along with it, of nearly all the commandments by which their parents were guided, without acquiring any substitute."

The warning contained in the latter sentences of this impressive passage should not be overlooked. The moral and ethical standards which have been built up in the last twenty centuries of human history are very imperfect. But they are incomparably better than no standards at all. They are, however, closely bound up with religious doctrines and sanctions. Now that those doctrines, and consequently their sanctions, are, whether we like it or not, fading from the minds of men, we run the grave risk, if we equivocate any longer, of discrediting all moral and ethical codes of conduct in the eyes of those who discover for themselves the unreality of supernaturalism. It is, it is often forgotten, a part of the anti-religious teaching of the Soviet Union, it is indeed a part of all communist and socialist teaching, to inculcate a very definite code of conduct, built upon rational, social and terrestrial, instead of traditional and supernatural, sanctions. And this code of conduct is at least as strict as the code which is inculcated, and is far stricter than the code which

Hs

is observed, in modern Britain and America. (Hence the surprise and disappointment over the Soviet attitude to life expressed by those indescribably superficial thinkers of the West who suppose that the time has come when men need no ethical or moral standards to help them to live in peace and decency with their fellow men.)

Communism and socialism are, in fact, more than economic and political systems. Since the effort to achieve these systems is occupying a whole epoch of history, and is absorbing the life work of whole generations of the intellectually and morally most alert men and women, communism and socialism become moral and intellectual disciplines, by which men may guide and evaluate their whole conduct.

To sum up: there is reason to suppose that religious belief will fade as and when men achieve as great a control over social and economic forces as they now possess over natural forces. We reserve the right to proclaim this view and to inform the whole population of the probable origins of religious belief, and of the part which organized religion has played in modern history.

But we are firmly opposed to any attempt forcibly to eradicate religious belief from men's minds: for we believe that this would be impossible to-day and unnecessary to-morrow. Consequently we avow the necessity of maintaining freedom of worship for every religious denomination, and, what is more, are willing to shoulder the arduous task of preventing any denomination from curtailing the religious liberties of other denominations, or the liberty of expression of those who have ceased to hold religious convictions. In order to carry out such a policy of liberty of opinion in religious matters, the political and psychological grip of certain formidable, aggressive, and intolerant religious monopolies, of which the Russian Orthodox Church was a leading example, must be broken. Finally, socialist and communist teaching inculcates a code of conduct at least as strict, although far more rational, than that aimed at by religious doctrine.

Chapter XX

Socialism and Peace

ONE of the highest and one of the most disputed of the claims of socialism is that it alone can bring permanent peace to the world. It is necessary to examine this claim with great care, for it amounts to nothing less than the allegation that the abolition of capitalism is a condition necessary to the continuance of human civilization.

On what grounds is it asserted that capitalism must inevitably produce war ? The purpose of this chapter is to state the precise objective grounds of this assertion; to show that the allegation that war is one of the necessary products of capitalism is not a mere piece of abuse, but is based upon a careful analysis of the way in which this economic system works. The general description of the workings of the capitalist system which we gave in Part I took us to the conclusion that as soon as a capitalist system has passed a certain point in its development it becomes impossible for it to dispose of all the consumers' goods which it could, and on occasion actually does, produce. The system can get out of the difficulty for a time by using a higher and higher proportion of its resources for the production of new means of production. But an increased sale of consumers' goods is ultimately a condition for the profitable operation of the new means of production which are so produced. Hence the ultimately decisive defect of capitalism is an inability to sell an adequate quantity of consumers' goods. A lack of adequate markets is the chronic, incurable, ever-growing difficulty with which every capitalist, and group of capitalists, is to-day visibly and undeniably contending.

So far, however, we have considered capitalism more or less in the abstract: we have considered it as a system. We have not yet considered it in particular detail as it exists in the contemporary world. We have considered " Capitalism " with a big " C," rather than contemporary capitalism as it exists in the world of 1936. Immediately, however, that we apply our analysis to the contemporary world we see that it needs qualifications. Our analysis would be exactly true of a perfectly capitalist world: of a world, that is to say, which had become a perfectly unified and evenly developed capitalist system. But the existing world is not perfectly unified economically, is not unified at all politically, and is most unevenly developed. Certain parts of it (e.g. parts of Asia and Africa) are not effectively in the capitalist stage of development at all. They are in various pre-capitalist stages of development, ranging all the way from the ancient gentile stage which we discussed in Chapter XVII, through complex feudal stages, to the characteristic transitional stages which mark the emergence of capitalism (e.g. India: the coastal region of China).

Moreover, those parts of the world which are already definitely capitalist have developed, and are developing exceedingly unevenly. Japan is rushing in a few years through the stages which it took Western countries decades to traverse. Britain is in the extreme old age of the system. Indian capitalism is being born into a world in which capitalism as a whole is already in full decline. Hence, Indian capitalism shows symptoms of decay, although it is hardly out of the womb. American capitalism, after sowing its grandiose wild oats, has suddenly lost its youth. German capitalism has come to a perilous old age, for it lacks those advantages with which other capitalisms have prolonged their days. No two capitalist communities are at the same point of economic development. Finally, one large part of the world, the Soviet Union, has passed out of the capitalist stage and is building up a socialist economic system of planned production for use.

Upon this sharp economic differentiation between different areas of the world is superimposed the fact that each one of the fully capitalist communities is under separate, wholly independent, management: that it is a politically sovereign State. *Moreover, each one of these fully evolved capitalist communities has acquired control over one or more of the under-developed, pre-capitalist areas, while the socialized area of the world is fully independent.* It is to this highly complex, and ever-changing, world situation that we must apply our analysis of the dynamics of a system of production for profit.

Let us first envisage the problem from the point of view of any one fully developed capitalist State. If we do so, we shall see at once that a possibility of relief from capitalism's supreme difficulty of finding a market presents itself.

We saw that the essential nature of the system prevents it disposing of its potential output of goods to its own population.[1] No capitalism, neither that of Britain, nor of America, nor of Japan, can provide itself with an adequate market for its output of goods. *It must, therefore, seek markets outside itself.* If it can find and retain them, a temporary solution, at any rate, for its essential difficulties will have been found. It will be possible both to hold down the purchasing of the home population, so as to make the production of new means of production possible and profitable, and yet to allow of the operation of these new means of production when they come into being. For the output of consumers' goods, which cannot be sold at home, can under these conditions be sold abroad. This is the explanation of that desperate search for markets in which every capitalist State is so visibly engaged.[2]

An objection at once presents itself. We say that the goods can be sold abroad. But how can they be paid for? For paid for they must be, or else they might just as well be given away at home. In principle, they can only be paid for by the return sale of goods to the exporting community. All sales must be, ultimately, but one half of an exchange. Therefore the capitalist State which solves its difficulties by selling abroad those goods which it cannot sell at home must sooner or later accept payment for them in the form of goods sent into itself. But how can the exporting capitalism take in such a return flow of goods? If its population has not the purchasing power to buy the goods which they themselves have produced, no more will they have the purchasing power to buy the equivalent goods which their outside customer must send them.

This objection is sound in principle. But we are now dealing,

---

[1] The reader will recall that this inability arises not through a failure to distribute sufficient total purchasing power, but because that purchasing power is distributed so unevenly that first the available output of consumers' goods, and, then, consequentially, the output of means of production, cannot be disposed of.

[2] The foreign markets sought can be, the reader should note, either for consumers' goods or for means of production. For a new outlet for means of production will relieve the congestion at home just as much as will an outlet for consumers' goods. For it will remove some of the means of production which would, if they were left at home, soon choke the market with their products.

not with questions of principle and general theory, but with questions of particular application. And a method for over-coming this difficulty, for a period, has been devised. It is possible for a particular capitalist community to sell to the rest of the world more goods than it buys from the rest of the world. It does so by means of taking payment in terms of IOUs, instead of by immediate payment in terms of equivalent goods. It takes its payments in the form of claims, cashable at some future date. It lends to its foreign customers the money necessary for the purchase of its own goods. (For all these are but different ways of describing what is fundamentally the same transaction.) Thus, for the time being, a solution is found for the dilemma of every capitalist community, namely that at one and the same time it dreads being paid for its exports, and yet cannot possibly give them away.

We must next distinguish between exports to other more or less highly developed capitalist communities and exports to under-developed or pre-capitalist parts of the world. It is apparent that the postponement of payment by way of a return flow of goods which is possible in the case of exports to another capitalist community is limited. For this second capitalist com-munity will have its own problem of markets. It will be searching more or less desperately, according to its stage of development, for outlets for its own products. Hence, in spite of the increase in purchasing power which its population will have received by way of the money loaned (in one way or another) from the first community, it will soon be unable to take any more imports unless it can itself sell more abroad.

But this is by no means equally true of undeveloped parts of the world. Their supreme advantage to capitalism is that they cannot yet produce very much. They lack the essential means of production. Accordingly, the great developed capitalist communities can lend them the money with which to buy the goods with which to build up their own productive systems. And, *until this is done*, these undeveloped areas will not need to send out any return flow of goods. This is the indispensable function performed by undeveloped areas in the economy of a capitalist world. They serve as sponges which can absorb the surplus pro-duction, unsaleable at home, of the developed communities. And they absorb these goods on credit, by paying over not actual goods or cash, but IOUs or claims on their future wealth.

This is a real relief to the recurrent crises of glut to which every capitalism is subject. It is a substantial relief because it may take many years to build up the productive resources of an undeveloped area. And during all this time such an area can be absorbing, on credit, goods from some otherwise choking capitalism. These goods will be, the reader will observe, predominantly means of production, not consumers' goods; they will consist of railway materials, machinery for power plants, textile machinery, and the like.

This possibility of prolonging the life of a particular capitalist community by undertaking the development of some precapitalist area of the world is further evidence, the reader will observe, that the sole function which capitalism can perform is the creation of a community's outfit of productive equipment. For once this task is accomplished at home the only thing which the system can do is to repeat the process somewhere else. Hence, in the later stages of capitalism a system has arisen by which one part of the world industrializes another. Each fully developed capitalism has acquired a ring of satellites revolving in its economic orbit, and providing it with those external markets which have become necessary to its survival.

This process has involved the political linking together of the pre-capitalist areas with one or other of the great capitalist communities. For this particular type of trade, as distinct from the ordinary reciprocal trade carried on between communities in approximately the same stage of economic development, almost inevitably involves the political control of the pre-capitalist area by the capitalist centre which is undertaking its development. For, as we have seen, this development may take decades to accomplish, and during all that time it must be conducted on credit. Hence, a formidable debt to the capitalist centre is piled up. Anxiety for the safety of this debt must be acute unless some form of political control over the debtor has been established.

Moreover, this process of the political linking together of a fully developed capitalism with one or more undeveloped areas of the world, the markets of which are thereby more or less monopolized to it, is closely associated with that profound change, in the nature of the capitalism of each great empire, which we described in Chapter VII. It is another aspect of that ever-growing concentration of the ownership of the means of production into fewer and fewer hands which both intensifies the maldistribution of purchasing power and, in the end, changes and dislocates the whole capitalist system by eliminating effective competition from whole spheres of production. In a word, the political acquisition of undeveloped territories, and the monopolization of their markets, is only the other face of that process of monopolization which is going on within every capitalism. Capitalism is transforming itself before our eyes from a system of competition into a system of monopoly. And this change in the economic structure of each capitalist empire is inextricably associated with the portioning out of all the undeveloped areas of the world as preserved markets for this or that empire. The political monopolization of markets follows, and is built upon, the economic monpolization of particular spheres of production.

If this latter process of economic monopoly had not, inevitably, taken place, then we might have conceived of an enormous number of separate firms, scattered throughout the industrial areas of the world, peacefully competing for the opportunities to develop the pre-capitalist areas. But the competitors are now for the most part vast national monopolies or semi-monopolies, so that their competition has become, in effect, the rivalry of their respective empires. Thus the present stage in the development of capitalism, in which the struggle for economic expansion and new markets between rival empires visibly dominates the world situation, can be called either imperialism or the monopoly stage of capitalism.

The development of the pre-capitalist areas of the world by the export to them of means of production (and some consumers' goods) financed by loans is the one method by which a capitalism which has grown into the monopolistic stage can obtain the relief of an outlet for its otherwise unsaleable products. It can be, however, the reader will observe, only a temporary relief. For, again, unless the goods are to be given away, the loans out of which they were purchased must some day be repaid.[1] And no one has ever been able to suggest how this can be done. Hence the capitalist exporters in one sense only *seem* to be paid by the undeveloped country. All they are really given are IOUs or claims, *and these claims can never be collected.* The interest on these ever-mounting claims can for a long time be paid, however, and so long as this is the case the debtor feels that his claim is sound.[2] But the claim itself is uncollectable.

The underlying reality is not apparent at the time at which the export of goods is made and it may take decades to emerge into view. Hence the finally contradictory character of the whole transaction does not prevent it being repeatedly made, and does not prevent it providing a real, although temporary, relief for a choking capitalism. For example, the British capitalist system would have stifled to death under a mountain of its own unsaleable products in the late eighteen-eighties had not this form of relief been resorted to on the largest scale.[3]

Finally, the export of their capital, mainly in the form of means of production, to undeveloped parts of the world which have passed under their control, enables the capitalists of the

---

[1] It is usual to speak of this whole process as the export of capital, and so it is. But the phrase " the export of capital " does not give us any clear idea of what is happening. Is it, for example, money or goods that is being exported ? The answer is that it is both, but that the money is, in this case, only the symbol of the goods. What happens is that a firm in the City of London hands 10 million pounds to a South American republic, the republic then spends the 10 million pounds on buying, say, railway materials from British iron and steel firms. But the financial transaction is, from our analytic point of view, merely a complication. All that has really happened is that the British capitalists have supplied the republic with means of production to the value of 10 million pounds while agreeing to postpone their right to be sent goods to the value of 10 million pounds in return. But, be it noted, since interest on the loan is charged, a *claim* for much more than 10 million pounds' worth of goods to be sent to Britain, from the republic, is established.

[2] For decades at a time the interest on such loans is often met by the simple expedient of contracting new loans. Hence, the absurd and familiar spectacle of the capitalists of some wealthy empire lending an undeveloped country the money with which to pay the interest on some former loan !

[3] The finally contradictory character of capitalist foreign trade has probably become apparent to many of the shrewder leaders of the capitalist world to-day. But they cannot possibly stop such trading, for if they did so the entire capitalist economic structure would collapse. Hence they go on piling up utterly uncollect-able debts, piously hoping that the interest payments will at any rate last their time. This is but one aspect of the ever-increasing tendency of capitalist trade to degenerate into gambling and then swindling.

major empire to reap otherwise unrealizable profits. For the capital when it arrives in the colonial area is typically employed in the extraction of some tropical raw material—such as rubber, for example. Partly because of the extreme exploitation of the native labour which is employed, and partly because of the semi-monopoly which the possession of the main sources of supply of the commodity may give it (as in the case of the British and Dutch empires with rubber), capital so employed can often earn astronomical returns. Hence, colonies have become a vitally important source of profit, and so of new capital, as well as a necessary market for goods. This extremely important aspect of imperialism is always conveniently ignored by the spokesmen of the possessing empires. These gentlemen (see Sir Samuel Hoare's well-known speech at Geneva in September 1935) always assure the world that the empires which they represent are only too ready to sell to all comers the tropical raw materials which they possess. So they are. But this does not help the excluded capitalists (the German capitalists, for example). In the first place (see note below), these capitalists cannot buy because they are now increasingly excluded from the only available markets in which they could sell. But the excluded capitalists do not merely desire the right to buy raw materials at their present owners' semi-monopoly prices. What they want is the right themselves to possess some of the sources of the supply of these raw materials and consequently to share in the very great profits to be made from their extraction. These, in briefest outline, are the economic causes of that striking phenomenon of our times, which we call imperialism.

The imperative need of every capitalism, when it has reached the monopoly stage, for perpetual expansion into new markets, both for its otherwise unsaleable consumers' goods and its otherwise unusable capital, is the basic cause of modern war.[1] For

[1] A hard-pressed empire may feel that it needs colonies chiefly in order to secure a supply of raw materials (as Germany does to-day, for example). But this is, in the last analysis, consequential upon her lack of adequate access to markets. For if she possessed these, and could therefore secure by selling her goods in them the wherewithal with which to buy, she would have no difficulty whatever in buying raw materials; for the sellers are anxious to sell if they can get paid. Hence, even in those extreme cases when the empire in question feels its difficulties as an inability to buy rather than to sell, the lack of sufficient access to markets is the essence of the matter.

it is not difficult to show that the attempt of several highly developed capitalist communities simultaneously to satisfy their need for such expansion must bring them into acute conflict. This is one of those propositions in which the content of truth is continually growing. It was always true that the attempt of the most highly developed capitalisms to seize and hold undeveloped areas might lead to disputes between them, and did in fact frequently lead to such disputes. But, compared to the conflicts which to-day convulse the world, these conflicts were soluble without a resort to war. For two factors in the world situation have changed, and are still changing, for the worse. First, both the number and the needs of the fully developed capitalist empires have sharply increased: second, the opportunities for satisfying the increased needs of the increased number of empires have sharply diminished. These two factors tend to bring the empires more rapidly into collision with each other. Moreover, the populations of the undeveloped areas of the world have turned recalcitrant. It is no longer easily possibly to take, or in some cases even to hold, great pre-capitalist tracts for the relief of this or that stifling empire. The inhabitants of such lands are more and more showing that they intend to become something more than conveniences for distressed empires. Hence, a whole series of conflicts between each empire and its subject peoples, or the peoples which it intends to make into its subjects, is engendered.

Comparing, for example, the world of the eighteen-eighties with the world of to-day, we notice that, while at that time there were only two fully developed capitalist empires, there are now, at the lowest computation, six. In the eighteen-eighties both British and, although to a lesser extent and for different reasons, French capitalism had exhausted their main possibilities of interior development and had had to turn outwards towards imperialist expansion, if they were to survive. Neither of them was destitute of colonial possessions, but both felt acutely the need to acquire more. Compare this situation with that of 1935 when four more capitalisms, namely those of Germany, America, Italy and Japan have also reached, or are now reaching, this point of internal saturation. Moreover, in spite of the acquisition by both France and Britain of vast and succulent colonies during the past fifty years, the needs of these two original empires for still more expansion are perhaps as great as ever. For their own internal productive forces have grown as rapidly as have their empires. Yet their need for expansion is small compared to the needs of such capitalisms as Japan, Italy, and, above all, Germany. For these capitalisms find themselves almost (in the case of Germany, quite) without colonial possessions, and yet equipped with well-developed productive apparatuses which must certainly choke them with unsaleable products if they cannot be given empty areas to fill. So much for the difference between 1880 and 1936 on the side of the numbers, and the intensity of the needs of the imperial powers.

Now compare the two periods in respect of the opportunities available for satisfying these needs. In 1880 the map of Africa was largely blank. A huge, vast, undeveloped continent stretched out to the South of Europe. Asia, also, with the exception of India, lay almost untouched by the Western powers, while South America seemed to offer enormous opportunities to the capitalists of the United States, whenever their own vast internal field of development should be exhausted. The prospect must have seemed one of inexhaustible opportunity. It seemed easy to satisfy the need for expansion of every capitalism which was sufficiently developed to support such claims. There seemed, and, for the moment, there was, enough room for everyone.

To-day, South America has been tilled and retilled by United States capital; nor has the process failed to make the expanding dollar press both against the pound, well entrenched in Argentina and Paraguay, and the nascent capitalisms of the South American republics themselves. All of Asia, with the large exception of China, has become the dominion of one or other of the great empires. And Japan, the newest of these empires, is now attempting to convert China into her own gigantic colony. That process is not taking place easily or without the risk of conflict, for it involves both the prejudice of those British, French, and American interests which were deeply entrenched, although without full political control, in all Eastern China, and the attempt, as yet by no means successful, to subjugate the Chinese people. But it may enable Japanese capitalism to subsist for a time. It is in Africa, however, that the most striking changes have taken place. What was then a virgin continent awaiting the exploiter has now been partitioned and re-partitioned down to the last Abyssinian acre.

Moreover, in those parts of the colonial world which have long been in the possession of one or other of the great empires a counter-movement of national independence has begun. India, the greatest of all colonies, affords the leading example of such a counter-movement by which a people attempts to free itself from a helpless subservience to an empire. The Indian movement towards independence has taken various shapes during the past thirty years. It has risen and fallen in intensity. But it has never disappeared. The British imperialists have had to meet it either with repression or concession. As usual, they have done both. And so far they have succeeded, though with great difficulty, in preventing the Indian people from making British rule in India impossible. But they have only succeeded in doing so by employing methods of coercion so odious that Indian resistance is certain to grow ever more fierce, and also by making concessions to the newly emerged native Indian capitalists. These concessions were necessary to the British in order to divide the Indian nationalist movement, but they have begun perceptibly to diminish the value of India as a colony to British capitalism. (For example, India has been allowed to charge a certain import duty on Lancashire cotton goods, even though giving them a substantial preference as against other imported cottons. Again, a certain amount of native capitalist industry has had to be allowed. It may be that the new Government of India Act, granting certain very limited parliamentary institutions to India, while it will certainly do nothing for the Indian people, will be used by the Indian capitalists to secure an extension of these concessions.)

Another example of substantial concessions being won by a colonial people is that of Egypt. Thus the movement of colonial resistance to capitalist imperialism can and does begin to embarrass the great empires long before particular colonial peoples are strong enough to achieve complete independence. Just when their economic situation requires the maximum extension of

their colonies as areas of exploitation they are forced by difficulties created not only by the ambitions of rival empires but
also by the resistance of their own subject peoples. And naturally
these two types of difficulties interlock. The subject peoples
begin to learn how to play off one empire against another. (As
the Egyptian Nationalists appear to be doing to-day—playing
off Britain and Italy, for example.) Hence, the major possessing
empires, such as the British, are forced towards concessions
which they can ill afford, while the hard-pressed, desperate
empires such as the German, Italian, and Japanese, are forced
into conflict not only with the possessing group of empires, but
with peoples, such as the Abyssinians or the Chinese, in pre-
capitalist stages of development. Thus the conflicts engendered by
the process of all-round expansion upon which every capitalism
is inevitably launched, so soon as it reaches the monopoly stage,
are not confined to wars between themselves. On the contrary,
the conflicts which capitalist imperialism most immediately and
directly engenders are those between a given empire and some
colonial or semi-colonial people. In the case of primitive peoples
like the Abyssinians such conflicts are, it is true, relatively small.
But in the case of the conflicts between vast and highly civilized
peoples in pre-capitalist stages of development, such as the
Chinese and Indian peoples, and, in these cases, the Japanese and
British Empires, they may prove to be some of the most serious,
prolonged and terrible conflicts of our epoch.

If, then, the relatively tolerable needs for expansion of a few
empires, in a relatively empty world, and without the present
degree of colonial resistance, produced many small wars, and
finally produced the Great War itself, what are the future
possibilities of peace in the present epoch of ever-growing
colonial resistance, and of many empires, some of them desperate
for expansion, in an almost completely occupied world? How
can we avoid the conclusion that if the present world of rival
imperialisms is allowed to continue in existence there is no
chance of peace? How can we doubt that whatever may have
been the causes of the wars of the past, the effective present
cause of war is the imperative need for economic expansion in

general, and for markets in particular, experienced by every fully developed capitalist empire as it enters the monopolist stage in its development?

It may, or may not, be true that if this present cause of war were removed there would remain other causes. But the fact that no capitalism, once it has reached the monopolist stage of development, can continue to exist without ceaseless economic and so political expansion, is a fact which in itself fully explains both why the wars of the recent past have occurred, and why to-day a new war is visibly almost upon us. Hence it is necessary to remove this cause of war in order to make peace possible. When that has been done we will tackle the other causes of war, if they turn out to exist. But, until that is done, every other attempt to abolish war must be unavailing. For here is a cause quite sufficient in itself to make war inevitable so long as it continues to exist.

It is important to notice that the word " inevitable " is here used with precision. The need for economic expansion of every monopoly-capitalism is absolute. Unless more and more un-developed territories can be made available to it every capitalism must collapse soon after reaching the monopoly stage of develop-ment. There do not remain in the world sufficient undeveloped territories to satisfy the minimum requirements for existence of all the capitalist empires. No re-partition of the available terri-tories can possibly solve the problem. Some empire must be so deprived that the collapse of its economy is certain. It can never be to the interest of any capitalist empire tamely to await its own collapse without attempting to win by force of arms areas for economic expansion from its rivals.

Hence war, so long as we allow the world to be dominated by such empires, but only so long, is in the strictest sense of the word inevitable. It must come, that is to say, even if all the imperial governments concerned behave with perfect good sense, goodwill, intelligence, and moderation. There is nothing which such governments can do, short of acquiescing in their own extinction, which can permanently prevent war.

The above reasoning does not mean, however, that the ques-tion of the more or less rational behaviour of capitalist govern-ments is unimportant. For if they behave irrationally, if, for example, they become slaves to the nationalist sentiments which they themselves have excited, so that they cannot make concessions even when they would, then war will break out much earlier than it need. And, in fact, our existing capitalist governments do exhibit many irrational characteristics. Thus contemporary wars always appear to arise, and in a sense do actually arise, from the mistakes, or crimes, of the governments concerned. But this does not alter the fact that even perfectly wise and benevolent governments, if they were compelled to maintain the existing world system of competing capitalist imperialisms, could not prevent war.

The above analysis of, first, the inevitability of the birth of imperialism out of the necessities of any fully developed capitalism, and of war as the equally determinate result of a world situation dominated by the rival activities of several formidable and desperate capitalist empires, constitutes the most important application of communist and socialist theory to existing reality. It is an analysis which, in one part or another, is admitted by many capitalist writers themselves. Indeed, no more than common observation is needed to see that the rivalries of the six existing major capitalist empires are leading the world to war. But nothing but a comprehension of the way in which capitalism works can explain what is the cause and object of these rivalries and why they must, if they are not ended, inevitably lead the world to war.

The basic argument of this book is, however, that the world system of these rival imperialisms can be ended. It can be ended by the peoples of each empire taking the means of production from their respective capitalists and organizing socialist economic systems of the type which we have described in Part I. If we do this before the present series of acute inter-imperialist conflicts breaks out into world war, then we can certainly preserve the peace of the world. There is nothing in the least inevitable about the outbreak of war. We have only to take the necessary steps to make such an event, on the contrary, impossible. But these steps do, in the end, involve the dispossession of the capitalists of the great empires and the ending of the system of production for profit. In a word, capitalism inevitably produces war. But this does not mean that war is inevitable. For there is nothing inevitable about the continuance of capitalism.

We must now turn to the other and positive side of our original claim. Can it be shown that a socialist economic system of planned production for use will show no tendency to drive communities which adopt it into war ? We have seen that the inability of a profit-making system, when it has developed into the monopolist stage, to distribute enough purchasing power to its own citizens to clear the market of consumers' goods, drives every capitalist empire to seek, and to fight to the death, for new markets, areas of exploitation and fields for every type of expansion. As we saw in Part I, no such inability can arise under a system of planned production for use. Whatever other difficulties such systems may suffer from, they can never be unable to put into the hands of their own citizens every single consumable good which they can get produced. No problem of finding markets can ever arise in a socialist economic system. The illimitable market provided by the infinitely extensible needs of their own citizens will always absorb every single good and service which can be produced.

Hence, such communities can experience no need whatever for the acquisition of undeveloped areas of the world. On the contrary, the addition to them of undeveloped areas might well appear to their citizens as a heavy burden: they would feel that, while it was no doubt their duty to aid the inhabitants of such areas in their arduous task of developing their productive resources, yet they could not, and would not, divert to them more than a certain proportion of their own available plant and labour; for to do so would be to diminish the standard of life to which they themselves might otherwise attain. Thus in a predominantly socialist world the difficulty might be to see that every advanced community took its proper share in the necessary, but heavy, work of aiding the development of the peoples of the backward areas. Far from there being a " grab " for such areas, there might be a certain tendency to avoid a proper measure of responsibility towards them !

Chapter XXI

The World before War

THE last chapter contained an analysis which appeared to account for the fact that war has been a recurrent feature of the capitalist system. Moreover, it was asserted that a socialist system is alone compatible with peace. In this chapter we must examine the present world situation in order to decide whether it appears to confirm this view. Do the various states which make up the contemporary world behave in the way which we should expect them to behave if this analysis were true ? Or is their actual behaviour more readily explicable on the basis of some other hypothesis ?

The dominating factor in the present world situation is the evident intention of three out of the six major capitalist empires to acquire new territories, new privileges, and new advantages— in general, to change the world situation in their favour. These dissatisfied empires are Germany, Japan, Italy.

We have named them in the order of the intensity of their need for expansion and of their power to expand. The three remaining major capitalist empires—France, Britain, and America—do not exhibit an equal desire for expansion and change. Their actions indicate that they have on the whole more to lose than to gain by change. And they are not slow to stigmatize as bellicose all those who do not acquiesce in the present division of the world.[1]

Now if our analysis of the motives which must actuate the governments of highly developed capitalist empires is correct, it should enable us to explain why it is that the rulers of Germany, Japan, and Italy are willing to hazard their existence, as they visibly are, on an attempt to re-divide the world, while the rulers of Britain, France, and America feel no such need. If our analysis is valid, we should expect to find that Germany, Italy, and Japan possessed opportunities for economic expansion

[1] There are many shades of difference within each of these two groups. Moreover, there is little community of interest between the members of either of them. The fact that Germany wishes to expand into Austria does not commend her to Italy. The desire of Great Britain to come to an agreement with Japan over the partition of China into British and Japanese spheres of influence does not endear her to the United States.

which, in relation to their degree of economic development, were small, while Britain, France, and America possessed relatively large opportunities. A glance at the map of the world will inform us that this is in fact the case. But let us examine the situation of the six empires in turn.

The most extreme case of a disparity between internal economic development and opportunity for expansion is afforded by Germany. The German capitalists possess the second most highly developed apparatus of production in the world (second only to that of the United States). Her capitalists must, if they are not to be ruined by the exorbitantly expensive idleness of their vast means of production, pour forth an enormous torrent of goods of all kinds. And who is to buy these goods ? No German capitalist is under the delusion that they can be disposed of at home, for more than a short period, so long as the population's purchasing power is held down to the level necessary to the existence of capitalism. The only possible way in which the immense and superb productive apparatus of Westphalia, of Central Germany, of Berlin, and of Silesia can be kept going on a capitalist basis is for the German capitalists to undertake the development of several of the undeveloped parts of the world. There is no other possibility of preventing this apparatus from eating off its head in an idleness so expensive that it must ruin its owners.

This disparity between Germany's economic development and her opportunities of expansion arose before the war. It is, indeed, no more than an over-simplification to call this disparity the cause of the last war. German capitalism is strongly and highly developed, partly because its development started later than that of Britain, France, and America; for the German capitalists, learning from the experience of others, achieved with unequalled swiftness a very high technical level. But for the same reason the German capitalists came to need opportunities for economic expansion only after the best of those opportunities had been seized by the firstcomers, namely France and Britain.

The German capitalists had in general to be content with the leavings of the undeveloped continents. But they were not, and could not, be content with such leavings, if they were to survive as capitalists. They had to have, not the worst, but the best fields for colonial development, for they had the most, not the least, developed productive system. It could be sustained by the largest markets alone.

The war of 1914 to 1918 was, in the last analysis, and besides being many other things as well, the formidable and almost successful attempt of the German capitalists to bring the territorial division of the world, and the general balance of world power, into harmony with their ever-growing economic predominance. But that attempt failed. By means of a world-wide coalition which came to include every other capitalist empire, and its peripheral states (except Austria-Hungary, which was destroyed), Germany was defeated. Accordingly the redivision of the world which actually took place after the war, instead of ending the disparity between the German capitalists' productive power and their opportunity of economic expansion, vastly intensified that disparity. Germany was stripped of even those colonies which she had been able to acquire. And her armed power, including her navy, and with it her ability to penetrate economically into regions like South America or China, which had not become the exclusive possessions of any one of the great empires, and to protect the interests which she might thus acquire, was destroyed. Yet the basic capacity to produce and, consequently, the imperative need for expansion into world markets of her capitalists were only slightly diminished.

What should we expect to be the consequences of these events? We should expect that, so long as the productive apparatus of Germany remained in the hands of her capitalists to operate on the basis of a system of production for profit, the German capitalists *must* make a new attempt to acquire markets. We should expect that they must make this attempt, however desperate the venture might seem, either to the prospects of their own survival or to the survival of capitalist civilization as a whole.

For there would be only these two alternatives to a war waged by the German capitalists for the re-division of the world: first, their own extinction as capitalists, and the voluntary handing over of their means of production to the German people to operate on the basis of production for use; or, second, the voluntary handing over by the other capitalist powers of markets to the German capitalists. And there is no record in all human history of anything remotely analogous to either of these events having taken place.[1]

The reader will see that we have in fact described the position of Germany. Her intensive rearmament, the enslavement of the German people to the one purpose of promoting military power, the ceaseless attempts of German diplomacy to break up the coalition of her opponents, are precisely the phenomena which we should expect to observe if the hypothesis stated above is valid. We can now understand that so long as Germany remains a capitalist state, there is nothing for her to do except to make a second and even more desperate bid for that world power which can alone give her adequate opportunity of economic expansion. Before our eyes Germany is preparing for such an attempt. No other hypothesis can account for her present actions. The hypothesis upon which we are working fully accounts for them.

Now let us take the case of Japan. Japanese capitalism is a much younger growth: her capitalists have only lately reached the stage in which they require economic expansion as a necessity of their existence. But they have reached it, and their consequent behaviour has become just what the behaviour of the British, the French, the German, the American, and every other capitalist class has always been in a similar situation. They possessed, five years ago, comparatively insignificant colonial areas for their exploitation. They had not, like Germany, lost their colonies in unsuccessful war, but they were too young to have been in a position to acquire, or to need, colonies, during the period in which most of the world was parcelled out.

When, therefore, the Japanese capitalist class came to maturity they were confronted by a world almost completely pre-empted by the original capitalist empires. But, knowing that their very existence as capitalists was at stake, they have thrust their way outward, no matter what the cost and what the risk. They have several times brought the world to the verge of war: but they have for the time being been enabled to acquire the vast undeveloped area of North China without producing a general inter-imperial war. For they had the enormous good

[1] For the retention of these markets is just as essential to the existence of the victorious capitalists as their acquisition is to the existence of the defeated capitalists. This is why no lasting " deal " or compromise between them is possible.

fortune of geographical proximity to this the last considerable pre-capitalist area which was not fully dominated by any one great empire. The hypothesis that every capitalist system, when it comes to a certain stage of development, can only continue to exist if it acquires outlets for its products by the acquisition of undeveloped areas, alone accounts for the recent and present behaviour of the Japanese capitalists.

Finally, how does this hypothesis account for the recent (1935) act of aggression of the Italian capitalists ? The map of Africa proffers us the explanation. We see that the Italian colonies consisted of wretched strips and patches, the mere selvedge of the African dominions of France and Britain. (Belgium and Portugal themselves had far more !) In " the grab for Africa " the Italian capitalists received the typical poor relation's portion; and it was, on the basis of the rules of the capitalist game, no more and no less than their due. For the Italian capitalists have never been more than poor relations of the three supreme European capitalist groups, namely the British, the German and the French. Hence the Italian capitalists could not lay effective claim to the extensive colonies of France, still less to the vast possessions of Great Britain.

Italian capitalism, however, though comparatively small, is not young. It has reached a fairly high degree of development. Hence it has begun to experience acutely the inevitable need for expansion. And the peculiarly arid and depressing strips of desert which it alone possessed offered no such opportunities. There was a real and typical disparity between the comparatively small, but considerably developed, Italian capitalism, and its extremely meagre opportunities for expansion. This disparity produced its invariable consequences. The Italian capitalists saw that they must expand or collapse. Like everyone else, they preferred the chance of survival, however desperate, to certain extinction. Their chief executive proclaimed the customary sacred mission. The attack upon Abyssinia was coldly undertaken.

As I write, it is not yet quite certain that this particular effort of a choking capitalism to hack its way out will not provoke an inter-imperial war. But the possibility that it will not arises only from the circumstance that Italy was able to find the one last remaining corner of Africa which had not yet been formally allotted to any of the great empires. But now that Abyssinia has gone, there is not one African acre left in the possession of the Africans.[1]

Now let us turn our attention to the other and comparatively satisfied group of empires, Britain, France, and the United States. An explanation for British satisfaction, based upon our hypothesis, is certainly not hard to discover. British capitalism is in 1936 in the least difficult, though not the most secure, position of any. How could it be otherwise when it possesses incomparably the largest and most useful markets and opportunities for expansion ?

The resultant relative prosperity of British capitalism is ceaselessly emphasized by every one of its spokesmen, from the present Prime Minister, Mr. Baldwin, to the humblest announcer of the British Broadcasting Corporation. " O Lord, we thank thee that we are not as other men," has become the reverberating anthem of the British Isles. An impenetrable and terrifying self-satisfaction has settled upon Britain. It is so easy, and it is, in itself, so true, to say that the comparative economic stability and, for about half of the population,[2] comparative plenty of Britain compare favourably with conditions in any other part of the capitalist world. But no hint is allowed to penetrate to the British people of the fact that their relative good fortune has been alone secured by the direct or indirect subjection to them of almost a quarter of the population of the world.[3] We are never allowed to know by those who control, in a monopoly of now unparalleled perfection, every considerable channel of publicity that those social services and other amenities, of which we ceaselessly boast, are made possible by the extreme degradation of the people of a whole sub-continent, such as India, and of a hundred other races throughout the world. Nor, when we compare our lot with that of the peoples of other capitalist states, with the lot of the Italian, the Czech or the German people, for

[1] With the doubtful exception of Liberia.
[2] See the figures of British income distribution on pp. 321–31.
[3] The British Empire contains some 450 million persons out of a world population of just under 2,000 millions.

example, is it ever breathed that it is by shutting their capitalists out from the exploitation of the races subject to ours that we have achieved our boasted advantages.

Moreover, the British people are given no inkling of the fact that the German and Italian, and for that matter almost every other, people are taught by their capitalists that the undoubted advantages enjoyed by the British are not the result of superior virtue but of successful greed. They are taught that the British have shut out everyone else from almost every part of the world worth having; that every advantage enjoyed by the British people could be conceded to the Germans and Italians by their capitalists—if only they had half what their British rivals possess.

Peace, our statesmen never tire of telling us, and not any sordid question of British interests, is the grand and holy objective of British policy. But we are never allowed to realize that what peace means in the contemporary world is the right of the British capitalists peacefully to possess those markets and opportunities of expansion which alone sustain them, and for want of which the other deprived capitalist groups must soon collapse. Our rulers are not indeed so foolish as to believe their own propaganda: they know that they must, sooner or later, be called upon to defend their vast possessions against the desperate assault of those capitalist empires which cannot any longer exist without expansion, and they are arming intensively for the inevitable struggle of life and death. But they use the fact that they already have possession of the spoils, and will merely have to defend them, as proof of their own guileless pacifism, and of the outrageous, unprovoked aggression of everyone else. The perfect incomprehension of the opinions, needs, struggles and passions of others exhibited by the contemporary leaders of opinion in Britain must dismay every Englishman who sincerely loves his country. And every British communist and socialist most certainly claims to love and to serve his country a thousand times better than do those who prefer to flatter and to deceive her people in the interests of the now tiny group of her owners and rulers.

The actions, and the propaganda, of the British capitalists, their iron determination to hold on to everything they have got, their comparative indifference to acquiring any more, their specious pacifism, and their now hurried preparations for war, are exactly what we should expect to find if our explanation of the motives which must govern the rulers of every capitalist empire is true.

The position of France is in some respects similar to that of Britain. She has a less extended empire; but, on the other hand, the productive resources of her capitalists are smaller. Hence they do not need such wide outlets. Their position is so much more favourable than that of the German or Italian capitalists that it is clear that the French capitalists consider that they have far more to lose than to gain by attempts to re-divide the world. Hence the French capitalist empire, although at the moment (1936) hard pressed by economic difficulties, finds itself in the camp of the satisfied. Nor could we expect anything else upon the basis of our hypothesis. For, after all, the French capitalists actually gained more from the settlement at the end of the last war than did any others.

The presence of the United States in the camp of the relatively satisfied may seem to require explanation. For her capitalists possess the most highly developed productive apparatus in the world, capable of pouring out an unparalleled torrent of goods. Yet the actual overseas possessions of the United States are insignficant. (They are relatively small even if we count, as we should, a large part of Central and South America as in fact, though not in form, an area exclusively reserved for the exploitation of the United States capitalists.) We might expect, then, to find a disparity between the tremendous American productive apparatus and its overseas outlets. The present economic situation of the United States confirms this expectation. For six years now it has been quite impossible either to sell nearly the whole possible output of goods at home —the Brookings Institution estimated (see p. 21) not more than between one half and two thirds—or to find an outlet for them abroad.

Why then do we not find the American capitalists moving strongly towards the opening up of opportunities of expansion by a policy of active imperialism ? The two obvious fields for the American imperialists are South and Central America, and China. The first has been, and is being, intensively cultivated. But it might at first sight be thought surprising that a more vigorous effort has not hitherto been made to cultivate the second. For the Japanese domination of much of China has been at any rate acquiesced in after somewhat feeble protest. America, indeed, is arming intensively as if for an active expansionist policy. (She is not in the remotest danger of attack.) But she has not yet developed the policy for which the armaments will be necessary.

Do we find in this American inaction evidence running counter to the hypothesis that the economic difficulties which every capitalism in its monopoly stage must encounter drive its rulers to attempt a policy of imperialist expansion ? I do not think that the evidence is substantial for the following reasons. It has become impossible for the American capitalists to sell their output at home: but this has only occurred very suddenly and very recently. The enormous extent of the American homeland, and the fact that it had been completely virgin territory, needing development of every kind, had enabled the American capitalists to dispose of a high percentage of their output at home right up till 1929. Then, with unparalleled suddenness, it was discovered that the process of developing the North American continent was nearing completion. American capitalism has almost done its job.

But this tremendous fact could not be, and has not been, immediately realized by the American capitalists themselves. They were and are quite unaccustomed to any other task than the industrialization of their own country. To them it seemed, and seems, inconceivable that this task is no longer there to do. Hence they have not realized that nothing more remains to them but the function upon which their British colleagues have long relied, namely the development, and exploitation, of overseas areas. They have not yet fully realized that their only hope of survival is to turn outwards, enter, even at this late hour, the imperialist race, and find, if they can, new worlds to conquer and to industrialize.

Moreover, we have stated their position in an over-simplified way. The development of North America is even now incomplete. There remain profitable opportunities for the employment of capital at home. It has been possible to effect a measure of recovery without acquiring new markets overseas. But such a recovery will be temporary and partial. There remains no substantial possibility of survival for the American capitalists but the conquest of vast, reserved foreign markets. This fact is, no doubt, now dawning upon the consciousness of their abler thinkers. Indeed, an important explanation of relative American passivity in Eastern Asia may already lie, not in an unawareness of the need for expansion in this field, but in the width of the Pacific Ocean. The military and technical difficulties in the way of an effective American challenge to Japan (and to Britain) in China are very great. These difficulties probably account in a large measure for her failure to make any decisive move. There are numerous signs, however, of persistent and formidable American naval and air efforts to overcome these difficulties. The American navy has had unprecedented sums spent upon it, and the American air force, which is considered by many experts to be the most formidable in the world, is continuously expanded. It may well be that, when these preparations have reached a certain degree of perfection, we may see a remarkable alteration in the world situation. The United States may leave the category of satisfied, relatively pacific, capitalist empires and enter the ranks of the hungry and aggressive.[1]

We must conclude that the present behaviour of the six capitalist empires is readily explicable on the basic hypothesis which we are pursuing, and is inexplicable on any other. The contemporary world presents, however, a still more interesting and significant opportunity for testing the truth of this hypothesis. There exists a non-capitalist community, a community which has passed on to a stage beyond capitalism, namely the Soviet Union. Does, or does not, the Soviet Union reveal by its behaviour that it is subject to the same need for markets, and for economic expansion in general, as do the capitalist empires ?

[1] But there is a substantial expectation that the American people, with their strongly anti-expansionist, and in that sense pacific, tradition will genuinely oppose the imperialism of their capitalists. It could only be by sleight of hand, and the trickery of propaganda, that the American people could be got to fight in a war of aggression.

If it does, then we had better abandon our hypothesis without more ado; if, on the other hand, it does not, we shall be encouraged to believe that we have discovered the true cause of the present behaviour of these empires.

Now the Soviet Union would, if it were a capitalist power, naturally find its place in the hungry and aggressive group (and was expected by all capitalist observers to do so). For the Soviet Union lost important and extensive territories by the post-war settlement. She lost, besides all Poland, important economic outlets in the Baltic, and she failed to gain the main prize for which Tsarism fought—an outlet into the Mediterranean, derived from the possession of Constantinople and the Straits. Hence, if she were still subject to the pressure to expand put upon every capitalist system by its inability to sell its goods at home, we should certainly expect to find her desperately attempting to recover what she had lost, and ready to join with every aggressive power whose interest it was to overturn the existing world settlement. Moreover, the productive apparatus of the Soviet Union has grown since 1918, when that settlement was made, far more rapidly than has that of any other nation. Hence, if she were still governed by the necessities of capitalism she would most urgently require economic expansion.

There is, we must fully recognize, one important counterbalancing factor. The Soviet Union possesses in Soviet Asia large undeveloped areas with the development of which she could, even if she were capitalist, help to occupy her industries. But we know that this would be insufficient to prevent a capitalist Russian government from seeking imperialist expansion. For the empty spaces of Siberia existed before 1917, and they did not prevent the Tsarist government from being intensely imperialistic. As a matter of fact, in the totally new conditions created by the existence in Russia of a planned socialist economic system, the duty and necessity of developing the industries of the Asiatic republics of the Soviet Union have become, in one sense, a heavy burden on the Soviet economy. If it were not for this duty the standard of life of the peoples of European Russia could be more rapidly raised. For the people of European Russia would not find the slightest difficulty in selling to, and consuming, themselves the extra supply of consumers' goods which they could produce with the resources which they now have to devote to industrializing Soviet Asia.

But this statement itself rests upon our general economic hypothesis as to the nature of capitalism and socialism, and so cannot be used as a proof of that hypothesis. When we have made all allowances for the counter-balancing fact of the existence of Soviet Asia, however, is there any doubt that if Russia were still under a capitalist régime, she would now be following the traditional line of Russian imperialism ? She would be pressing southwards towards the Mediterranean, eastwards towards China, southwards again towards India, south-west towards the Balkans, and westwards towards her lost Polish and Baltic provinces.

Observers who have no comprehension of the difference which a new social and economic system makes to a community's foreign policy have in the past sought to read into the Soviet Union's actual policy some subtle continuation of this traditional Tsarist line. They have talked of " Red imperialism " and expected every year to find the Soviet Union behaving in the way in which they knew from experience a capitalist government placed in the Soviet's circumstances would behave.

But of recent years it has become difficult to pretend that the Soviet government is pursuing a policy of imperialist expansion. For the facts are exactly contrary. In the West the Soviet government, far from trying to recover lost provinces, has made a series of pacts of non-agression with the new Baltic States. It has striven persistently to conclude such a pact with Poland, the historic vassal of Russian imperialism. In the South, far from pushing forward the traditional Russian policy of acquiring Constantinople and the Straits, the Soviets have established especially close and cordial relations with Turkey. Indeed, Soviet Russian support and her own military prowess are now Turkey's chief assurance that she will be able to retain the Dardanelles and the Bosphorus. Towards the Balkans it is clear that the Soviets have no expansionist aims. For they have lately established close relations with Roumania, which lies completely across their path towards the South-East; and they have established these relations despite the fact that Roumania holds a large area, Bessarabia, which had been for centuries a part of Russia.

But it is in the Far East that the incomprehensibly pacific nature of Russian policy, if judged on ordinary capitalist standards, has been most strikingly developed. The Soviets inherited as a legacy from Tsarist imperialism the Manchurian railway as the last link in the trans-Siberian system joining the Far East to Western Europe. In 1932 Japanese imperialism, as part of its inevitable expansion, took Manchuria. Here, then, was a typical cause of war. If the Soviet Union had been a capitalist empire, it is almost impossible to believe that war could have been averted. (And such a war was confidently and eagerly awaited by every capitalist observer.[1]) The imperative need of Japanese imperialism for economic expansion had brought it sharp up against the interests of another state. If that other state had been itself an expanding capitalist empire, subject to the same economic pressures and necessities, a collision would have been unavoidable. No capitalist state in the position of the Soviet Union would have been willing, or could have afforded, to withdraw from Manchuria. Relentless economic necessities would have driven it, on the contrary, to press forward. Nothing could have prevented the clash between the two expanding forces. In fact, however, one of the states concerned was a socialist community, totally exempt from these pressures. Hence it was possible for the Soviet Union to withdraw from Manchuria, sell the railway to Japan, and preserve the peace.

But was not this, it may be objected, merely a sign of Soviet Russia's weakness ? Would not any capitalist state in the Soviet's condition have done the same thing in order to avoid fighting at a disadvantage ? The answer to this is that, if Russia's sale of the railway to Japan had been the result of weakness, of an inability to face and fight Japan, she would have lost, not merely the Manchurian railway, but Vladivostock and the whole Maritime province as well ! The truth is that weakness does not, and cannot, avert the necessity of fighting from capitalist states. For, if they yield in small things, they are invariably driven to

---

[1] It is said that the recognition of the Soviet Union by the American Government in 1933 was motivated by a confident belief that the Soviets must immediately engage the Japanese Empire in war, and so fight America's battles for her. It is further suggested that the subsequent and notable cooling in the American Government's attitude to the Soviet Union was in turn due to the Soviet's refusal to play the rôle assigned to her.

yield in big until before long they are compelled to yield their very existence. In the ferocious internecine struggle of capitalist empires a state which begins to make substantial concessions to its neighbours is rightly assumed to be powerless: for it is known that substantial concessions must be fatal to its existence. And powerless states are soon not left even their eyes to weep with.[1]

The concession of the Manchurian railway to Japan was in fact accompanied by the mobilization of formidable Soviet forces in the Far East: forces which succeeded in convincing the incredulous Japanese that here was a concession of a different kind, made not out of weakness, but out of the unique strength of a socialist state, the inner economic stability of which made external expansion unnecessary to it.[2]

The steadfast, energetic, and unremitting peace policy of the Soviet Union has now become one of the most important factors in the world situation. The Soviet Union is able to align herself, not with the necessarily aggressive capitalist states, which like Germany were deprived of large possessions by the last world settlement, but with the relatively satisfied states. For, despite her losses of territory, the Soviet Union, too, is a satisfied state —for her innate constitution is such that she needs no expansion. The hungry and aggressive states cast their eyes both at her and at the possessions of their more fortunate capitalist

[1] Small capitalist states, e.g. Portugal, Denmark, Czecho-Slovakia, exist as clients or semi-protectorates of one or other of the great empires. Thus the first two of the above states exist under the British and the third under the French aegis.

[2] Those who accuse the Soviet Union of Red imperialism, being unable to find in the Far East any evidence which does not directly contradict their accusation, have now shifted their field of vision to Central Asia. We are now told that the growing influence of the Soviet Union in Sinkiang, Outer Mongolia, and throughout Central Asia, is proof of Soviet imperialism. In fact, the undoubted growth of this influence is due in the main to two factors. First, the rapid economic growth of Soviet Central Asia, including, above all, its railway development, of which the building of the Turk-Sib line, and the double tracking of the Trans-Siberian, are only two examples, has inevitably come to dominate, and enormously to assist, the economic life of the peoples of Central Asia outside the Soviet Eastern border. Second, the presence in Western China of a vigorous communist movement, including several successful communist armies, means that communism is taking deeper and deeper root in this whole gigantic area. Finally, this area is pressed upon from the North-East by the invading Japanese imperialists. Hence it is very possible that Soviet influence will grow in this area and that, if the struggle of its people against Japanese imperialism, and the Nanking Government in Eastern China, is successful, parts of this area may become Soviet Republics and join the Soviet Union. We shall then be told, I suppose, that they have been annexed by the Soviet Union !

neighbours. An inevitable community of interest grows up between the relatively satisfied capitalist states, who wish to keep the peace because they wish to keep the spoils, and the Soviet Union, which wishes to keep the peace because she has no need of the spoils. Hence there arise such instruments as the present Franco–Soviet pact of mutual assistance. The Soviet Union is enabled to break the serried ranks of the capitalist powers which have so long opposed her. But the Soviet Union is only enabled to pursue this policy because her socialist economy, with its ability to sell internally every single good it can produce, frees her from any need whatever for imperialist expansion.

We must, then, regard the unique ability of the Soviet Union to pursue a genuinely pacific policy as the supreme confirmation of that view of the cause of contemporary war which we stated in the last chapter.

CHAPTER XXII

War, Nationalism, and Human Nature

THOSE who do not accept the view that modern wars are caused by the economic necessities of capitalism put forward several alternative explanations. The recurrence of war is often ascribed, for example, to the existence of nationalism. Now the existence and the strength, in the contemporary world, of the spirit of nationalism are undeniable facts. What part, then, does nationalism play in the origin of modern war?

In order to answer this question satisfactorily we must enquire what nationalism is; we must enquire when, how and why this important emotional attitude has arisen. Now it is an historical commonplace that the rise of nationalism has occurred simultaneously, and has been associated, with the rise of the capitalist class. Pre-capitalist Europe was divided into states which had little or no relation to the various nationalities which were then just emerging as distinct and self-conscious entities. The feudal landowners, lay and ecclesiastical, who formed the ruling class had little sense of solidarity with the particular peoples over whom they ruled; and they had a considerable sense of solidarity with each other. Partly because of this non-national character of the old feudal governing class, the nascent capitalist class came to represent and to lead their respective peoples or nations. In many places the revolutions by which the capitalist class came to power involved the freeing, not only of the native capitalists from the native feudalists, but also the freeing of the nation as a whole from foreign domination. For the feudal overlords were, as often as not, the representatives of some sprawling feudal empire, the territories of which bore no relation to national boundaries (e.g. the Habsburg Empire).

Such, for example, was the character of the first of all successful capitalist revolutions, the founding of the Dutch Republic by the expulsion of the Spanish. Such was the American Revolution. Such was the Italian Revolution of the nineteenth century, by which an independent capitalist Italy arose on the termination of the Austrian domination. Of such a character was the

Is

slow and distorted emergence to power of the German capitalists. For Germany was only able to become a unified, modern, capitalist state after the power, first of the still semi-feudal Austrian Empire, and then of imperial France, had been cleared out of the way. Moreover, even when, as in the case of the great French Revolution, there was no question of the expulsion of foreign feudalists, the capitalist class when it first effected its revolution was always in danger of attack from the alarmed feudalists of surrounding states. Because of these factors an intensive nationalism inevitably came to be associated with the emergence to power of the capitalist class.

Now the rise of nationalism between, say, 1400 and 1850 was a progressive and beneficial event. The capitalist revolutions with which the process was associated marked long steps forward in the evolution of human society. It was essential that the huge, tyrannous, reactionary, stifling feudal empires should be broken up in order that the creative energies of the peoples of the world should be freed. This is the historical justification of that glorification of the nationalistic spirit which the capitalist class has everywhere undertaken.

But this historical justification of nationalism is by no means valid in the entirely different conditions of the twentieth century. The world no longer consists of young capitalist nation-states struggling to be free. On the contrary, many capitalist nations have themselves become empires which hold down more subject peoples than ever the feudalists managed to acquire. Nothing could be more unjustifiable than to ask men to defend these sprawling and heterogeneous empires in the name of patriotism and love of country. For the patriotism of a dozen subject peoples is perpetually violated by the maintenance of these empires. To invoke, for example, the principle and spirit of nationalism on behalf of the British Empire seems a mockery to the Hindu and the Irishman: and the Moor and the Senegalee sing with a double meaning that verse of the Marseillaise which begins:

> *Quoi ces cohortes étrangères*
> *Feraient le loi dans nos foyers.*

Yet so strong is the tradition of nationalism, and so potent are the modern means of preserving and exciting that tradition, that nationalist sentiment is frequently and successfully used by every capitalist class to reinforce its own position. It cannot be denied that the hold of the nationalist spirit over the minds of the peoples of Western Europe presents one of the great problems which face these peoples in their task of finding their way out of their present plight. But this recognition, both of the strength of nationalism and of the way in which the capitalist class can distort, for its own ends, this often generous emotion, must not make us into nationalists. However strong nationalist sentiment may be, it is necessary to explain to the peoples of the great empires that their patriotism is being used, not to save their own country, but their masters' profits. The immediate denunciation as a traitor to his country of everyone who questions the capitalists' absolute power is evidence that what the capitalists are intent that the people should defend is a country which belongs lock, stock, and barrel to them.

Thus socialists and communists do not question the right of men to defend their country; but we do recommend that they should first acquire a country to defend. Till then we are bound to protest and to struggle against the exploitation of nationalist sentiment by the capitalists for their own benefit. We must assure men that it is neither their duty nor their destiny to be slaughtered in the internecine wars made inevitable by the necessity for economic expansion of every capitalist empire. Such wars can merely settle, and that but temporarily, which of two different national groups of capitalists shall have the opportunities of expansion necessary to their survival. To tell men, when they die in such a cause, that they are dying for their country is a most odious deception.

Contemporary wars are never wars of national liberation; they are seldom wars of national defence. They are essentially wars of imperialist expansion, or, in the case of the possessing states, of imperialist retention. The profound national traditions of the peoples of the West are, however, used effectively by the contending capitalists to mobilize their peoples for willing sacrifice. Thus the existence of nationalism is certainly an aid to those who have to lead the peoples into war in order to maintain themselves as capitalists. But it is certainly not itself the cause of war.[1]

We may turn to the example of the Soviet Union for proof that there is nothing in nationalism, in itself, to cause wars. For it has been a deliberate and important part of the policy of the Soviets to give the fullest scope and encouragement to the hitherto suppressed, and so fervid, nationalisms of the peoples formally subject to the Tsarist Empire. The Usbecks, the Tartars, the Ukranians, the Karelians, and the men of a dozen other of the nations of Eastern Europe or Western Asia, have been actively helped to develop a distinctive national culture of their own. But this has not resulted in any tendency towards the disruption of the Soviet Union. On the contrary, since none of these races are exploited, and each is free to develop its cultural life as much as it likes, the nationalisms of the Soviet Union are complementary, not competitive; they exercise a centripetal instead of a centrifugal influence.

For this side of nationalism, for the aspiration of a suppressed people to emancipate itself and to develop its own proper, distinctive, cultural life, communists and socialists must show comprehension and respect. Moreover, they can now demonstrate from the indubitable evidence of the Soviet Union that the abolition of capitalism alone gives every people the practical opportunity for such national development. The practical support which communists and socialists can thus give to the genuine and profound national instincts of the peoples of the West is to-day a question of great practical importance. For capitalist imperialism, in spite of its ceaseless pretensions to the contrary, has, we repeat, become a profoundly anti-national force. The liberating rôle which capitalism at one time played, came to a final conclusion in 1918. The break up of the Austro-Hungarian Empire was the ultimate achievement of capitalism

---

[1] It is true, however, that nationalist sentiment plays a part in the causation of war. For, as we pointed out above, the nationalism which the capitalists themselves promote sometimes proves unmanageable. It may restrict the possibilities of manœuvre which a given capitalist group might wish to explore, if it had not to consider the frenzied emotions which its own propaganda has excited. But this is a secondary effect consequential upon the basic need for expansion of the contending empires.

in this respect. By it the Czech, and some of the Slavonic peoples, gained their independence.

But now capitalist imperialism has become a wholly enslaving force. For example, an opportunity of survival for the German capitalists is presented by the attempt to reconquer these precariously freed Slavonic peoples, and this attempt is being prepared. Thus the struggle of the smaller peoples of Central and Eastern Europe to retain their independence will be one which every communist and socialist must support. They will not forget, however, to advise these peoples that they can never make their national freedom secure, nor achieve their social freedom, until they take over their means of production and operate them for their own use. But the advisability of doing this does not alter the fact that these peoples need to prevent their re-enslavement by German imperialism. The struggle of the smaller, and now acutely threatened, nations of Europe, and the struggle of the subjected peoples of the other continents, against the great, predatory empires, is an important part of the general struggle for the abolition of capitalism, and so for relief from its torturing wars. For the peoples of the great empires, when they are asked to fight for their countries, are in fact being asked to trample upon the patriotisms of a dozen other races, in order to decide whether their masters, or their " enemies' " masters, shall hold these races in subjection. Moreover, the subjection of one race by another is as injurious for the conquerors as the conquered: the true interests of the British people, for example, are identical with those of the Hindus: the emancipation of the subject nations from foreign domination will make possible the emancipation of the peoples of the great empires from their own capitalist rulers as well.

There is no meaning, then, in so loosely formulated a question as whether nationalism is good or bad. We must always demand that such abstract enquiries descend to historical particulars. We shall be ready to say without hesitation that the emancipation of the nations from the feudal empires was good: that the exploitation of nationalist sentiment on behalf of the great capitalist empires of to-day is bad: that the struggles of the small independent, and striving subject, peoples of the world against these empires are good.

The last cause to be adduced for the occurrence of war by those who do not accept its economic causation is the most general. We are told that wars occur, not because of the need of the capitalist empires for economic expansion, nor because of the existence of nationalist sentiments amongst the population, but because of " human nature." This argument is now advanced both by some of the simplest and by some of the subtlest of those who express opinions on this subject.

The innate combativeness of man is a favourite theme of those whose way of life and professional interests are bound up with the waging of war. The military and naval officer (more especially, perhaps, the retired military and naval officer) frequently elaborates this view. Reflection will suggest, however, that this is a proposition of so general a character as to contain little or no significance. It is perfectly true that men, in common with the other large, carnivorous animals, are combative. It is true that for both men and animals combativeness and courage have had, and still have, a high survival value. But then so much else is also true of human and animal nature, and of the parts of that nature which have survival value. Men and the larger, stronger animals are lazy, timid, erotic, inquisitive and greedy as well as combative. And each of these qualities had or has survival value.

The same type of consideration applies to the argument that our alleged present combativeness is a necessary survival from our relatively recent state of savagery. On this point the evidence of anthropology could hardly be more conflicting. Some savages are extremely combative. Others are extremely pacific. As anthropological research proceeds, almost every conceivable kind of human nature is discovered to exist or to have existed. It seems that human nature is incomparably more variable than we had supposed. The types of conduct which different men in the same circumstances, and the same men in different circumstances, exhibit seem inexhaustible in number and variety. It is hard to attach much importance to a view which bases itself upon the existence of one particular, fixed " human nature," which will in all circumstances produce a particular result.

In recent years, however, a far more elaborate argument, seeking to demonstrate that modern war is caused by the innate nature of man, has been adduced. Some psychologists of the psycho-analytical school contend that the effective cause of war is to be found in men's innate, but unconscious, aggression. A leading British psycho-analyst, Dr. Glover, has given us the clearest available statement of this view in his essay, *War, Sadism, and Pacifism*. He believes that all men possess an unsuspected fund of repressed, and wholly unconscious, aggressive impulses. Some of us control our repressed aggression fairly well, but there are other types who, for reasons connected with an unconscious fear of their own inferiority or impotence, are liable to develop an extraordinary and irrational degree of aggression if they get the opportunity. War, which has been aptly called " legalized murder," clearly provides them with the sanction of society for the liberation of such ill-repressed aggression.

Hence, Dr. Glover believes that this type of men (and women) have a strong, unconscious urge towards war for its own sake. Dr. Glover considers that great danger of war arises if and when an individual of this type occupies an important government position, such as Foreign Secretary or Prime Minister. And, as he believes that this type is numerous, he considers that he has adduced a sufficient cause of war.

Dr. Ernest Jones, another leading figure of the British psycho-analytical school, has applied this general point of view to certain historical incidents. In a recent lecture (as yet unpublished, so far as I am aware) he referred to the Fashoda incident. This incident occurred in 1898 during the aforementioned " grab for Africa." At the oasis of Fashoda a party of French imperialists under General Marchand, pushing eastwards from French Tunisia, encountered a party of British imperialists pushing westwards across the Sudan. Both parties claimed this part of the continent for their countries. France and Britain were brought to the verge of war. But in the event a treaty was negotiated by which France received the larger area, which consisted predominantly of desert, while Great Britain retained smaller but much more fertile domains.

Dr. Jones enquired how it was that in this sharp conflict of interest the British and French Empires yet managed to avoid war. The main emphasis of his explanation was laid upon the character of the British Prime Minister of the day, the late Lord

Salisbury. Lord Salisbury was, Dr. Jones considers, an eminently well-adjusted man, conspicuously free from repressed, unconscious impulses to aggression arising from feelings of inferiority or unconscious fear of impotence. Thus Lord Salisbury was enabled to follow a cool, reasonable line of diplomatic policy, and war was avoided.

It is instructive to compare this view of the Fashoda incident with the view of it which follows naturally from the socialist and communist theory of the economic causation of war. We notice that while the psycho-analyst puts the main emphasis on the character of Lord Salisbury, the communist and socialist will put it upon the size of Africa. We believe that Britain and France were just able to avoid war during "the grab for Africa" because, after all, there was so much to grab, and because there were as yet only two important grabbers in the field.[1] The one school of thought puts its emphasis upon a subjective, the other upon an objective, factor. And this difference is of great practical importance. For, while finding it unnecessary to deny that Lord Salisbury was a cool and able imperialist, we are sure that, even if he had been still a hundred times cooler and abler, he could not have averted war if the favourable objective factors of a large divisible prize and only two disputants had been absent.

We may appreciate the great importance of the difference between the two explanations by noticing the view which their respective acceptance will incline us to take of the cause of the great war of 1914, and of the greater war which menaces us to-day. The psycho-analyst will naturally suppose that the question of whether a type of man similar to Lord Salisbury was in power in 1914, and is in power to-day, was and is of great importance. He will suppose that the British statesmen who became involved in war in 1914, and the statesmen who may become involved in war to-morrow, were, or are, inferior in psychological stability to Lord Salisbury. We, on the other hand, while not finding it necessary to deny that Sir Edward Grey and Mr. Asquith may (or may not, the point is arguable) have been

[1] At the same time, the appearance just at that moment (1898) in the imperialist arena of a third and most formidable grabber, in the shape of the then rapidly rising German imperialism, was on this occasion an influence driving the two older, and individually weaker, imperialisms of France and Britain to sink their difference for mutual defence against the newcomer.

less cool and able in 1914 than Lord Salisbury was in 1898, will not admit for an instant that the presumed inferiority of these later statesmen was a significant cause of the Great War.

The Great War was caused by the increasing exhaustion of the opportunities for economic expansion open to the capitalist empires, and the increasing number, power, and need for expansion of these empires. The calibre of the individuals holding high office may have an effect on the moment of outbreak of any given war. If these individuals are of an inferior and unstable type, if they suffer from repressed aggression, they may well precipitate war *before* it is theoretically inevitable. But that is all. Reincarnate Lord Salisbury in 1914, or, still more, in 1936, and he would be confronted by a situation in which there was no possibility of achieving such peaceful solutions as he achieved up till the turn of the century. (Incidentally, were not Mr. Asquith and Lord Salisbury men of a very similar, and about equally stable, psychological type—and is not Mr. Baldwin also a man of this type ?)

The psycho-analytic view of the causation of war overlooks factors of such primary and widely recognized importance, that, as it is at present presented to us, we must characterize it as false. Moreover, it is disastrously false, for its adoption would blind men to the real, effective cause of war, namely the capitalist system of production for profit. That cause can be eradicated. And unless it is eradicated it will cause wars in which all of us, the well-adjusted and the neurotic, the analyst and his patients, shall be destroyed.

The question of whether or not our minds do contain unconscious and repressed impulses of the sort described by Drs. Jones and Glover is largely, though no doubt not wholly, irrelevant to the question of the causation of modern war. I, personally, happen to believe that our minds do contain these impulses, and that these are the impulses which are appealed to by the war propaganda carried on by every capitalist class. But that these impulses are dominant, in the sense that they would cause international wars in the absence of the objective economic factors which we have analysed above, I do not for one moment believe. We cannot, no doubt, have perfect proof on the point until these objective factors are removed. But already we have a good deal of evidence. For example, it is necessary to conscript the population of modern states in order to get them to engage in war, and to threaten them with death if they refuse. But why should this be necessary if their repressed aggressions were dominating their whole psychology ? Surely the evidence of the actions and propaganda which are undertaken by capitalist governments in war time points to the conclusion that, while aggressive impulses, upon which such propaganda can play, do exist, they are only occasionally and temporarily dominant and are quickly replaced by other powerful impulses, such as those of self-preservation, fear, and, ultimately, by positive impulses towards an attitude of fraternization (i.e. love instead of hate) with the enemy ?

On the other hand, we have, in the specific character of capitalist production for profit, with its need for economic expansion as an absolute condition of its further existence, an entirely sufficient cause of modern war. Hence, it is contradictory to the primary principles of logical enquiry to seek for other and more elaborate hypotheses as to the cause of war. It would have been necessary to Dr. Glover, in order to establish a real connection between our repressed aggressions and the causation of modern war, to have first advanced grounds for believing that the economic causes of war were ineffective or insufficient. But Dr. Glover made no attempt to do this. On the contrary, it is clear from his essay that he has never heard of the economic causes of war. Like most British intellectuals, his semi-explicit hypothesis is that the present economic system is perfectly compatible with peace. He has no inkling that there are any serious grounds for supposing that communities of perfectly adjusted angels could not keep the peace if it were stipulated that they had to maintain the existing world of rival systems of private production for profit.

It is deeply to be regretted that Dr. Glover was, when he wrote his essay, unacquainted with communist and socialist thought on this subject. For individual and neurotic maladjustments play a part, not indeed in causing war, but in making it possible to force the mass of the population to go and fight their masters' battles for them. This, in my view, is a fruitful field of enquiry. But to attribute to the maladjustments of individuals (themselves to an unknown but certainly very considerable extent created by present-day society) a primary importance in causing war is to overlook a mountain of overwhelmingly convincing evidence of the objective inevitability of war between competing capitalist empires.

When capitalist production for profit, which must in theory cause, and is visibly in practice causing, ever-recurrent inter-imperialist wars, has been abolished, we shall be able usefully to approach the important question of whether or not there exist other causes of war which might in themselves be dangerous. Personally, I believe that we shall find that our habitual nationalism, and our unconscious aggressions, while they will undoubtedly continue to exist for a very long time, will be manageable. They may cause friction and difficulty between various more or less separately organized communities; but that they will be sufficiently potent to drive men to the extreme and hazardous course of international war is hard to believe. What we shall probably find is that these impulses, which are to-day made use of for the purposes of international war, whilst not ceasing to exist, will, in a different social environment, find new forms of expression. No one has laid more emphasis on the variety of the forms of expression which a repressed impulse may take than have the analysts. The sublimation of impulses which to-day find one of their modes of expression in war can be confidently expected; we may deduce the character which these sublimations will take from sublimations which already exist. Competitive games of an athletic and preferably violent character are, undoubtedly, the characteristic British and American sublimation of repressed aggressive impulses. It would no doubt be over-optimistic to suppose that all these impulses can be diverted into this harmless and delightful channel. But that they can, and will, find adequate channels of expression (of which the principal one will no doubt be the struggle with nature), other than the fatal channel of international war, seems clear.

These, then, are the grounds of the assertion that socialism, and nothing but socialism,[1] can prevent a new and endless

---

[1] And, of course, communism itself; but socialism is the only immediately available alternative to capitalism.

series of world-wide wars. No one, surely, will be so mad as to deny that, if this claim can be proved, it is in itself sufficient to demonstrate the necessity of abolishing capitalism and building up for ourselves a socialist system of production for use? For, in all soberness, can we deny that modern war promises to be the ultimate evil? We do not, and cannot, know what the next war will be like. But we catch some inkling of its probable character from the type of preparations for it which our governments require us to make. Behind the quietly written paragraphs of the instructions for air raid drill with which we are being provided, we cannot fail to catch a glimpse of masked figures crouching and stifling in their cellars, while London, Paris, Berlin, and New York burn and crumble and crash above them.

Such, it is submitted, must be the final consequences of maintaining the capitalist system. In these three chapters the grounds for this assertion have been stated rather than demonstrated. Yet the issue is of our life or of our death. Would it not be well, then, closely to examine the full analysis of the ultimate consequences of capitalism, lest it be true, and we in rejecting it are destroyed?

Part III
SOCIALISM AND THE WORKING CLASS

Chapter XXIII

The Birth of an Idea

THE idea of a new and better form of human society beyond capitalism is as old as capitalism itself. Moreover, the history of capitalism has been marked by a series of revolts against the conditions of life which capitalism has produced for the greater part of the population. Hence, an essential part of such a book as this must be to survey, however briefly, the intertwined development of the idea of socialism and the revolt against capitalism. For without such a survey the description of a new economic and political system given in the first two parts would remain thin, doctrinaire, and academic; it must be clothed in the flesh and blood of human experience.

The idea of a socialist or communist form of society was born at the very moment of the birth of capitalism, and of capitalism's shadow, a property-less working class. Capitalism and the working class first appeared at the end of the Middle Ages, when the old feudal relationships began to loosen and disintegrate. In England they began to be visible about the middle of the fifteenth century. And this is what they looked like to a contemporary observer :

" the husbandmen be thrust out of their own, or else either by cunning and fraud, or by violent oppression they be put besides it, or by wrongs and injuries they be so wearied, that they be compelled to sell all ; by one means therefore or by other, either by hook or crook, they must needs depart away, poor, silly, wretched souls, men, women, husbands, wives, fatherless children, widows, woeful mothers, with their young babes, and their whole household small in substance and much in number, as husbandry requireth many hands. Away they trudge, I say, out of their known and accustomed houses, finding no place to rest in. All their household stuff, which is very little worth, though it might well abide the sale : yet being suddenly thrust out, they be constrained to sell it for a thing of nought. And when they have wandered abroad till that be spent, what can they then else do but steal, and then justly pardy be hanged, or else go about a begging. And yet then also they be cast in prison as vagabonds."

This description of the formation of the first property-less working class which England had ever known is from Sir Thomas More's *Utopia*, and follows immediately the famous passage in which More makes his character, the Portuguese mariner, Raphael Hythloday, explain to Cardinal Morton, one of the last great Catholic Archbishops of Canterbury, why there is so much stealing in England :

" But yet this is not only the necessary cause of stealing. There is another, which, as I suppose, is proper and peculiar to you Englishmen alone. What is that, quoth the Cardinal ? Forsooth my lord (quoth I) your sheep that were wont to be so meek and tame, and so small eaters, now, as I hear say, be become so great devourers and so wild, that they eat up, and swallow down the very men themselves. They consume, destroy, and devour whole fields, houses, and cities. For look in what parts of the realm doth grow the finest and therefore dearest wool, there noblemen and gentlemen, yea and certain abbots, holy men no doubt, not contenting themselves with the yearly revenues and profits that were wont to grow to their forefathers and predecessors of their lands, nor being content that they live in rest and pleasure nothing profiting, yea much annoying the weal public, leave no ground for tillage, they inclose all into pastures; they throw down houses; they pluck down towns, and leave nothing standing, but only the church to be made a sheep-house."

These passages reveal the degree to which the apperceptive genius of More had comprehended the nature of the extraordinary social change which was going on around him. He realized perfectly that the peasants (and they had been Chaucer's peasants) were being thrown into destitution because the use of the land was being denied them by the lords, lay and ecclesiastical. These lords had up till then been no more than the general overlords of the land, enjoying a feudal tribute or a fixed rent from the peasants, but no more. But now they claimed to be the direct owners of the land—to be landlords or land-owners in the modern sense—able to turn off the peasants, become mere tenants-at-will, and to use the land for their own purposes. And their purposes were to turn the land into sheep runs under the care of a few shepherds working for fixed money wages. For the raising of wool had become by far the most profitable use to which the land of England could be put. The temptation of profit had floated before the eyes of the lords and abbots ("holy men, no doubt") who up till then had simply lived well off the feudal dues paid to them by the peasant husband-men, but had had no thought of accumulating a money profit— of becoming capitalists. But now it had become apparent to them that they had only to " inclose all into pastures," turn off the husbandmen, replace them by sheep, and wealth would be theirs. " Therefore," More continues, " that one covetous and insatiable cormorant and very plague of his native country may compass all together within one pale or hedge."

The enormous process of the enclosure of the land of England had begun. Hitherto it had been tilled on the basis of production for use ; now it was to be tilled on the basis of production for profit. This process began before 1500 and was not finally com-pleted until about 1850. It was the true and indispensable parent of British capitalism. This was the process by which feudal society split up into the capitalist and working classes. The clear and sensitive mind of Thomas More saw and understood the frightful consequences for the mass of the population of their exclusion from independent access to the means of production for the purpose of this transformation from production for use to production for profit. The horror, which More felt at the sights and sounds of the process, engen-dered in his brilliant, quick-footed imagination the dream of a society in which such things should not be: of a society in which the land and all other means of production should be the common property of the whole people.[1] The appearance of property-less

---

[1] The prophetic genius of More consists in the fact that the sights and sounds of the early enclosures did not make him desire to restore the individual owner-ship of land to the English peasants. He somehow grasped the fact that this system was inevitably doomed. Thus he escaped that futile, if often eloquent, advocacy of the return to individual peasant proprietorship which has occupied so many Englishmen from John Ball, to Cobbett, to the Chartist leaders, and to, in our own day, Mr. Belloc and Mr. Chesterton. More wanted to go forward beyond capitalism, not backward to pre-capitalist conditions. Few of his co-religionists have ever again seen so far.

masses, bereft of all access to the means of production, could alone have engendered such a conception. So long as the population consisted predominantly of peasants, owning or, at any rate, using their land to grow their own food, the very idea of the abolition of private property in the means of production could not arise. And even in 1516 (the date of the first publication of the *Utopia*) the idea of abolishing all private ownership of the means of production, as the only effective way of restoring the entire population's access to these means, could arise as no more than a dream; for it was the dream of a society designed for the benefit of the working class. And the immediate future belonged, not to the embryonic working class, but to the emergent capitalist class. For four long centuries the capitalists were to inherit the earth—for only so could the economic and technical progress necessary to the realization of More's dream be achieved. But how ominous was it that at the very moment of the birth of capitalism, when the capitalist class had only just begun to fulfil its historical function, the idea of a society which should need this class no longer should be conceived in the mind of a man.

During the whole four centuries of the emergence, the struggle for power, and then the dominance of the capitalist class, that conception of a possible world beyond capitalism was never to be wholly extinguished. At every critical juncture, at every moment when the developing necessities of capitalism imposed especially heavy burdens upon the working population, the dream of a world beyond capitalism was redreamt. And not only was the dream redreamt; at each succeeding crisis of capitalism, as at its painful birth, a movement of the revolt of the dispossessed was spontaneously generated.

For, as More saw so vividly, capitalist private property in the means of production could only be established by the confiscation of the scattered, small-scale means of production hitherto belonging to the mass of the population. For you cannot use any given means of production simultaneously for the two purposes of production for use and production for profit. The land of England, for example, could not be used for the production of a profit, until and unless it was taken from the peasants, who were using it to produce food. In the same way, the production of clothes, tools, and luxuries could not be organised upon a profit-making basis until and unless the existing system of production was abolished. For under the then existing system of production these goods were made for use, by small masters, employing an apprentice or so, and organized in self-governing guilds, the ordinances of which were expressly designed to prevent the accumulation of considerable profit. The property of the guild members in the means of production of their trade had to be directly or indirectly confiscated if the new, large-scale masters were ever to get a start.[1]

At first the reaction of those classes of the community who were thus dispossessed of their property was feeble and, above all, blind. There was no apparent connection between such dispersed efforts at resistance as they made and the dream of socialism. But gradually the revolt has become stronger and the dream more precise, until at length the revolt and the dream have become linked; the workers have become increasingly conscious of the kind of society which they would establish if and when their revolt succeeded, and the dreamers have come to realize that apart from the workers they can only dream. They have begun to understand that the social dynamic of the workers' spontaneous resistance to their lot under capitalism can alone make their word flesh. In so doing they have ceased to be dreamers and become the first social scientists that the world has yet known.

But the process has not been a short one. It was four centuries and one year after the publication of Thomas More's book that the revolt of the dispossessed became so strong, and the knowledge of the necessary method and purpose of that revolt so clear, that the two could perfectly fuse. In October 1917 the capitalists of

[1] Marx, in the famous peroration of *Capital*, when he speaks of " the expropriators being expropriated," is referring to the historical fact that the private property of the capitalists had necessarily been built up by the gradual destruction of the much more diffused private property of the mass of the population in simpler means of production. The passage is often found puzzling to-day because the memory that there was a time when private property in the means of production was general throughout the population, is in Britain almost extinct. And naturally the historians of the capitalists give us no hint that the property of their class is built upon expropriation. (Some account, although little comprehension, of the process may be found, however, in the works of the Catholic historians such as Mr. Hilaire Belloc, for they have sufficient grudge against the Protestant tradition of English capitalism to wash some of the dirty linen of their class in public.)

one-sixth of the world were dispossessed and for the first time in all history the way was opened for the building up of a socialist community.

It has taken four hundred years for men to discover what are the conditions necessary to the establishment first of socialism and then of communism. This was what proved difficult. For the conception of the ultimate goal—of communism itself—was clear enough from the outset.[1] More knew as well as Lenin all that either of them, or anyone else, can know of the general outline of the fully developed communist society to which mankind shall some day attain. But it took centuries of combined historical experience and technical achievement to discover the stages through which mankind had to pass on the way to that goal.

Already in 1516 Thomas More knew well enough that common ownership of the means of production is the one great condition precedent to any effective alteration of society to the advantage of property-less workers. Private property, he declares, is at the root of all social evil. But he has not yet distinguished between private property in the means of production and private property in consumable goods. Hence his Utopia has necessarily to be organized upon the basis of full communism. In the island of Utopia there are great communal storehouses into which all products flow and out of which every citizen can take what he needs. His Utopia is organized upon the basis of " to each according to his needs, from each according to his abilities." The possibility of an intermediate stage such as socialism, in which the means of production, which in the sixteenth century meant essentially the land, should be held in common, but in which the products themselves should pass into private hands in proportion to the work done, could not have occurred to More. For one of the essential conditions of such a society is the development of large-scale industry. Until such a development has taken place such a society cannot even be imagined. All this makes More's conception remote and, in a sense, fanciful.

---

[1] It is, of course, more or less arbitrary to take More's *Utopia* as the first conception of communism. But the ideal states of antiquity, such as in Plato's *Republic*, have no connection with the struggle against capitalism, of the dispossessed part of the population, which More's book definitely has. For both were generated by the same great event—the beginning of the enclosure of the land of England.

But yet what remarkable insight into the nature of social and economic forces his book contains! For example, More had realized the evils of insecurity and instability which must arise (as we saw in Chapter XVII) from the establishment of the division of labour, even while the accumulation of profit is still so small that capitalism itself has not appeared. For the inhabitants of these pre-capitalist, but commodity producing, societies, must satisfy their needs by exchanges mediated by money: and with the institution of money and the market they lose control of their economic life.

" Yea poverty itself, which only seemed to lack money, if money were gone, it also would decrease and vanish away. And that you may perceive this more plainly, consider with yourselves some barren and unfruitful year, wherein many thousands of people have starved for hunger. I dare be bold to say, that in the end of that penury so much corn or grain might have been found in the rich men's barns, if they had been searched, as being divided among them whom famine and pestilence then consumed, no man at all should have felt that plague and penury. So easily might men get their living, if that same worthy princess, lady money, did not alone stop up the way between us and our living, which a God's name was very excellently devised and invented, that by her the way thereto should be opened."

The continuity of communist and socialist thought, from its germ in More's *Utopia*, to its full maturity in the theory and practice of Lenin, is very extraordinary. To take an example. As we saw in the case of the Attic peasants, money, in all unplanned societies, must inevitably become a tyrant—to be cajoled and fawned upon, entreated and desired, but also to be feared and hated. So More makes his Utopians revenge him upon money— " of gold and silver they make chamber pots, and other vessels that serve for most vile uses—thus by all means possible they procure to have gold and silver among them in reproach and infamy." Lenin, echoing More, suggested that in a communist world gold might be used as a pleasant material for lavatory seats. More, however, knew as well as Lenin that gold would have to be used by a communist or socialist community in a non-communist world for foreign trade, and actually makes his Utopians so use it.

There are other remarkable passages in the *Utopia* which show the extent to which More had thought out some of the implications of a classless society. For they describe practices which are actually developing in the Soviet Union to-day. The Utopians fought their wars largely by means of propaganda against the rulers of enemy states, conducted amongst the population of these states. More, in other words, had realized the great strength of a homogeneous, classless society when at war with a society based on class domination. For only a classless society dares to use the weapon of revolutionary propaganda against the rulers of the opposing state. Again, More, as a lawyer, was shocked by the barbarity of the civil code of his time. Hence, he makes the principal form of punishment in his Utopia the deprivation of civil rights. A man who had committed a crime was not killed or locked up, but was forced to work as a " bondsman " for a definite period, until by good conduct he might regain his freedom. We have a development of this system in the Soviet Union to-day, where punishment consists in the re-training of the individual by constructive work, either in an institution or in the outside world, but with a loss of civil rights. How striking it is that More foresaw that in a classless society, based on common ownership, where there is no question of one man's work competing with another's, this solution of the question of punishment (for it is little less) would become possible.

Socialism was to remain an idea for four hundred years after the publication of More's *Utopia*. But it was a developing idea. It developed as the working class developed, and as the crises in the development of capitalism put pressure upon that class. The next great crisis in the development of the British capitalist class occurred in the seventeenth century. The English civil war of 1640 to 1660 again brought every social issue out into the open. And once again the intolerable pressure of the crisis upon the lowest class of society made a man conceive of the idea of socialism or communism. And at this second appearance the idea had come appreciably nearer to the revolt.

The man was Gerrard Winstanley, the "Digger," or "Leveller," and the book in which he described his proposed communist community was called *The Law of Freedom*. Winstanley's community is to have the same basic economic system as More's Utopia. All products are to be taken to communal storehouses, and all citizens are to draw what they will from the storehouses, "without buying or selling." Winstanley goes on to describe a community of the same general pattern as that of More's *Utopia* (which he may have read), although with considerably less fullness and precision of detail.

But the particular details of these ideal systems are of little importance. Moreover, any inferiority of description in Winstanley is more than compensated for by an immense gain in actuality. More placed his Utopia in the undiscovered Southern Hemisphere; Winstanley put his at St. George's Hill, Weybridge, Surrey. While More knew that he was telling an allegory, Winstanley believed that he was drafting the laws for a state of society which should, and well might, be immediately inaugurated in England. The act of revolt had come a step closer to the still vaguely conceived objective. Indeed, in Winstanley's case, the act preceded the dream. Winstanley was a digger before he was a writer. He only took up his pen to describe what he considered England ought to be, when the spades with which he and his friends were seeking actually to remodel her were struck from their hands.

The Digger movement,[1] of which Winstanley was the leader, arose on the morrow of Parliament's final victory over what Winstanley calls "the kingly power." The Diggers arose to assert their interpretation of the "freedom" which Parliament had won. For that freedom meant one thing to one man and another thing to another man. To the squires in Parliament it had originally meant freedom from arbitrary taxation, and had come to mean freedom to rule: to many men in the middle of English society, to shopkeepers, traders, farmers, and the like,

[1] Not to be confused with the Leveller movement (although they were often confused at the time). The Levellers, associated with the names of Colonels Lilburne and Rainborow, were the extreme left wing of the New Model Army. The Diggers were an independent, spontaneous movement of dispossessed peasants and artisans.

it meant religious freedom, freedom to worship as they wished. But to Winstanley and his friends, poor men, men ruined in the wars, or never having had enough to be ruined, freedom meant something different. It meant nothing more nor less than freedom to dig: freedom to dig the common lands of England; it meant that freedom which the heartrending procession of their peasant ancestors had lost a hundred and twenty years earlier.

Freedom to dig the common lands of England: that was what Winstanley asked: no more and no less. And he put the matter to the touch. On April 16th, 1649, one month after the execution of Charles, the Council of State, then the sovereign body for all England, received a letter from a Mr. Henry Sanders of Walton-upon-Thames which began as follows:

" Informeth, that on Sunday was sennight last, there was one Everard, once of the army but was cashiered, who termeth himself a prophet, one Stewer and Colton, and two more, all living at Cobham, came to St. George's Hill in Surrey, and began to dig on that side of the hill next to Campe Close, and sowed the ground with parsnips, carrots, and beans."

The Diggers had begun to dig. To Winstanley and his followers their position seemed perfectly clear. A heavy civil war had just been fought in which the mass of the population, under the leadership of some of the squires, had finally defeated, dethroned, and executed the King. For what purpose had the civil war been fought ? It had been fought, said Winstanley, in order that the people of England might resume those rights of which they had been gradually deprived by the usurpations of successive generations of the privileged classes: and, above all, of the right to live by tilling the land.

But Winstanley was a man of peace. He did not propose to take back into common possession that two-thirds of the land of England which had, it was estimated (I do not know with what accuracy) already been enclosed as private property. He proposed to dig only that one-third which was still common land, but over which the lords of the manors, and certain privileged freeholders and copyholders, had now acquired exclusive rights of grazing and the like.

The new rulers of England thought differently. They were no

mean social theorists themselves (we know that from the record of their debates on the franchise). They knew that if Winstanley and his friends were allowed to dig the common lands the thing would not stop there. They would very soon claim the right to hold all land in common and cultivate all for the common stock. (They had only to turn to Winstanley's writings to discover that this was indeed the ultimate purpose of the Diggers.) And where then would be the gentry, whether cavalier or Parliament man? They took no notice of Winstanley's protestations that he did not mean to touch private, enclosed land, and ordered their General, Lord Fairfax, to send a troop of horse to turn the Diggers off the common.

Winstanley's major work, *The Law of Freedom in a Platform: or True Magistracie Restored,* was written after the Diggers had been finally harried off St. George's Hill by the magistrate's court, sitting at Kingston.[1] *The Law of Freedom* has an elegiac note; its author seems to know that the tide is running against him. He writes as one wishing to have his full say this once before he dies, to go on record for the truth as he sees it. For the Diggers of St. George's Hill had not found imitators. I suppose that the memory of an effective possession of the land had already become dim in the minds of the English poor, or else a nation-wide movement for the reoccupation of the common land might well have led to a formidable English Jacquerrie. The Surrey Diggers were, it is true, feebly imitated by the poor of the town of Wellingborough in Northamptonshire, but in spite of the fact that they sent missionaries to the surrounding counties, that was all. Long before the Restoration the movement had disappeared. It left only Winstanley's beautiful and neglected little book as its monument, the second communist fantasy to be born of the land hunger and misery of the dispossessed English peasants.

Winstanley lacked the polish and elegance of the scholarly More, but he was at least as eloquent a writer and was in many respects a more profound thinker. Winstanley, like every Englishman of his generation, had approached social and economic

---

[1] It still sits there, and tries, principally, the motoring offences of those city men who have now covered St. George's Hill with their particularly comfortable villas.

questions through theology and the Bible. He had abandoned, however, by the time that he wrote *The Law of Freedom*, his original mystical, Quakerish views for a magnificently expressed materialism. For example, the function of the ministry in his ideal community turns out to be simply that of educating the population in politics, economics and the natural sciences. He thus anticipates the objection of the sacerdotalists:

" ' I,' but saith the zealous but ignorant Professor, ' this is a low and carnal Ministry indeed; this leads men to know nothing but the knowledge of the earth and the secrets of nature; but we are to look after spiritual and heavenly things.'

" I answer: ' To know the secrets of nature is to know the works of God; and to know the works of God within the Creation, is to know God himself; for God dwells in every visible work or body. Indeed, if you would know spiritual things, it is to know how the Spirit or Power of Wisdom and Life, causing motion or growth, dwells within and governs both the several bodies of the stars and planets in the heavens above, and the several bodies of the earth below, as grass, plants, fishes, beasts, birds and mankind. For to reach God beyond the Creation, or to know what he will be to a man after the man is dead, if any other wise than to scatter him into his essences of fire, water, earth and air, of which he is composed, is a knowledge beyond the line or capacity of man to attain to while he lives in his compounded body. . . .

" ' God manifests Himself in actual Knowledge, not in Imagination. He is still in motion, either in bodies upon earth or in the bodies in the heavens, or in both; in the night and in the day, in Winter, in Summer, in cold, in heat, in growth or not in growth.' "[1]

After the publication of *The Law of Freedom* there is no further record either of Winstanley or his movement. Soon the great coalition of the noblemen, gentry, and great merchants of

[1] Just as More anticipated some of the social legislation of the Soviet Union, so Winstanley stated the basis of the philosophical attitude of any workers' community. Compare, for example, the attitude towards science of the Soviet Union (as described, for example, in *Soviet Communism: A New Civilization?* by S. and B. Webb) with this passage of Winstanley's.

England, temporarily broken up by the civil war, was to be knit up again more strongly than ever before. The process by which the peasants of England were to be steadily deprived of the land, almost to the last acre, was resumed and went on for two hundred years more. In such a future Winstanley had no place. But it was to be long before any Englishman again attained to so simple and direct a conception of man's relation to the universe. Winstanley spoke for those workers who, if once the pall of ignorance which is imposed upon them can be lifted, must be natural materialists. For they live by understanding and controlling the forces of nature. For them knowledge and practice can never be separated, for they do not live, as do the *savants* of all possessing classes, upon the labours of other men: they can never be what Winstanley gloriously called the clerical philosophers of his day, " monsters who are all tongue and no hand." With Winstanley, materialism, the typical and inevitable characteristic of working class thought, pushed its way up for a moment through the gap made in the ranks of the privileged classes of England by the civil war. Quickly, and of necessity, however, it was submerged again, for the capitalist class had yet to come to maturity, and to the fulfilment of its mission.

CHAPTER XXIV

Robert Owen and the Communist Colonies

THE next substantial appearance of communist and socialist thought, and of working class activity, inextricably associated as before, occurred at the next great crisis in the development of capitalism.

At the end of the eighteenth century it became clear that an almost wholly new technique of production had been evolved in the preceding fifty years and that this new technique was shaking the existing social structure to its foundations. It was discovered that the development of industrial production by steam power was incompatible with the still semi-feudal structure of society; that this method of production was both endowing society with extraordinary wealth, and was creating vast urban aggregations of men and women living in conditions of un-exampled misery. Finally it was found that this new technique of production was everywhere becoming associated with the emergence of the capitalists as the exclusive rulers of society. In the period from 1770 to 1870 the capitalists achieved their paramountcy all over Western Europe and North America, by a series of movements, more or less revolutionary according to local circumstances, of which the French Revolution is the type.

The prophets and thinkers of the capitalists had promised and believed that their final conquest of power would produce the millennium for everyone. What it did produce was something very near heaven for the capitalists, and something very near hell for the workers. And hardly had the victory been won than three men stepped forward to point out this discrepancy between promise and performance. Their names were Saint-Simon, Fourier, and Robert Owen. These three great men saw more clearly than any of their contemporaries what was the nature of the new, fully capitalist, society which had just been created. It is true that their proposed remedies for its ills, which it was their immortal service to expose, were all more or less fantastic and Utopian. But this was only because at that time there were *no* effective remedies for the evils which the rule of the capitalists was creating.

Capitalist production was only now blossoming forth. In a novitiate of three hundred years it had existed as one form, and that not the most important, of the productive activities carried on by society. But now it entered into its heritage: it unceasingly pressed forward with its mission, namely to industrialize the world, and so to raise a thousand-fold the productive powers of man. Saint-Simon, Fourier, and Owen could show that the capitalists were only accomplishing this task at the cost of inflicting tortures upon the mass of the population worse than any which had existed under the feudal monarchies. Whole generations of workers became the living fuel with which the crude steam engines of early capitalism were stoked. It did not matter. Capitalism was launched on its meteoric ascent. Until the possibilities of development inherent in the system were exhausted, the most that could be done was to mitigate the tortures inflicted upon the working population.

Of the three great Utopian socialists of the dawn of the industrial era, we shall select Robert Owen for brief consideration. For not only is he, on the whole, the most important, but his career naturally concerns more closely the fortunes of the British and American workers. Moreover, it is above all from a study of the career of Robert Owen that we may derive evidence of the truth of some of the main principles which we laid down more or less arbitrarily in Parts I and II. It is from Owen's misfortunes that we may learn what actually does happen if such guiding principles as the necessity of changing the political system of a community if you wish to change its economic system, or of the primacy of the working class as an agent of social change, are disregarded.

Robert Owen and his generation had not yet discovered these principles, and consequently their work ended in apparent futility. Hence they have been called Utopian socialists— socialists of fancy rather than of fact. Now it is sometimes supposed that Marx and Engels, whose work for ever superseded that of the Utopian socialists, despised them and sneered at their doctrines. Nothing could be further from the truth. For it is precisely from the experience and, above all, the errors of these great men that we, their descendants, have been enabled to acquire scientific knowledge of how social change can be effected. This, for example, is how Engels describes the appearance of Robert Owen upon the stage of English public life. Engels refers to the murk, squalor, confusion, and misery of the Manchester, the Glasgow, and the Birmingham of 1800 :

"Then a twenty-nine-year-old manufacturer came on the scene as a reformer, a man of almost sublimely childlike simplicity of character and at the same time a born leader of men such as is rarely seen. Robert Owen had adopted the teachings of the materialist philosophers of the enlightenment that man's character is the product on the one hand of his hereditary constitution, and the other of his environment during his lifetime, and particularly during the period of his development. In the industrial revolution most of his class saw only confusion and chaos, enabling them to fish in troubled waters and get rich quickly. He saw in it the opportunity to put his favourite theory into practice, and thereby to bring order out of chaos."

In truth the dews of the morning were upon the young Robert Owen. There is something of a fairy-tale quality about the first half of his career. It is a modern success story, which happens to have a saint for its hero. It is a little as if St. Francis of Assisi had absent-mindedly made good as a textile manufacturer.

Owen left home at the age of ten, and he supported himself entirely by his own labours from that moment. By the age of twenty-nine he was managing partner of the large and prosperous textile concern of New Lanark, and on the way to making a great fortune. So far there was nothing strange about his story. It was something that was happening to dozens of the poor boys of his time. But to them making their fortunes was the object of their careers, the be-all and end-all of their activities. To Owen it was something quite incidental, to which he gave less and less of his attention. From the moment of his accession to the management of New Lanark, almost his whole real interest was devoted, as Engels says, to trying out his theory of the exclusive formation of character by environment. (For at that time this was his view; see his first book, *A New View of Society* (1813), though by the time he wrote *The New Moral World*

(1836) he had come round to the view which Engels attributes to him and admitted, although grudgingly, the influence of hereditary factors.)

There now appears a fantastic element in the career of Robert Owen. His theory was over-simplified to the extent of being false, but the practical demonstration of it was an unqualified success ! By treating the workers, and, above all, the workers' children, of New Lanark like decent human beings, instead of like valueless slaves, he utterly transformed them. Treated as civilized beings, they behaved as civilized beings. Owen, not unnaturally, concluded that all that was needed in order to produce an earthly paradise was that a similar environment should be provided for the rest of the population. And he forthwith suggested to the Government, and to prominent persons in what we, but not he, should call the governing class, that they should get on with the job. For with Owen a thing was no sooner thought than done.

Owen's remarkable illusion that a Government composed of such men as Lords Liverpool and Castlereagh, plus Mr. Canning, might immediately, and would certainly by the time of the next session of Parliament at the very latest, lay the foundations of a socialist commonwealth for Britain, persisted until the day of his death. As late as 1844, for example, he was writing:

" The Imperial British Parliament, properly constituted, is, by far, the best existing power to effect peacefully, and most beneficially for the human race, this great change in the constitution of society over the world. It may now commence, with great advantage, at the opening of the next session of the present parliament, to prepare the minds of the public to abandon, in due time, upon a magnificent scale, the errors of our inexperienced ancestors, and to adopt, on a scale yet more magnificent, the fundamental principles of truth in accordance with all nature, and the glorious practices which will necessarily emanate from this true source of knowledge and happiness." (*Book of the New Moral World*, Part V, p. 24.)

This passage is a tragic epitome of all Robert Owen's political thinking. This apparently supremely practical man had as much conception of the politically possible as an inhabitant of another planet. He saw not the slightest reason why the capitalists and their Government should not inaugurate socialism. After all, he was a great capitalist and he was prepared to inaugurate socialism. Why should not they ?

The incredible, if endearing, mistake of judging others by himself vitiated, so far as immediate results were concerned, almost the whole of Owen's public activities. But in his early years even this illusion seemed to be on the point of proving itself well founded. When in 1816 the inevitable post-war industrial crisis and prolonged depression struck Britain, Owen was at the height of his reputation. At New Lanark he had made a fortune for himself and a paradise for his employees—a paradise, at any rate, when compared to conditions in the other factories of Britain. When such a man proposed a scheme for remedying the dangerous distresses of the time he had to be listened to. He seemed to be, after all, merely a great capitalist and philanthropist who, although he was known to hold strange and extreme doctrines on such abstract questions as the formation of human character, had never been suspected of a subversive thought.

All Owen's early schemes (there were several) were proposals for the establishment, by the British Government, of mixed agricultural and industrial colonies into which the unemployed were to be sent, to be put on to such productive work as would make them self-supporting, while they were to be housed, fed, educated, and generally treated on the model of the conditions established at New Lanark. These proposals certainly seemed to the Government to be daring, not to say hazardous. But until Owen himself pointed it out, it was not realized that they were socialist or subversive. They were seriously considered by the Cabinet and found warm supporters in such exalted personages as the Royal Duke of Kent, Queen Victoria's father. Parliament, it is true, refused on a division to appoint a committee to enquire into them, but even there they found distinguished supporters, Mr. David Ricardo, for example, voting with the minority.

The measure of support which they received was at any rate enough to confirm Owen's delusion of a socialism imposed by the capitalists. (Or, for that matter, by the feudalists; at various times he had high hopes of Metternich and the Tsar of Russia, and bombarded them with memoranda.) Moreover, Owen had himself only just realized that the establishment, " on a magnificent scale," of his communes, or colonies, in which non-profit-making production for use was to be carried on, was incompatible with the existing order of society, with, that is to say, capitalist production for profit, private property in the means of production, and the institutions and ideas associated with such a system.[1]

About 1820, however, Owen did come to realize this fact. But this did not shake his faith that the capitalists would themselves establish socialism as soon as they had been taught by him how much nicer socialism would be. But he did come to see that if the communist colonies were to supersede private property in the means of production, every idea and habit of mind associated with capitalist private property would, sooner rather than later, have to go. This capacity of Owen's to realize the indissoluble connections between the economic system used by any society and its social and moral ideas showed him to be a real social thinker. It places him far above the shallow generations of British socialists who supposed that socialism was a mere matter of a readjustment of the economic mechanism of the community's life. But, since Owen combined this social insight with his illusion that the governing class could be converted to socialism, it made still more tragically absurd that always impossible task.

For Owen was not the man to keep his conclusions to himself. No sooner had he reached them than he announced that three things stood in the way of the realization of universal happiness, to wit, private property, religion, and marriage in its present form. That was all. The effect of this conclusion, as it gradually emerged from Owen's enormous, but not very precise, addresses, upon his wealthy and influential supporters, can be imagined. He does seem to have realized that his active advocacy of anti-religious views, in particular, would make his task of converting the British Government to socialism no easier. But he was far from supposing that it would make it impossible.

---

[1] The reader will notice that Mr. Upton Sinclair's scheme for the employment of the unemployed of California on socialist production for use in government-owned establishments, while leaving the Californian capitalists in possession of their present means of production, is a lineal descendant of Owen's proposals.

Ks

Still, about 1823, Owen did begin to notice that the British Government seemed so fully occupied in enforcing the Combination Laws and passing the Six Acts that it had no time to inaugurate a socialist commonwealth. Hence, ever impatient of delay, he decided (in 1824) to set the Cabinet an example by establishing the first communist colony himself. Accordingly, the next phase of Owen's career was occupied by a series of attempts to set up an initial, model, communist colony.

Owen's first and greatest experiment was in the United States. At Harmony, on the banks of the Wabash river[1] there was established the most famous of a series of abortive communist colonies, founded by Owen, Fourier, or their disciples. Owen himself was to be associated with several more and to take an active part in directing another, Harmony Hall, or Queenwood, in Hampshire, England.

It is not necessary to describe these colonies individually. For they were all of the same basic pattern, and they all failed for the same reasons. Any attempt to abolish capitalism by means of setting up colonies of persons producing for use is in fact foredoomed to failure, both for political and for economic reasons. It is an attempt to alter the economic system of a community without simultaneously altering its political system. Hence, even if it were economically feasible, it could not succeed, for it would be suppressed by the governing class. As a matter of fact, however, there are also economic reasons which make it impossible for capitalism to be abolished by the establishment of a chain of socialist or communist colonies. There are, to put the point the

---

[1] The young Abraham Lincoln is said to have seen the colonists pass up the river on their way to Harmony and to have begged his father to let him join them —not because he was interested in communism (he had almost certainly never heard of it), but because the colonists had books—and he was desperate to learn. In the event, the one thing which the colony did succeed in doing was to establish a considerable cultural centre round the *savants* (including Owen's sons) who came out with the colonists, but stayed on after the break up of the colony, in what were then the primitive middle Western States.

It is curious to speculate on what influence, if any, contact with Robert Owen and his communist ideas might have had upon the man who was destined to be the chief instrument in destroying the servile system of society, and consequently establishing capitalism, over the Southern half of the United States. Lincoln was as earnest, direct, and, in the highest sense of the word, as simple a man as Owen, but he was much more intelligent. Moreover, he lived in a society in which the pre-requisites of socialism were still less developed than they were in early nineteenth-century Britain. He would probably have admired Owen, but given little heed to his ideas.

other way round, economic reasons why socialism, a system, that is to say, of planned production for use, can only be established on an, at any rate, national scale. And the story of the Owenite colonies demonstrates exactly hat these economic reasons are.[1]

Owen's colonies, like the Utopias of More and Winstanley, were organized upon the basis of full communism. The colonists were, if possible, housed in a large central building, or group of buildings, and their members ate in common and lived a largely communal life. Moreover, they worked communally. No record, that is to say, was kept of the contribution of each to the work of the community, and their share in the product bore no relation to their individual effort. It was apportioned either on the basis of need or of equality.[2] No such colonies, surrounded by a capitalist environment, and composed of members who had been brought up in that environment, could in any case have succeeded. But when we examine the actual causes for the failure of the Owenite colonies (I do not know if this is true of the others), we find that they did not break up (as they probably would ultimately have done in any case) from the idleness, or quarrelsomeness, of the colonists, but from the quite startling improvidence of their management. Owen managed both New Harmony and Queenwood with an astonishing disregard of elementary financial prudence. He squandered the available capital, both his own and other people's, upon luxurious buildings, upon buying more and more land, before the original land was properly cultivated or stocked, and generally upon a policy of wild over-expansion.

Now this repeated wrecking of the communist colonies by over-expansion was the direct result of reliance upon fallacious economic theory. Owen and his followers based most of their propaganda as to the desirability and possibility of communism

[1] The most interesting communist colonies of the contemporary world are to be found in Palestine amongst some of the Jewish immigrants. Some of these colonies are over half a century old. Hence they demonstrate that in exceptional circumstances it is possible for such colonies to exist, in the sense of providing a living for their members, and to acquire the toleration of a still dominant capitalist class. But the Palestine colonies also demonstrate that such enclaves in a capitalist society have very little effect upon that society—and this no doubt is why they have been tolerated.

[2] This may not be true of every colony, but it was typical.

or socialism (the words were used indiscriminately) upon the enormous increase in the productivity of labour which had resulted from the application of steam power and the other basic discoveries of the industrial revolution. " The working part of the population of 2,500 persons," Owen wrote of New Lanark, " was daily producing as much real wealth for society as, less than half a century before, it would have required the working part of a population of 500,000 to create." Therefore, the Owenites concluded, people ought now to be some two hundred times as well off as they were fifty years ago. They were not starving fifty years ago. Indeed, as Owen deduced from his own childhood in an agricultural community, they were then better off than they had ever been since. Hence, there must now exist the possibility of general plenty and security, as we put it in the early chapters of this book. Society must be immediately re-organized to make actual this possibility. " As," the Owenites reasoned (if we may venture to epitomize a number of typical statements), " neither Lords Liverpool, Grey, nor Melbourne, nor the Tsar Alexander, nor Prince Metternich, has been sufficiently convinced of this necessity by the memoranda which Mr. Owen has repeatedly submitted to them, we must demonstrate in practice the possibility of universal plenty by establishing model communist communities in which everyone will live in plenty with very little work. Then at last everybody, both rich and poor, will surely be convinced and become communists."

Three distinct, though related, economic fallacies are contained in this Owenite reasoning.[1] These economic fallacies are worth analysis, not only in order to trace how present-day communist and socialist doctrine has been built up out of the trials and errors of successive generations, but also because the failure of the communist colonies is still sometimes raised (especially in America, where they are less wholly forgotten than in Britain) as an argument against the possibility of the abolition of capitalism.

[1] We are dealing here, let it be repeated, with *economic* fallacies alone. Owen's supreme *political* error was to suppose that socialism could, in any event, be established without the transference of power from the capitalist to the working class. For the success of the communist experiments, had it been possible, far from converting the capitalist class to communism, as the Owenites innocently supposed, would undoubtedly have excited the frenzied and terrified opposition of that class.

The first fallacy is suggested by the question with which Owen continues his estimate of the enormous increase in man's capacity to create wealth which had taken place in the course of his lifetime. " I asked myself," he writes, " what became of the difference between the wealth consumed by 2,500 persons and that which would have been consumed by 500,000." Owen knew very well what had happened to this wealth. It had afforded himself and his partners 5 per cent per annum interest on their capital, and, besides, a profit of over £300,000. Owen did not, however, pause to recollect what the partners of New Lanark had proceeded to do with their share of this accumulated wealth. (Owen, it is true, had put his share into founding a communist colony in Indiana. But this was exceptional—indeed, unique!) His partners, and all the other capitalists of Britain, had reinvested the greater part of their money. They had, to use the terminology of Part I, bought new means of production with it. They had used it to build new textile mills, or to build the first railways of Britain, or to build the early iron steamships, or to build the first mechanized ironworks. Their profits were used, in other words, for the continued industrialization of Britain, which had only just begun.

It was true that the money had gone into the pockets of the rich. But most of it had soon come out again. (Leaving behind it, of course, a nice sediment on which the rich, then as now, did themselves very well.) The pockets of the rich were, in fact, only a clumsily designed channel by which the money went to the further development of industrialization. Moreover, those very textile mills, including New Lanark, which had made possible the original two-hundredfold increase in the productivity of labour, had not built themselves. They had only been built by laying aside the surpluses made possible by still earlier technical improvements.

In other words, if the results of the earlier improvements of the industrial revolution had been used to increase the standard of living of the population, these improvements could never have been made at all—if an economic Hibernianism be permitted. It was only by devoting, in the form of private profit, the fruits of the earlier improvements in production to developing still further improvements, that the industrial revolution, which was itself the major premise of Owen's hopes, had been begun, or could be continued. Thus to devote the fruits of industrial development, not to still further development, but to raising the standard of life, was as yet an historical impossibility. Not until the development of man's productive powers had gone much further would the enjoyment of a high proportion of its fruits, such as socialism alone can ensure, become first compatible with, and then (as we saw in Chapter VII) an actual necessity for, the further development of those powers of production. In Owen's day, capitalism was still fulfilling, in the only way then possible, what Marx calls its " historic task and privilege " of industrializing the world. It could not yet be deflected from that task.

This initial fallacy in Owen's economics was, perhaps, an obstacle to the success of socialism in general in his day rather than to the success of particular communist colonies. But it is closely connected with his second mistake. This was to assume that the increase in the productivity of labour which had been achieved in the textile industry, had also been achieved in all other branches of production. The converse of this assumption was nearer the truth. In Owen's youth the textile industry almost alone had been put on to a mechanized basis. As his long life wore on, one industry after another revolutionized its technique. But they were only enabled to do so because nearly all the resources of production which were saved by the improved technique of the textile industry (and the other early improved industries) were devoted, not to raising the general standard of life, but to the task of revolutionizing, and then re-revolutionizing, the technique of all the other industries. The building of the railways alone, which was going on all through the latter part of Owen's life, absorbed an enormous proportion of the labour, skill, and other resources of production freed from the earlier improved industries.

Owen, in a word, sanguinely assumed that the industrial revolution had already taken place, when, in fact, it had only just begun. In particular, he assumed that the same two-hundredfold increase in the productivity of human labour which had so struck his imagination in the textile industry, had taken place in agriculture also. But it was just in the sphere of agriculture that this assumption was least of all true. For just as textile technique had improved most, agricultural technique had improved least. And yet the communist colonists had necessarily to devote themselves predominantly to agriculture if they were to be self-supporting. Hence the enormous errors of Owen's management. Hence his fantastic optimism as to the return which labour and capital devoted to agriculture would reap. Hence the over-expansion, and squandering of resources, almost on principle, which ruined all the colonies. For it was a principle of the Owenites that there was now enough and to spare for everyone. So why hoard, niggle, and make do with uncomfortable or unseemly houses ? Away with such parsimony—and on with the beautification and glorification of the colonies.

The third, and perhaps the gravest, of Owen's economic errors was to suppose that the colonists of an economically isolated, self-supporting community could expect the same return on their labour as could be achieved by workers in the outside world, exchanging their products on the world market. Owen, in other words, forgot entirely the second great factor which, associated with the revolution in technique, had made possible the two-hundredfold increase in productivity. He forgot the division of labour. The wealth which the British textile manufacturers, and the other British capitalists of his epoch were piling up, was not only due to their improved technique. It was also due to the fact that the markets of the world were theirs to buy and sell in. This great extension of the division of labour had been as necessary a condition of the new wealth as had been the revolution in production itself. They had been indissolubly associated developments, for the new, large-scale, productive technique would have been impossible without the extension of the market. But Owen assumed that he could retain all the advantages of a world-wide division of labour, while resorting in his colonies to a division of labour upon the most primitive scale alone. This was at least as serious a miscalculation as the assumption that agricultural technique had undergone that degree of improvement which textile technique had in fact alone achieved.

In sum, then, the Owenites neglected three facts : first, that the industrial revolution could never have begun, and could not be continued, unless the bulk of the new wealth was devoted, not to raising the standard of life, but to creating new means of production. Second, that anything like a two-hundredfold increase in men's capacity to produce wealth had occurred in the textile industry alone. And, third, that the startling increase in wealth production which they observed around them was as dependent upon a wide division of labour as upon a new industrial technique.

These are the explanations of the extraordinary improvidence of the communist colonists. They had been taught to believe in the possibility of realizing immediately in their colonies a plenty and security which was at that time and by that method totally impossible of attainment. Owen was a true prophet. His vision foresaw what the industrial revolution would in a hundred years of development make possible. But he took the tendency for the accomplished fact. And he neglected, not only all of the political conditions, but also the economic conditions, for the attainment of plenty and security.

The third phase of Owen's career (it began before he had been forced to abandon finally his attempt to found communist colonies) was one of co-operation with the working class movement of resistance to capitalism which was going on all through the first three-quarters of his life. In fact, Owen, for a short time, led the most important section of this movement. And yet his co-operation with the working class always remained limited and, on the whole, reluctant. Engels writes that when a realization of Owen's communist views dawned on the British governing class and they would have little more to do with him, " he turned directly to the working class and worked amongst them for another thirty years." In this passage Engels does Owen more than justice. Owen did work energetically amongst the Producers' Co-operative Societies—which for a time assumed the functions of Trade Unions—of his day.[1] And it was through their help that he set up his later colonies and experiments, such as the labour exchange bazaars. But he

[1] See p. 337 below.

almost entirely refused to enter into the political activities of the working class. Between 1830 and 1850 the Chartist movement stirred the British working class to its depths. Working class political activity reached a height to which it was not to attain again till the present century. But Owen remained aloof from all this. Just as he could see no reason why Liverpool and Castlereagh should not support socialism, so he could see no special reason why the working class should.

It was this extreme political blindness which destroyed the effectiveness of Owen's career. What possibilities would not have been opened if Owen, with his enormous energy and prestige, had become a Chartist : if he had been willing to learn what O'Brien, O'Connor, Harney, and the other Chartist leaders had to teach him, and had become one of the leaders of their movement. It is conceivable that effective political democracy might have been achieved in Britain fifty years earlier than it was, with all the incalculable effects upon the history of the world which this would have had. But it was not to be. Owen was the essential type of the English practical man. He had the greatest contempt for what he called " closet philosophers." He prided himself, above all, on being a man of action, who had the great concrete achievement of New Lanark behind him. He spent his life and his entire fortune in ceaseless and selfless activity for the cause which he had at heart, and which he rightly believed to be the cause of all humanity. And yet, just because he neglected to think out the nature of the problems with which he had to deal, nine-tenths of that activity was tragically wasted. It is hardly too much to say that Robert Owen's main service to the world was to show conclusively how the process of the abolition of capitalism and the establishment of socialism cannot be accomplished. He proved to demonstration that it cannot be done either by trying to convince the capitalists and their government that socialism would be better for everybody, or by founding communist colonies. He showed by process of elimination, by trial and error, that socialism can only be established as the inevitable resistance of the working class to the conditions of their lives under capitalism deepens and strengthens into conscious revolt. But it was a long and tragic process, and poor Owen was only in the end saved from heartbreak by retreating into a world of fantasy where the unrelieved failure of all his enterprises meant nothing to him.

It is interesting to contrast the failures of this supremely practical man with what the man who immediately succeeded him as the leading socialist in the world was able to accomplish. Marx (though he was extremely practical whenever he got an effective opportunity) was precisely what Owen would have called a closet philosopher. While Owen spent the years of his vigour ranging over Britain and America, making a great fortune, organizing the model industrial establishment of the world, bombarding every government with memoranda, founding communist colonies, and finally speaking, lecturing and debating without cease, Marx spent a great part of the same years of his life sitting in the reading room of the British Museum. Yet, while the memory of Robert Owen is dim and faint, the name of Marx, either as aspiration or as menace, dominates the world. The example must not lead us to despise action[1] or to suppose that the world can be saved merely by sitting and thinking. But it should warn us of the urgent necessity to discover before, or at any rate whilst, we act what are the essential conditions within which alone our actions can be effective.

Owen is remembered as a Utopian differing from Thomas More, for example, chiefly in that he tried to construct his ideal community of bricks and mortar instead of paper and ink. (The stouter materials proved the more transitory.) But he was not the last great Englishman to project his imagination towards a future society. Thirty-three years after his death the poet and socialist, William Morris, published *News from Nowhere*. It would be impossible to end even the most cursory and selective sketch of the development of the communist and socialist idea without mentioning this remarkable book.

William Morris cannot, however, be called a Utopian. He was, on the contrary, one of the first, and one of the greatest,

---

[1] Marx was intensely active whenever objective circumstances gave him even half a chance for effective action. And when they did not he never ceased to work for the creation of such an opportunity.

of the Englishmen who have whole-heartedly thrown in their lot with the international working class movement, because they saw in that movement the only force which could transform society. Moreover, Morris was one of the first Englishmen to make himself acquainted with the body of scientific social thought which the international working class movement evolved (almost entirely through the agency of its two leading figures, Marx and Engels) during his lifetime.

A man who had made these decisive steps forward could alone have written *News from Nowhere*. On the other hand, Morris's book is, in one sense, not a particularly satisfying example of the accounts of a future society. The old gibe that, according to Morris, the inhabitants of the twenty-second century will find their exclusive occupation in haymaking is not entirely unjustified. Morris's mediævalism and his generally anti-scientific attitude may make some parts of his account of a communist Britain irritating to-day. But we must remember that Morris was reacting not so much against science itself as against the prostitution of science to the overwhelming " commercialism," as he called it, which then, as now, characterized British capitalism. Thus Morris's inability even to guess at the major scientific endeavours which will probably form an important occupation of the citizens of socialist and communist communities, his view that æsthetically pleasing production must necessarily be conducted on a handicraft basis, and his failure to realize how highly any classless community, which is not supported by the labour of human slaves, will value its mechanized slaves, were the almost inevitable attitudes of a sensitive man of his class and day.

But there is much that is shrewd—and indeed profound— in his description of the England of A.D. 2000 odd. Moreover, no lack of realism can mar the lyricism of his ode to the beauty of the English countryside, or his denunciation of the odious, crass barbarity of the profit-making process which, in his day, (as it is now) was remorselessly destroying that beauty. For such an ode and such a denunciation embellish every page of his *News from Nowhere*.

It is not mainly, however, in its account of his ideal community that Morris's book differs from all its predecessing

Utopias. It differs from them, and surpasses them, and indeed ceases to be a Utopia at all, in this respect: it contains a clear and realistic description of how the abolition of capitalism and the establishment of socialism can be brought about. The chapter in *News from Nowhere* on " How the Change Came " demonstrates how far more clearly the poet may see into the nature of political reality than can the practical men of his day. Morris's book was published in 1891, in the first blush of the Fabian movement, when every English socialist was being taught by Mr. and Mrs. Sidney Webb, by Mr. Bernard Shaw, and by a dozen others, that socialism could undoubtedly be achieved by a process of cumulative reform at once so gradual that the capitalist class would never resist it, and so thorough that nothing of capitalism should remain.

Morris foresaw whither these cumulative reforms must lead. He saw that a point would come when these reforms would become incompatible with the further working of the profits system. He saw that then matters must come to a head, that either the workers must lose all that they had gained by the reforms, or must achieve the political power necessary to the abolition of capitalism and the establishment of socialism. He foresaw, moreover, that the actual conflict would be precipitated, not by the workers, but by the capitalists. For the capitalists would be sure to attempt to keep their system going by revoking all their concessions to the workers. More striking still he foresaw that the regular armed forces would become unreliable instruments for the suppression of the workers and that the capitalists would then recruit special armed bands of the middle class for the purpose. Under the name of " The Friends of Order," Morris gives a most acute forecast of the rise of Fascism. The civil war which he foresees is fought out primarily between the workers' forces and the " Friends of Order."

Moreover, Morris had an excellent realization of what it is that turns the scale in a revolutionary situation; of how the very defeats of the workers often serve as the decisive factor in arousing so widespread a horror of the Government that they lead to the workers' ultimate victory. In 1891 Morris prophesied that the Government would one day in the twentieth century open fire on a great workers' demonstration in Trafalgar Square and kill over a thousand people. (Very much as was to happen fourteen years later on Bloody Sunday in St. Petersburg.) " How fearful," comments Morris to his informant of the future. " And I suppose that this measure put an end to the whole revolution for that time." " No, no," cried old Hammond; " it began it," and he goes on to describe how the Government was made so odious by this deed that its forces were never afterwards able to reassert their hold over the loyalty of the population, until gradually their authority became completely worn out, their instruments of force had nothing upon which to base themselves, and became useless for lack of reliable hands to direct them.

The four hundred years which separate William Morris from Thomas More produced an instrument capable of transforming society, and so making actual the longing dreams of men: they produced the working class. By the eighteen-nineties they had also produced a consciousness in the minds of communist and socialist thinkers that it was the workers alone who could lead the world to socialism. But, so far as most British socialists and communists were concerned, they had done no more. No adequate science of social transformation, which could be used to show men how to rid themselves of capitalism, and build up socialism, had been evolved. Meanwhile, however, and almost unknown to British socialists, Marx and Engels, by mating English experience with the main achievements of French and German thought, had been able to bring such a science to birth.

CHAPTER **XXV**

The Working Class

THE misfortunes of the Utopian socialists demonstrated that the
working class must be the chief agent of social change. For no
other class or group has ever shown either the desire or the
capacity to lead the community in the task of abolishing capitalism and building up socialism. Socialism must be established
under the leadership of the working class, or it will not be
established at all.

This is why the establishment of socialism is only now a
practical proposition; for it is only now that the working class
of the world has come of age, as a leading class of society,
capable of remaking society according to its own interests and
desires. For the working class itself is an historical product. It
has not always existed, and it will not always continue to exist.[1]
It is true that there have always been poor, overworked and,
ever since civilization arose, oppressed people in the world; it
is true that such persons have always comprised by far the
larger part of the population. But they have not constituted a
working class in the, perhaps, technical sense of that term
which communists and socialists use. As we saw in Part I a
working class is composed of persons who live on a wage; or, to
be more scientific, of persons who are compelled to live by selling
their ability to work, and to work in other men's factories or
fields, since they have no access to fields or factories of their
own in which they might work for themselves.

Now the poor of previous epochs have not consisted of such
persons. The poor of classical antiquity, for example, consisted
of slaves, who were not paid wages, and of peasants, who,
although they often had too little land, had some land of their
own on which they worked.[2] Again, the poor of the middle ages
consisted of serfs, or villains, who worked upon land which they
possessed, or, which, in a sense, possessed them. For they were
bound to it. But they did not work for wages paid to them by

[1] For with the achievement of a classless society the working class ceases to
exist by merging into a homogeneous community.
[2] In the later centuries of antiquity they also consisted of state pensioners
see p. 320 below).

someone else who did own the land, and the other means of production, with which they worked. The wage-earning working class, a class of persons neither owning nor attached to any of the means of production, that is to say, made its appearance with capitalism. It remained small and undeveloped so long as capitalism remained small and undeveloped; it grew as capitalism grew, and finally it became the largest class in society when capitalism became the predominant economic system. And necessarily so, for the existence of such a propertyless, but legally free, class is a pre-requisite for carrying on capitalist production.

This class of legally free persons, without independent access to means of production, came into existence, as we saw, in the fifteenth century. But the working class did not become a wholly distinct, completely integrated, social entity until about a hundred and fifty years ago. Just as the inventions of the last half of the eighteenth century put capitalism upon its feet, so also they for the first time established work for wages in other men's factories or farms as the predominant way of life for the mass of the population, first of Great Britain and then of all Western Europe and North America.

A working class appears, then, only when an intermediate stage is set between the direct producer and the consumer. So long as the man who bakes the bread, or weaves the cloth, or forges the plough, makes these commodities with his own tools and out of his own raw materials, owns them when he has made them, and sells them to the consumer, the working class has not appeared. It is only when a third party to the transaction has arisen, it is only when one man, or group of men, makes the commodity, and another man, or group of men, owns both the means of production with which the commodity is made, and consequently the commodity itself, when it has been made, that the working class emerges.

The critical importance of this distinction is illustrated by the opening chapters of Mr. and Mrs. Webb's standard work, *The History of Trade Unionism*. These investigators discovered that the Trade Union, the characteristic form of organization of the working class, nowhere and never appears until this intermediate class of capitalists has been set between the producer (in the sense of the actual manipulator of the raw material) and the consumer of commodities. They show that the mediæval guild, an organization fundamentally different from a Trade Union, is the characteristic organization of direct producers who work with their own tools, own the commodity when they have made it, and themselves sell it to the consumers.

This form of economic organization was destroyed by the development of technique which became marked in the fifteenth century. For nearly three hundred years, however, it was predominantly the technique of transportation, rather than of production itself, which changed. The development of the technique of transportation (the invention of the effective ocean-going ship especially) enormously increased the size of the market for which the direct producers worked. This in turn permitted a great increase in the division of labour and specialization. It became profitable for whole groups of men, instead of single individuals, to work at producing, although still by hand, particular commodities, in order to satisfy the new and larger market. Such groups of associated workers arose in the form of the hired employees of those men who owned the means of production.

We have already described how this process happened in the case of agriculture. In the other fields of production the same process took place. Commodities came to be turned out, not in tiny workshops in which a master and his apprentice worked up their own raw material with their own means of production, but in larger and larger workshops in which a whole group of apprentices worked up their masters' raw material with their masters' means of production. These groups of hired apprentices were the embryo of the working class. For the gradual growth in the number of apprentices changed the whole character of their relationship to their masters, or employers. While there were approximately the same number of masters as apprentices, the apprentice was assured of ultimately becoming a master himself. He was an apprentice in the original sense of the term: a young man learning his craft so that in due course he might set up in production on his own account. But, clearly, so soon as the number of apprentices had become much larger than the number of masters it became impossible for all the apprentices ever to become masters. Some of them were bound to remain hired wage workers, working up other men's raw materials, with other men's tools. This profound change in the social structure took place very gradually over the three hundred years between 1500 and 1800. It was not until the eighteenth century that an important part of production came to be carried on in fairly large workshops employing (still on hand work) considerable groups of workers. This was what Marx distinguished as the manufacturing period. (He used the term " manufacturing " in its strict, original sense of " making by hand.") And it was in this period that the Trade Union, or combination of wage workers, arose.

The size of the wages, the working conditions, and the hours of work of the gradually more numerous and more permanent class of journeymen (literally workers paid by the day), or apprentices, were regulated during most of this long transitional period by the great Elizabethan Statute of Apprentices. Up till about 1730 technical, and therefore economic, conditions were still sufficiently stable to make it possible to regulate prices, wages, and conditions of work by law. Moreover, and this is the neglected essence of the matter, the owners of the means of production were in this period in urgent need of regulations primarily intended to prevent a rise in wages such as would make the use of their means unprofitable. For the whole of the rest of the population had not yet been deprived of independent access to the means of production. There was still a great deal of individual, scattered ownership of land, and of other means of production, worked not for profit, but by their owners with their own labour. Hence the bargaining position even of those who had become entirely dispossessed wage workers was by no means hopeless. They were not overwhelmingly numerous, and they had a chance, at any rate, of getting back into independent production on their own account if the wages which they were offered were too low. Hence the owners had pressing reasons for supporting a system of the legal regulation of hours and conditions of work.

Slowly but surely, however, the process of dispossession went on. Except in the case of the land, where forcible enclosures went on into the nineteenth century, the process now took place, in the main, by means of the superior competitive power of the newer, larger, more concentrated means of production which were already in the hands of capitalists. And then suddenly, in the second half of the eighteenth century, the process of dispossession was accelerated a hundredfold. Suddenly the technique of production was revolutionized. The most economically important series of inventions recorded in human history occurred in England between 1750 and 1800. The older, still individually owned, means of production became wholly obsolete almost overnight. The entire stock in trade, and independent livelihood, of the central mass of the still independently producing population were silently and secretly dispersed. The classical example is that afforded by the hand-loom weavers. No one went and took their hand looms from them by act of parliament, as it was still necessary to do in the case of the land of the peasant cultivators. What happened was that the new power looms and spindles so lowered the price of cotton goods that no one could now live by weaving by hand.

In this way an unknown but certainly extraordinarily high proportion of the population suddenly became dispossessed wage workers. They flooded into the labour market. Naturally their competition instantly destroyed the bargaining power of the wage workers as against the owners of the means of production. The danger of wages being driven up by the demand for wage labour exceeding the supply abruptly disappeared. Wages, on the contrary, tended to fall sharply. What need was there for the capitalists to maintain any longer the system of the regulation of wages by law to which they had hitherto strongly adhered? It was suddenly discovered that such |regulations were contrary to the eternal laws of the universe. By a series of extraordinary decisions, Parliament repealed every effective clause of the Statute of Apprentices, and of the other regulatory statutes. It had been discovered that if the labour market was left free the owners of the means of production could now impose almost any terms they liked upon the wage workers. For the class of men and women, and above all of children, who had to live by working for wages, determined in amount by the supply of, and the demand for, labour, had suddenly doubled and then redoubled its numbers. The working class had ended its long period of inter-uterine development, and had been cast out into the world.

To-day the fact that the workers are, actually or potentially, the only force which can seriously challenge the continued existence of capitalism is generally, although more or less tacitly, realized. No one thinks of appealing, as Owen never ceased to do, to the contemporary Lord Castlereagh or to Mr. Pierpont Morgan to establish socialism. (And as for the Tsar of Russia, another object of Owen's petitions, he is no longer there to appeal to.) Most people feel instinctively that, although the workers evidently do not always or everywhere attempt to replace capitalism with socialism, no one else will do so if they will not.

But in England and America this sociological, or psychological, fact was, we saw, only discovered by long experience, and even now most people do not attempt to ascertain the reason for it. Moreover, even to-day (more especially in America) the fact that the workers are in actual practice the only people who ever lead a sustained and serious opposition to capitalism is from time to time forgotten again. New schemes are hatched by which capitalism is to be got rid of, if not, as with Owen, by appealing to the capitalists themselves, then by appeals to the technicians, the civil servants, or this or that category of the intermediate sub-classes. The same considerations which caused Owen to appeal to kings and parliaments make our modern Utopians appeal to the technicians or the civil servants. They see, as Owen did, that those people who already enjoy a measure of power are in the best position to effect the necessary social transformation " peacefully, with the greatest advantage and on the most magnificent scale." They see, as Owen did, that the workers are poor, and, so long as capitalism lasts, relatively ignorant and apparently powerless. They see that if society is to be transformed under their leadership the process must be long, stormy, and painful. They recoil from such a prospect. How much nicer it would be, they reflect, if the job could be done in a polite manner by the " trained minds " of the middle classes. (Mr. H. G. Wells is, in England, the leading exponent of this attractive view.)

Unfortunately, however, appeals to these trained minds remain almost, though not quite, as futile as did Owen's appeals to the Prince Regent, to Metternich, and to the Tsar Alexander. For those who make them forget the all-important fact that the greater number of these trained minds have been so trained that they do not desire, and indeed cannot even imagine, any system of society other than capitalism. They have, to return to Veblen's phrase, a trained incapacity for the job which they are asked to do. It is only the un-mistrained workers who can in a majority desire, or even conceive of, the total replacement of the present economic and social system by another. And, in historical fact, all serious attempts to replace capitalism, including the one successful attempt, have relied upon the social dynamic of the resistance of the working class to the conditions of life imposed upon them by capitalism. It is, then, by an enquiry into the way of life of the working class under capitalism that we may achieve a comprehension of this remarkable, but undoubted, historical fact. For we shall find that the conditions of life which capitalism always has, and does now, impose upon the working class are such as inevitably to cause that class to struggle continually against those conditions of life. This struggle becomes, in the end, a struggle for existence. For in the end capitalism creates conditions in which whole sections of the working class cannot live. This struggle for existence in turn becomes a struggle to destroy capitalism, since it is capitalism which is creating the impossible situation for the workers. Finally this long struggle *against* capitalism becomes a positive struggle *for* socialism, becomes a struggle to realize on this earth a socialist economic and social system as the alternative to capitalism.

So much has been written about the conditions of the first generations of the English factory workers that it is as unnecessary as it would be intolerable to darken these pages with another description of their miseries. For in this, the childhood of the working class, a great part of the workers were in fact children. The new machines demanded, above all, cheap, light, but immensely prolonged, labour. The textile industry (then known as " the great industry ") dominated the situation. For this industry alone had become mechanized. And for labour at the new power looms and spindles young children, if they could be driven without limit, were exactly suitable.

We have indicated the reaction of the generous spirit of Robert Owen to the conditions of the child workers of the textile industry of his day. It is some measure of those conditions that Owen's greatest reform at New Lanark was to increase the age of his working children to ten years, and to fix their hours of work first at fourteen, and then at twelve. We may measure the standard of the times by the fact that one of the most humane and, in this matter at any rate, one of the most intelligent of men could accomplish no more.[1]

The descriptions of the working to death of many hundreds of thousands of children in the early decades of the nineteenth century given by such social historians as Mr. and Mrs. Hammond are now taught in many British schools and universities.[2] In many factories an average of sixteen hours a day was worked by children from six years of age upwards. Mr. and Mrs. Hammond describe the conditions of the child workers as follows:

" The punishments for arriving late in the morning had to be made cruel enough to overcome the temptation to tired children to take more than three or four hours in bed. One witness before Sadler's Committee had known a child, who had reached home at eleven o'clock one night, get up at two o'clock

---

[1] " At the outset, Owen had resolved to take on no more parish apprentices, but to draw the necessary supply of child labour from the population resident in Lanark, and it does not appear that he ever found difficulty in procuring the services of as many children as were required. As we have already seen, he fixed the limit of age at ten: below that age the children might, if the parents chose, attend the school, but there was no work for them in the factory. On a point of scarcely less importance he was compelled to defer to the wishes of his partners. Dale had worked the mills thirteen hours, with intervals of one and a half hours for meals. Monstrous as those hours appear to us, especially when we remember that a large proportion of those employed were young children, they were too merciful for the ordinary manufacturer of that day. Owen told the Committee of 1816 that for some time during his management the hours of work at the New Lanark Mills were fixed at fourteen a day (including two hours' intervals for meals). It was not until January 1816 that he was enabled to reduce the hours to twelve a day, with one and a quarter hours for meals, leaving ten and three-quarter hours for actual work." (*Robert Owen: A Biography*, by Frank Podmore, pp. 92–3.)

[2] The still unsurpassed descriptions given by Marx in the first volume of *Capital*, and by Engels in *The Condition of the English Working Class*, are never referred to; for if the student read them he might read on.

next morning in panic and limp to the mill gate. In some mills scarcely an hour passed in the long day without the sound of beating and cries of pain. Fathers beat their own children to save them from a worse beating by the overseers. In the afternoon the strain grew so severe that the heavy iron stick known as the billy-roller was in constant use, and, even then, it happened not infrequently that a small child, as he dozed, tumbled into the machine beside him to be mangled for life, or, if he were more fortunate, to find a longer Lethe than his stolen sleep. In one mill, indeed, where the owner, a Mr. Gott, had forbidden the use of anything but a ferule, some of the slubbers tried to keep the children awake, when they worked from 5 in the morning to 9 at night, by encouraging them to sing hymns. As the evening wore on, the pain and fatigue and tension on the mind became insupportable. Children would implore anyone who came near to tell them how many hours there were still before them. A witness told Sadler's Committee that his child, a boy of six, would say to him, ' Father, what o'clock is it ? ' I have said perhaps it is seven o'clock. ' Oh, it is two hours to nine o'clock ? I cannot bear it.' "

(The Town Labourer, p. 160.)

It is clear that such conditions could only have been imposed upon the children of a population whose resistance had been morally and physically broken; which had been, in fact, if not in form, enslaved. We cannot imagine for example the sturdy and rebellious peasants of fourteenth-century England allowing their children to be so treated. We cannot even imagine the hand-loom weavers, or the agricultural workers, of the first half of the eighteenth century being forced to suffer such things. For these classes still in some measure possessed that indispensable condition of liberty—an independent access to the means of production. Only a class whose possibility of independent existence had wholly disappeared could have been forced to submit to the wholesale destruction of their own children. And such an enslavement had indeed taken place. The contemporary revolution in the way in which production was organized had enabled a relatively small class to deprive the British people of independent access to the means of production.

The British people had such access when they, individually, owned the small, easily devisable means of production of the pre-industrial period: they will have such access again when they collectively own the gigantic means of production of to-day and to-morrow. But, in the meanwhile, during the painful centuries when the means of production were already too big to own individually, and yet were not sufficiently developed to serve as a basis for collective ownership, the mass of the population inevitably became enslaved to the limited class of persons whose private property the means of production necessarily became.

But this enslavement was economic and invisible, not legal and political. Indeed, the people's loss of access to the means of production was represented as a liberation. The casting of the people of England, bound and gagged, into the furnace of industrialism was accomplished in the name of human emancipation. The brief and stunted generations of the early nineteenth century were much freer, according to the law, than their forefathers had been. The elaborate regulations of wages and of conditions of work contained in the eighteenth-century Statute Book had been one by one repealed by Parliament in the name of freedom of contract. The Government which finally destroyed the last of the old regulatory statutes had been created in order to liberalize the British Constitution. It had done so. From 1832 onwards, liberty of contract reigned supreme in Britain, and by 1844 the contemporary Lord Londonderry could order the inhabitants of " his town of Seaham " to refuse to succour some miners who were engaged in a transient strike, and were thus, Lord Londonderry wrote, waging " an unjust and senseless warfare against their proprietors and masters."[1] Perfect liberty of contract had produced an effective and, in the heat of the moment, admitted serfdom, such as had not been known in England since the dark ages.

Such, then, were the miseries and the servitude of the British workers in the youth and early manhood of capitalism. To what extent have these miseries ceased or changed in character ? For the moral which is always drawn from their recital in our schools

[1] Quoted by S. and B. Webb in their *History of Trade Unionism*, p. 166

and universities is that the present condition of the British people is relatively paradisial. The present generation of the British governing class continually congratulates itself that it is not as its grandfathers were. And it is true that the dramatic terrors of child torture and of industrial serfdom have been abolished. They have been abolished by a long series of measures, every one of which was obstinately and passionately resisted by the capitalist class. Nor were the capitalists, from their point of view, mistaken in this resistance. For the legal restrictions of the hours of labour by the Factory Acts, the creation of an educational system, and the development of a system of social services, were all in principle anti-capitalist measures. They were laws which limited, that is to say, that freedom of contract, between those who own and those who do not own the means of production, which is an essential feature of capitalism. They were all measures designed to prevent the unmodified operation of capitalism as a system. Both in theory and in practice they flouted the basic principles of capitalism.

We are now habitually told that the enactment and, in a sense, successful operation of these measures of reform demonstrates the contention that capitalism can be so modified as to eliminate its abuses and yet preserve its general and effective principle of production for profit. This was not the view of the earlier spokesmen of capitalism. The men who resisted these reforms said that if they were enacted they would so curtail and burden the operations of capital as to slow down the whole profit-making system and thus, by causing wholesale dismissals of workers, create more misery than they abolished. For a time these prophecies of some of the best theorists and the ablest practical men of capitalism failed to materialize. But to-day we are beginning to realize that they were not devoid of substance.

In capitalist Britain to-day torture by over-work has largely disappeared.[1] An elaborate system of legal and Trade Union regulations of the conditions and remuneration of work is in effect. And a system of insurances and pensions alleviates the

---

[1] Or rather, we should write torture by immoderately long hours of work has largely disappeared. For, above all in the United States, but also now and to an ever increasing extent in Britain, the pace set in such great plants as those of Mr. Ford is so great that the length of time which a worker remains in his otherwise attractive employment is said to average under one year.

miseries of those who are denied work. These great reforms have in themselves immensely benefited the British workers; but they have not done so to anything approaching the extent that was expected of them, and to-day they are beginning to benefit the British workers less and less. For to the torture of destitution combined with racking overwork has succeeded the torture of destitution combined with enforced idleness. No infernal scenes of six-year-old children working for fifteen hours a day under the lash can be found in modern Lancashire. But walk the back streets of its cities, where the physical decay of almost every house proclaims the ruin of the " great industry," and you will discover a slower but hardly less awful torture of the men, women, and children of Lancashire. A gentle torture of enforced idleness, a listlessness and aimlessness born of under-nourishment combined with the frustration of every possibility of creative effort—these are the conditions of life to which the attempt to reform the capitalist system without abolishing it has in the end brought considerable and growing sections of the British working class.

No doubt it would be a far less terrifying prospect to be born the child of an unemployed weaver of Lancashire to-day than it was to be born the child of a ruined hand-loom weaver of the same county in 1800. To-day your prospect would be physical and mental stunting by periodic under-nourishment, over-crowding, and deprivation of light and air. From your fourteenth year you would probably experience more or less permanent idleness, varied by occasional casual labour. You would almost certainly receive enough of one sort of relief or another to prevent any great danger of actual starvation. It would be a far less terrifying prospect, but it would be a far more hopeless one. For we must not forget that if the child of a worker in 1800 some-how survived into manhood a considerable degree of oppor-tunity was open to him. Industrialization was going forward at an ever-accelerating speed. The possibility of a worker's son acquiring a substantial share of the means of production (as Owen did[1]), and becoming a capitalist was, as always, very

[1] But Owen was the son of a skilled handicraft worker, a sadler, in a still agri-cultural district. This was a very different thing from being born the son of a worker in one of the new industries or of a worker in one of the old industries, such as hand-loom weaving, which were being destroyed.

small, but it existed. And the opportunity to become a comparatively well paid, skilled worker, overseer or manager was, no doubt, considerable. At any rate, society would not then, as it does so often now, meet the worker with a blank refusal to give him any opportunity of advancement.

But, it will be suggested, is it not true that there was, at any rate for Britain and America, an intermediate period when the horrors of capitalism's youth had been abolished, and our contemporary horrors, caused by capitalism's decay, had not begun ? Was there not a period in the latter half of the nineteenth century when British capitalism in particular provided the mass of the working class with very much better conditions than it has ever done before or since ?

If we were to judge by the degree to which British capitalism succeeded in that period in acquiring the support of the workers, we should suppose that it greatly improved their conditions. But the facts do not support this conclusion. This was the very period in which elaborate investigations into the living conditions of the British workers were undertaken. For example, it was at the very apex of this, the most triumphant period of British capitalism (in 1866), that Charles Booth started his famous investigation into the *Labour and Life of the People*, and discovered that the conditions of both were degraded beyond his belief.[1]

The social investigators of that period discovered that there stretched beneath and all about them an ocean of human misery of which neither they nor anyone else articulate in Britain had any knowledge. At the very zenith of the prosperity of British capitalism there existed a vast and dark region of hunger, insecurity, and perpetual overwork from which no cry arose. The millions of unskilled, unorganized, uneducated men and women who inhabited it had no way of making their point of view articulate; indeed, they had no way of becoming fully conscious themselves that they had a distinct and separate point of view.

[1] From 1850 onwards there also appeared a series of authoritative Government reports describing the conditions of the life and work of the wage-earning population, e.g. the series of reports of the Child Employment Commission; the annual reports of the inspectors appointed under the Factory Acts, and the seven Public Health Reports. It was from these unimpeachable sources that Marx drew his deadly quotations in the first volume of *Capital*.

Their minds were almost as perfectly enslaved as their bodies: they kissed the imperial rod by which they were ruled, and tried to nourish themselves upon their barmecidal share in the enormous prosperity which surrounded them. Their silence and acquiescence were due, not to any adequate improvement in the lot of the majority of the working class, but to special causes which we shall investigate in the next chapter.

CHAPTER XXVI

The Conditions of the Working Class under Capitalism

THE conditions of the British workers have twice altered decisively since the rise of capitalism.[1] From 1800 to 1850 the horrors of early industrialism continued substantially unalleviated. For if the conditions of the wage workers were in some respects improved, as by the gradual limitation of child labour, in other respects they grew worse. (By the imposition of the new Poor Law in 1833, for example.) But from 1850, or, to be precise, from the surmounting of the complex and severe crisis of 1848, with the repeal of the Corn Laws and the passage of the Ten Hours Act, British capitalism got fairly into its stride. From that time onwards it succeeded in raising somewhat the general level of the whole working class, and in substantially improving the conditions of a sub-class of skilled workers. The wages of these skilled workers rose steadily from 1850 to 1875, and their Trade Union organizations were gradually and reluctantly, but in the end effectively, granted the right to speak in their name and to protect their interests. From 1875 onwards the increase in the money wages of the skilled workers became much slower and, in some cases, ceased. But to compensate for this a steady and substantial decline in prices began, so that the rise in real wages continued steadily, and even at an accelerated pace, until 1900.[2]

[1] It would, no doubt, be preferable to describe the conditions of the working class in all the well developed capitalist states, or, at any rate, to make a comparative study of those conditions in Britain since 1850 and America since 1865. Both for reasons of space, however, and also for the sufficient reason that I have neither the theoretical nor the practical knowledge necessary to write of working class conditions elsewhere, this chapter contains an estimate of the conditions of the British working class alone. We can safely assume that where working class conditions under capitalism have greatly deviated from those of the British workers they have been worse rather than better.

[2] The late Mr. Theodore Rothstein, in his indispensable work, *From Chartism to Labourism* (Lawrence & Wishart), makes 1875 an important turning-point in the economic fortunes of the British working class. He is intent to prove that the reactionary, non-political Trade Unionism of the British workers during the last quarter of the nineteenth century failed even in its own limited purpose of raising the standard of life of the skilled workers. Accordingly, he devotes two elaborately documented chapters entitled " The Fruits of Opportunism " to showing that money wages ceased to rise appreciably after 1875. He then dilates upon the undeniable sloth and arrogance of the British Trade Union leadership between 1870 and 1890.

But in the following chapter, which he calls " The Roots of Opportunism," he

This was the period of general working class acquiescence in capitalism. For the new and alone articulate sub-class, consisting of skilled workers in the basic industries, the engineers, the cotton operatives, the hewers in the coal pits, and the skilled iron and steel operatives, had little or nothing in common either with their own fathers, who had laboured and suffered in the first half of the century, or with the unskilled workers of their own day, who were labouring and suffering still. If the whole British working class had shared in the outrageous conditions of life and labour endured by the unskilled, their helpless resignation would have been inconceivable. If the highly skilled, organized workers in the great basic industries had been subjected to conditions even similar to those endured by the rest of the working class, a formidable anti-capitalist working class movement would certainly have arisen.

For the skilled, organized workers in the great industries are the natural leaders of a working class. And, in fact, until 1850, when the conditions of the skilled, organized workers were not greatly superior, a formidable anti-capitalist movement did, as we shall see, exist. It was not until British capitalism succeeded in raising, it is hardly too much to say, half out of the working class, a whole section of the workers, by giving them relatively very favourable conditions, that this movement of revolt against capitalism was checked. But between 1850 and 1900 the British capitalists, by thus dividing the working class, by isolating the mass from its natural leaders, succeeded in winning from the British workers a greater degree of acquiescence than has ever been given to capitalism by any other working class at any other time. (With the exception, perhaps, of the American working class between 1921 and 1929.)

The acquiescence of the British workers in capitalism proved

is naturally constrained to enquire why it was that the alleged failure of their leaders to do anything for them did not provoke a more substantial movement of revolt amongst the rank and file of the skilled workers. He discovers an explanation in the fact that from 1875 to 1900, whilst money wages remained almost constant, prices, more especially of working class necessities, fell by 40 to 50 per cent. Real wages increased, then, by this substantial amount.

Hence he is forced in this chapter to destroy his own previous argument. For it is just as useful to the workers if their Trade Unions maintain their wages in a period of falling prices as if they raise their wages in a period of constant prices. It is a thousand pities that Mr. Rothstein marred his book with this absurd bit of special pleading.

as transitory, however, as did the relatively satisfactory conditions of their upper section.

Exactly in 1900, prices began to rise again, whilst wages failed increasingly to keep pace with them. For the first time in half a century the conditions of the British working class, including the skilled workers, began to deteriorate. And in just over two decades a new, apparently anti-capitalist, and undoubtedly working class, movement, such as had not existed in Britain since 1850, had grown from nothing into the second largest political party in the state.

The progress of this movement has, however, been checked and deflected by various and substantial economic and political concessions granted by the British capitalists to the workers. Between 1906 and 1914 the foundations of the present elaborate British system of social services were laid down. Health insurance, old age pensions, and a very limited scheme of unemployment insurance were enacted. Immediately after the war this system of social services was widely extended. Housing subsidies were instituted, the number of Trade Boards (by which minimum wage rates are fixed in certain industries) were greatly increased, and, above all, a comparatively wide system of unemployment insurance was enacted. In subsequent years Old Age pensions have been increased, widows' pensions created, and the provision of various forms of public relief extended.

These reforms have been intended to prevent a sudden decline in the standard of life of the British working class. For if they had not been enacted the standard of life of the British workers would, no doubt, have fallen fast and far in the post-war years. The economic position of British capitalism, in spite of its victory in the war, had so deteriorated (basically for the reasons which we analysed in Part I) that, if economic forces had been allowed free play, the British workers would have found their conditions of life regressing rapidly to those which their ancestors had endured before 1850. The fear that, if the British workers' conditions should return to what they then were, so also would their opinions, has driven the British governing class to take more elaborate measures for the maintenance of the standard of life of the workers than have ever been taken by any other capitalist class in any country.

But how, the reader will object, was the economically hard-pressed British governing class able to afford to prop up the workers' standard of life by extended social services ? The answer is that the funds out of which the British social services are paid come, in the ultimate economic analysis, not from competitively derived profit, every penny of which is now urgently needed to maintain an adequate rate of profit on the British capitalists' vast total capital, but from monopolistic, semi-feudal tribute derived from Britain's vast dependent Empire. The exploitation of a whole sub-continent such as India, in which wealth is to a large extent taken from the workers and peasants by direct, monopolistic methods, without the check of effective competition, modifies the working of the laws of capitalism in favour of the British capitalists—so long as they possess their Empire.

When we examine the workings of the British economic system to-day we are confronted with a situation which has similarities to the economy of the later Roman Empire as well as to that of a normal, typical capitalist system, in which the ordinary laws of a competition are still almost exclusively predominant. If the British capitalists had no other way of extracting their wealth than by the normal workings of competitive capitalism, they would not have a penny to spare for concessions to the British workers. But the dependent Empire, by allowing them to sell a substantial proportion of their exports well above their price of production, since they sell in semi-monopoly conditions, provides them with a fund which can, and is, used to prevent the British workers from becoming desperate. " *Panis et circenses* " are distributed in the old Roman way, although in money instead of kind. Marx has a very suggestive comment (written in 1877) in this connection. He says that at the end of the Republican period, the Roman, like the English, peasants lost their land to the landlords (who also became possessed of money capital), and thus became " free " men, apparently only able to live if they were employed by these landlords. The stage seemed set for the birth of Roman capitalism, for its pre-condition, viz. the concentration of the means of production in a few hands and the consequent appearance of a propertyless mass, was accomplished. But capitalism did not appear. The Roman proletarians, instead of becoming wage workers, became, as Marx puts it, " a mob of do-nothings," maintained by doles from the public treasury. (Meanwhile slaves carried on the productive system.) But this development was only possible because Rome had laid the whole world in tribute, and so had available apparently inexhaustible funds out of which to maintain her proletarians in idleness. Can anyone deny the resemblance of this situation to that of contemporary Britain ? When the British governing class congratulates itself, as it does not cease to do, on the quiescence of the dole-maintained workers of the " distressed areas," does it ever reflect on what it is endeavouring to make of the British people ?

However, the economy of modern Britain resembles only very partially that of ancient Rome. Capitalism *did* come to birth in Britain. Over 80 per cent of the British proletariat are still wage workers, not dole drawers.[1] Above all, the British Empire does not reign unchallenged over the whole civilized world as Rome once did. On the contrary, her power and her wealth are, as we saw, acutely challenged everywhere both by other powerful and ravenous capitalist empires and by increasing intransigence on the part of the colonial peoples. Hence the ability of the British capitalists to keep their workers quiet with timely doses of bread and circuses is relatively limited.

It has been essential for the British governing class, if they would prevent the growth of a new revolutionary movement amongst the workers, not only to provide a minimum subsistence for the worst-off workers, but to continue to maintain a favoured sub-section in work and good wages. And this also they have so far succeeded in doing. There still exists in Britain a distinct sub-class of better-paid, better-treated, workers whose point of view may be expected to differ from that of the mass of their class. But this elevated sub-section is not composed of workers in the same trades as it was from 1850 to 1900. Then the favoured workers were engaged in the great staple industries of coal, cotton, shipbuilding, and general engineering. The conditions of these workers have now immensely deteriorated. Some of them,

---

[1] Nor, of course, are there anything like 20 per cent of permanently unemployed workers. Seven per cent or 8 per cent would be nearer the figure of what might be called the permanently unemployed, i.e. of workers who get no opportunity of work for years together.

notably the skilled miners, have almost sunk to the conditions of unskilled labourers. All of them are decimated by unemployment. But in their place there has arisen a distinct class of favoured workers, concentrated geographically in the South of England, especially around London, and engaged chiefly in light, secondary industries. To them must be added a substantial and ever-growing body of relatively well-paid workers engaged in luxury trades, producing services rather than goods, for the property-owning class of the imperial metropolis.

What must be our estimate of the net effect of these various counteracting influences upon the present conditions of the British workers ? Have their conditions regressed to those which they endured before 1850 ? Or has the progress made between 1850 and 1900 been continued ? Taking the broadest and most general view, and disregarding all secondary movements, I incline to the following estimate of the contemporary (1936) condition of the British working class: It would be untrue to suggest that there has been any general regression to pre-1850 standards. On the other hand, the general improvement of the standard of life provided by British capitalism, which lasted half a century, stopped in 1900 and has never been resumed. Would it, then, be true to say that there has been some general regression, although not to the level of the first half of the nineteenth century, during the last thirty-five years ?

This is an extremely difficult question to answer; indeed, the answer must depend on what weight the enquirer attaches to particular factors. For some of the conditions of the British workers have notably improved in the last thirty-five years, whilst others have as notably deteriorated. Let us take the credit side of the account first. The level of real wages remains the predominant factor in determining the working class standard of life. Money wages were calculated by the Labour Research Department, using official figures,[1] to have been, at the end of 1934, 179 per cent of what they were in 1900. The Ministry of Labour's cost of living figure stood at that time at 160 per cent

[1] See *The Two Classes* (L.R.D., 2d.).

Ls

of 1900. So that on this basis there had been, for employed workers, an appreciable increase in real wages.[1] In addition, there has been a substantial, although varying, reduction in hours of work. A relatively comprehensive system of social services including, above all, unemployment benefit, old age pensions, health insurances, and improved educational facilities has been established. Finally, dwellings (for perhaps seven or eight million persons) of a very much superior type to anything which has ever before been available to the British workers[2] have been built. Another and usually neglected source of increased incomes is the increase of the number of workers employed, or seeking employment (and often, therefore, entitled to unemployment benefit), per family, due to the fall in the birth rate and to the increase in women's employment. (The extent of this increase can be exaggerated, however. For there has been an offsetting decrease in women's employment due to the decline of the textile industry.)

On the debit side must be set first the formidable increase in the incidence of unemployment. As no national statistics of the number of unemployed existed before 1921, it is again impossible to make any exact comparison. But it seems probable that unemployment is nearly four times as great as it was thirty-six years ago.[3] Three or four decades before that, unemployment was probably much lower, while the rate seems to have almost doubled in the last six or seven years. Thus unemployment seems to have been growing steadily during the whole of this century, and to be growing to-day at a sharply accelerating speed.[4]

The Labour Research Department pamphlet cited above

[1] Sir John Orr's report (see below) shows that there has been an increase of 6 per cent in the total calories of food eaten per head per day by the population since 1909, and an increase of 25 per cent in the consumption of animal fats. When the reader has seen the extreme inadequacy of the present diet of the population (see p. 325), he will realize what it must have been like in 1909.

[2] It is not so much that the houses themselves are superior as that, being (up till 1931) for the most part publicly built, the housing estates are decently planned and spaced so that the houses have gardens, light, and air.

[3] For the Trade Union records show that the number of their members who suffered from unemployment seldom rose to 5 per cent, whilst between 10 per cent and 20 per cent of the insured population are to-day unemployed in what we are assured is a time of great prosperity.

[4] In these comparisons we must ignore the cyclical fluctuations: we must, that is to say, compare boom with boom, and slump with slump.

attempts to correlate the increase of unemployment with the rise in the real wages of the employed workers since 1900. At the end of 1934 the percentage of insured workers unemployed was 17·7 per cent. Thus the total weekly earnings of the working class as a whole, taking employed and unemployed together, were only 82·3 per cent of 179 per cent of their 1900 earning. In other words, the working class's money earnings in 1934 were 145·5 per cent of what they were in 1900. But in 1934 the cost of living was, we repeat, 160 per cent of what it was in 1900. So that the real earnings of the working class in 1934 were only 91·1 per cent of what they were in 1900. According to this calculation, the growth of unemployment since 1900 has converted a rise of 19 per cent in real wages for the employed workers into a drop of 9 per cent in the real earnings from wages of the working class as a whole. The calculation avowedly takes no account of the growth of social services, which must be set against this drop of 9 per cent in earnings from wages.[1]

In any case, however, the effect of the enormous increase in the level of unemployment which has taken place in the last thirty-six years cannot be fully shown in figures. The growth of insecurity for the whole working class, including those who seldom or never have themselves been unemployed, is perhaps its most serious feature. Its sheer economic effect has, of course, been mitigated by unemployment insurance benefit, as indeed it had to be, if the stark alternative of starvation or revolt was not to be presented to considerable sections of the British workers. But benefit has always been kept sufficiently low, and sufficiently difficult to obtain, to make the life of the unemployed very wretched. It is certain that in those areas where unemployment has towered up to something approaching 30 per cent, all the other gains which have been made by the working class have been entirely offset.

The second adverse factor is the increased and increasing intensity of work. This has gone far to offset the decrease of hours. It is felt most, perhaps, in the hard-pressed industries, such as coal mining, but it extends to the prosperous industries such as motor-car production and light engineering. Third, the

---

[1] It is also clearly imperfect in that it takes no account of unemployment in 1900, which was quite appreciable.

system of social services has lately been itself curtailed. Beginning with the extension of miners' hours in 1926, and continuing with the tightening up of the conditions of the receipt of unemployment benefit, and the imposition of a family means test on its recipients, a series of measures have in the past ten years reversed the tendency to extend the social services which had existed ever since 1906.

I shall not attempt to strike a balance between these counteracting factors. But, even if we were to come to the conclusion that, on the whole, the condition of the British workers has never been appreciably better than it is to-day, then that would be a deadly comment upon the past record of British capitalism rather than a panegyric on its present achievements. For as soon as we examine it we find that the present condition of the great majority of the British workers, judged, not by a comparison with their former condition, but on any absolute standard of human need, is a very wretched one.

The general level of purchasing power of the class is best envisaged by the income figures, quoted in Chapter I, of an average of £25 a year per head, or a family income of £100 a year, for a family of four, for the poorer two-thirds of the British population. But such an average figure tells us little of the actual living standards of the eight million or so families which comprise the mass of the population. The best available picture of their present situation is given in a report entitled *Food, Health and Income,* by Sir John Boyd Orr (Macmillan). This report is the result of an investigation conducted by official bodies such as the Rowett Institute and the Market Supply Committee. The object of this investigation was to show how much, and what kinds of, food the different sections of the British population were able to buy. For this purpose the population was divided in six groups according, not to the income received per family, but according to the income available per head. Thus full account was taken of the decisive effect upon the amount of purchasing power available per head, of the number of earners in relation to the number of dependants which a family contains. The following table was compiled.

TABLE IV

Classification of the Population by Income Groups and Average Food Expenditure per head in each Group

Group	Income per head per week	Estimated average expenditure on food	Estimated population of group Numbers	Percentage
I	Up to 10s.	4s.	4,500,000	10
II	10s. to 15s.	6s.	9,000,000	20
III	15s. to 20s.	8s.	9,000,000	20
IV	20s. to 30s.	10s.	9,000,000	20
V	30s. to 45s.	12s.	9,000,000	20
VI	Over 45s.	14s.	4,500,000	10
Average	30s.	9s.	—	—

The reader will see that Sir John Orr takes a much more favourable view of the total amount of income available to the poorer two-thirds of the population than does Mr. O. R. Hobson (see p. 23). Mr. Hobson simply divided the number of non-income tax payers into the amount of the national income not subject to income tax. His result of £25 a year, or under 10s. a week, per head would clearly place a much larger percentage of the population in Group I that does the Orr report. (The discrepancy may be partly accounted for by the fact that Sir John Orr makes no allowances for reductions in income due to sickness and short-time working. See Appendix V, p. 59.) In any case, we shall be in no danger of exaggerating the gravity of the position if we accept Sir John Orr's figures of income distribution. Sir John Orr is a skilled dietician. Here are his conclusions on the adequacy of the food which the above distribution of income will buy in the different groups. His standard of adequacy is, it should be explained, a diet such that no improvement in health could be expected by an increase in the quantity of any foodstuff contained in it.

" The average diet of group I is inadequate for health in all the constituents considered; group II is adequate only in total proteins and total fat; group III is adequate in energy value, protein and fat, but below standard in minerals and vitamins; group IV is adequate in iron, phosphorus and

vitamins, but probably below standard in calcium; group V
has an ample margin of safety in everything with the possible
exception of calcium; in group VI the standard requirements
are exceeded in every case."

(Orr Report, pp. 33 and 36.)

Sir John Orr and his colleagues are public servants. Hence we
may say that in 1936 the British Government announced that
10 per cent of the British people were getting inadequate
quantities of every kind of food, and that a further 20 per cent
got inadequate quantities of all the body-building and health-
preserving foods. Thus 13,500,000 British subjects, 30 per cent
of the entire population, are very seriously under-nourished.
Another 20 per cent (Group III) get inadequate minerals and
vitamins: another 20 per cent get enough of everything except
calcium (which means in practice that the one important foodstuff of which they cannot afford an adequate supply is milk);
the next 20 per cent have plenty of everything except milk, but
hardly enough of that, while only the top 10 per cent of the
population enjoy real plenty.

The situation is, moreover, more serious in one respect than
these facts and figures would suggest. For the number of children
in the lower income groups is very large. Sir John Orr tells us
that no less than 20 to 25 per cent of all the children in the
country are in the first group, which has an average income of
under 10s. a week per head, and which, he calculates, can spend
no more than 4s. per head on food. (The British Ministry of
Health calculated, in 1933, that 5s. 1½d. was the minimum sum
necessary to buy a week's supply of food just capable of sustaining one person, while the British Medical Association put the
figure at 5s. 10½d.) He does not calculate what proportion of the
nation's children are in the first two groups taken together, but
it seems probable that, if 20 per cent to 25 per cent are in the
bottom 10 per cent of the population, at least 50 per cent must
be in the bottom 30 per cent of the population. *And the whole of
this 30 per cent of the population is unable to buy an adequate
supply of those body-building foods which growing children imperatively need.* Thus it seems probable that one half of the children
of one of the two richest capitalist communities in the world,

which has developed an extraordinary capacity for wealth production, cannot get an adequate supply of the most elementary of all human necessities, food.[1]

The Orr report gives us an indication of the amount of this deficiency by listing the percentage increases in the consumption of various foodstuffs which would be necessary to raise the amount of food eaten by the rest of the population to the amount actually eaten to-day by the richest 10 per cent of us, whose diet is alone wholly satisfactory. *In order to have enough to eat, the British people would have to consume 80 per cent more milk, 41 per cent more butter, 55 per cent more eggs, 124 per cent more fruit, 87 per cent more vegetables, 29 per cent more meat.* It will be seen that neither bread nor potatoes are mentioned. This is because even the members of the lowest income group consume enough bread and potatoes, if they could buy enough of other foodstuffs. But, as Sir John Orr notices, this group does not eat any more bread or potatoes than do the groups above it, which eat far larger amounts of all the other, more expensive, foods.

It may be imagined that such deficiencies, particularly in the diet of children, must have a visible effect upon health. And so they do. According to the graph printed on p. 40 of the Orr report, elementary schoolboys of thirteen years of age average about 57 inches in height, while public school boys of the same age average 63 inches in height. (For the benefit of non-English readers it should be explained that elementary schools are state-provided schools for the working class, while public schools are private schools. They are schools, that is to say, reserved, as

[1] Competent professional authorities unite in dismissing the pleasant allegation (frequently made in the capitalist Press) that working-class malnutrition is not due to poverty, but to the ignorance and folly of working-class housewives. Thus Dr. G. C. M. M'Gonigle (Medical Officer of Health for Stockton-on-Tees) and Dr. J. Kirby, M.R.S.I., in their authoritative study *Poverty and Public Health* (Gollancz, 6s.), write:

" The statement is frequently made that more advantageous spending of small incomes is possible and that much existing under-nourishment is due to ignorance of marketing and of food values, combined with lack of skill in cooking. Careful analysis of food budgets shows that such statements are, to a very large extent, wide of the mark. . . . Graphs have been prepared showing the quantities of various foodstuffs purchased by families at each income level . . . they are clearly indicative of the sound knowledge of the elements of satisfactory dietetics possessed by women of the working classes. The rule of thumb methods used by these women work well, and it is doubtful if education in the principles of nutrition would enable them materially to improve the nutritional condition of their families."

Sir John Orr estimates, almost exclusively for boys coming from the richest 10 per cent of the population.) Thus a difference of 6 inches in height at the age of 13 years appears to be associated with the difference between adequate and inadequate diet.

There are, of course, many diseases, such as rickets, the incidence of which is known to be closely associated with inadequate diet. Unfortunately, however, there seems to be no objective standard by which the question of whether or not a given child is in fact rickety can be judged. For example, the medical advisers of the London County Council robustly announced in 1933 that only 0·3 per cent of children in London County Council schools suffered from rickets. On the other hand, a Board of Education report, published in 1931 (Committee on Adenoids and Enlarged Tonsils, 2 Interim Report) stated that a special examination of 1,638 unselected school children had showed one or more signs of rickets to be present in 87·5 per cent of the children examined. It is clear that we have here no possible standard of reference.

In the case of one disease closely associated with inadequate diet, namely anæmia, an objective standard does exist, however. It is possible to measure the hæmoglobin content of the blood. A healthy child should have a hæmoglobin value of at least 90. In " a routine medical inspection group," which represents, it seems, an average sample of the children of the working population, 25 per cent of the children examined had a hæmoglobin value of under 70, and in a group of children taken from the poorest sections of the population 48·5 per cent had a hæmoglobin value of under 70. In Newcastle an investigation was carried out on children of pre-school age (under five years). Of the children from the poorest class who were examined 23 per cent were anæmic and of the children taken from the well-to-do class none were anæmic.

We do not possess comparable statistics for adults and their diseases. But the Registrar-General's report for 1927 shows that the mortality from tuberculosis was nearly three times as high amongst the low paid, unskilled workers as in the higher ranks of business and professional life. We do, however, possess one important piece of evidence as to the general condition of health of the adult male population. This evidence was obtained by the National Service Medical Boards which examined the men of military age in the years 1917 and 1918. The report of these Boards sums up its conclusions as follows: "Medical examination showed that, of every nine men of military age in Great Britain, on the average three were perfectly fit and healthy; two were upon a definitely inferior plane of health and strength, whether from some disability or some failure in development; three were incapable of undergoing more than a very moderate degree of physical exertion and could almost (in view of their age) be described with justice as physical wrecks; and the remaining man was a chronic invalid with a precarious hold on life." (Quoted in *Poverty and Public Health*, by G. C. M. M'Gonigle and J. Kirby.) In a word, all the available evidence tends to show that the malnutrition of a very substantial proportion of the population has just the effect which we should expect it to have; it first stunts the workers as children, and then renders them far more susceptible to disease than they need be in adult life.

We have devoted attention to the expenditure upon food of the British working class to-day because we can easily deduce from its level of food-buying what the other living conditions of any group of persons must be. For food is the prime necessity: men will, rightly, go without everything else, including adequate shelter or clothing, before they will go without adequate food.

Such, then, are the conditions in which live the working mass of the population of the oldest, most fully developed and, in many respects, richest capitalist empire in the world. It is true that the conditions which the Orr report reveals probably represent an improvement over the pre-war conditions of the British workers, and certainly represent a substantial improvement over their conditions throughout the nineteenth century. Hence the main defence that can be made for the present semi-starvation of 30 per cent of the population, and the malnutrition of at least another 20 per cent, is that, in the past, British capitalism has starved even more of its workers, and starved them even worse.

We, however, are not primarily concerned with the question of whether or not the conditions of the workers have varied to a significant extent between different periods in the development of British capitalism. We have seen that there have been considerable variations, but we have also seen that at the best level reached, which is probably that of to-day, their conditions remain abominable. The truth is that the lot of the great majority of those who in a capitalist society live by selling their ability to labour has always been, and still is, almost unendurable.

This is why the working class is driven to become the chief agent of social change. It seeks to change society because it finds the lot assigned to it in existing society intolerable. This is the primary reason why all those who desire that society should be changed, and have envisaged more or less clearly the type of society which might take the place of capitalism, have come to realize that the only dynamic principle capable of effecting this change is the resistance of the working class to the conditions of life assigned to it by capitalism. It is by infusing this resistance, which will take place in any case, with a full consciousness of the cause of the workers' present miseries, and of the type of economic and social system which could end these miseries, that the change can be effected.

NOTE.—I hazard the following suggestion for a comparative study of the living conditions of the British and American working class. The later, although more rapid, development of American capitalism may have produced conditions for the mass of the American workers in the latter part of the nineteenth century roughly analogous to the conditions suffered by the British workers in the eighteen-thirties and forties. For the violently, if blindly, anti-capitalist movements of the American workers in the latter half of the nineteenth century bear a recognizable resemblance to the British working class movements before 1850. In particular, the meteoric career of the Owenite Grand National Consolidated Trades Union (see next chapter) in the thirties is strikingly analogous to the equally brief and meteoric career of the American Knights of Labour in the sixties and the seventies. (This resemblance is pointed out by the Webbs in their *History of Trade Unionism*, p. 135 note.) And there is a similar resemblance between many aspects of Chartism and the I.W.W. (On the other hand, the existence of free land, all through this period, in America prevented the growth of any movement of equal scope and depth to Chartism.) Moreover, just as the British revolutionary movements were swallowed up in the mighty surge of the development of British capitalism between 1850 and 1900, and were succeeded by a pro-capitalist trade unionism, so the Knights of Labour and the I.W.W. were submerged in the 1900–29 prosperity of America, and were succeeded by the equally pro-capitalist American Federation of Labour. Again, the prosperity which caused this transformation was in America, as in Britain, a prosperity largely confined to the skilled, organized workers—a prosperity which left largely unameliorated the conditions of the great mass of the unskilled labourers. On this reckoning, 1929 in America would correspond to 1880–1900 in Great Britain. Hence we may now confidently expect the emergence of an American working class and anti-capitalist movement.

Chapter XXVII

The Working Class Begins to Think

ROBERT OWEN, having conceived of the idea of communism and socialism, wasted his life because he failed to make adequate contact with the working class movement of resistance to capitalism. But the working class movement of Owen's lifetime failed because (amongst other reasons) it did not make adequate contact with the idea of communism and socialism.

Between 1850 and 1900, Marx and Engels effected the synthesis between the idea and the movement; but this happened too late for their essential discoveries to be used by the working class during the first half of the nineteenth century. Indeed, the gropings of the British workers before 1850 were an essential factor in enabling Marx and Engels to discover the types of political activity by which capitalism can be abolished and socialism established. Hence it is essential that we should pay attention to the ideas and actions of those early working class leaders who, before 1850, strove, though never with complete success, to achieve an adequate conception of the goal of working class action and who, with a much greater measure of success, fought and toiled to organize the resistance of the working class to capitalism.

Chartism was the principal, although not the only, anti-capitalist movement to be generated by the sufferings of the early generations of British workers. A series of movements, taking different forms, sprang from the British working class between 1800 and 1850. And each one of these movements was met and suppressed by a prolonged governing class terror. Indeed, it must be clear that a working class could only have been forced to submit to such miseries as those alluded to in a preceding chapter by a policy of terror. This terror reached its culmination in the decade between 1815 and 1825. But it had started as early as 1799 (when the right of association in Trade Unions, which had existed all through the eighteenth century, was withdrawn), and it continued right through the eighteen-thirties and forties, only ending after 1850, when British capitalism began rapidly to solve its difficulties.

Thus the reign of terror of British capitalism lasted a full half-century. It was, however, on modern standards, relatively mild. For example, the famous six Dorsetshire labourers who tried to form a trade union were not beheaded, as they would be in modern Germany, but merely sentenced to transportation. A number of British workers were executed, however, and a very large number imprisoned for long periods, for anti-capitalist activities during this period. It is only by modern German, Polish, Californian, or Italian standards that the number of prosecutions can be considered small, or the sentences mild. We are fully justified then, in describing these years as years of terror ; for the British government's essential policy between 1800 and 1850 consisted in preventing the working class by means of executions, imprisonments, and transportations, from influencing public policy. During the first fifty years of the existence of British capitalism it was not possible to win any degree of consent from the working class, and it was necessary for the governing class to rule by force.

The success of the British government's fifty years' terror aptly illustrates both the possibilities and limitations of this method of class rule. The terror did not in itself enable the contemporary British capitalists to solve their economic problems. It did not enable them to surmount the cyclical crises that struck them, or to avoid having to impose such vile conditions upon the workers as to cause their resistance. Nor would it, if the economic conditions which necessitated it had endured, have prevented that resistance from turning into ultimately successful revolt. But the policy of terror did give the British capitalists time in which to lay down a firm foundation for their system, and thus gradually to solve, for a period, their economic problem.

We may perhaps make a generalization in this connection. If the situation of a ruling class is basically sound (as was that of the British capitalists in the early nineteenth century) : if their characteristic economic system still has a period of development before it, a policy of terror can succeed. It can tide over periods of crisis due to the early growing pains inevitable to any economic system ; it can give time for the slow but steady improvement which will certainly occur if the economy in question has not exhausted its possibilities of growth. The resistance of the subject class can be held in check until the conditions which are generating that resistance become ameliorated. In these historical circumstances the familiar view that repression and terror never succeed in their object is unfounded.

There are conditions, however, in which this view is correct. No policy of terror can permanently maintain in power a governing class whose characteristic economic system has exhausted its possibilities of development. If the general, secular curve of the economy has turned downwards, if its recurrent crises are becoming graver and more prolonged, instead of slighter and shorter; if each period of recovery is less, instead of more, stable, and has to be purchased by more painful sacrifices imposed upon the subjected class, then no repression, however efficient and ferocious, can succeed. For the movement of revolt springs up anew each time that it is beaten down, and springs up more quickly and more strongly. There is no chance of the eradication of the causes of revolt, since the conditions of the subjected class cannot be ameliorated.[1]

The movements of revolt of the British workers before 1850, and the ideas which these movements generated, are of the highest importance. For they afford the first examples in history of the activity of a working class. It would be beyond our scope to attempt to describe the profoundly interesting, but relatively small, scattered and sporadic working class activities of the early years of the century, such as the Corresponding Societies, the Spencean Clubs and the Luddite movement. On a different scale to these was the sudden anti-capitalist movement which flared up in the eighteen-thirties. This movement was distinct both from Chartism, which already existed, but which did not become dominant until a few years later, and from the Trade Unionism of the skilled handicraft workers, which had existed since the beginning of the eighteenth century.

---

[1] Even in these circumstances a policy of terror can succeed in the sense that it can prevent the subjected class from coming to power and creating its new economic system. But terror cannot, in the above historical circumstances, succeed in preserving the power of the governing class. For its continued success merely results in the common ruin of both classes. (Marx was careful to note this possibility; *vide* the *Communist Manifesto*.) There are, however, specific circumstances which make it certain that this will not be the outcome of the present struggle between the capitalist and working classes.

The movement was organized in the " Grand National Consolidated Trades Union," led, half reluctantly and wholly disastrously, by Robert Owen. In it, therefore, the idea of Utopian communism, personified by Owen, made its first contact with the working class movement of resistance to capitalism. How inadequate, precarious, and transient that contact was, the brief history of the Grand National Consolidated was to show. This extraordinary organization was founded in the year 1834. It was the culmination of a series of attempts to bring to birth a *Trades Union*, as opposed to a *movement of Trade Unions*. The grammatical distinction is important. For a Trade Union means an organization of men working at one particular trade, while a Trades Union means an organization uniting the workers of each and all of the different trades of the country.

The formation of a Trades Union, as distinct from a Trade Union, is an idea which up till very recently haunted the imagination of the militant workers of the American continent— the idea of the One Big Union. Nowhere and at no time has this idea come nearer to realization than it did in Britain between January and July 1834. In the first few weeks of that year over half a million workers were enrolled in " the Trades Union." No part of England was left unaffected, and it was for the attempt to carry " the Trades Union " into a far-away, west country hamlet that the six Dorsetshire labourers were transported. The extreme rapidity of the growth of the Trades Union was due to the terrible disillusionment of the British workers at the result of the Reform Bill of 1832. By the threat of revolution the British workers had enabled the middle class to force the aristocracy to share their power. And they were repaid by the New Poor Law, the most severe penal enactment under which the British workers have ever suffered. No wonder the workers rushed into an organization which promised them protection, strength, and emancipation.

The ideas which animated the tactics and strategy of the Grand National Consolidated Trades Union were confused and inchoate. A Trades Union, as distinct from a Trade Union, is however, an implicitly revolutionary thing. An organization claiming to comprise, and to speak for, the whole working class is inevitably a challenge to the existence of capitalism. In a

sense, the spokesmen of the Grand National Consolidated
Trades Union realized this fact: for they proclaimed revolutionary intentions. Their avowed purpose was to declare a
general strike by which the capitalists should be expropriated
and the means of production reassumed by the working class.
Their object was, they wrote, " not to condition " (i.e. bargain)
" with the master producers of wealth and knowledge for some
paltry advance in the artificial money price in exchange for
their labour, health, liberty, natural enjoyment, and life; but to
ensure to everyone the best cultivation of all their faculties and
the most advantageous exercise of all their powers."

In these fatally vague and typically Owenite phrases, the
Grand National repudiated the ordinary function of a Trade
Union and proclaimed itself a Trades Union, or union of trades,
with aims which were flatly incompatible with the continuance
of capitalism. It is interesting to observe how Owen found himself at the head of this first great movement of the British
working class. He had always refused to have anything to do
with either the political or the industrial agitation of the workers.
Trade Unions were, he considered, as useless as political parties,
for both were concerned with mere " conditioning " with the
employers about hours and wages—a proceeding which could
only prejudice the governing class against themselves undertaking their own abolition, as he had repeatedly advised them to
do. Since, however, the *felo de se* of the British capitalists tarried
awhile, it was useful, Owen came to think, to organize examples
of communism in practice, preferably, as we saw, in the form of
communist colonies; but, if that proved impossible, then by
means of Producers' Co-operative Societies. These societies consisted of groups of workers who ceased working for their employers and, while still living in their own homes, began making
goods for themselves, which they should exchange within the
society according to the labour time involved in making them.[1]

[1] As the reader will notice, Owen simply ignored the fact that the essential
means of production were in the hands of the capitalists and were, therefore,
inaccessible. But his mistake was not quite so glaring as it would be to-day, for
in the thirties of the last century a good deal of production was still carried on
on a handicraft basis. Hence it was just possible for workers, in some cases, to
scrape together a few inadequate tools and a precarious supply of raw material,
and to start up work on their own. But they were never able, of course, to get
hold of means of production adequate to give them a chance of success in competition with capitalist industry.

This idea caught the imagination of the workers, and hundreds of these Producers' Co-operative Societies were founded.

The conception of Producers', as distinct from Consumers', Co-operative Societies recurs constantly to the working class as a method by which it may emancipate itself from capitalism. As such it is a delusion. It can never be possible for the workers to lay hold of sufficient means of production to start up in competition with the capitalists by self-employing themselves. Moreover, as in the case of communist colonies (of which they are variants), if these economic difficulties did not render the success of Producers' Co-operative Societies impossible, no capitalist class, while yet holding political power in its hands, would ever tolerate their growth. This does not mean, however, that the idea of Producers' Co-operation—of groups of workers voluntarily associating themselves together for production on the basis of self-employment—is not of great value. For we now know that, once political power has been assumed by the workers, and the main industries of the country have been taken over by the community for operation on a planned basis, an important sphere of production is left available for Producers' Co-operative Societies. As we saw in Part I, such Producers' Co-operative Societies exist in large numbers in the Soviet Union, living in the interstices of the great nationalized industries. Some three million Russian workers find their employment in them, and they carry on production for the market provided for them, both by the general consuming public and by the need of the great industries themselves for specialized goods, which it is still best to produce on a small scale. Moreover, as we saw, in agriculture, Producers' Co-operative Societies have become the predominant form. Thus in this case also Owen's concept was in itself no delusion: his error was to have overlooked the political transformation necessary to its realization.

It was out of a federation of these Producers' Co-operative Societies, and not out of the existing Trade Union movement, that the Grand National Consolidated Trades Union largely originated. At least, that was how matters looked to Owen. It seemed to him that he was leading a mass movement of communist co-operators: that half a million people had suddenly become converted to his ideas. Elated, he composed a programme

of immediate action by which the Grand National Consolidated
should forthwith take over the entire industries of the country
and run them on what we should now call Syndicalist or Guild
Socialist lines. " This is the outline for individual trades—they
shall be arranged in Companies or families: thus all those trades
which relate to clothing shall form a company, such as tailors,
shoemakers, hatters, milliners and mantua-makers; and all the
different manufactures shall be arranged in a similar way."
(From Owen's newspaper, *The Crisis*.)

His biographer, Podmore, informs us that Owen explained
later that he expected the employers to join these guilds themselves, but whether on the basis of the surrender of the ownership of their businesses or not he does not say. This little detail is
not clear to us—and possibly was not clear to Owen ! As usual,
Owen could not believe that any capitalist would object to so
reasonable a proposal as the surrender of his entire property in
the means of production to common ownership.

This is how the thing looked to Owen: but to many of its other
leaders, some of whom were later to become prominent Chartists,
the Grand National Consolidated was essentially a Trades
Union, a centralized fighting organization of the working class,
which should " condition " (i.e. bargain) with the employers over
hours and wages, but only as a step to their proximate expropriation. A Trades Union was not a central organization of
Trade Unions, of associations of workers according to their trades,
that is to say—such as the Trades Union Congress is to-day.
It was an all-inclusive organization of the Western One Big
Union type, which everybody and anybody might join, whether
by the affiliation of their existing organizations, such as co-
operative societies or Trade Unions, or individually.

Now this conception of a Trades Union, or " One Big Union,"
with its inevitably revolutionary implications, is a step beyond
ordinary Trade Unionism. It is an expression of the workers'
growing realization that, if they want to do more than " condition " with their employers on hours and wages, they must equip
themselves with some wider organization than a Trade Union.
But the One Big Union succeeds in uniting the workers on an
industrial basis alone. If the workers are to organize themselves
as a class; if they are to set up an association capable of

exercising power on their behalf, they must find a definitely political form of organization.

They must in fact create a party, in the new and definite sense of that word which we described in Chapter XV. For nothing but the construction of an organization of this type, equipped for every kind of political struggle, can enable the working class to take the power of the State out of the hands of the capitalists. And this, as we have seen, is the preliminary to everything else.

It was a very great achievement for the young British working class to have created an organization as inclusive as the Grand National Consolidated. But it was not enough. Its leaders had no adequate conception of what they wished to accomplish, or of the means they should use. Owen, their reluctant chief, had, it is true, a fairly clear conception of ultimate communism. But he had never had any conception of an intermediate stage of socialism. And in 1834 he was momentarily obsessed with the illusory and misty syndicalist scheme which we have just described. It is doubtful if many of the members of the organization took much interest in Owen's scheme. They were blindly in revolt against the treachery of their new rulers, who had promised them freedom and given them the workhouse. If they imagined at all the kind of society which they would establish when they overthrew the power of their employers, they probably dreamed of a return to pre-capitalist peasant and handicraft conditions.

But the rank and file of the organization had, at any rate, a solid knowledge of the necessity for struggle against the employers if they were to accomplish anything. Yet, as we have seen, Owen, and the other Owenite leaders, expressly denied the necessity of any form of struggle. They expected that the employers would be just as ready as the workers to join in the work of abolishing capitalism. They felt that the only thing which prevented anybody from being a communist was ignorance and misunderstanding, and that these difficulties would be met with amongst both the employers and the workers. No one was more surprised than they when half a million workers, and no employers, joined their organization! No one was more dismayed than they when the employers threw themselves with relentless determination into the task of destroying the Grand National Consolidated Trades Union.

Nor did that task prove difficult. It was accomplished within six months by a series of lock-outs (of which " the Derby Turn-outs " of February 1834 was the most important) by which the employers simply dismissed all members of the Union. The Union's leadership was quite unprepared for such an attack: they perforce had to support their locked out members, but they had never thought out any general plan of campaign, any principles of strategy or tactics upon which to meet the employers' inevitable attack. They had not dreamed that any such attack was inevitable; they felt that it must all be due to some terrible misunderstanding. With such leadership the struggle could have only one end. By August the Grand National Consolidated was in ruins, and its delegates, meeting in London under Owen's presidency, wound up its affairs and passed a resolution in which they wrote that they had " experienced much more opposition from the employers of industry and from the wealthy portion of the public, as well as from the Government, than its promoters anticipated." Such are the pitiable results of failing to realize that the workers, and the workers alone, will strive for the abolition of capitalism, and that the capitalists will inevitably resist their own expropriation with relentless energy.[1]

The collapse of the Grand National Consolidated Trades Union marked the end of the first crude attempt to fuse the idea of communism and socialism with the dynamic thrust of the workers' resistance to capitalism. It showed how disastrous was the leadership of a communist or socialist such as Owen who, although he had achieved a relatively clear conception of the right objective for the working class movement, had no idea of the necessary means of achieving that objective.

The next movement of the British workers was led by men who, compared to Owen, had a remarkably clear and realistic knowledge of the means necessary to the struggle to abolish

[1] This does not mean that the workers will always and everywhere strive to abolish capitalism. As we have seen, few of the British workers had any such impulse between 1850 and 1900, and some of the British workers and most of the American workers have no such conscious impulse to-day—though both of them have the impulse to resist the more and more intolerable conditions of life which capitalism imposes on them. But it does mean that no other class but the workers will effectively oppose capitalism.

capitalism. But, unfortunately, they lacked Owen's knowledge of the proper objective of that struggle. The Chartists leaders were for the most part not communists or socialists : they did not aim at establishing a new economic system of planned production for use, based upon the technical advances achieved by capitalism, but rather (in so far as they formulated their social objective at all) at returning to the pre-capitalist peasant society out of which capitalism had emerged. Yet it is in the writings and speeches of the Chartists that we discover the first substantial step towards the evolution of a characteristic working class body of political doctrine. In the person of the Chartist leaders the young working class began to think. And this thinking was an essential preparation for that all-important synthesis of the idea of communism and socialism, and the resistance of the workers to capitalism, which was to be effected immediately after their epoch. O'Connor, O'Brien, George Julian Harney and Ernest Jones, to mention four of the most talented of the Chartist leaders, actually discovered, although they failed to record their discovery in any systematic way, the nature of the political situation in any capitalist community. Their thinking marks the beginning of a genuine political science such as the academic political scientists of the capitalist world have never attained to.

As early as 1819 a working class newspaper, *The Black Dwarf*,[1] was thus brilliantly satirizing Owen's plans for communist colonies :

" ' See what a pretty plan I have drawn out *on paper*. And at what equal distances I have placed such and such buildings. How imposing they are. There are all the offices, attached and detached, that could be wished. There are schools and lecture rooms, and Committee rooms and brewhouses and workhouses and granaries. There you will put the women, there the men and there the children. They will be called to dinner every day regularly, and they will be clothed and taught and not worked very much. Oh, how happy they must be ! There is nothing to prevent it whatever.

[1] What a magnificent title, itself a symbol of class consciousness—the Black Dwarf—the factory worker upon whom rests the whole of society !

All the bad passions will be eradicated and I should like to
live there myself. Nobody that *understands* it can for a moment
object to it. Why, there is to be a chapel in which only the
truth is to be taught; and schools where nothing but *useful*
knowledge is to be inculcated.' "

(See Podmore's *Robert Owen*, pp. 239–40.)

The moment we begin to read these working class newspapers
and speeches we leave behind us that immature element which
mars so much of Owen's thought; we enter the adult world.

It can be no part of this book to attempt to write even the
briefest history of the Chartist movement. We must limit ourselves to discerning the birth-pangs of a body of political knowledge and experience, and to a lesser extent of economic insight
into the nature of capitalism, such as can alone enable the working class to carry out its objectives. Chartism lightly sketched
the outlines of those political and economic concepts, by the
aid of which alone the workers are able to see their way to power.
Above all, none of the Chartists had any illusion as to the necessity of achieving political power before any attempt to alter the
nature of society could be made. All of them realized that the
industrial and agricultural workers living on weekly wages were
the only people who would ever undertake that task. But the
best minds amongst them got considerably further than this.
One of the leading political theorists of the Chartist movement
was undoubtedly Bronterre O'Brien. And O'Brien went far
towards the discovery of that conception of historical evolution
which, now that it has been fully developed, makes impossible
to all except the most naïve the kind of political illusions from
which the Owenites suffered. "The history of mankind,"
O'Brien wrote,

" shows that from the beginning of the world, the rich of
all countries have been in a permanent state of conspiracy
to keep down the poor of all countries, and for this plain
reason—because the poverty of the poor man is essential
to the riches of the rich man. No matter by what means they
may disguise their operations, the rich are everlastingly
plundering, debasing, and brutalising the poor. All the crimes

and superstitions of human nature have their origin in this cannibal warfare of riches against poverty. The desire of one man to live on the fruits of another's labour is the original sin of the world. It is this which fills the world with faction and hypocrisy and has made all past history to be what Gibbon so justly described it—'a record of the crimes, absurdities, and calamities of mankind.' It is the parent injustice from which all injustice springs."

The author of such a passage is evidently safeguarded, by his comprehension of the nature of historical conflicts, from spending his life in petitioning the governing class to expropriate itself. Moreover, on some occasions O'Brien showed that he understood that the miseries of the workers were not due to the malice aforethought of the capitalists, but to the automatic operation of an economic system based upon the private ownership of the means of production:

"We do not," he writes, "accuse the moneyed capitalists of intentional robbery. To do this would be as unjust as it would be malignant. . . . These spoliations they commit, not from sinister design, but from accidental position in society; or, rather, the spoliations are committed *for* them by the silent operation of causes over which they have no control under the existing arrangements of society. Those of the middle class are, like all other men, the creatures of circumstances. Their characters are formed by institutions and their *relative positions* in society to other classes."

This passage may sound familiar enough to-day. But to write it in 1835 required the insight of genius.

O'Brien had evolved a distinct conception of classes, in the exact sense in which that term has been used in these pages; what is more, he knew that it is these classes, and not individuals or governments, which obtain and retain power. People, he complained, commit the error

" of imputing to *individuals* the glory and the guilt of these political acts and systems of government, which are, in reality, the work of whole classes, and in the execution of which the individuals are but the chosen tools or instruments of these classes."

Nor did O'Brien fail to apply this general principle to the great events of his own epoch :

" Fools, indeed, imagine that Pitt or Bonaparte caused it " (the eighteen years' war against France), " or that it was the work of Cabinets or a few individuals in power. With such imbeciles we have nothing to do. Men capable of believing such stuff are not worth our notice. *Rulers and Cabinets have no power whatever beyond that society gives them.* The ' statesmen' who made war on France in 1793 did so because war was agreeable to the capitalists and profit-hunters. . . . It was for the double purpose of crushing that revolution and of opening a new field for the ' enterprise of commerce ' that our moneyed interests urged that war against France."

This passage probably marks the highest level of O'Brien's political genius.[1] In it he clearly enunciates a truth of which only a tiny minority of mankind is yet seized. Millions of men are still incapable of realizing that neither Hitler nor Mussolini, nor Baldwin, nor Roosevelt, nor Stalin, rules according to his own sweet will, *but on behalf of the different classes which sustain him in power.* O'Brien wrote that he would have nothing to do with " such imbeciles." He must have led a lonely life.[2]

Political theory was O'Brien's great strength. The economics upon which he grounded his politics were inadequate. He has, it is true, a passage of great insight into the nature of capitalist wealth in which he says that

" the upper and middle classes have no wealth but what consists of subtractions wrung from industry, through institutions of their own making. Those of them who have sprung from the ' lower ranks ' may boast as much as they like of

---

[1] Note the unsurpassed analysis of the characteristic double purpose of British policy; to stand in with the other eighteenth-century monarchies in attempting to crush the French Revolution, and at the same time to overreach these allies by conquering new markets.

[2] He did.

their habits of industry as *workmen* and ascribe their wealth to that industry, but all who know anything know well enough that it is not as *workmen* they acquired it, but as *hirers of workmen.*"

In this passage we catch a glimpse of an essential principle of realistic economic theory: of the fact that capitalist wealth is formed, not by the capitalists, but by the workers for them: that it is not created by any magical philoprogenitive qualities said to inhere in capital, but from the fact that the capitalists are enabled by their exclusive ownership of the means of production to retain the difference between the value of what the workers produce and of what the workers need for their sustenance. But it would, no doubt, be fanciful to suggest that O'Brien had more than a glimpse of this great truth. Indeed, as he grew older, and as the sustaining power of a militant and growing working class movement was, after 1850, withdrawn from him, he began to fall under every kind of economic illusion, such as land schemes, co-operative banks, currency reforms, and the like—illusions which in the end obscured his originally intense political insight. It was in this last, sad period that he drew upon himself the scorn of Marx, a scorn which blinded Marx to his former great achievements.[1]

Even in his best period, however, O'Brien's economics were scanty. He did not fully understand the nature of capitalism, and, above all, he never clearly conceived of socialism or communism—of an organisation of society based on a public, pooled ownership of the means of production worked according to a pre-determined plan. On the whole, he identified capitalism with industrialism. "The system I combat," he wrote as late as 1847, "and which I wish to combat is that by which your profit-mongering oppressors have turned you from agriculturists into manufacturers for all the world." The longing look of the English people still ran backward towards the land they had lost, rather than forward to the socialism they might gain.[2] As a dozen

---

[1] This, at any rate, is Mr. Theodore Rothstein's view.
[2] Note the superior emotional appeal of the simple concrete term " the land " to the abstraction " socialism." The psychological genius of Lenin enabled him to teach the Russian workers to win socialism by fighting for " Peace, Bread and the Land."

statements both of O'Brien's and of most of the other Chartist leaders show, the main social and economic purpose for which they proposed to use political power, when the enactment of the Charter had given it them, was to restore the land to the people.[1] To the Chartists, capitalism was still what it was to More, to Winstanley, and to Spence—the filching of the land from the people of England. There was, as we have seen, a profound historical truth in this view.[2] But there was an equally profound error in supposing that the emancipation of the workers could be achieved by a resumption of their ownership of the land alone.[3] With every year that passed, the land became more and more only *one* of those indispensable means of production which it was necessary for the workers to possess if they would achieve their emancipation. But it was hard for the Chartists to realize this. O'Brien, it is true, was not opposed to machinery. He grasped the fact that it was not the machines themselves, but their ownership by the capitalists which was the trouble. But he had no clear idea of how the workers were to assume the ownership of the means of production: of whether they should own them collectively or individually: nor had he any conception of a planned economic system.

Moreover, O'Brien was considerably ahead of many of the other Chartist leaders. O'Connor, the real leader of the movement, expressly declared that he was neither a socialist nor a communist. His objective was a return to universal peasant proprietorship in which everyone should have his own plot of land. Thus, while the Chartists knew the correct means of social transformation, they did not know the goal, and while Owen knew the goal he had no conception of the means of approaching it.[4]

[1] The immediate programme of the Chartists was the establishment of full democratic rights based upon universal franchise.

[2] " The expropriation of the masses of the people from the land forms the basis of the capitalist method of production." (*Capital*, Vol. I, p. 852.)

[3] It is an illusion which flared up again at the end of the nineteenth century in the movement led by Henry George, and which lingers on in odd corners of English political life to this day.

[4] But Engels seems to me to exaggerate when, in defending the memory of Robert Owen from the illiterate attack of Dühring, he says that Owen's *Book of the New Moral World* contained " the most clear-cut communism possible." This, no doubt, is true of the economic arrangements proposed for use within the colonies, but Owen nowhere, so far as I know, showed any consciousness of the necessity for a general economic plan for the community as a whole.

On the other hand, the Chartists made important contributions to the construction of a science of economics which, by giving the workers a real understanding of how capitalism works, should enable them to abolish it. (For men can seldom or never overcome that which they cannot comprehend.) The whole Chartist movement had a profound realization that they, the workers, were being exploited. This sense of irredeemably unjust exploitation inspired almost all their utterances. When they said that " Chartism was a knife and fork question " they meant much more than that the workers were struggling for bread. They meant that the Chartist protest was not merely, and in the end not principally, directed against the denial of political rights to the British workers. They meant that they were fighting the whole economic and social system of exploitation upon which the political subjection of the workers was based. It is true that they never quite achieved a comprehension of how the capitalists effected the exploitation of the workers. But the two best-known Chartist economists, Hodgkin and Thomson, came near to such a comprehension. These writers based their economic analysis on Ricardo, and the labour theory of value, which he, of all the classical capitalist economists, had most clearly formulated. They took Ricardo at his word. IF, they said, labour is the source of value, as you tell us, then how is it that the capitalist owners of the means of production, who may themselves perform no labour at all, receive far more value than anyone else ? Something, on the capitalist economists' own showing, must be very wrong with a system which produced results like that. But what it was exactly that was wrong with capitalism, or how the actual exploitation of the workers occurred, they were never quite able to demonstrate.

We cannot forbear to return to the speculation as to what would have happened if Owen had been even normally willing to learn anything from anybody and had become a Chartist.[1] Such a conversion would not, of course, have resulted in the creation of a socialist Britain in 1840. It was altogether inevitable

[1] As Mr. Rothstein well says, " In history it is preposterous to use the conditional mood "—but he then immediately indulges in a piece of retrospective historical speculation: his example shall be our excuse for rejecting his precept.

that capitalism should unfold its possibilities of development. But it might have resulted in the enactment of some at least of the essential democratic reforms of the Charter. Consequently, the development of British capitalism might have taken place in an incomparably more democratic political environment, perhaps even under a republic instead of a constitutional monarchy. But it was not to be. The working class forces remained disunited during the whole of the period of the weakness of British capitalism up till 1850, when a well-applied, united, pressure might have extorted major concessions. From about 1842 the stability of British capitalism, under Peel's able guidance, began to increase. And, when the last profound crisis, that of 1848, occurred, the Chartist forces were already in decline and the British capitalists had no real difficulty in combining a necessary struggle with the landlords for the repeal of the Corn Laws, with a united front of all property owners against the workers.

After about 1845, the real strength behind the Chartist movement steadily declined. The leadership, however, was in many respects developing and improving its comprehension of the situation. The older generation of leaders, such as O'Brien and O'Connor—particularly the latter—were, it is true, becoming exhausted. Their thought made no further progress, and with the end of the period they began rapidly to regress. A younger generation of leaders now appeared, however, of which Harney and Ernest Jones were the most talented. These leaders began to be influenced by the thinking of Marx and Engels, who were living in England, and with whom they were in fairly close contact. Indeed, it is hardly too much to say that the Left Wing of Chartism, led by Harney and Jones, was coming close to the modern communist conception of the nature and functions of the working class movement. But before that conception was reached Chartism itself was extinguished by the triumphs of British capitalism in the second half of the nineteenth century. Harney, in particular, achieved some admirably clear political formulations. He was even able splendidly to express the proper goal of working class effort, although not to define the economic system under which that goal would be reached. " Emancipation of labour," he wrote, " is the only worthy object of political warfare . . . that those who till the soil shall be its first masters, that those who raise the food shall be its first partakers, that those who build mansions shall live in them. . . ."

The fate of this younger generation of Chartist leaders was an almost unbearably tragic one. After 1850 they saw their movement growing yearly smaller and smaller. Their older leaders were destroyed. O'Connor went mad, O'Brien became an ineffectual crank. Harney and Jones spent themselves in desperately trying to keep an ever-dwindling agitation alive. Jones, in the most extreme poverty, wrote an account of what his life was like in this period which, as Mr. Rothstein eloquently writes, " even to-day echoes to the sound of weeping."

To-day we can see that the Chartists were, after 1850, engaged in an inherently hopeless task. But it was not possible for them to realize this. They had not achieved sufficient insight into the nature of capitalism to perceive that it had entered into a long, ascendant phase. Hence they believed that the old conditions of crisis, instability and mass agitation might at any moment return. In their lifetime such conditions never did return, and they and all their inspired political thinking went down into half a century of oblivion.

For their own countrymen this oblivion has been so complete that even to-day we owe much of our knowledge of their real views to the researches of a Russian resident in this country, Mr. Theodore Rothstein, from whose work, *From Chartism to Labourism*, all the quotations from the Chartists' writings in this chapter have been taken.[1] It is, indeed, shameful that the ideas of these great Englishmen and Irishmen should still be inadequately known to us. Even such writers as Mr. and Mrs. Webb abuse the Chartists most ignorantly. In their *History*

[1] There are now several histories of the Chartist movement by Englishmen in which some of the actions of the Chartists are accurately recorded. But their authors suffer from the disadvantage of being unable to understand a single one of the ideas expressed by the Chartists.

There appeared, however, in the autumn of 1935, Mr. Allen Hutt's volume, *This Final Crisis*, chapter iii of which removes the reproach that no Englishman has yet written with understanding on the political conceptions of the Chartists. Mr. Hutt shows at least as adequate a comprehension of the ideas of the Chartists as did Mr. Rothstein, and not only corrects him on certain questions of fact, but also shows very clearly the relationship between the Utopian communism of Owen and the political realism, combined with economic romanticism, of the Chartists. We still lack, however, a full-dress history of Chartism written by a British historian competent to understand his subject.

of Trade Unionism they write that Chartism " was disgraced by the fustian of many of its orators and the political and economic quackery of its pretentious and incompetent leaders whose jealousies and intrigues, by successively excluding all the nobler elements, finally brought it to naught."

The reader will be able to judge for himself how monstrous is such a verdict upon men of the intellectual calibre of O'Brien and Harney. Our real complaint against these men is that they did not embody their invaluable political thinking in a permanent form. If O'Brien, for example, had given systematic shape to his conception of history in a book, it would have survived him and been rediscovered at the end of the nineteenth century to enlighten the new anti-capitalist movement of the British workers. Or, again, if Harney and Jones had devoted themselves after 1850 to mastering the real nature of the capitalist system, they might have bequeathed to the British working class an invaluable body of economic knowledge. But to have done so would have required a belief in the importance of economic and political theory which the Chartist leaders never achieved.

The names of the Chartists were writ on water. For they failed to erect that monument more enduring than brass, a developed, consistent system of ideas capable of elucidating the historical movement of their times. There were, however, two men in England, although neither of them was an Englishman, who knew what to do when the possibility of immediate working class action, which had hitherto seemed so great, began to fade and fail in the middle of the nineteenth century. Marx and Engels, when they realized that the revolutionary movement of 1848 was spent, and that a revolutionary situation was not likely to recur for some time, did not either leave the working class movement in despair, or spend themselves in necessarily ineffective agitation with ever-dwindling forces. They set themselves down to the exhaustive and scientific study of the capitalist system, its origins, nature and probable course of development; of the type of economic system which might replace it, and of the nature of the political activity which could alone enable the working class to change the one into the other. Their discoveries have changed the history of the world.

PART IV
THE SCIENCE OF SOCIAL CHANGE

Chapter XXVIII

The Materialist Conception of History

On the eve of its publication Marx referred to *Capital* as " the task to which I have sacrificed my health, my happiness in life, and my family."[1]

Extreme poverty, recurrent illness, the death in childhood of two sons, and the gradual breakdown from overwork of a beloved wife were the price which Marx paid for devoting over thirty years to the discovery of that science of social change which now so justly bears the name of Marxism. For a new science does not come into the world without both physical and intellectual birth pangs. It does not spring fully formed from the heads of its discoverers. On the contrary, its first principles can only be slowly deduced from an enormous quantity of accumulated data and experience by the lifelong labours of a man of genius, or, as in this case, of two men of genius working in the closest association.

As a result of the work of Marx, Engels, and the men who have built upon the foundations which they laid down, there now exists a body of ascertained fact, of repeatedly tested deduction, and, above all perhaps, a methodology which is known to be fruitful, in the field of social science. Never again need men fumble helplessly with the problems presented by the need for social change. It is the immortal glory of Marx and Engels to have discovered and proclaimed both the basic features of that social system which can take the place of capitalism and the basic methods by which that new system can be established. This science is indispensable. We shall not avoid such errors as those into which Owen on the one hand, and the Chartists on the other, so disastrously fell unless we make use of it. The experience of the last half-century has conclusively shown that the ever recurrent working class movement of resistance to capitalism must remain sporadic and inchoate; must fail to achieve its ends, or even to become clearly conscious of what those ends are, if it does not use these discoveries. Wherever and whenever working class movements have failed to learn and to use them, futility and failure have been their harvest. It has been proved to

[1] *Marx–Engels Correspondence*, p. 219.

demonstration that success can only be achieved by a working class movement which is permeated with a realization of its own position in capitalist society, and which can develop out of itself a party which can in turn use the all-important discoveries of Marx, Engels, and their successors as to how capitalism may be abolished and socialism established.

This is not to say, however, that an acceptance of Marxism is enough to bring success to the struggle of a working class movement. For the social science of which Marx and Engels discovered the basic principles is still very young: and, like all young sciences, it is still striving adequately to subsume its subject matter in reliable generalizations. Hence its use requires the greatest caution, resolution, and intelligence. Even those who seem to have mastered it may show (as the German Marxists showed) that they are totally incapable of successfully applying its general principles to a given situation. But what repeatedly tested experience does enable us to say with confidence is that, although this science gives no guarantees of success to those who use it, consciously desired social change is impossible of accomplishment unless it is used.

The newly evolved science might be called social dynamics, for it is essentially a body of knowledge of how social change takes place, rather than a description of existing social institutions, such as might be called social statics. Social dynamics, we repeat, is one of the newest of the sciences. Its first principles are themselves only now firmly established, and many secondary problems remain unsolved. It is in a stage of development comparable to that of physics in the seventeenth century, or biology sixty years ago.

As was the case with both of these sciences, the claim of social dynamics, or Marxism, to have discovered relatively invariable laws governing the relationships of phenomena in its own field is bitterly disputed. In just the same way the exponents of previously existing modes of thought, organized on a predominantly religious basis, furiously denied the validity of the seventeenth-century physicists' claim to have established laws according to which matter invariably behaved. The same religiously minded thinkers, having gradually accepted the view that inorganic matter behaved in a regular, predictable way, as furiously denied the claim of the nineteenth-century biologists and physiologists that they were now discovering invariable laws according to which living organisms behaved. But these furies were trivial compared to the passion with which it is now denied that it is possible to deduce relatively invariable laws as to the way in which human societies arise, develop and decay.

The science of social dynamics, is however, slowly making headway, and for the same reason as did physics and biology. The discoveries of Newton and his contemporaries were found to have prediction value. By their use it became possible to predict some natural events (i.e. eclipses), and actually to control others (i.e. the spot upon which a missile, thrown with a certain velocity at a certain angle, would fall). The discoveries of Darwin and the biologists who have succeeded him have been found to have the same capacity. And now the discoveries of Marx and Engels, who stand in very much the same relation to social dynamics as does Newton to physics and Darwin to biology, have also been found to have this same decisive capacity of enabling the prediction, and hence, if appropriate action is taken, the control, of events.

The comparison of Marx and Engels to Newton and Darwin indicates that social dynamics is an incomplete, imperfect science. But this qualification must not suggest that we are making but a small claim for the new science. For the difference between an incomplete and a fully developed science is almost trivial when compared to the difference between science and no science. The superiority of Einstein's conception of the universe over Newton's is no doubt very great. But it is dwarfed by the superiority of Newton's conception over that of a mediæval alchemist. As the science of social dynamics develops, it will become, and indeed is now becoming, much richer, more complete, more capable of accounting for all the phenomena within its field. But its most perfect formulations will still be based upon the primary concepts discovered by the great pioneers of the science, although in amplifying and perfecting them they will, no doubt, also modify them. But they will be based on the work of Marx and Engels in the same sense in which the work of the modern biologist is based on the work of Darwin and his contemporaries.

In a word, the claim made for the work of Marx and Engels is not that they completed or perfected a science of sociology. It is, on the contrary, the much larger claim that they took that critical and enormously difficult initial step by which scientific methods are for the first time made applicable in a given field. Their work marks that critical point, which occurs in every field of human knowledge, when the gradually accumulating mass of data (in this case of ascertained historical facts, and of economic and philosophical knowledge) is suddenly seized on by powerful minds who, both classifying and synthesizing, demonstrate that relatively invariable relationships are inherent in it. Their inspired vision sees " the pattern in the carpet "— to use a literary simile. And once that pattern is discerned, once it is realized that one type of phenomena is invariably associated with another and that there are links of a causal nature between them, it becomes possible both to predict the future results of existing tendencies, if these are left unmodified, and to control these future results by modifying existing variable factors.

Preceding chapters of this book have stated (more or less dogmatically) the conclusions of social dynamics as to why our existing society is breaking down, what type of society can replace it, and how this social transformation can be effected. It has not been the function of this book to describe the methods by which these conclusions have been arrived at. Something must, however, be said of the science of social change as a science.

All that we can here attempt, it is evident, is to awaken the interest of the reader in the science. Moreover, any attempt to outline Marxism[1] (as the science is usually called) faces peculiar difficulties. Marxism is a highly unified and integrated outlook upon the world. It is a seamless coat, which cannot be cut up without spoiling. Still, purely for the purpose of preliminary

[1] The science is now sometimes referred to as " Marxism-Leninism." But, if we wished to do justice to each of those men who have made major contributions to it, we should have to call it " Marxism-Engelism-Leninism-Stalinism " ! Is it not simpler, then, to stick to Marxism as a name ? Alternatively we can use its characteristic expression in the philosophical field and call it Dialectical Materialism (see Chapter XXX), or again, as suggested above, it might be called Social Dynamics.

exposition, it is possible to differentiate three particular aspects of the science. There is first a particular view of human history, best known as the materialist conception of history. This conception gives expression to the discovery that constant associations exist between certain technical, economic, social and political phenomena. It enables us to understand the rise and fall of that succession of social systems under which men have lived during the long, complex, history of human development.

The second aspect of Marxism consists of its specifically economic theory as to how our present social and economic system (namely, capitalism) works. This is what Marx called the law of motion of capitalism. While the materialist conception of history gives us the first ordered and comprehensive bird's-eye view of the whole of human development—a macroscopic view—the law of motion of capitalism gives us a close, detailed, microscopic view of the way in which we are all here and now producing and exchanging our products, selling our ability to labour, or drawing values produced by others from ownership of the means of production. Moreover, it enables us to plot the curve of the, within certain limits, determinate course of capitalism: to see why capitalism continues to produce such phenomena, as for example permanent and ever growing unemployment and imperialist aggression.

The third aspect of Marxism is of an even more comprehensive and generalized character than the materialist conception of history. This is what may be conveniently called the philosophy of Marxism, or dialectical materialism. A general pattern has been found to inhere in reality in general. More precisely, this pattern has been found to be characteristic of the movements, or changes, which occur to all types of phenomena. It is a pattern which can be discerned alike in the movement and changes of inorganic and organic matter and in the movements and changes through time of human societies and institutions. Unless we have discerned this pattern, it is suggested, we shall find these movements incomprehensible. We shall fail to see any relationship between different classes of phenomena, and our comprehension of their interactions will be limited to mechanical cause and effect. But mechanical movement is only one of a number of the ways in which phenomena interact; there are other, more subtle, but more important, interactions which can be accounted for upon the hypotheses of dialectical materialism alone.

It remains to set up serviceable signposts indicating the nature of these three aspects of Marxist thought. It would be logically correct to begin with dialectical materialism—since this is the most general and abstract aspect of Marxism. It explains the methodology with which Marxists tackle their problems. But, in accordance with the general scheme of this book, we shall instead discuss first the more concrete and particular aspects of Marxism, and then return to an explanation of the methodology of the science. This group of chapters consists, then, in an attempt to clear away certain obstacles which many British and American readers encounter when they turn to Marxism, and not in any attempt at a formal exposition of the science. We begin with the materialist conception of history.

The materialist conception of history marks such an immense advance on any previous historical conception that to-day many people more or less unconsciously adopt its general standpoint. Hence there is some danger of an elaborate definition of it raising problems and difficulties where none really exist. For example, preceding chapters on the origin and development of the working class are an elementary application of the materialist conception of history. We traced, for example, an association between the appearance of persons earning their livings by working for other persons for wages, and the development of modern methods of transport and production. Again we saw that a large number of important phenomena appeared in history at about the same time. The appearance of capitalists and wage-workers, of a world-wide exchange of products, of changes and improvements in the technique of production, of clearings of the peasants off the land, of a change in religious belief from Catholicism to Protestantism, and of a change in political institutions from absolute monarchies to republics or constitutional monarchies, were all events which began to occur at about the same time, viz. between four and five hundred years ago. Now the first thing asserted by the materialist conception of history is that the simultaneous appearance of these phenomena was not a coincidence: that there was an inevitable and necessary inter-connection between these things.

For historians who do not accept this conception no such inter-connections between historical events exist. For them it is just an accident that these tendencies began to develop at the same time. Some of them might easily have developed without the others. It is hardly too much to say that their attitude implies that modern, mechanized methods of production might have developed without capitalists or wage-workers. The establish-ment of republics or constitutional monarchies might, for them, have happened at any time and is not connected with the development of the capitalist class. The change of religion from Catholicism to Protestantism occurred, they suggest, because of King Henry VIII's prejudice in favour of marrying his mis-tresses, and happened to coincide in time with the change in the technique of transportation, the opening up of the world market, and the appearance of agricultural production for profit.

Thus the simplest thing to say about the materialist concep-tion of history is that it reveals hitherto unperceived inter-connections between historical events. It is not so much that we assert that A causes B, as that we assert that A and B are in-separably linked together—that the one cannot appear without the other, and that they continually interact upon each other. For example, the important thing asserted is not that the in-creased profitability of wool growing caused the dispossession of the English peasants from the land and the overthrow of the Roman Catholic Church in Britain, or vice versa that the overthrow of the Roman Catholic Church made possible the dispossession of the peasants, and so enabled the sixteenth-century landowners to make increased profits from growing wool. The important thing asserted is that these three events were interconnected—that each of them could not have happened without the others.[1]

Marxists do, it is true, consider that the economic event is

---

[1] As will become apparent in the next two chapters, Marxists do not admit a rigid antithesis between cause and effect. " Cause and effect are conceptions which only have validity in their application to a particular case as such, but when we consider the particular case in its general connection with the world as a whole, they merge and dissolve in the conception of universal action and inter-action, in which cause and effect are constantly changing places, and what is now or here an effect becomes there or then a cause, and vice versa." (Engels in the *Anti-Dühring*, p. 29.)

primary in time: that, for example, the increased profitability of wool growing was the event which in fact started off this particular series.[1] But once the series has started off, political and social changes often react back powerfully upon the economic situation, again changing it radically.

Engels has a particularly explicit passage in which he refutes the foolish misconception that Marxists suppose that economic, and ultimately technical, changes are the sole dynamic factors in history.

" According to the materialist conception of history," he writes, " the determining element in history is *ultimately* the production and reproduction in real life. More than this neither Marx nor I have ever asserted. If therefore somebody twists this into the statement that the economic element is the *only* determining one, he transforms it into a meaningless, abstract and absurd phrase. The economic situation is the basis, but the various elements of the superstructure—political forms of the class struggle and its consequences, constitutions established by the victorious class after a successful battle, etc.—forms of law—and then even the reflexes of all these actual struggles in the brains of the combatants: political, legal, philosophical theories, religious ideas and their further development into systems of dogma—also exercise their influence upon the course of the historical struggles and in many cases preponderate in determining th ir *form*. There is an interaction of all these elements, in which, amid all the endless host of accidents (i.e. of things and events whose inner connection is so remote or so impossible to prove that we regard it as absent and can neglect it), the economic movement finally asserts itself as necessary. Otherwise the application of the theory to any period of history one chose would be easier than the solution of a simple equation of the first degree.

" We make our own history, but in the first place under very definite presuppositions and conditions. Among these the economic ones are finally decisive."

(*The Correspondence of Marx and Engels*, pp. 475–6.)

[1] But it was itself caused, as we have seen, by prior changes in technique—such as improved navigation opening up wider markets. And it might be possible to trace the social events which themselves gave rise to these changes in technique (the Black Death is often suggested as one of them) and so on and so on.

In fine, the materialist conception does not assert that history is a one way street in which every political change is caused by a social change, and every social change by an economic change, and every economic change by a technical change. It asserts, on the contrary, that history is a complex of reciprocating inter-actions between technical, economic, social and political events. Moreover (and this is the respect in which it differs most from the *soi-disant* scientific conception of history now dominant in British and American universities), the materialist conception asserts that history is a complex of interactions the general mechanism of which can now be understood, at any rate in its main outlines; it asserts that history is not a mere jumble of unrelated, and so incomprehensible, events.

Engels, in another place, examines the whole question of the motives of men as they appear in history. The older conception of history accepted at their face value the motives which his-torical characters, whether individual leaders or masses of men, gave for their actions. " It judges everything," Engels writes of this pre-scientific view of history, " according to the motives of the action: it divides men in their historical activity into noble and ignoble, and then finds that as a rule the noble are defrauded and the ignoble are victorious." (*Ludwig Feuerbach*, p. 59.)

Let us take an example. The older conception of history (in the hands of an historian of the liberal school) supposes that Danton and the great French revolutionaries were fighting for liberty, equality, and fraternity. When a Marxist historian comes along and asserts that, on the contrary, these men were fighting for the dominance of their class over both the nobility and the workers, the liberal historian is both shocked and incredulous. He supposes that the Marxist is alleging that such a man as Condorcet, for example, was a hypocrite. That his passionate assertion that he was willing to die for truth, justice and liberty was a lie. And this odious imputation cannot be true, the liberal historian continues, for Condorcet, and a hundred others, actually did die for their cause.

But the Marxist historian is not alleging that Condorcet did not fight and die for his ideal. He demands, however, that we

ask why that particular ideal seemed to Condorcet, at that time
and place, worth dying for. He denies that ideals are an historical
first cause coming from nowhere and therefore incomprehensible.
He accuses the older type of historian of taking (to return to
Engels' words) " the ideal driving forces which operate (in
history) as ultimate causes, instead of investigating what is
behind them, *what are the driving forces of the driving forces* "
(my italics). The error, Engels continues, " does not lie in the
fact that ideal driving forces are recognized, but in the investigation not being carried back behind them into their motive
causes." (*Ludwig Feuerbach.*)

Thus the materialist conception of history does not, as is
vulgarly supposed, assert that men always act from their
material interests. It is an incomparably more subtle and
developed conception than that. It gives the fullest weight to the
ideals which have actuated men and women, but it insists on
investigating the question of why different ideals have actuated
them at different times and places. It suggests that the leaders
of rising classes have, on the whole, fought and died for those
ideals which embodied the principles upon which it was necessary, then and there, to found human society; which cor-
responded to, and were the only adequate expression of, the
particular stage of technical, economic, and cultural development which man had then reached.

These considerations throw light on the real nature of political
motive. Men think that they overthrow, say, a feudalistic
monarchy for the sake of the ideal of liberty, equality and
fraternity. And so they do. This is the only conscious motive in
their heads and it is absurd to deny that it is their real motive.
The " ideology " (the general world outlook) of which the slogan,
" liberty, equality, and fraternity " is the epitome, has filled
their consciousness completely. It is only if we go behind this
ideology that we discover that it has grown up out of the
conflict between changing, developing, technical and economic
conditions and a static political structure. It is only then that
we shall recognize that what the victory of the idealists will do is
to bring the political structure into line with the technical and
economic developments which have taken place. And it will do
so by putting into power the class with whom the idealists have,

consciously or unconsciously, become identified. But this is far from saying that the idealists are conscious hypocrites.

The truth is that the historical conflict between social classes has as yet been mainly unconscious. The combatants have not hitherto known why they found themselves in conflict with one another. Or, rather, they have only known the most proximate causes of the conflict. Oppressed classes have come into conflict with their oppressors because they found themselves denied some or all of the necessaries of life. Their conscious motive for struggle has been simple self-preservation. Or a rising class, such, for example, as the young capitalist classes of England in the seventeenth, and of France in the eighteenth, centuries, has found itself denied possibilities of development and enrichment by laws and regulations which have become irrational, and so unjust.

In the past all that such classes have been conscious of is the necessity to change the existing social and economic situation. Still, the self-consciousness of struggling classes has steadily increased. Classes have become more and more conscious of the fact that the struggles into which they found themselves impelled by such pressing necessities as self-preservation, or the abolition of intolerable restrictions upon their activities, had necessarily to become struggles for the power to mould society to suit themselves.

With the nineteenth century this consciousness of the nature of historical struggles began to grow rapidly. We have seen how it dawned amongst the British workers—finding its first expression in the writings of the Chartist leaders such as O'Brien. But to a certain extent such consciousness also began to appear in the minds of the nineteenth-century capitalists themselves. For the inter-class nature of political conflicts was becoming unmistakably clear. History was simplifying itself. The twisting thread of class conflict, which had been hidden by the labyrinthine inter-connections of earlier societies, was becoming unmistakable. Engels thus describes this increasing consciousness of the dynamics of history :

" But while in all earlier periods the investigation of these driving causes was almost impossible—on account of the complicated and concealed inter-connections between them and their effects—our present period has so far simplified these inter-connections that the riddle could be solved. Since the establishment of large-scale industry, i.e. at least since the peace of Europe in 1815, it has been no longer a secret to any man in England that the whole political struggle there has turned on the claims of the supremacy of two classes: the landed aristocracy and the middle class. In France, with the return of the Bourbons, the same fact was perceived; the historians of the Restoration period, from Thierry to Guizot, Mignet and Thiers, speak of it everywhere as the key to the understanding of all French history since the Middle Ages. And since 1830 the working class, the proletariat, has been recognized in both countries as a third competitor for power. Conditions have become so simplified that one would have had to close one's eyes deliberately not to see in the fight of these two great classes and the conflict of their interests the driving force of modern history—at least in the two most advanced countries."   (*Ludwig Feuerbach.*)

The essential conclusion which can be drawn from the materialist conception of history is, then, that the dynamic factor in history is the attempt of successive social classes, themselves set in motion by technical and economic changes, to remould society to suit themselves. But once this great scientific discovery had been made, it was important that Marxists should not neglect the form which historical struggles have taken. It was important that Marxists should recognize that the economic developments which threw social classes into conflict did so by breeding particular ideas in the minds of the ablest members of those classes; and that these ideas themselves became to some extent independently variable factors in the complex of inter-acting forces. Engels wrote a letter to Mehring (Marx's principal biographer) politely criticizing him for neglecting this ideal link in the chain of interactions which constitutes the historical process.

" Otherwise there is only one other point lacking, which, however, Marx and I always failed to stress enough in our writings and in regard to which we are all equally guilty. We all, that is to say, laid and were bound to lay the main emphasis at first on the derivation of political, juridical and other ideological notions, and of the actions arising through the medium of these notions, from basic economic facts. But in so doing we neglected the formal side—the way in which these notions come about—for the sake of the content. This has given our adversaries a welcome opportunity for misunderstandings, of which Paul Barth is a striking example.

" Ideology is a process accomplished by the so-called thinker consciously, indeed, but with a false consciousness. The real motives impelling him remain unknown to him, otherwise it would not be an ideological process at all. Hence he imagines false or apparent motives."[1]

(*Marx-Engels Correspondence*, pp. 510–11.)

Engels' conception of " a false consciousness " is particularly noteworthy. Modern psychological discoveries have revealed the capacity of motives of which we remain unconscious powerfully to influence our conduct. These discoveries have made Engels' conception much easier to understand. In particular, it has been found that men have a remarkable faculty for substituting, quite unconsciously, motives which carry social approval, for their real motives. They " rationalize." They drape, even from their own eyes, their over-sharp desires in the robes of respectable aspirations. They fight for liberty, equality, and fraternity, and if their victory brings them instead rent, interest, and profit, no one is more genuinely surprised than themselves.

In conclusion it will be worth while to quote two precise definitions of the materialist conception of history. The first is by Engels :

" The materialist conception of history starts from the principle that production, and with production the exchange of its products, is the basis of every social order; that in every society which has appeared in history the distribution of the

[1] A little further on Engels talks of " the fatuous notion that because we deny an independent historical development to the various ideological spheres which play a part in history we also deny them any effect upon history."

products, and with it the division of society into classes or estates, is determined by what is produced and how it is produced, and how the product is exchanged. According to this conception, the ultimate causes of all social changes and political revolutions are to be sought, not in the minds of men, in their increasing insight into eternal truth and justice, but in changes in the mode of production and exchange; they are to be sought not in the *philosophy* but in the *economics* of the epoch concerned."

(*Anti-Dühring*, p. 300.)

Finally, we must cite the best known of all the formulations of the materialist conception of history. Marx placed it in the preface of one of his earlier published works, *The Critique of Political Economy*, and called it " the leading thread in my studies."

" In the social production which men carry on they enter into definite relations that are indispensable and independent of their will; these relations of production correspond to a definite stage of development of their material powers of production. The sum total of these relations of production constitutes the economic structure of society—the real foundation, on which rise legal and political superstructures and to which correspond definite forms of social consciousness. The mode of production in material life determines the general character of the social, political and spiritual processes of life. It is not the consciousness of men that determines their existence, but, on the contrary, their social existence determines their consciousness."

(Op. cit., p. 11.)

So far, the reader will notice, we have a static analysis. Marx is asserting that certain powers of production force men to associate themselves in certain particular ways. For instance, handicraft production, the stage of development reached in the Middle Ages, habitually gives rise to institutions of which the mediæval guild is the type. Or, again, agriculture at the " open field " stage of development habitually gives rise to some sort of feudalism. On the other hand, if they are using modern methods of production men find themselves associating in institutions such as Joint Stock Companies and Trades Unions. And on top of these directly economic forms of association there arise corresponding political, religious, legal, and philosophical ideas. So far Marx is simply asserting the interconnections of historical phenomena. He is making the point that it is idle to suppose that you can have mediæval guilds as your form of association and automatic, electrically driven machinery as your method of production: or, vice versa, handicraft methods of production and Joint Stock Companies, international trusts, and nation-wide Trades Unions as your forms of association. But now he goes on to describe the way the thing moves, to give the dynamic analysis.

" At a certain stage of their development, the material forces of production in society come into conflict with the existing relations of production, or—what is but a legal expression for the same thing—with the property relations within which they had been at work before. From forms of development of the forces of production these relations turn into their fetters. Then comes the period of social revolution. With the change of the economic foundation the entire immense superstructure is more or less rapidly transformed. In considering such transformations the distinction should always be made between the material transformation of the economic conditions of production which can be determined with the precision of natural science, and the legal, political, religious, æsthetic or philosophic—in short, ideological forms in which men become conscious of this conflict and fight it out."

Once the foundation upon which the social structure rests is disturbed—once, that is to say, the technique of production changes—a complex, reciprocating interaction is set up between all the parts of the social structure. History is under way.[1]

---

[1] Marx goes on to make the point that we have been discussing above, and which Engels makes with his concept of " false consciousness." He goes on to assert that you cannot, for example, judge of the real motives of a class struggling for power by what the spokesmen of that class think are their motives. This is how Marx, somewhat obscurely, puts the point:

" Just as our opinion of an individual is not based on what he thinks of himself, so can we not judge of such a period of transformation by its own consciousness: on the contrary, this consciousness must rather be explained from the contradictions of material life, from the existing conflict between the social forces of production and the relations of production."

Chapter XXIX

The Law of Motion of Capitalism

THE specifically economic aspect of Marxism is best defined as the law of motion of capitalist society. To the discovery of this law Marx devoted the very flower of his genius. It amounts to a full description of the way in which capitalism works. Those who have mastered it, and they alone, experience has now shown, can predict the direction in which capitalism will develop.

The unique predictive power of Marxist economic theory is based not so much on a superior acuteness or subtlety of analysis as on a distinctive approach. The science of political economy, as it was developed in France and Britain during the eighteenth, and the beginning of the nineteenth, centuries was in essence a criticism of the economic system then in existence, a system which was only semi-capitalist. This system was called the mercantile, or mercantilist, system, and it was the last of the numerous transition stages between feudalism and capitalism. The characteristic feature of this economic system was an elaborate structure of rules and regulations, both for foreign and domestic trade, within the framework of which alone production and exchange could be carried on. A pervasive system of tariffs and regulations for foreign trade is often thought of as the most important part of this network of laws. But equally significant were the laws and regulations which established particular rates of wages, conditions of work, and in many cases selling prices, for home production. In England, as we have seen, these regulations were mainly based upon the Elizabethan Statute of Apprentices. Continually revised and adjusted, they constituted a very complete regulation of the productive system.

The essential message of the great economists who appeared in both England and France in the latter half of the eighteenth century was this: sweep away all these rules and regulations: allow the owners of the means of production to employ labour on any terms on which they can secure it; allow them to sell in any market they can reach, and at any price they can get, and everything will go better: " Laissez faire—laissez aller,"[1] as the French economists summed up the precept. The wealth of nations will be enormously increased, as Adam Smith summed up the promise.

The economists were right. As the event showed, the wealth of nations was prodigiously increased when their advice was taken. But what *is* the wealth of nations ? The wealth of nations turned out to be the maximum possible accumulation of profit in the hands of the capitalists. For it was out of this privately accumulated profit that the world was industrialized. And an obvious condition for the utmost possible amount of profit was the lowest possible wages. Hence the maximum augmentation of the wealth of the nation was seen in theory, and turned out in practice, to depend upon the imposition of the utmost possible poverty upon the people. It was the familiar paradox of the individual miser, who must starve himself in order to get rich, reproduced upon a social scale.

The essential point for us is that the body of economic doctrine which was thus established, and which is still the core of all capitalist economics, was not a critique of capitalism. It was, on the contrary, a critique of pre-capitalist, mercantilist, or, in the case of France, semi-feudal, conditions—and a plea for the establishment of fully fledged capitalism. Now the body of economic doctrines which Marx worked out begins where capitalist economic theory leaves off. Just as capitalist economics are, in essence, a critique of pre-capitalist conditions and a demand for capitalism, so Marxist economics are a critique of capitalism and a demand for socialism. Capitalist economics, by contrasting capitalism to earlier conditions, show us how capitalism will work if only we will let it. Marx shows us whither capitalism will take us, if we do not stop it. Adam Smith and Ricardo demonstrated that capitalism would industrialize the world at the maximum possible rate. Marx accepts their conclusion: and then shows what must happen when this job of industrializing the world is substantially accomplished.[2]

[1] Which means, let it be noted, not " Let everything alone," but " Let make, let go "—viz. " Let the capitalists make what they like and do what they like with it."

[2] Another difference is that, naturally, the classical capitalist economists placed all their stress on the wealth which capitalism would bring to the capitalists

This explains why Marx wrote comparatively little about the socialist economic system which, he declared, should succeed capitalism. To describe a future socialist economic system in detail was not his business. For it is only possible to foresee economic systems in the broadest outline. The classical capitalist economists foresaw the basic principles of capitalism, for they derived those principles from their critique of the mercantilist system. In just the same way Marx derived the basic principles of socialism (viz. planned production for use from publicly owned means of production, the products to be distributed according to the quality and quantity of the work done) from his critique of capitalism. But he would have forfeited his right to be called a scientist, and become a mere spinner of fancies, if he had claimed to be able to describe the society of the future in any greater detail than this. And if we are now able to fill in a certain amount of that detail, that is only because a socialist society, the actual practice of which we can study, is now arising in the Soviet Union.

In the course of the first part of this book we attempted to outline (especially in Chapter VII) the essential point of Marx's critique of capitalism. Here we need only indicate how Marx arrived at his economic discoveries.

Marx's economics are a particular application of the materialist conception of history. Someone who was seized of this conception could alone have conceived of the existing, contemporary economic system having a law of motion at all. The concept that economic systems have a determinate cycle of growth and decay, and that consequently a social morphology is possible, was Marx's first great contribution to economics.

The body of Marx's economics, as expounded in the three volumes of *Capital*, is concerned with tracing out what happens if and when a class of persons owning almost all the means of

during the time in which it was performing its task and privilege of industrialization. Marx, on the other hand, reveals the other side of the picture—the atrocious poverty which this same process, conducted by these means, must bring to the workers.

But here there is no real disagreement between them; they are only concentrating their attention on different aspects of the same phenomenon, i.e. industrialization, or the accumulation of capital—which both agree is the function of capitalism. But the classical capitalist economists stop at this point. Marx goes on, and shows that once this job of industrializing the world is done, there is nothing more which capitalism can accomplish.

production buys the labour power of a much more numerous class of persons who have no other way of maintaining their existence. Marx showed, by a far more rigorous and thorough application of the law of value which the classical capitalist economists had themselves discovered, that the effect must be the ever more rapid piling up of immense masses of capital in the hands of the owners of the means of production, and the holding down of the standard of life of the workers to what sufficed to enable them to provide an effective labour supply in perpetuity. The theory of value which was, up till about 1830, common ground between Marx and the capitalist economists declares that the value of commodities is determined by the number of hours of socially necessary labour which have been expended in producing them. The reader will have noticed that we made no direct attempt to expound the labour theory of value in Part I. It was, however, implicit in our investigation of the problems raised by the conscious application of a community's productive resources to the satisfaction of its wants in the order of their urgency. For human labour of hand and brain is, in the ultimate analysis, the basic, limited and therefore precious, productive resource which has to be allocated between alternative uses.

Indeed, so soon as we think in terms of society as a whole, the labour theory of value is self-evident. The total number of man-hours of work is undeniably the ultimate factor of production which must be distributed amongst the necessary tasks to be accomplished by any social group. It is above all necessary, that is to say, for anybody who is planning the economic life of any community, whether large or small, whether a family group of settlers or a whole nation, to decide on how the work of the community is to be shared out amongst the available workers. Units of labour time inevitably become his units of measurement. He will inevitably reckon the cost of alternative acts of production according to the amount of labour time which they directly or indirectly absorb. Thus, since in Part I we were intent to describe a planned system of production for use, rather than to give any exhaustive analysis of capitalism, an exposition of the labour theory of value was unnecessary to our limited purpose. Such an exposition is, however, essential to any final understanding of capitalism and its present difficulties.

To achieve such an understanding of capitalism is not the purpose of this book, however. Here, therefore, we may be content merely to point out that the chief difficulty to an acceptance of the labour theory of value arises from the delusion that Marx stated that commodities, in a fully developed capitalism such as ours, exchanged in proportion to the amount of socially necessary labour time contained in them. Or, to put the point in another way, it is supposed that Marx thought that the prices of commodities in a capitalist economy fluctuated round their values.

Marx, however, was far from supposing any such thing. He declared that the only way in which men living under a system of buying and selling (or exchanging) can rationally allocate the necessary work of the community between its members is by exchanging their products in proportion to the labour time contained in them. The eighteenth-century economists had discovered that this was what men were, unconsciously, doing. They saw that the essential, basic ratios of exchange between commodities must be, and were, determined by the amount of socially necessary labour time which men had had to put into their production.

But Marx was far from suggesting that, under the capitalist variant of such a system of buying and selling, commodities do tend to exchange at these ratios. He expressly pointed out that as capitalism develops, and more especially as the unevenness of its development becomes greater and greater, the points round which the prices of commodities fluctuate diverge more and more from their values. So much the worse for capitalism ! For this divergence of prices from values is evidence of the ever growing irrationality of the system. But this aspect of the workings of capitalism was not the one which principally interested Marx. For he had been able to prove that, even if all commodities in a capitalist society were sold at their values, as in certain conditions (viz. if the composition of capital were the same in all branches of production) they would be, the exploitation of those who did not own the means of production, by those who did, would still occur.

The labour theory of value explains *how* the flagrant injustice and waste of the capitalist system (the existence of which needs no demonstration) have arisen. It does so by showing that the rapidly accumulating masses of capital which characterize every capitalist system are produced by the unpaid labour of the workers. Marx christened the product of this unpaid labour, surplus value.

The standard, or yard stick, provided by the labour theory of value enabled Marx to predict the ever growing difficulties into which capitalism must get, as and when industrialization became complete. Marx was able to predict the exact condition of capitalism which we can now observe. The labour theory of value enabled him to realize that the holding down of the workers' standard of life to the minimum possible level was, *up to a certain point*, a necessary condition of industrialization at the most rapid pace possible. For thus alone could all available productive resources be freed for the production of means of production, or, to put the same point in financial terms, for the accumulation of capital. But Marx predicted that after a certain point was reached, this holding down of the standard of life of the great majority of the population to a minimum level would turn into a barrier to the further process of industrialization.[1] For the essential fact, that the only ultimate purpose of industrialization is to increase the supply of consumers' goods, and so raise the standard of life of the population, would begin to make itself felt. It would become absurd, and in the end actually unprofitable, to go on producing new factories which could not sell their products, because the process of their own erection had necessitated the holding down of the general standard of life to so low a point that the population could not hope to buy the products.

This is the core of that central " contradiction," as he called it, which, Marx predicted, would more and more press upon capitalism. For there is no way of overcoming this difficulty which does not land capitalism in even worse troubles. In particular, the often advocated, but, significantly, never adopted remedy of raising the wages of the workers in order to enable

---

[1] " From forms of development of the forces of production these relations turn into their fetters." (See p. 367 above.)

them to buy all the consumers' goods which industry can produce is not open to the capitalists, even if they should be so generous and so intelligent as to attempt it. For contemporary capitalism, in spite of the immense profits which the owners of the means of production appropriate, is always and everywhere hard pressed. Even in the richest empires, such as Britain, it feels, and in one sense correctly, that it has nothing to give to the workers. On the contrary, we invariably notice that the practice of all capitalists, however much they may talk of solving their difficulties by raising wages, is to attempt to solve them by still further lowering wages.

This remarkable contradiction between capitalist theory and capitalist practice is based upon the fact that the owners of the means of production have now accumulated such immense masses of capital that vast sums of profit are now necessary even to pay a minimum rate of profit, or interest, on them. And it is imperatively necessary for capitalism to prevent the *rate of profit*, which is the mainspring or driving motor of the whole system, from going below the point at which the whole massive and complex mechanism can be kept in motion. Hence, however much it may escape from it *in fancy*, by the expedient of paying more to the workers, capitalism is, *in fact*, continually being driven back on to its basic inability to dispose of its products. The difficulty asserts itself in what we are accustomed to call a lack of markets. There are, however, as we noticed in Chapter XX, various ways in which its onset can be postponed. The main one is the acquisition abroad of those markets which cannot be provided at home. But this temporary solution of the difficulty leads to international conflicts insoluble except by war.

We can now observe the series of fateful and tragic developments, which Marx predicted, taking place before our eyes. We do not need the theoretical apparatus, which he built up upon the basis of the labour theory of value, in order to know that they exist. But this apparatus was necessary in order to enable Marx to predict their appearance, and is still necessary to us if we would not only recognize but comprehend them. At the same time it is this theoretical apparatus which makes Marx's work difficult, often to the point of incomprehensibility, to many present-day readers. The first part of *Capital* in particular requires the greatest effort of comprehension. In the opinion of Engels this is partly due to defects in Marx's methods of presentation, which are themselves attributable to the dreadful conditions of poverty and ill health in which this part of *Capital* was written. But the initial difficulties of *Capital* are basically due to the deductive method which Marx had necessarily to adopt for his task of prediction. For the inductive method is clearly not available till the necessary phenomena from which the induction can be made have developed.

In any case what excites our wonder is not that Marx was unable to plot the curve of the determinate development of capitalism without introducing difficult conceptions: the wonder is that he was able to do it at all. Indeed, Marx's substantially correct prediction of the future course of capitalist development, considered as a sheer feat of intellect, has never been surpassed. The limits of rational explanation are strained to the utmost in order to account for the ability of Marx to have discovered the law of motion of capitalism as early as 1850.[1] For at that time capitalism had still well over half a century to run before the symptoms produced by its central contradiction became acute. We can only marvel at, and delight in, the startling mental powers which certain men have possessed. What future triumphs for the mind of man are not promised us by these at present exceptional phenomena !

[1] There is evidence that he knew all the essential parts of his economic system by 1850—although his analysis was only completed in the third volume of *Capital* published in 1894.

CHAPTER XXX

Dialectical Materialism

THE materialist conception of history and the law of motion of capitalism describe the general movement of human society. The first gives us a general, perspective view, the second an exhaustive study of the foreground. But neither of them analyses the nature of that movement: nor do they, even taken together, amount to a comprehensive outlook on the world.

We now come to the third and most generalized aspect of the science of social change, namely Dialectical Materialism. In order of discovery, however, Dialectical Materialism came first.[1] Marx and Engels, like all young Germans of their generation, received a predominantly philosophical education. They were legitimate heirs to the great tradition of German classical philosophy. Now German classical philosophy belonged to the idealist as opposed to the materialist philosophical school. The difference between these two schools is in essence this. Idealist philosophers believe that the primary stuff of the universe consists of thoughts or ideas, and that material reality is only a reflection of this thought stuff. Materialist philosophers believe, on the contrary, that our thoughts and ideas are the reflection of a material reality which exists outside and independently of our consciousness.[2] Materialist philosophy is associated with the scientific, investigatory, experimental attitude towards the

---

[1] This was inevitable, for only men possessed of the dialectical theory of evolution could ever have even asked themselves the questions which Marx and Engels answered. Hence, again, we should logically have attempted to deal with dialectical materialism first. The advantage of the present order of treatment is simply that by using it we can move from the familiar, the concrete and the specific towards the abstract and general. Its disadvantage is that it may suggest that dialectics are a sort of philosophical ornament superimposed upon the more " practical " aspects of Marxism. In fact there is no part of the Marxist theoretical structure which is not dialectical, or which could have been created by men who did not think dialectically.

[2] Philosophical schools are to-day more usually divided into dualists and monists; viz. persons who respectively believe that the stuff of the universe is of two kinds —mind and matter (to use the terms which are now most usually employed)— which cannot be resolved into a unity, and those who think that they can be so resolved. Monists may in turn be sub-divided into those who think that the basic stuff of the universe is mind: those who think that it is matter, and those who think that it is of a neutral character as between mind and matter. But these distinctions are not relevant to our field of interest. The historically important and significant distinction is undoubtedly that between materialists and idealists.

world. Indeed, the early seventeenth-century scientists were many of them philosophers of this school (for example, Bacon). Marx and Engels were, however, brought up idealists. Yet obviously they were natural born materialists. Their whole cast of mind revolted at the idea that external reality was a mere mirror image of something inside the human head. Their outlook was essentially investigatory and experimental—extrovert, as we should say now. As soon as they began to think independently they became materialists. But, and this was the first sign of their genius, they did not, as would have most young men in revolt against the intellectual tradition in which they had been brought up, simply fling away their heritage in idealist philosophy. On the contrary, they realized that idealist philosophy had preserved and developed an extremely important aspect of the truth which materialism, and the scientific outlook built upon it, had hitherto neglected. This is how Engels expressed the view, from which they never departed, that the then existing scientific, materialist outlook was by itself inadequate :

" The analysis of Nature into its individual parts, the grouping of the different natural processes and natural objects in definite classes, the study of the internal anatomy of organic bodies in their manifold forms—these were the fundamental conditions of the gigantic strides in our knowledge of Nature which have been made during the last four hundred years. But this method of investigation has also left us as a legacy the habit of observing natural objects and natural processes in their isolation, detached from the whole vast interconnection of things; and therefore not in their motion, but in their repose; not as essentially changing, but as fixed constants; not in their life, but in their death. . . .

" . . . And this is so because in considering individual things it loses sight of their connections; in contemplating their existence it forgets their coming into being and passing away; in looking at them in rest it leaves their motion out of account; because it cannot see the wood for the trees."

(*Anti-Dühring*, pp. 27–8.)

Marx and Engels considered that the materialist, scientific outlook had only achieved its triumphs at a price. In immensely increasing our knowledge of each one of the trees, it had progressively blinded us to the wood. The pre-scientific epoch had possessed a superior vision of the complex of reality. The philosophers of ancient Greece, for example, had only the most meagre knowledge of the nature of the component parts of the universe; but they had a vivid sense of the whole. They had, above all, a grasp of the fact that the universe is not a structure but a flux: that it is a complex of moving, and therefore interacting, parts. The philosophers of ancient Greece gave, Engels goes on to say, incomparably the best expression to this original, pre-scientific conception of the universe. They expressed superbly what everyone must feel when he reflects upon the picture presented to him by the totality of his objective experience.

" When we reflect on Nature, or the history of mankind, or our own intellectual activity, the first picture presented to us is of an endless maze of relations and interactions, in which nothing remains what, where, and as it was, but everything moves, changes, comes into being, and passes out of existence . . . everything is and also is not, for everything is in *flux*, is constantly changing, constantly coming into being and passing away." (*Anti-Dühring*, p. 27.)

This conception of reality as an infinitely interconnected, continuously developing process was lost when the materialist, scientific attitude became dominant. In order to see what its parts were like, men had, as it were, to take the universe to pieces, much as a student lays out the interacting parts of a machine which he is studying upon his work bench. This process of taking to pieces was absolutely necessary; without it we could never have got any exact knowledge of what reality was made up of. But it entailed a process of dissection; it entailed the taking apart of each particular minute sub-division of the whole in order to investigate it separately and in isolation. It entailed losing sight of the fact that each of these parts was both interacting with all the rest, and was also itself coming into existence and passing out of existence again.

But the older, better integrated, although far less precise, way of looking at things was not entirely lost. From the revival of learning at the time of the Renaissance the idealist school of philosophy began to develop. And this school preserved, although in a distorted form, the older, integral conception of the universe. It conceived of reality as a mere reflection of the thought process going on in the heads of its philosophers. But it conceived of their thought as a process; as an uninterrupted development, as an organic whole made up of interacting parts. Moreover, as the primary thought process was of this character, so also must be the reality which mirrored it. Hence the idealist philosophers, by a devious route, came to look at reality more dynamically and more integrally than did anyone else.

This way of thinking culminated in the German philosopher, Hegel, in whose elaborate discipline Marx and Engels were brought up. Hegel was a man of formidable intellectual powers and of encyclopædic learning. In his system, Engels writes,

" the whole natural, historical, and spiritual world was presented as a process; that is, as in constant motion, change, transformation and development; and the attempt was made to show the internal interconnections in this motion and development. From this standpoint the history of mankind no longer appeared as a confused whirl of senseless deeds of violence, all equally condemnable before the judgment seat of the now matured philosophic reason, and best forgotten as quickly as possible, but as the process of development of humanity itself. It now became the task of thought to follow the gradual stages of this process through all its devious ways, and to trace out the inner regularities running through all its apparently fortuitous phenomena.

" That Hegel did not succeed in this task is here immaterial. His epoch-making service was that he propounded it."

(*Anti-Dühring*, p. 30.)

Hegel propounded the problem of seeking over the whole field of knowledge for regularities, for invariable laws, which might be found to govern the way in which phenomena interacted, changed and developed. It was, above all, this attitude of mind which Marx and Engels admired in the idealist school, and determined to preserve when they abandoned its basic postulate of the unreality of matter. They determined to preserve, Engels writes in his essay on Ludwig Feuerbach,

" the great basic thought that the world is not to be comprehended as a complex of ready-made *things*, but as a complex of *processes*, in which the things apparently stable, no less than their mind-images in our heads, the concepts, go through an uninterrupted change of coming into being and passing away."

Moreover, they felt there was a great deal of evidence to suggest that the interconnections and the laws of motion which Hegel and his school had declared to inhere in the world of thought (in the self-development of the idea, as Hegel put it) were laws which could be observed to be operating in the objective world—both in the sphere of historical events and of nature. Marx and Engels devoted much of the rest of their lives to the investigation of the question of whether these suggested laws of motion really were objective phenomena. Marx took especially the field of historical and economic development, and Engels that of the natural sciences. They came to the conclusion that both historical events and natural forces did move, change, and interact according to a general, observable pattern.

It is clear that nothing can exceed the importance of this discovery, if it can be verified; for it provides an invaluable guiding hypothesis for investigation. Moreover, in fields in which past events are well known, it provides the basis for scientific prediction, and so for the control of phenomena. Since the pattern which Marx and Engels observed in all classes of phenomena was of a particular kind known by Hegel as " dialectical,"[1] they

---

[1] Hegel's choice of the word dialectical to express his basic concept that ideas and (for him) consequently reality had developed, and always must develop, through a synthesizing of opposites, was a curious one. He took the word from the classical Greek philosophers; but they had used it in a much more restricted, and, indeed, somewhat different, sense. They had maintained that truth could be best *discovered* by the clash of argument—by the full recognition of the opposite sides of propositions and phenomena. From this came the Socratic method of philosophical investigation, and, in the decline of classical philosophy, the use of " dialectics," i.e. the scoring of debating points, in the sense of the word most widely current to-day. Hence no little confusion arises for those who hear of dialectical materialism for the first time. It is true, however (see below), that the greatest Greek philosophers had an essentially dialectical concept of t he universe, using the term in the far wider sense first given to it by Hegel and now used by Marxists. Hence Hegel was justified in his choice of terms.

called this view of the world " dialectical materialism." In their hands, Engels writes,

" dialectics reduced itself to the science of the general laws of motion—both of the external world and of human thought —two sets of laws which are identical in substance, but differ in their expression in so far as the human mind can apply them consciously, while in nature and also up to now for the most part in human history, these laws assert themselves unconsciously in the form of external necessity in the midst of an endless series of seeming accidents."

(*Ludwig Feuerbach*, p. 54.)

In this way Marx and Engels married the materialist, scientific tradition, as it had developed in France and England, with the dialectical method of German idealist philosophy. The result, " dialectica materialism," is a body of knowledge which claims to describe the way in which phenomena have, and hence presumably will, interact and develop. This is what things in general are like, Marx and Engels declare; or rather, this is the way they move. Dialectical materialism is a theory of evolution.[1] It claims to be a strictly scientific hypothesis deduced from the ever accumulating data provided by all the sciences. " There could be no question of building the laws of dialectics into nature, but of discovering them in it and evolving them from it," Engels writes (*Anti-Dühring*). Dialectical materialism is not, then, a philosophy; it is, rather, the methodology of scientific thought. Engels elaborates this point as follows:

" In both cases modern materialism is essentially dialectical, and no longer needs any philosophy standing above the other sciences. As soon as each separate science is required to get clarity as to its position in the great totality of things, a special science dealing with this totality is superfluous. What still independently survives of all former philosophy is the science of thought and its law—formal logic and dialectics. Everything else is merged in the positive science of Nature and history." (*Anti-Dühring*, p. 32.)

This is how Lenin describes it. (See the *Teachings of Karl Marx*.)

The philosophic temper and approach is preserved, but philosophy itself becomes redundant. " Dialectics is nothing more than the science of the general laws of motion and development of Nature, human society and thought." (*Ludwig Feuerbach.*)

What, then, are these extremely general laws of motion which, Marx and Engels assert, both organic and inorganic nature, and human society, exhibit in their evolution ? First of all, it can be observed, it is suggested, that both of these classes of phenomena do not evolve in a straight line. Human society, for example, has not, as is often supposed, slowly but steadily evolved from lower and more primitive to higher and higher forms. On the contrary, the movement has been of a zig-zag character. It is not that successive civilizations have arisen and collapsed. That is a commonplace. The historical fact upon which dialectical materialism insists is that the rise of each civilization has represented a loss as well as a gain, and the fall of each civilization has represented a gain as well as a loss.

We noticed this in the case of the rise of Athenian civilization. We discussed the well-known fact that the essential foundation upon which one of the most beautiful of all civilizations was based was the brutal and horrible degradation, the ruin and eventual enslavement, of the people of Attica, till then organized in the relatively free and equal gentile order. We noticed that an analogous process happened in Britain five hundred years ago. The gain in learning, accumulated wealth, amenities, command over nature—in a word, in civilization in general—which began about 1450, was only achieved at the cost of the degradation of the mass of the population. Chaucer's hearty, healthy, sturdy peasants, who were the admiration of all Europe, became in little more than a century the wretched paupers of whose universal presence Queen Elizabeth had to complain: paupers who then, as ever afterwards, had to be supported out of public funds by special legislation. The same thing, again, took place with the introduction of power-driven machinery around 1800. The standard of civilization was in one way immensely raised; but only at the cost of the frightful degradation of whole sections of the population, including the torture of generations of children.

Every step forward in human development seems to have been bought at so high a price that we are often inclined to doubt if there has been any net gain. But this tragic doctrine is not the whole story. There is a relationship, an interaction, between the different stages of historical development. The loss which humanity suffers each time it makes a step forward is not necessarily a permanent one. The next step in advance may remedy the evils produced in the previous one, while retaining its achievements.

For example, the societies of almost independent peasants (and of handicraft workers in the free towns) which developed in favourable conditions at the end of the Middle Ages (as in fifteenth-century England) recovered much of that freedom and equality which had been lost at the dawn of civilization and the decay of the *gens*. But the thirteenth- and fourteenth-century societies retained the enormous advances in civilization which had meanwhile been achieved. They retained field agriculture, the highly developed manipulation of wood and metals, the capacity for the exchange of surplus products, the power to store knowledge in written records, and all the other fundamental advances which had been made during the intervening two or three thousand years.[1]

Again—and this is, of course, the example on which Marx and Engels laid the greatest stress—the startling gains in the technique of production and in the accumulation of wealth which have been made by means of the filching of the means of production from the mass of the population during the last five hundred years will not be lost when that expropriation is reversed by the establishment of socialism. Capitalism, as we saw, established itself by taking (originally by force, subsequently by allowing economic tendencies to act without restraint) their essential means of production from some seven-tenths of the population. It was a mistake, however, said Marx and Engels, to think, as did the Chartists, that when the British people recovered their means of production, they would break up the relatively large-scale agriculture, and the extremely large-scale industry, which

---

[1] The high level of classical civilization had been lost meanwhile, but by 1500 the technical knowledge which makes civilization possible had in certain vital respects (e.g. printing) already been pushed beyond the level reached by the ancients.

had in the meanwhile been established, and return to peasant agriculture and tiny, scattered, handicraft industry. They would have to do just this if they attempted to divide up amongst themselves the means of production—to parcel them out for individual ownership again. But this would involve the abandonment of most of the unparalleled technical advances of the last five hundred years. Not only would this be a crime against human progress; it would be a sheer physical impossibility. For the population had in the meanwhile grown six- or seven-fold. It would now be physically impossible to maintain us all, even on the lowest standard of life, by means of the technical methods of the Middle Ages such as are alone compatible with scattered, individual ownership of tiny means of production.

The peoples of the capitalist states would not, then, when they recovered possession of the means of production, attempt to re-establish individual ownership by physically breaking up the great aggregated means of production. They would, on the contrary, operate them as their common property—dividing only the *products* amongst themselves. (And this is what has actually been done in the only case in which the people of a community have regained possession of the means of production —in the case of the people of the Soviet Union.) In this way, and in this way alone, Marx and Engels taught, can the people of Europe regain all that they have lost in the last five hundred years and yet retain, and at long last get the benefit of, the immense gains which have been made in the same period.

Thus the general pattern of human history is seen to consist, not of any even line of upward development, but of a complex interaction in which every step forward is only achieved at the cost of a step back—but in which these inevitable retrogressions are remedied at the next stage. Another way of picturing this type of movement is that of a spiral. The movement comes back to the place at which it started, but at a higher level. For example, in the historical sequence which we have instanced we may take freedom and equality in the old gentile societies as the starting-point. This type of society had to be dissolved in order to start civilization on its upward path. The slave civilizations of antiquity arose. These dissolved into the comparatively free societies of the barbarian invaders. But, by the end of the Middle Ages, human society, while retaining a relative freedom and equality, had regained a measure of civilization. Freedom and social equality[1] were, necessarily, soon lost again, however. They had to be lost if our recent giant steps in technical and economic progress were to be achieved. Nor could they be recovered until, with the overthrow of capitalism, the wheel comes full circle and social equality and freedom again become possible on the basis of the common ownership of the giant means of production evolved in the capitalist epoch.

Or, again, we may look at the historical process as progress through a series of contradictions. (This is how Hegel and the older dialecticians thought of it.) The gentile society is dissolved, is contradicted, or " negated," as the philosophers called it in their curious terminology, by the ancient forms of civilization. These in turn dissolve into the Dark Ages. For the evils which those civilizations have created become insupportable, and the ancient civilizations are negated. But their basic technical and cultural achievements are not lost, and civilization reappears during the Middle Ages on a relatively tolerable basis. But this new stage is in its turn " negated," and so on and so on. Each stage is a contradiction, or negation, of the one before it. But it is not a flat contradiction—an absolute negation. It does not wipe out completely the stage which it supplants.

The re-establishment of a relatively free society in the Dark Ages by no means entailed the regression of the technical basis of civilization to the old gentile level. The basic achievements of antiquity survived,[2] and relative freedom and equality were re-established on a higher level. Or, again, the overthrow of capitalism does not mean the destruction of our gigantic modern means of production which were accumulated in the form of private capital: on the contrary, while changing the ownership and use of this capital, it will mean the re-establishment of

[1] Equality in the sense of a relative diffusion of the means of production.

[2] We are accustomed to think of the main achievements of classical antiquity as cultural, and these cultural achievements were, temporarily, almost completely lost in the Dark Ages. But the basic achievements of antiquity were technical, were such things as the invention of field agriculture, the domestication of some animals, the invention of coasting ships and the like. And these achievements were not lost, but transmitted by the conquered Roman provincials to their barbarian conquerors.

Ns

freedom and equality on the higher basis afforded by these massed productive resources.

This is the general pattern which Marx and Engels discerned in the development of human society through time. It is called a dialectical movement, and this particular aspect of it was called by Hegel " the negation of the negation." For each stage contradicted or negated the one before it, and then was contradicted or negated itself.

The question is, has history really been like that ? Marx and Engels believed that it has. They believed that this pattern was not something to which they fitted and twisted the record of the human past, but was something which emerged as inherent in that past so soon as the historical record had become sufficiently long and full to make its general character visible. The test must be, as usual, one of prediction value. If this really is the pattern of history, exhibited in coil after coil, in spiral after spiral, of ascending development, it must surely be possible to predict the general character of the next phase ? By producing the present curve of development it must be possible to see how and when society will return, though on a higher level, to a given point on a previous spiral. Marx and Engels did not hesitate to put the matter to this test. For example, they confidently predicted that the next phase of historical development would return to the mass of the population those means of production which had been gradually taken from them during the last five hundred years. The capitalist class, in order to perform its historical function, had expropriated the people. But the expropriators, as Marx puts it, in the peroration to the first volume of *Capital*, would themselves be expropriated. This is how (writing in the eighteen-sixties) he characterizes this future counter-expropriation of the capitalists by the people. " It is the negation of the negation. This does not re-establish private property for the producer, but gives him individual property based on the acquisitions of the capitalist era; i.e. on co-operation and the possession in common of the land and of the means of production."

In Britain and America the counter-expropriation remains a prediction and an aspiration. But over one-sixth of the world's surface this event has now happened. Moreover, in most of the other five-sixths of the world the struggle[1] of the mass of the population to resume the ownership of the land and the other means of production dominates the political scene.

Engels has a passage in which he deals with the dialectical character of the successive stages through which the ownership of one essential factor of production, namely the land, has passed.

" All civilized peoples begin with the common ownership of the land. With all peoples who have passed a certain primitive stage in the course of the development of agriculture, this common ownership becomes a fetter on production. It is abolished, negated, and after a longer or shorter series of intermediate stages is transformed into private property. But at a higher stage of agricultural development, brought about by private property in land itself, private property in turn becomes a fetter on production as is the case to-day, both with small and large landownership. The demand that it also should be negated, that it should once again be transformed into common property, necessarily arises. But this demand does not mean the restoration of the old original common ownership, but the institution of a far higher and more developed form of possession in common which, far from being a hindrance to production, on the contrary for the first time frees production from all fetters and gives it the possibility of making full use of modern chemical discoveries and mechanical inventions."

(Anti-Dühring, pp. 156–7.)

This passage, let us not forget, was written just half a century before the collectivization of the land of Russia. It was written while the breakdown of the early, primitive, common ownership of the Russian land into individual holdings (which was not quite completed till the revolution) was still going on. Yet it foretold, with an accuracy which would be uncanny if it had not been based upon a scientific, observed law, what has now occurred. For how could the present collectivization of the land

[1] In some countries we can discern the conscious struggle of the people to regain the means of production: in others all that is as yet visible is an unconscious struggle against the sufferings entailed by their alienation.

of Russia be more accurately and vividly described than in these words of Engels, viz. " the institution of a far higher and more developed form of possession in common which, far from being a hindrance to production, on the contrary for the first time frees production from all fetters and gives it the possibility of making full use of modern chemical discoveries and mechanical inventions " ?

It is upon this ability to foretell the general direction of historical development that dialectical materialism bases its claim to proved validity. I cannot resist the conclusion that this claim is now established.

But dialectical materialism makes wider claims than this: it claims that the above law of " the negation of the negation " applies not only to historical development, but also to the development of organic and inorganic nature. And it also claims to have observed two other laws which are also applicable to all classes of phenomena, and without which their motions and interactions cannot be understood. Let us deal with these claims separately.

It is claimed that natural as well as historical phenomena have evolved; that, if they are to be understood, they must be studied, not only as they are, but as they have been and as they will be. This is now, of course, a commonplace, admitted by every scientist. The doctrine of the evolution of all life from a few parental stocks is now universally accepted. The doctrine of the evolution through time of the inorganic matter of the universe, from original nebular clouds to the ever hardening, cooling masses of the stars and planets, is also not questioned. Science has come to look at both classes of phenomena in their becoming and their motion, their change, their life histories. We should remember, however, that this is a new development in scientific thought. Until the second half of the nineteenth century no such evolutionary view had been developed by the scientists. The only people who had this view (although they held it in their peculiar and inverted form) were the idealist, dialectical philosophers such as Hegel.

Moreover, dialectical materialism does not merely insist upon the study of the evolution of natural phenomena. It insists that their evolution, their motion through time, is of a dialectical character: that it too exhibits the principle of reciprocating or spiral movement, which Hegel called the negation of the negation. Engels in the *Anti-Dühring* gives a number of examples. He takes first the life history of those kinds of plants which propagate by a seeding process.

" Let us take a grain of barley. Millions of such grains of barley are milled, boiled and brewed and then consumed. But if such a grain of barley meets with conditions which for it are normal, if it falls on suitable soil, then under the influence of heat and moisture a specific change takes place, it germinates; the grain as such ceases to exist, it is negated, and in its place appears the plant which has arisen from it, the negation of the grain. But what is the normal life-process of this plant ? It grows, flowers, is fertilized and finally once more produces grains of barley, and, as soon as these have ripened, the stalk dies, is in its turn negated. As a result of this negation of the negation we have once again the original grain of barley, but not as a single unit, but ten, twenty or thirty fold."

(Anti-Dühring, p. 154.)

The barley lives and evolves by means of returning to its starting-point—but at a higher level. One seed has produced many. Moreover, as Engels goes on to point out, over long periods plants have evolved qualitatively as well as quantitatively. Successive generation of seeds have shown variations, becoming minutely more adapted to their environment. And the skilled horticulturist can immensely speed up this process, producing appreciably better seed from the evolution of a comparatively few generations.

Engels' next example is from the insect world.

" Butterflies, for example, spring from the egg through a negation of the egg, they pass through certain transformations until they reach sexual maturity, they pair and are in turn negated, dying as soon as the pairing process has been completed and the female has laid its numerous eggs."

(Anti-Dühring, p. 154.)

The story of the evolution of inorganic nature reveals, Engels continues, the same pattern.

" The whole of geology is a series of negated negations, a series arising from the successive shattering of old and the depositing of new rock formations. First the original earth-crust brought into existence was broken up by oceanic, meteorological and atmospherico-chemical action, and these disintegrated masses were deposited on the ocean floor. Local elevations of the ocean floor above the surface of the sea subjected portions of these first strata once more to the action of rain, the changing temperature of the seasons and the oxygen and carbonic acid of the atmosphere. These same influences acted on the molten masses of rock which issued from the interior of the earth, broke through the strata and subsequently solidified. In this way, in the course of millions of centuries, ever new strata are formed and in turn are for the most part destroyed, ever anew serving as material for the formation of new strata. But the result of the process has been a very positive one: the creation, out of the most varied chemical elements, of a mixed and mechanically pulverized soil which makes possible the most abundant and diverse vegetation."

(Anti-Dühring, p. 155.)

Engels next turns to mathematics. He attached, I think, great importance to these mathematical examples, for, if the dialectical pattern can be perceived in the precise and abstract movements of numbers and symbols, it must be inherent in the very bones of reality.

" Let us take any algebraical magnitude whatever : for example, a. If this is negated, we get $-a$ (minus a). If we negate that negation by multiplying $-a$ by $-a$, we get a^2, i.e. the original positive magnitude, but at a higher degree, raised to its second power. In this case also it makes no difference that we can reach the same a^2 by multiplying the positive a by itself, thus also getting a^2. For the negated negation is so securely entrenched in the a^2 that the latter always has two square roots, namely a and $-a$. And the fact that it is impossible to get rid of the negated negation, the negative root of the square, acquires very obvious significance as soon as we get as far as quadratic equations."

(Anti-Dühring, p. 155.)

Engels then gives another example from the higher mathematics of the differential and integral calculus. Finally Engels, by a neat turn, shows that the evolution of philosophical thought, of which dialectical materialism itself is the end product, has followed this same pattern.

"The philosophy of antiquity was primitive, natural materialism. As such, it was incapable of clearing up the relation between thought and matter. But the need to get clarity on this question led to the doctrine of a soul separable from the body, then to the assertion of the immortality of this soul, and finally to monotheism. The old materialism was therefore negated by idealism. But in the course of the further development of philosophy, idealism too became untenable and was negated by modern materialism. This modern materialism, the negation of the negation, is not the mere re-establishment of the old, but adds to the permanent foundations of this old materialism the whole thought content of two thousand years. It is in fact no longer a philosophy, but a simple conception of the world which has to establish its validity and be applied, not in a science of sciences standing apart, but within the positive sciences. In this development philosophy is therefore ' sublated '—that is, ' both abolished and preserved ' ; abolished as regards its form, and preserved as regards its real content."

(Anti-Dühring, p. 157.)

So much for the universality of the dialectical pattern in the evolution of organic and inorganic matter. It is suggested, however, that two other laws of motion may be perceived from the study of the movements of all types of phenomena. The one deals with the question of the nature of contradiction, and is often referred to as " the interpenetration of opposites." The other deals with the relationship of quantitative to qualitative changes. It is based on the observation that in many cases a quantitative change pushed beyond a certain point constitutes, or amounts to, a change in quality.

Engels exhibits the first of these laws by pointing out that so long as we regard phenomena in repose, statically, no contradictory characteristics present themselves. But this no longer holds good so soon as we look at their motion and interaction. For motion itself, as the ancient Greeks did not fail to observe, is a contradiction.

> " Even simple mechanical change of place can only come about through a body at one and the same moment of time being both in one place and also not in it. And the continuous assertion and simultaneous solution of this contradiction is precisely what motion is."
>
> (*Anti-Dühring*, p. 137.)

In the same way Engels observes that the eating and excreting processes, which every living thing must continually maintain, mean that the actual physical structure of every man (for example) is continually changing. A man is not composed of the same cells as he was thirty years ago. Not a single one of the atoms of matter which then constituted the man are left. And yet we say without hesitation that it is the same man. The movement, or evolution, through time of a living organism seems to present an analogous contradiction to the movement of an object through space. " Life is therefore also a contradiction which is present in things and processes themselves, and which constantly asserts and solves itself ; and as soon as the contradiction ceases, life too comes to an end, and death steps in." (*Anti-Dühring*, p. 138.)

The point of these examples is to show that, whether we like it or not, contradictions abound in objective phenomena just so soon as we regard them in their movements and interconnections. This is, no doubt, very awkward. It would make everything easier and simpler if the ordinary laws of formal logic, with their first principle of the exclusion of contradictions, gave a complete and adequate account of objective reality. But, demonstrably, they do not. Accordingly, the dialectical materialist urges, we must not try to cram reality into the

Procrustean bed of formal logic, but must face up to the contradictory character of its development, and elaborate a system of concepts which will fit it.

This insistence on the necessity to allow for the existence of contradictions in objective reality can be put in another way. We can talk instead of the " interpenetration of opposites." The two poles of the contradictory antithesis manage to co-exist by interpenetrating each other. Popular wisdom, with its insistence on paradox, has always had an insight into this. For paradox is the recognition that two contradictory, or opposite, considerations may both be true ; that, indeed, in the recognition of both of them lies the only possibility of an adequately comprehensive, and therefore true, description of reality.

This law is, clearly, one aspect of the general hypothesis of dialectical development, the pattern of the negation of the negation described above. A pattern consisting of successive negations can, clearly, only be a pattern of development if each negation does not simply cancel out the stage preceding it, but, instead, both contradicts it and includes it in itself. But we can only recognize such a movement as possible if we have also recognized that reality exhibits numberless contradictions of this character : contradictions which are solved by the introduction of a new element into the proposition.

For example, in the above-mentioned case of motion we noticed the logically insurmountable difficulty that an object cannot be at any given moment of time both in position A and position B. How, then, can it ever get from A to B ? The problem is dissolved in the endless succession of infinitely minute sub-divisions into which time can be split up ; it is soluble just because time knows no " moments," no " quanta," no primary units, but is infinitely divisible : the contradiction of motion is washed away in the ever-flowing waters of the temporal river.

Finally we come to what is perhaps the best known and the simplest of the laws, or generalizations, which the dialectical materialist draws from his observation of reality. This is the generalization which affirms that, if you go on changing the quantity of units of which a certain phenomenon is built up, you sooner or later change the whole character, or quality, of that phenomenon. Or, again, if you subject a phenomenon to quantitative changes, in temperature, for example, it sooner or later suffers a qualitative change. This is the easiest to exemplify of the laws of dialectical materialism. An obvious example is afforded by the changes exhibited by water at different temperatures. If you heat some water, all that happens for some time is that, degree by degree, it gets hotter. You add one degree after another to the heat of the water. But if you go on doing this long enough something else happens. The water is at, say, a temperature of 98°C. You add another degree of heat and get 99°C. Then you add another degree of heat and get—steam. At 100°C water boils. It turns from a liquid into a gas. In order to make this startling qualitative change in the water you have not added a single drop of any new element. You have simply gone on heating it. And the same thing happens if you begin by cooling the water. For a long time it stays just as it was : it stays water. But then, suddenly, when its temperature has dropped to 0°C, it becomes ice. It changes from a liquid to a solid state.

The main example, in the field of inorganic nature, of the generalization that quantitative changes sooner or later amount to qualitative ones is afforded, however, by the basic discovery of modern chemistry that all matter is built up of different combinations of a very limited number of atoms. All the innumerable and apparently very different kinds of matter which we encounter are merely different permutations and combinations of the one limited series of atoms. In other words, if you can make the purely quantitative change of adding or subtracting so many atoms to the molecules of a given substance you can change one kind of matter into quite a different kind.[1] Engels gives some examples. He takes, for instance, the series of normal paraffins, which range from a gas called methane, a molecule of which is composed of one atom of carbon and four

[1] The further possibility has now arisen of transmuting not merely the compounds—by changing the number of atoms in the molecules, but of transmuting the elements themselves by changing the number of electrons in their atoms. This is a new and very striking confirmation of the ability of quantitative changes to produce fundamental qualitative changes—a confirmation which has arisen since Engels' death.

atoms of hydrogen, to hexadecane, a crystal formed of 16 atoms of carbon and 34 atoms of hydrogen. Between these two substances are a whole series of other and apparently very different substances. But each one of these different substances is formed by the addition to the preceding one of CH_2 (one atom of carbon and two atoms of hydrogen). " This quantitative change in molecular composition produces at each step a qualitatively different body." (*Anti-Dühring*, p. 145.)

As in the case of the other dialectical laws, the observation that quantitative changes amount at a certain point to qualitative changes is not confined to the field of natural phenomena. Engels gives two more examples, one from the field of economics, and one from the field of military history.

In *Capital*, Marx observed that any sum of money, however small, does not constitute capital. Every business man knows this very well from experience. For any particular line of enterprise, at any given time and place, a certain minimum sum is necessary as the capital required for setting up in independent business. The sum necessary was, of course, much smaller in the early stages in the development of capitalist industry than it is to-day. But there was always some definite minimum. For it was always necessary for the intending capitalist to command enough resources to employ a sufficient number of labourers to enable him to live off their surplus produce, viz. the amount they produced minus the amount they consumed. Indeed, he must do a little better than this, for the characteristic object of the capitalist is not merely to live off his labourers, but to put something by as well—to accumulate capital. Hence the initial sum at his command, if it is to become capital, must be sufficiently large to set this minimum number of workers on to work in the average conditions of the time and place in question. Therefore a sum of money can only become capital when it reaches a certain definite size. You go on adding pound to pound for some time, and then a particular final pound makes your fund of savings into capital—into something apparently capable of growing by itself. Your quantitative additions have made a qualitative change.

Finally Engels instances the fact that Napoleon discovered that a purely quantitative change in the numbers engaged on both sides in a battle, with all the other factors remaining constant, made the decidedly qualitative change of transforming defeat into victory. Napoleon, Engels writes,

"makes the following reference to the fights between the French cavalry, who were bad riders, but disciplined, and the Mamelukes, who were undoubtedly the best horsemen of their time for single combat, but lacked discipline : ' Two Mamelukes were undoubtedly more than a match for three Frenchmen : 100 Mamelukes were equal to 100 Frenchmen ; 300 Frenchmen could generally beat 300 Mamelukes, and 1,000 Frenchmen invariably defeated 1,500 Mamelukes.' Just as with Marx a definite, though varying, minimum sum of exchange value was necessary to make possible its transformation into capital, so with Napoleon a detachment of cavalry had to be of a definite minimum number in order to make it possible for the force of discipline, embodied in closed order and planned action, to manifest itself and rise superior even to greater numbers of irregular cavalry, in spite of the latter being better mounted, more experienced horsemen and fighters, and at least as brave as the former."

(Anti-Dühring, p. 146.)

These examples suffice to show that the principle that quantitative changes when pushed beyond a certain point cause a change of quality, is applicable to the most diverse types of phenomena —to cavalry tactics no less than to molecular theory.

Both this quantity-quality law and the law which recognizes the objective presence in reality of contradictions insoluble to formal logic (the law of the interpenetration of opposites) are supplementary to the general observation as to the character of all processes of development and change which we discussed under the Hegelian title of the negation of the negation. For example, the observation that quantitative changes in the end amount to qualitative ones gives us a comprehension of how those great reversals in the general tendency of historical events, those negations which we just now discussed, in fact occurred. How, for example, did the early gentile social order, with its freedom and equality, and its inability to allow of free technical and economic development, break down ? It happened, as we saw in Chapter XVII, by the gradual piling up of new technical and economic factors which in the end made the gentile order impossible. After a long period of mere quantitative change, in which these factors slowly got more and more numerous, a sudden qualitative change, namely the destruction of the gentile order, the appearance of the state, and with it a hierarchy of social classes, based on private property in the means of production, appeared. It was the same with the next major negation —the destruction of the state system of antiquity by the barbarian conquest of the Roman world. The bad or negative features of ancient civilization, its destruction of freedom and equality, piled up and up until they came to overshadow its achievements (namely the immense advances in the arts and sciences which it had made possible). At a certain point this quantitative piling up of negative elements resulted in a qualitative change—the restoration of relative freedom and equality by the barbarian conquest.

The same process is at work to-day. The bad or negative features of capitalism, its reduction of the population to a dependent, propertyless, unstable, under-employed mass, and its inherent drive towards war, have now overshadowed its positive achievements—namely the industrialization of the world. The negative features pile up until they cause the qualitative change of the abolition of capitalism and the establishment of a planned system of production for use, based upon the restoration of the means of production to the whole population in collective ownership.

Finally the law is applicable to the way in which social change takes place. Non-Marxist socialists, or " reformists " as they are often called, believed, and even still believe, that capitalism can be abolished by a process of cumulative reform: that we shall go on and on reforming capitalism until one day we shall wake up in a socialist community. Now Marxists do not for one moment deny the need for, and the importance of, wringing reforms and concessions from the capitalists. They realize to the full that this is how the workers necessarily carry on their struggle. But they maintain that a point inevitably arrives when the quantitative changes in capitalism made by the reforms extorted from the capitalists set up a qualitative change. At this point the capitalists must stop the reforms or cease to be capitalists. This is the critical point. For at this point the two great classes of capitalist society will decide by struggle the question of whether the process of reform is to go on, and capitalism is to end, or the reforms are to end and capitalism is to survive. Who, in the light of the last twenty-five years of European history, can possibly doubt that this piece of dialectical thinking corresponds to reality !

Thus the three laws of dialectical materialism, namely the negation of the negation, the interpenetration of opposites, and the transformation of quantitative into qualitative changes, are closely bound together. They form one consistent view of reality. It remains to enquire what is the use of dialectical materialism. Its use is that it enables us to understand reality more adequately than does any other hypothesis yet devised. On the basis of that more adequate comprehension, we can predict the lines of future development, and then modify and control that development by appropriate action. It enables man to take his first conscious step towards the control of his destiny.

NOTE.—It may amuse the reader to notice passages in these pages where dialectical conceptions appear. See p. 304, for example, on the question of the growth in the number of apprentices employed by a master, at length changing the status of apprenticeship: converting it from a state in which each man was assured of becoming a master, to one in which there was little or no chance of his becoming a master. Or see p. 276 for More's grasp of the fact that it was necessary to abolish all private property in the means of production in order to restore the means of production to the collective ownership of the people. Or, again, see p. 277 for More's epigram as to the necessity of abolishing money in order to destroy poverty. Or see p. 311 for the reimposition of an effective serfdom upon a large section of the British working class by the final perfection of the system of freedom of contract.

Then there is the major instance given in Chapter VII. The whole development of capitalism is dialectical. The holding down of the purchasing power of the workers to a subsistence level, from being a condition of successful accumulation and industrialization, turns into an impassable barrier to further accumulation and industrialization.

CHAPTER XXXI

The Class Struggle

SUCH are the leading concepts of the science of social change. Marx and Engels stated the main conclusion which they drew from their science in an opening sentence of their first considered summary of their view. After its famous introduction, the *Communist Manifesto* of 1848 begins with these words:

" The history of all hitherto existing society is the history of class struggles.

" Freeman and slave, patrician and plebeian, lord and serf, guild master and journeyman, in a word, oppressor and oppressed, stood in constant opposition to one another, carried on an uninterrupted, now hidden, now open fight, a fight that each time ended, either in a revolutionary reconstruction of society at large, or in the common ruin of the contending classes."

Unless we realize that this conclusion is inevitable from the materialist conception of history, the law of motion of capitalism, and from dialectical materialism itself, we shall have missed the main bearing of these concepts.

It is essential to realize, for example, that each one of those turning-points in history, in which men realized, in a new and more developed way of living, their growing command over nature, was indissolubly associated with the rise to power of a new class. For example, the old lords could not, and did not, develop the gigantic forces of production which in the fifteenth century quickened within the womb of feudal society. For that it was necessary that a new class of men should come to political power in the State. The history of the last five hundred years is the history of the simultaneous development of our modern powers of production, and of the struggle for supremacy of the new class of men who alone could wield these powers.

The reader need only turn to the *Communist Manifesto* to see the contrast between it and any socialist or communist pronouncement which we have as yet encountered. He will see that it could only have been written by men who had already discovered the basic principles of the science of social change. The

Communist Manifesto is the first application of that science; it calls for action based upon and guided by the ascertained facts of social change. Hence a good way of envisaging what, in broad principle, such an application of the science must be is to summarize the *Manifesto*.

After the announcement of the theme, which we have just quoted, the *Manifesto* rapidly sketches the rise to power of the modern capitalist class until " in the modern representative state " the bourgeoisie[1] " has conquered for itself exclusive political sway. The executive of the modern state is but a committee for managing the common affairs of the whole bourgeoisie."

Then follows a description of the way in which the capitalists,[1] having taken power, have constructed a new world in their own image. The capitalist class " has been the first to show what man's activity can bring about. It has accomplished wonders far surpassing Egyptian pyramids, Roman aqueducts, and Gothic cathedrals; it has conducted expeditions that put in the shade all former Exoduses of nations and crusades. . . . The bourgeoisie, during its rule of scarce one hundred years, has created more massive and more colossal productive forces than have all preceding generations together. Subjection of nature's forces to man, machinery, application of chemistry to industry and agriculture, steam navigation, railways, electric telegraphs, clearing of whole continents for cultivation, canalization of rivers, whole populations conjured out of the ground—what earlier century had even a presentiment that such productive forces slumbered in the lap of social labour ? "

But will the capitalist class be able to direct the giant forces which it has developed ? Already, says the *Manifesto*, it does so very ill. " Modern bourgeois society . . . is like the sorcerer who is no longer able to control the powers of the nether world which he has called up by his spells." Recurrent crises rack the capitalist economic system. These crises are becoming, and will become, more severe. They presage a time in which the capitalists will find it permanently impossible to use the gigantic productive forces which they have created. Then will come the time when,

---

[1] We are here using the terms " capitalists " and " bourgeoisie " interchangeably.

just as the capitalist class had to burst the bonds of feudalism in order to use the new productive forces of that epoch, so now some class will have to break through the bonds of capitalism in order to use our new and gigantic productive forces. Who can accomplish this task ? It can only be the new class which capitalism has called into existence—" a class of labourers who live only so long as they find work, and who find work only so long as their labour increases capital."

The *Manifesto* then sketches the emergence of the working class upon the political scene. At first the workers become the allies of the capitalists in the latter's struggle against feudalism. "At this stage the proletarians do not fight their enemies, but the enemies of their enemies." As, however, capitalism becomes the more and more exclusive economic system of every advanced country, as the last lingering feudalists are defeated, as the working class becomes ever larger, more homogeneous and more devoid of independent access to the means of production, and as finally the difficulties of capitalism grow greater and greater, the working class breaks from its alliance with the capitalists and becomes their most formidable antagonist. The workers are inexorably driven into a fiercer and fiercer struggle with the capitalists, for the workers' position becomes ever more intolerable with the declining fortunes of capitalism. "At this stage it becomes evident that the bourgeoisie is unfit any longer to be the ruling class in society and to impose its conditions of existence upon society as an overriding law. It is unfit to rule because it is incompetent to assure an existence to its slave within his slavery, because it cannot help letting him sink into such a state that it has to feed him, instead of being fed by him."

(It is difficult to believe that that last sentence was written, not in 1936, but in 1848 !¹) It becomes a matter of life and death for the workers to take the power of the state out of the more and more incapable hands of the capitalists.

This ends the first part of the *Manifesto*. The second part describes the general position of communists and socialists in

¹ The prescience of Marx and Engels is astoundingly illustrated by it. But the limits of the powers of prediction given to them by their scientific insight into the law of motion of capitalism are also illustrated. They could see that the present epoch of dole-fed unemployed must be the pre-determined last phase of capitalism; but (until events made them correct their view) they expected that last phase to begin some seventy years before it did.

relation to the working class, and answers, often very wittily,[1] the various misconceptions, current then as now, as to our aims. This part ends with a programme of " immediate aims," aims the attainment of which will mark, that is to say, the political conquest of power by the working class and will thus open the way to socialism.

There follows a third part which describes and criticizes the various types of socialist thought then in existence. Marx and Engels list: " Feudal Socialism," by which they mean the anti-bourgeois propaganda emitted by the retreating feudalists as they finally leave the field to the bourgeoisie; " Petty-bourgeois Socialism " as it developed in France; " German or ' true ' Socialism," of the particularly anæmic brand which had developed in still feudal Germany before 1848; " Bourgeois Socialism," and finally " Critical, Utopian, Socialism and Communism," by which they mean the views of Owen, St. Simon and Fourier, such as we discussed in Chapter XXIV. This part of the *Manifesto* is brilliantly written.[2] It contains the first clear differentiations between modern scientific Socialism and every other variety. Moreover, it is astonishing to notice how directly applicable these characterizations of the various socialist groups of the first half of the nineteenth century are to the non-Marxist socialists of to-day. But because these early nineteenth-century groups were necessarily the subject matter of Marx's and Engels' definitions, present-day readers of the *Manifesto* often find this section confusing. In order to get the full value from it, the reader must substitute contemporary groups and tendencies for those which Marx and Engels so devastatingly describe. The document ends with a short fourth part on the relations of the communists to each of the parties of the Left in each of the European countries. This part, although largely irrelevant to any period but 1848, was naturally of great importance when the *Manifesto* was written.

---

[1] See, for example, the passage on the bourgeois real objection to the abolition of private property in the means of production.

[2] What could be better, for example, than this characterization of that brand of Tory or feudal socialism which periodically pops up in England ?—" . . . half lamentation, half lampoon; half echo of the past, half menace of the future; at times, by its bitter, witty and incisive criticism, striking the bourgeoisie to the very heart's core, but always ludicrous in its effect through total incapacity to comprehend the march of modern history."

The *Communist Manifesto* marked an advance in working class thinking to an entirely new level. The *Manifesto*, and the books in which Marx and Engels for the next fifty years amplified and demonstrated the ideas contained in it (for the germ of almost every conception of Marxism can be found in it) mark the point at which the scientific method is made applicable to human society. For, in spite of the vigour of its language, the real difference between the *Manifesto* and all previous socialist and communist pronouncements lies in its scientific approach. By far the larger part of the *Manifesto* is concerned to show, not what ought to be, but what has been and what is. It is only after revealing the nature of the great social driving forces at work, after gauging their respective thrust and counter-thrust, after revealing the dynamics of the whole historical movement, that the *Manifesto* goes on to show how the conscious human will can intervene to remodel the world.

Let us then sum up the attitude of communists and socialists to the class struggle, both as originally expressed in the *Communist Manifesto*, and as expressed in every responsible Marxist pronouncement to-day.

Communists and socialists do not cause, advocate, or like the class struggle: on the contrary, they diagnose the class struggle: they diagnose the class struggle as the essential and incurable sickness of modern society. The existing economic system impels the two main classes of modern society into conflict with one another. This is the reason why men are starving, clubbing, shooting, and sometimes torturing, each other. This is the reason, whether the participants in the struggle know it or not. At some times, and in some places, they are conscious that they are engaged in class struggles. In a South Wales mining strike to-day, for example, both sides have a fairly adequate consciousness of the reasons which are impelling them to attempt to impose their wills upon each other. In Nazi Germany, again, when the German secret police arrest and proceed to torture a group of German workers engaged in Trade Union or political activity, neither side can have many illusions about the cause of the conflict. The German workers know perfectly, at any rate, that they are being tortured because that is the only way left of preserving the power and privileges of the German capitalist class. And it must be a particularly slow-witted Nazi policeman who has not by now a general consciousness that he is torturing for the same object.

On the other hand, such a consciousness is often almost entirely lacking in an American strike or lock-out. But, and this is a point worth noting, an absence of class consciousness does not make an outbreak of the class struggle less violent. On the contrary, the violence used in American industrial disputes, in which neither side may have any consciousness of why they are fighting, beyond the immediate issue of hours and wages, is notoriously far greater than the violence customary in, say, South Wales, where the level of class consciousness on both sides is relatively high. Again, there are frequent instances in all countries where one side in the class struggle may have achieved a considerable degree of consciousness of its cause and nature, while the other remains quite unconscious. This situation is common in America, where the employers sometimes achieve a high degree of class consciousness, while the workers remain quite unaware that they are faced, not simply by the desire of their own employers to, say, prevent Trade Union organization, but by the determined application of a consciously arrived at decision made by the capitalists of the whole country, acting as a class. It would be possible to multiply indefinitely examples showing that workers and employers are impelled into conflicts of all degrees of violence quite without reference to whether or not either or both of them know why they are fighting each other.

Now, it is a primary object of communists and socialists to bring the cause of the conflicts in which the workers continually find themselves engaged into their consciousness, to make the workers, as the phrase goes, " class conscious." What is our purpose in doing this ? Our purpose is, precisely, to end the class conflict. The analogy with a doctor diagnosing a disease is exact. A doctor diagnoses that his patient is suffering from, say, tuberculosis, in order to cure him. Until and unless the cause of the patient's ill-health can be traced to the action of the tubercle germs in his lungs, there is no hope of a cure. In exactly the same way, there is no hope of men ceasing to attempt to starve, torture, and kill each other until they realize what it is that is making them do these things. For their present social and economic conditions are making them do these things. And until and unless those social and economic conditions are altered, nothing can prevent them being impelled into ever more violent conflicts.

But, as we saw in Part I, it is now possible so to modify our social and economic environment as to remove the cause of the class struggle. In order to do so it is necessary to pool the means of production, to preserve them undivided in public hands, and to operate them for use on a planned basis. Such a modification of the economic system will eradicate the cause of class conflict, for, as we saw, it will result in the appearance of a homogeneous, classless society, all of whose members derive their incomes from the same source, viz. their labour. Thus the ever-repeated capitalist, and now specifically Fascist, accusation that communists and socialists foment, or actually create, the class struggle is the exact reverse of the truth. The class struggle is an objective fact which has existed ever since primitive society split up into separate classes at the birth of civilization. What communists and socialists do is to bring this struggle and its causes into consciousness, in order to end it. It is precisely because they regard the class struggle as the most frightful evil of our time that they turn the searchlight of scientific analysis upon it.

It is inevitable that this determined facing of the facts will arouse hostility. Moreover, it is inevitable that it will arouse hostility, not only in the minds of those who benefit by the continuance of the conditions which make class conflict inevitable. Just as a doctor who tells a patient that he has a serious disease, in order that he may take appropriate measures for its cure, must face the possibility of that patient's hostility, so communists and socialists must face the fact that even the workers will not like being told that they must inevitably become involved in more and more violent conflicts until and unless they transform the economic system. Men much prefer to be told that their troubles are slight and easily remediable. They dislike being told that they are grave, increasing, and incurable without a drastic and difficult alteration in their environment. But if the former information is false and the latter true, they will in the end be forced to listen to those who have the courage to tell them the truth. For they will discover by painful experience that the nostrums of those who tell them smooth things give no relief. It is only, however, under the lash of experience that men have ever yet faced unpleasant facts.

The above simple psychological facts are used to the full in the propaganda of Fascist parties, intent to preserve the private ownership of the means of production. Fascist propaganda tells men what they want to hear—namely, that the painful and terrifying fact of the class struggle is an illusion conjured up by wicked agitators : that consequently they need make no large and difficult change in their environment in order to rid themselves of it ; that all they need do is to suppress these agitators, who speak of the class struggle, in order to make the struggle itself disappear. Moreover, the Fascists promise that specific enactments will be passed forbidding the class struggle to break out. Strikes and lock-outs will be prohibited by penal laws. In a word, the Fascists repress the class struggle. They repress it not only physically; they also repress it in the sense of that word used in modern psychology. Without changing any of the objective conditions which produce the class struggle, they systematically pretend that it does not exist. They take energetic measures to banish a consciousness of it from men's minds. But these measures can do nothing whatever to abolish the struggle itself. All the objective forces which in any capitalist society must drive those who do not own the means of production into conflict with those who do, continue to operate in Fascist countries with undiminished force.

It is true that it is often possible for a time to prevent by terror these forces from expressing themselves directly in strikes and lock-outs. But this merely diverts them into other channels. A main effort of all Fascist propaganda is, for example, to divert, or, as the psychologists would say, to displace, the workers antagonism to the class which excludes them from the means of production, on to other nationalities. When this propaganda is backed by all the resources of a modern state, and is conducted with great skill, it can achieve considerable success. It leads, of course, directly to war.

In general, however, we may say that the difference between the attitude of Fascists on the one hand, and communists and socialists on the other, to the class struggle is analogous to the difference in the attitude of the scientist and the medicine man in regard to any unpleasant natural phenomenon. Take the case of a flood. The scientist will recommend that appropriate steps of river control should be taken; steps which will modify the objective environment in such a way that the flood will not recur. The medicine man, on the contrary, will advise that such spells and incantations should be said as will diminish, or remove altogether, the fear of floods in the minds of the population. He recommends, and often actually effects, a subjective change in people's minds while leaving their objective environment as it was. Now the medicine man's technique is often extremely effective. It often does make the population feel secure against floods. It may actually be more effective for this purpose than the long and difficult job of river control advocated by the scientist. Moreover, it is far quicker, easier, cheaper, and less arduous. The immediate advantage is all with the medicine man. His technique has, however, the ultimately prohibitive disadvantage that the floods will recur.

Very much the same considerations apply to the Fascist exorcism of the class struggle. The highly skilled Fascist propagandists have shown the possibility of leading whole nations down the path of fantasy and wish-fulfilment. They have promised everything to everybody, and they have been believed. They have promised, above all, the abolition of the internecine conflict of class with class and the creation of a homogeneous, classless community; and they have promised to accomplish all this without having to go through the admittedly difficult and painful process of so transforming the economic system that classes will in fact cease to exist. And again they have been believed. The Nazis, in particular, have simply proclaimed that all classes, high and low, rich and poor, have been merged in one great homogeneous German folk. Just this was the profound wish of the German population. All those who had no comprehension of what it is which causes communities to be divided into social classes responded with enthusiasm. They did not notice that the Nazis did nothing whatever actually to modify those relations of ownership and non-ownership of the means of production which make some people rich and others poor.

Experience derived from individual psychology should enable us to understand how a whole people may be successfully induced to take the word for the deed, to accept a subjective change in their own psychologies in lieu of an objective change in their environment; to make believe, to pretend, as a child does, that a passionately desired change has taken place. Such deceptions as this, the Fascists have shown, can be perpetrated upon a whole nation. But they can only be perpetrated at the price of an ever growing divergence between the ideas in the minds of the members of such a nation and their real environment. Such a divergence between concept and reality, when pushed beyond a certain point, is called madness. And it is an undeniable fact that the Fascist propagandists are able to produce collective delusions in the population subjected to them, delusions which have pathological aspects.

Moreover, the divergence between the state of mind produced by successful Fascist propaganda, and the reality created by the fundamental Fascist policy of preserving the private ownership of the means of production, becomes ever greater. The population has been induced to believe that the class conflict has been abolished and that a homogeneous society has been produced. Meanwhile the standard of life of the non-owning populating sinks, while the profits of the owners of the means of production rise. Moreover, the operation of the general law of motion of capitalism continues to produce recurrent and ever more severe crises, soluble, even temporarily, by means of wars of conquest alone. Sooner or later the purely subjective, delusional attainment of social peace and homogeniety achieved by Fascist propaganda is wrecked by the intrusion of the old, unmodified reality of capitalist class relations. The more perfectly the consciousness of what is causing the bloody conflicts of our epoch is repressed, the more bloody, because the more blind, those conflicts necessarily become.

The repressed class conflict blazes forth from the social unconscious with frightful force. We have yet to experience the fall of a major Fascist régime. When we do so we shall see what are the ultimate consequences of the attempted repression, in the interests of preserving capitalism, of all consciousness and all manifestations of the class struggle.

CHAPTER XXXII

Force and Violence in Human Affairs

COMMUNISTS and socialists, like everybody else, live in a world in which violence between man and man is unceasing. In the theory of the class struggle they offer an analysis of the cause of by far the larger part of that violence. And upon that analysis they base recommendations as to how this cause can be eradicated. Hence they tend to be impatient at the familiar charge that they are promotors of the use of force and violence. For the truth is the very opposite.

We claim that the working class, as it becomes conscious of its own purposes (which are to found a classless society) can alone show humanity how to eliminate violence from its affairs. All that we can admit is that, in common with all other men except complete Tolstoyian non-resisters, we must, until the objective conditions of social peace have been achieved, reserve to ourselves the right to reply in kind to the methods of force and violence which are so unhesitatingly used against us. For we do not claim that social violence can be ended before its cause, which is the division of the population into rich owners, and poor non-owners, of the means of production, has been abolished. Hence we predict that, unfortunately, the process of that abolition will be accompanied by the same violence which to-day characterizes all the major activities of human life. To suppose anything else would be to suppose that human beings could suddenly change their nature before the environment which so largely determines that nature had itself been changed. Nor will it help us in the extremely important task of minimizing as quickly as we can the violence that everywhere surrounds us if we ignore the fact that the historical record declares that no great change in the way of life of human communities has hitherto been achieved without the pains and travails of a birth process. Force, said Marx in a famous phrase, has always been the midwife of every old society pregnant with the new. But he did not mean, as he is sometimes thought to have done, that he advocated the use of force and violence by the oppressed class on behalf of the attempt to establish a new society. There are many historical examples to show that the initial and predominating use of force has always come from the previously dominant class attempting at all costs to prevent the birth of a new epoch.

An essential part, then, of the general Marxist view is the assertion that we do but deceive ourselves if we suppose that we have already entered the kingdom of peace, where men will be able to carry on their affairs in a wholly rational and so wholly pacific way. For this presupposes the conscious control of our social and economic life. And who can pretend that any such control has yet been established? It is, on the contrary, only too clear that the formidable forces generated by the intricate and massive economic and social relations of the contemporary world control us. The only too familiar truth is that these forces are playing ball with our lives, are hurling us into destitution by slump, or into death by war, with little or no conscious control on our part. It will not be until we have mastered them, until we have put our economic life upon the basis of a consciously determined plan, that we can hope for permanent social peace.

But this does not mean that we need to be indifferent to the degree of violence which exists in the world to-day and which cannot in principle disappear until the above major social and economic change has actually been effected. On the contrary, as we value both the very fabric of human civilization and, for that matter, our own lives, we shall strive by every means in our power to lessen the amount of violence which is now being, and which will be, used. But how can we do this? *The one way by which both the violence of the struggles generated by capitalist society as it exists to-day, and the violence accompanying social change, can be minimized, is by increasing the consciousness of the cause and character of this violence.* It is largely because we have to-day a relatively clear and relatively widespread consciousness[1] of the character of social processes that we may legitimately hope and expect that the social transformation for which our century cries out will be achieved with incomparably less

---

[1] Relative, that is to say, to men's almost complete unconsciousness of the real nature of social processes up to a hundred and fifty years ago. The absolute level, and the degree of diffusion, of such consciousness is still painfully low.

violence, destruction and horror than has always hitherto accompanied such events.

The violence which accompanied, for example, the last great process of social transformation which history records was almost illimitable. Towards the end of the first volume of *Capital*, Marx describes the desperate violence, lasting for over three hundred years, by which the new capitalist class conquered political power, acquired the exclusive ownership of the means of production, and so set up capitalism. We have alluded to some part of this process in our sketch of the birth of the working class. The huge process of the dispossession of the peasants, and the herding of generations of the men, women, and children, first of Britain, and then of all Europe and North America, into the factory-prisons of the early industrialists, was one side of this violence. But, in addition, the rise of capitalism involved a whole series of wars and revolutions. The devastating conflicts of the Reformation and the Renaissance, the English civil war, the eighteenth-century wars for colonial supremacy, the American Revolution, the French Revolution, and the wars, civil wars, and revolutions of the nineteenth century were all incidental to the establishment of capitalism as a world system. It was by means of ever-recurrent domestic and international violence alone that the capitalist class of the world hacked its way to power. In addition to this long series of wars and revolutions, an unceasing violence was necessary to the actual process of the accumulation of the initial capital without which capitalism, as a system, could not have come into existence. Marx, in the great historical chapter of *Capital*, describes the gruesome details of the methods of colonial spoliation and exploitation, based, above all, upon slavery and the slave trade, by which the European and American capitalist class collected their initial capital.

All this endless tale of human suffering proved to be necessary to the establishment of capitalism. For the centralization, the mobilization, of the means of production into a few hands, involving their removal from the hands of millions of men, was an enormously difficult business. But the removal of the means of production from their present owners and their restoration, in the form of common property, to all, will be a far less difficult and violent process. " The transformation of scattered private property," Marx writes, " based upon individual labour, into capitalist private property is, of course, a far more protracted process, a far more violent and difficult process, than the transformation of capitalist private property (already in fact based upon a social method of production) into social property. In the former case we are concerned with the expropriation of the mass of the people by a few usurpers; in the latter case we are concerned with the expropriation of a few usurpers by the mass of the people." (*Capital*, p. 847.)

Moreover, we repeat, not only have the workers of to-day an intrinsically easier task, they are also, thanks to the genius of Marx and Engels, much more conscious of that task, and of the necessary conditions for its fulfilment, than could be any previous class on the road to power. Hence we may be assured that the abolition of capitalism and the establishment of socialism will be a far less terrible and violent process than was the abolition of feudalism and the establishment of capitalism. But to say this is not, perhaps, to say very much. Nor have we any knowledge of the actual degree of suffering and violence in which capitalism will involve us before it is abolished. Indeed, I believe that we have this question very largely in our own hands. The decision depends upon our intelligence and courage. For, although to-day the political consciousness of the workers is relatively high (for the capitalist class, at any rate in the earlier stages of its struggle, had no consciousness at all of its historical mission), it is absolutely very low. Only a tiny handful of the workers in every advanced capitalist state are fully conscious of the cause, nature, and object of the struggles into which they find themselves impelled by the necessities of their life. Hence the great majority of the working class still struggles more or less blindly, for the immediate and necessary object of preserving and protecting their livelihoods, without an adequate realization of those interconnections which make their struggle part of an immensely wide historical process by means of which the working class is called on to remake the world.

In America, in particular, the great mass of the workers are still almost wholly unconscious of the general aspects of their struggle. (Though this, as we have seen, does not prevent them from often having to struggle very desperately.) In Britain and

Western Europe there is a far wider consciousness amongst the workers that they are not merely, and not only, struggling for better conditions of work, but are also struggling for power to abolish the capitalist system and build up a socialist system of production. Perhaps 50 per cent of the British workers have reached this stage of consciousness. Judging by the electoral returns, from a third to a half of the British working class have become socialists, in the sense that they have a conception of some alternative economic system to put in the place of capitalism. As yet, however, political consciousness in the mass of the workers of Britain stops at this point. (I do not think that this is any longer true of the workers of continental Europe. But it was largely true of them until four or five years ago.) The nature and necessities of such a struggle as that involved in the expropriation of the means of production from the capitalists are still only realized by a tiny minority of the British working class. The greater part, even, have as yet no sense of the fact that the line of development of capitalism is downwards towards war and chaos, and not upwards, through ever increasing social reforms, to its own abolition in socialism. They have never been enabled to realize that from now on to the last day of its existence British capitalism must necessarily give the British people, not reforms, concessions and reliefs, but ever worsening conditions of life, punctuated by war.[1] They have no realization that the great forces of the modern world are moving on broadly determinate lines towards a conflict which can only be avoided by a far higher and more widely diffused consciousness of the nature of social processes than has yet been achieved.

Moreover, we now know what this absence in a working class of a consciousness of the inevitability of social crisis must lead to. For it was this fact which, above all, made it possible for the capitalist class of Italy and Germany to prolong their régimes beyond their natural term, by means of the ultra-violent

---

[1] It would be very strange if the British workers did yet realize this fact, for it is only now becoming a fact. Indeed, during the periods of the upward movement of the trade cycle, British capitalism can still perceptibly improve the conditions of the working population as against their conditions in the preceding slump. Thus during these periods it can still give the illusion of continuing, or, at any rate, of resumed, progress. It is only when we look at the longer, secular trend, comparing recovery with recovery and slump with slump, and, above all, when we look at the capitalist world as a whole, that it becomes apparent that the line of development has turned downwards.

suppression of all working class opposition. The fact that the Italian and German workers did not face the inevitability of the use of violence by their capitalists (and therefore did not prepare for it) did not avoid or even diminish the amount of violence which has occurred, and is occurring, in those unhappy countries. It merely meant that the workers were offered up, almost helpless, to the relentless violence of their opponents. Nor is the unceasing violence of the Fascist terror within Germany and Italy the only, or even the chief, part of the enormously increased violence which has resulted, or which is about to result, from the European workers' inadequate consciousness of political realities. As I write these sentences the Italian armies are still in action in Abyssinia, after having provided a textbook example of the Imperialist conquests which, as we saw in Chapter XX, are to-day the inevitable consequence of leaving capitalism in continued existence. The far vaster war machine of German Fascism has not yet, it is true, come into action. But it is being prepared in day and night activity for the day on which it shall drown the world in human blood. Such have been the actual consequences of the failure of the European working class to realize the inevitability of the use of violence by the capitalists, and the consequent necessity for the workers to develop the capacity to meet and break that violence.

We may venture a generalization as to the way in which force and violence in human affairs can be increased or diminished. The more clearly we face the fact that violence is now used to preserve the capitalist system, and that nothing we can do can prevent it being so used during the process of the abolition of capitalism, the less violence that process will actually entail. Conversely, the more we fail to become conscious of the causes, nature, necessities and objects of contemporary social struggle, the more of civil violence and international war that struggle will involve.

Let us demonstrate this generalization by considering the two extreme cases, first of such consciousness and then of its absence. Let us first examine what the consequences would be in the impossible event of all consciousness of the nature of political, economic and social development being wiped out. Then let us examine what would be the consequences of the, unfortunately, equally impossible event of such consciousness being universally achieved.

Let us, then, first suppose that every communist and socialist is either killed or silenced: that means are found by which every vestige of class consciousness is removed from the mind of every worker; that, above all, every worker is perfectly imbued with the doctrine that in no circumstances whatever shall he use violence to attain any ends which may seem desirable to him, or to prevent the occurrence of events which may seem undesirable to him. Would this prevent the use of force and violence in human affairs ? On the contrary, its immediate effect would be the outbreak of the unparalleled violence of international war. For the main restraining influence upon every capitalist government to-day is the fear of revolution in the event of war. Indeed, those capitalist governments (e.g. Germany and Italy) which realize that they must fight in the near future in order to reverse a, to them, intolerable world settlement, have gone to any length to suppress the working class movement, and to extirpate class consciousness and scientific socialist thought, as the precondition to their ability to make war. The principal influence to-day postponing the outbreak of inter-Imperialist war, or of a joint Imperialist attack upon the Soviet Union, is the knowledge of the European governing class, born of the experience of the closing phase of the last war, that in the end the workers grow weary of killing each other, and begin to kill those who have ordered them to kill.

But let us push our hypothesis still further. Let us suppose that the extirpation of class or socialist consciousness now being attempted in Germany and Italy were fully to succeed, and that it was successfully imitated in every other country of the world including a Russia reconquered for capitalism. Then inter-Imperialist war would be free to sweep unhindered across the face of the earth. No one can foretell the character or the results of such wars. But, it is surely incontestable that the whole political, economic, and administrative apparatuses of the defeated capitalist states, and with them human civilization itself, would crumble and dissolve. For, on our hypothesis that the consciousness of any alternative, socialist type of civilization had been wiped out of the minds of men, there would be nothing to take the place of the apparatuses of the capitalist states. The broken, starving, pestilence-ridden armies, the panic-stricken, decimated populations, streaming out of the gas-ridden cities, would not indeed be able to keep their pledge of non-violence. Spontaneous revolts would spring up everywhere. But, again on our hypothesis, they would be blind, incoherent revolts, bereft of conscious purpose, leaderless, or with leaders unable to conceive of anything to do when they had destroyed the remnant of the old rulers. Such working class revolts, lacking all scientific understanding of social processes, lacking all hope of another type of social order beyond capitalist Imperialism, could only hasten the destruction of human civilization.

Such a prospect is entirely fantastic to-day. The Soviet Union, a major non-capitalist state, which has existed for eighteen years, is itself a perfect guarantee that the hope and knowledge of a form of human existence beyond capitalism can never again be removed from the minds of men. Even if the Soviet Union was destroyed to-morrow: even if every means of disseminating communist and socialist knowledge was made impossible, the workers' consciousness that they can, *and have*, built a state of their own would return to them at every moment of spontaneous revolt. Hence the prospect of the destruction of human civilization is to-day a wholly unreal one. Still, it is not a useless fantasy. For in the past, in different conditions, the fabric of civilization has again and again been torn to bits, first by the internecine wars of the governing class, and then by the inevitable but incoherent, purposeless, and therefore necessarily unsuccessful, revolts of the oppressed. The most recent example is, of course, the break up of the civilization of the ancient world during the long-drawn-out process of the destruction of the Roman Empire. One has only to read Gibbon to envisage the prospect of unending, unmitigated, purposeless, nauseating violence which the extinction of communist and socialist consciousness would to-day entail.[1]

[1] Gibbon was, in one sense, the perfect historian of the process, for he had no more consciousness of the real causes or character of the decline of Roman civilization than had the Romans themselves. Western European consciousness had, by the second half of the eighteenth century, just about returned to the highest level

Now let us consider our other hypothesis, namely, that every worker in the world should become convinced of the necessity of abolishing capitalism and should become free from illusions as to the inevitability of the use of violence by the capitalists. Why, in that case the thing could be done almost over night, and probably without a blow being struck! The workers' numerical preponderance is so overwhelming, the economic power which they derive from the fact that they do the work of the world is so great, that if everyone to whose interest it really was to establish socialism were conscious of that fact, the resistance of the capitalists could be but trivial.[1]

In other words, the power of the capitalist class now rests predominantly upon their control over what we have called the means of production of opinion; upon their control over men's minds. If this power to keep men in ignorance and unconsciousness of social processes could be removed, then the process of social transformation could be swift, easy, and bloodless. The tragedy is that, so long as their economic and political power remains, there exists no way by which the capitalists' hold over men's minds can be broken. Hence we must take it as a constant factor in the social equation that the capitalists will succeed in obscuring, both from the workers and from themselves, that vital knowledge without which the process of social change is bound to be arduous, blind, and therefore to some extent violent.

Our two hypotheses of a total absence of the knowledge of the necessary conditions and character of social change, and of the perfect diffusion of such knowledge, were made solely in order to demonstrate our basic proposition, namely, that social change will be violent or peaceful in proportion as the character,

reached in the ancient world. Hence the almost eerie sense which the reader experiences, that *The Decline and Fall* was written by a contemporary of the events described in it.

[1] This raises the interesting question of whether the abolition of capitalism (since capitalism entails war) is not now in the true interests of the capitalists themselves. It can be very reasonably argued that it is. But we must, I fear, take the violent opposition of the capitalist class as a whole to the abolition of their class privileges as a datum—although we must not for a moment suppose that this will be true of every individual member of the capitalist class. On the contrary, as Marx clearly recognized, both in the *Communist Manifesto* and elsewhere, more and more individual members, both of the capitalist class and of the intermediate groups, will break away from their class and join the workers as and when they realize the nature of the issues which are being decided in our epoch.

Os

objects, and conditions of the process are known. The fact is, of course, that the capitalists will not be able to extirpate this knowledge, but that they will be able to prevent its universal diffusion. And between these two limits there is an enormously wide margin.

Moreover, some parts of the body of essential knowledge may become much more widely diffused than others. For example, in Great Britain, we repeat, a general sense of the possibility and desirability of socialism is common enough. But a knowledge of the conditions in which social transformation can possibly take place is narrowly restricted. And, by one of those paradoxes which, we suggested, are the elementary form of the dialectic, only in so far as a knowledge of the inevitability of violence in social transformation is diffused, can violence be avoided. Nor, surely, is there anything to be surprised at in this conclusion. The use of violence in human affairs is always the result of men's failure to achieve a conscious control of their situation. Violence always does, and always must, result when men's physical or social environments get out of their control. In such circumstances men are dominated by forces which they do not understand, whose effects they cannot forsee; desperate and blind, they strike out upon each other with the fury of the instinct of individual self-preservation.

The truth of the matter is that the position of communists and socialists in regard to the use of force and violence is in essence the same as that of all sensible men and women. They abhor violence. But they are not so foolish as to pretend to themselves that, in the present stage of the development of human consciousness, violence has been abolished. They differ from other people, however, in that they do believe that violence can be abolished from human affairs when new economic, political and cultural conditions, amounting to the conscious control of our whole environment, have been established. Till that is done a self-denying ordinance by one class that it alone, and no matter how violently its most vital interests are attacked, will never use violence, is not only an invitation to its own perpetual enslavement, but will actually result in the use of illimitable, and ever more purposeless, violence by the other class, in the form of international war.

CHAPTER XXXIII

The Development of Marxism

MARXISM was not imagined out of nothing by the brains of two nineteenth-century savants. It is a living, developing science, compounded of data gathered from the social struggles of all mankind. These social struggles have continued after the death of Marx and Engels, and they are continuing to-day. Hence Marxism has continually to be extended and developed in order to keep it abreast of the continually accumulating body of social data which become available. The developments in Marxist thought which have occurred since the first announcement of its basic discoveries, in the middle of the nineteenth century, have been very important. Those who wish to use the science to-day cannot possibly ignore them.

Marx and Engels were Germans, writing in German and using a German intellectual idiom. Hence it was natural that they should have their first influence in Germany. Up till 1914 the German working class movement was the main instrument by which Marx's and Engels' discoveries were preserved and popularized. If it had not been for the work done by German Marxists, the science of social change might almost have passed out of men's consciousness during the second half of the nineteenth century. For in Britain and America, at any rate so far as the world of the governing class was concerned, they might never have been made. (We shall discuss in the next chapter the only half-successful effort of the revived British working class movement from 1880 to 1914 to acquaint itself with Marxism.) The fate of Marxism in Germany was a hard one, however. From the moment of their first appearance in Germany, in the eighteen-fifties, the basic conceptions of Marxism were subjected to an extraordinary and disastrous process of distortion. Three separate attempts were made by German Marxists, or rather pseudo-Marxists, to change the essential content of the message of Marx and Engels while preserving its form and name.

The first of these attempts was made by that talented,

adventurous, but essentially self-seeking, workers' leader, Ferdinand Lassalle. Lassalle was quick to pick out the simpler propositions of Marxism, and he made effective use of them in his agitation for the creation of a working class party. But it is now clear that Marx was right in believing that Lassalle neither understood nor cared about the historical and philosophical conceptions of Marxism: that he neither realized nor was interested in the destiny of the working class as the liberator of mankind from its centuries of poverty and fratricidal class strife. For it is now known that Lassalle was at the time of his death making strenuous efforts to sell out to Bismarck the German workers' party which he had created.

The second attempt to turn Marxism into something quite different, while preserving its form, was made in the last decade of the nineteenth century. This attempt was in a sense a tribute to the strength of Marxism in the German working class movement. For when some of the German socialist leaders felt an urgent necessity to get rid of Marxist influence they did not dare openly to repudiate Marxism. This attempt was led by a group of German social democratic writers and economists of whom Edward Bernstein is the best known name. (But, as Lenin noted at the time,[1] the struggle over Marxism was this time on an international scale.) In Germany, and indeed throughout continental Europe, those who were at heart profoundly hostile to the essential concepts of Marxism called themselves " revisionists." Their real object was to revise Marxism in such a way as to reconcile it with the view that the development of capitalism was leading, not to increasing economic crises, worsening conditions for the mass of the population, and consequently to new wars and revolutions, but to a greater economic stability, improving standards of living, the reconciliation of the competing capitalist empires, and so to a gradual, cumulative transformation of the system along socialist lines.

The revisionists reached conclusions which were, the reader will see, substantially identical with those of the British Fabians. Nor was this by any means accidental. Bernstein, their intellectual leader, lived for many years in London and was strongly

---

[1] See his footnote on the international character of the controversy in *What is to be Done ?*

influenced by Fabian thought[1]—particularly by the work of Mr. and Mrs. Webb. Indeed what he really did was to translate Fabianism, not only into the German language, but also into Marxist terminology. It was no accident that this tendency to emasculate Marxism was international. And it was no accident that it drew its real inspiration from non-Marxist, British socialist thought. For the real basis of both revisionist and Fabian thinking was the temporary, imperialist, phase of expansion through which capitalism was passing. And, of the fruits of Imperialism, Britain had always the lion's share.

Indeed, although the revisionists became influential in the German working class movement, they never succeeded in capturing it. They were strongly combated by a group of leaders and thinkers who appeared to remain true to the essential conceptions of Marxism. The intellectual leader of this orthodox Marxist tendency was Karl Kautsky, a man of high intellectual gifts and monumental erudition. It seemed that in Kautsky the German working class movement possessed a man who could be relied upon to make effective use of Marxism as a guiding principle in its struggles, who could and would resist every tendency to bend and twist Marxism into an acceptance of the basic postulates of capitalism.

But when the decisive events of the twentieth century put the matter to the test it was found that Kautsky and the main body of the leaders of the German working class movement had revised Marxism hardly less drastically, if far more discreetly, than had the revisionists whom they had derided and defeated. By a subtle process[2] by means of which unwelcome aspects of Marxist thought had been quietly suppressed, more " moderate " statements emphasized, and often quietly reinterpreted, the official German Marxists had, by 1914, transformed Marxism into a harmless, toothless description of the capitalist system, which led to a demand, not for the abolition of capitalism, as the essential condition for the maintenance and development of human civilization, but to an adaptation of the working class movement to capitalism's presumed, upward,

[1] We shall discuss the Fabian influence in England below (p. 439).
[2] The process could be crude enough at times, however. Indeed, it did not stop short of the suppression of Engels' later works or what amounted to their falsification on one occasion. (See p. 462 below.)

evolutionary course. Now, however, a third tendency arose within the German working class movement. Two leaders, Liebknecht and Rosa Luxemburg, inspired a section of the movement with an urgent sense that the basic principles on which their movement was founded were being undermined. A vigorous attempt was made to get back to the real outlook of Marx and Engels. It is on this third tendency within German Social Democracy that the German Communist Party, which has alone survived the Fascist terror, was founded. But this left wing of German Social Democracy was not able to prevent the domination of the German working class by Kautsky and those for whom he spoke.

The deadly work of the German Social Democratic leaders played a predominant part in preventing the German, and consequently the whole European, working class movement from effectively opposing the preparations of every capitalist state for the last war. Although in words the socialist leaders pledged themselves to oppose their own war-making governments, they took no practical steps to mobilize the mass of the population, which was under their influence, for resistance to the command for mutual slaughter. And when that command was duly issued they almost with one accord placed themselves and their movements at the disposition of their respective masters. It is true that their masters' eventual defeat hoisted the German socialist leaders, largely against their wills, into the position of successful revolutionary leaders. Then it was seen how profoundly they had forgotten every shred of the real significance of Marxism. They were at heart so perfectly convinced of the immortality and omnipotence of capitalism that, even when Marx's prediction of its overthrow by the workers had actually taken place—when in 1918 the German governing class was prostrate and the workers were in occupation of every important position of power,—these leaders laboured at nothing but to restore the shattered structure of German capitalism, and in the end, although with great difficulty, succeeded. The horrible Europe in which we exist is the direct result of their work.

Such were the appalling effects of the third German effort to transform, and in the final effects to turn into its very opposite, the science discovered by Marx and Engels. But why, we must ask, did there arise even in Germany, even in the country where Marxism first struck root, these three successive attempts to distort and reverse its meaning ? The answer is that, though in Germany the storm and stress of the establishment of large-scale industry, and the birth into those difficult conditions of an industrial working class, did provide soil in which Marxism could grow, yet the successful development of German capitalism created an environment hostile to the essential revolutionary message of the science. Hence these persistent attempts to adapt Marxism, to make it over into a theory of the workability and tolerability of the capitalist system. The German workers were permeated with Marxism and they expected their leaders to use its terminology. But when it became apparent to these leaders that German captalism had a period of growth and development before it, they began to seek for a means of so modifying their Marxism as to make it consistent with a practical working arrangement with capitalism. To have done anything else would have required men of the foresight and integrity of Marx and Engels themselves, men prepared to hold their essential position through long, unrewarding years, to be content to know that their view might not be vindicated until after their own deaths.

For the Marxist view of the inevitability of the decline, decay and eventual break up of capitalism is only true in the end. The contradictory elements in capitalism which we have described in these pages only become fatal to the existence of the system after some decades of development. It is only when *all* the factors in the situation, both objective and subjective, are taken into consideration that the impossibility of the indefinite continuance of capitalism can be demonstrated. It is only the interaction of *all* the factors in the social equation which makes the continuance of capitalism as the basis of human civilization impossible. And these factors have only begun powerfully to interact in our own time, from say 1914, when capitalism entered into a period of general and chronic crisis from which it shows no sign of emergence.

Thus revolutionary Marxism, as Marx and Engels discovered it, is applicable to the development of capitalism as a whole, over its entire life history. It does not exclude the possibility of periods of successful capitalist expansion at particular times and in particular places. The small men who succeeded to the leadership of the German working class movement about 1900 could see that they lived in such a period: and this was all that interested them. They were quite incapable of long or impersonal views. They knew that, if they committed themselves to, and acted upon, the precepts of revolutionary Marxism, they would make things very unpleasant for themselves. For it was true that for the moment it was impossible to overthrow capitalism. They did not foresee that, if they failed to maintain the revolutionary position during the period of relatively peaceful and successful capitalist development, they would betray, when that period ended, everything for which Marx and Engels had stood. They did so betray both their teachers and the unfortunate workers who trusted them. And their betrayal was merely made the more difficult to expose, by the fact that they continually uttered impeccably Marxist opinions.

Marx's and Engels' discoveries fell, then, upon stony ground. In the English-speaking world they were wholly ignored. In Germany they were grossly or subtly distorted.

There was, however, another country in which Marx and Engels were read. Their works were translated into Russian soon after their appearance: and they were eagerly read by an emerging class of Russian intellectuals.[1] A group of Russian Marxists soon arose. This group went through the same processes of division as did the German Marxists. The Russians also produced their revisionists (such as Struve) who turned Marxism into a harmless description of the workings of the capitalist system. Russia also produced, however, the best Marxist of the second half of the nineteenth century—Plechanov. This brilliant and incisive writer made important contributions to Marxism, especially in the fields of literature and philosophy. When the hour of action struck, however, it was found that

[1] It is interesting to notice that the preface to the second (German) edition of *Capital* contains an appreciative comment on a review of the book in the St. Petersburg *European Messenger*.

Plechanov's character was by no means the equal of his intellect. He disgracefully betrayed the working class cause by becoming an extreme Russian patriot, protesting violently against the Bolshevists' determination to make peace. But this does not prevent his books from being of great importance and value.

The group of Russian Marxists which Plechanov at one time inspired (and indeed in a sense founded) will always be indissolubly associated with the name of Lenin. Lenin studied the works of Marx and Engels as did the other young Russian intellectuals of his time. He brought to that study, however, a formidable intellectual force. He did not pause nor rest until he had mastered the whole essence of the science. And, as the event showed, almost alone of that generation of Marxist scholars he grasped its revolutionary kernel. That kernel consists in the economic theorems upon which Marx rested his prediction of the decline of capitalism into crisis and war, and in the deduction that a revolutionary epoch will return in which the working class, in order to preserve itself from extermination, will have to take state power, establish its dictatorship, and on this basis socialize the means of production.

Lenin, almost alone of his generation of Marxists,[1] grasped the fact that this was what Marxism meant. But he did more than this. He realized that the great discoveries of Marx and Engels must be preserved and defended from adulteration and distortion to suit the comfort of socialist leaders who had made their peace with capitalism. But he also realized that Marxism must be developed, must be kept up to date; that the strong foundation which Marx and Engels had provided gave their successors the opportunity to rear a structure of thought which would be fully capable of guiding the working class, both in its struggle for power, and, after the successful issue of that struggle, in its enormously difficult task of building up a new social and economic system. For Lenin, Marxism was no dead body of dogma to be learned by rote. Just because he achieved so perfect a mastery of it, just because he could detect the often

[1] Rosa Luxemburg preserved better than anyone else after Lenin the revolutionary edge of the science.

subtle modifications and dilutions of Marxism which were going on all around him, he was able at the same time to see where Marxist theory needed extension so that it could cover new phenomena in the development of capitalism.

In the first place Lenin developed, both in theory (as in his book *What is to be Done?*) and in practice, by his vehement controversies inside the Russian Social Democratic movement, that new and vital conception of a working class party which we have striven to describe (Chapter XV). In so doing, Lenin for the first time made the workers conscious of the kind of instrument which they had to forge if they were ever really to get rid of capitalism. They had to create a political organization of a new and incomparably more developed type than anything the world had as yet seen.

Lenin's second great contribution to Marxism was his study of the new, monopolist or imperialist phase into which capitalism had passed. Marx had died in 1883, a few years before capitalism entered upon a new phase. Engels lived on till 1895. He, therefore, saw in his closing years the first stages of this new phase. He was aware that capitalism was undergoing modifications, and was profoundly interested by them. But he, too, died too soon for it to be possible for him to undertake a full study of what was happening. One of Lenin's essential contributions to Marxist thought was his study of this new and, as he named it, Imperialist phase of capitalist development. We attempted to give the essence of his conclusions in Chapters XX and XXI of this book. But Lenin's approach to the subject was necessarily opposite to ours. Instead of discussing Socialism and Peace, as the existence of the Soviet Union enabled us to do, Lenin had to discuss Capitalism and War. For these were the only actual phenomena of the then existing world. His conclusion was that the temporary revival of capitalism which took place from about 1895 onwards had been achieved upon the basis of rapid imperialist expansion alone. Moreover, imperialist expansion was intimately associated with an important modification in the internal structure of the economic system of every expanding empire. Free competition between the producing units within each state was gradually replaced by a system of partial (or sometimes complete) monopolies, so that each imperialist state tended to become a loosely, but effectively, consolidated firm, ready for competitive struggle with every other. Such a line of development, Lenin showed, must certainly produce war. Not only would the whole land surface of the earth be sooner or later partitioned out between the rival empires, but the existing partial division did not correspond to these empires' needs for expansion. Intense disproportions had arisen. Economically weaker empires, like the French and the British, had been able, because of their priority of development, to take up the major exploitable areas of the globe. Economically stronger empires, such as the German, were being left with a share hopelessly inadequate to their needs. Such disproportions were ever growing and inappeasable. For, although the British and French empires were relatively large, they were, even so, inadequate to the needs of their capitalisms for expansion.

The study of imperialism as a new, monopolistic, stage in the development of capitalism was Lenin's great contribution to Marxist economic theory. But he made political deductions of the highest importance from this piece of economic analysis. If imperialism was a phenomenon of this nature; if imperialist expansion, far from providing a road by which capitalism could peacefully evolve into socialism, by giving ever greater and greater concessions to the workers (as all the revisionists, open and tacit, declared it to be); if imperialism was bound, on the contrary, to produce the break up of world capitalism in a series of shattering wars—then the world was re-entering an epoch more stormy and revolutionary even than the epoch out of which Marxism had been born. Far from it being necessary to tone down, as the revisionists suggested, the revolutionary political conceptions of Marx and Engels, it was urgently necessary, if Marxism was to keep abreast of ever changing reality, to emphasize and to develop precisely this part of the science.

This work Lenin accomplished both with his pen and with his sword. During the months between the February and the March revolutions in Russia, when he was carrying through what even his closest colleagues supposed to be a desperate, not to say foolhardy, revolutionary policy, he was at the same time working out the theoretical basis of such a policy. He had written the main part of his book, *The State and Revolution*, when he came to the conclusion that the hour for the actual seizure of power by the Russian working class had come. Accordingly he broke off his writing. In December 1917, a month after Lenin had become the leading figure in the first stable workers' government in the history of the world, the book was published. It contained the following postscript:

" This pamphlet was written in August and September 1917. I had already drawn up the plan for the next, the seventh chapter, on ' the Experience of the Russian Revolutions of 1905 and 1917.' But, outside of the title, I did not succeed in writing a single line of the chapter; what ' interfered ' was the political crisis—the eve of the October Revolution of 1917. Such ' interference ' can only be welcomed. However, the second part of the pamphlet (devoted to the experience of the Russian Revolutions of 1905 and 1917) will probably have to be put off for a long time. It is more pleasant and useful to go through the ' experience of the revolution ' than to write about it."

These sentences must ever remain the classical example of the application of the Marxist principle of the unity of theory and practice.

We attempted in Chapters XVI and XVII to give the essence of the Marxist view of the State, as first formulated by Engels and then, it is hardly too much to say, rediscovered, or at any rate re-emphasized and reapplied, by Lenin. For it was upon Engels' work that Lenin based the theoretical part of his demonstration of the necessity of establishing a workers' dictatorship.

Lenin's fourth contribution to Marxism lay in the philosophical field. Here he met and defeated the determined attempt of many of the other Marxists of his time to retreat from the real position of dialectical materialism, into a concealed idealism which could provide no philosophical basis for a revolutionary movement. It is clear that these four aspects of Lenin's work are closely interrelated. Indeed, their differentiation for purposes of exposition is artificial. Taken together they amount to a complete working over of Marxism so that it may live and guide in the present epoch.

Marxism, however, was not completed or perfected by Lenin. Such an all-embracing science never can be completed ; it must for ever live, grow and change. Already it has passed into a new, third, stage of development. Lenin died too soon after the consolidation of the political power of the Russian workers to be able to do conclusive work, either practically or theoretically upon the problem of how a socialist economic system might be built up. He did, it is true, in the very first months of Soviet power sketch out some ingenious transitional forms of economic organization. But before ever these could take shape they were swept away by the emergency of civil war. Lenin survived the conclusion of the civil war only long enough to evolve the compromise, transitional stage of the New Economic Policy (which was itself largely a return to his original economic programme as proposed before the civil war broke out).

An analogous transitional economic system may well prove to be a necessary first stage after the conquest of political power by the workers in the capitalist states of the Western World. Hence the lessons which can be learnt from the Russian New Economic Policy will well repay the study of the communists and socialists of all other countries. But the establishment of the New Economic Policy was only the preliminary stage in the actual building up of a planned socialist economic system. As we saw (Chapter IV) the planning of the entire economic life of the Soviet Union did not become possible until 1928. It was in that year that the structure of the New Economic Policy was broken up and the first Five Years Plan was instituted. And by that time Lenin had been dead for four years.

Hence, just as the application of Marxism to the specific problems of our Imperialist stage in the development of capitalism, and the elaboration of the tactics and strategy necessary to the conquest of power by the working class, will always be associated with the name of Lenin, so the application of Marxism to the problems of the creation of the first socialist economic system in the history of the world will always be associated with the name of Stalin.[1]

[1] Hence the afore-mentioned barbarism of calling the science " Marxism-Leninism-Stalinism " ! It is only with the addition of this new body of theory and experience to the science of social change that the positive approach attempted in the first two parts of this book has become practicable. It is only

Stalin's contribution to Marxism began before the establishment of socialism in the Soviet Union, however. His first contribution was his detailed study of the National Question. Himself the member of an oppressed nation he was naturally deeply interested in relating the national struggles of such peoples as a whole to the international struggle of the working class. He fought strongly and successfully against the attempt of certain socialists to deny a value to these national struggles and to assert that a socialist community must necessarily be so highly centralized that it would be unable to give autonomy to national groups within it. He took a prominent part in drafting the first Soviet Constitution in which the national question was, it is not too much to say, solved. The way in which the Soviet Union has known how to reconcile the claims for cultural, educational and administrative autonomy made by the subject peoples of the Tsarist Empire, without sacrificing any of its essential strength and unity, has been one of its greatest triumphs. This work has been, above all, inspired by Stalin.

Stalin's second, and greatest, achievement was that he found the way forward for socialism in the difficult period of the temporary stabilization of capitalism between 1923 and 1929. Lenin, Stalin, and all the other Russian leaders had hoped and expected that the achievement of power by the Russian workers would be followed by revolutions over much of Europe. Nor did these revolutions fail to occur. In exactly a year from the Bolshevist revolution the German and Austrian peoples rose and ended both the war and the Habsburg and Hohenzollern dynasties. If these revolutions had not taken place it would have been quite impossible for the workers to have maintained their power in the Soviet Union. But because the German and Austrian workers were led by men who at heart feared nothing so much as the abolition of capitalism, their revolutions were

now that Marxism has been applied to the positive task of building up a socialist economic system that we can describe that application: it is only now that a socialist economic system has come into being that we can use the comparative method for the study of economic problems. Hence the indulgence of the reader of the first two parts of this book is requested for a pioneer attempt to state the conclusions of the science of social change as a (for the moment) completed whole. For in describing first the economic and then the political general plan of a socialist society, we attempted, in effect, to bring together the economic and political conclusions of Marx and Engels, their development by Lenin and their application by Stalin to the creation of a socialist society.

halted at the stage of the establishment of ordinary capitalist republics. German and Austrian capitalism were miraculously preserved. They were preserved by the only people who could possibly have preserved them in the *débâcle* of the immediately post-war years in the defeated empires, namely, the workers' own leaders. This halting of the German and Austrian revolutions gave time for their profit-making systems to be patched up. They survived into the brief period of capitalist revival in the nineteen-twenties. This event, itself made possible by the combined treachery and poltroonery of the German and Austrian Social Democratic leaders, put the Soviet Union in a very difficult situation. The rule of the capitalist had been overthrown over one-sixth of the world's surface. But that sixth was a relatively backward area. Was it possible for socialism to survive there if capitalism had been enabled to enter another definite, even if brief, period of expansion in Western Europe ?

As so often, something which no one had exactly foreseen, had happened. As Lenin said, history is always more cunning than any of the prophets; it always has some surprise up its sleeve for us. On the one hand the working class régime in the Soviet Union, aided by the semi-revolutions of Western Europe, had beaten off its enemies and was securely established in power. On the other hand Western Europe was evidently going to remain in capitalist hands for some time. What was to be done ? What was the way forward for the international working class movement ? Could the political power which the workers had won in the Soviet Union be used to build up the first socialist economic and social system which the world had ever seen, in spite of the fact that all the most advanced countries remained in capitalist hands ? Or must the workers either largely abandon their power in the Soviet Union or jeopardise it by trying artificially, and from the outside, to create revolutions in the rest of the world ? An important section of the Russian Communist party, led by Trotsky, who had become a leading member of the party in 1917, took the view that only these two latter courses were possible. They violently denied the possibility of building up a system of socialist planned production for use in the Soviet Union in isolation.

And indeed that task was sufficiently daunting. Only the most determined and courageous men could have set their hands to it. They had to build up, in a decade or so at the most, a socialist system which should surpass the capitalisms of Britain, America and Germany, with their century and more of development behind them. And they had as raw material the half-ruined industries and railways of a never well developed industrial system, standing amidst a vast sea of pre-capitalist agriculture and handicraft. Moreover, the Russian workers, though of thrice-proven courage and energy, suffered in their technical capacities from the backwardness of the whole Tsarist epoch, while the peasants were illiterate and primitive.

And yet, Stalin and his collaborators realized, socialism had to be built up in the Soviet Union if the gigantic opportunity afforded of the first firmly established working class régime was not to be thrown away. The proposals of Trotsky and his followers amounted, for all their extremely revolutionary terminology, either to a surrender to anti-working class forces in the Soviet Union, or to a fore-doomed and profoundly un-Marxist *sortie* upon the capitalist world. Stalin's claim to rank as one of the decisive figures in history is that he has found the way to overcome the extraordinary difficulties which ten years ago stood in the way of establishing socialism in the Soviet Union. He had first to defeat the formidable opposition within his own party to making even the attempt " to build socialism in one country," as the phrase ran. He had then to launch a gigantic programme to industrialize the country. And finally he had to find some way of bringing socialism to the vast Soviet countryside.

Stalin began his work by launching the First Five Year Plan. The plan itself may be said to be his *magnum opus* as a Marxist. (The First Five Year Plan was a document of over 1,000 closely printed pages.) Its preparation was essentially a technical task. It was, however, a task which only convinced and courageous Marxists, conscious both of the inherent feasibility of a planned economic system and of its necessity, would have had the courage to embark upon.[1] Next came the problems of the proper distribution of income in such a system. We have already described how Stalin and his colleagues, applying and developing the definite, but brief, principles laid down by Marx and Engels on this subject, have evolved a carefully designed system of the distribution of income in accordance with the quality and quantity of work done.

But all this did not solve the vitally important question of how the vast field of Russian agriculture was to be brought into the ambit of a planned, socialist economic system. The problem was in essence one of how Russian agriculture could skip the capitalist stage of development altogether; of how it could leap from the stage of peasant commodity production, newly emerged from communal ownership, and showing only the earlier signs of the development of capitalist farming, into some form of socialist agriculture. Stalin solved this problem with the collective farm. This is another of his greatest contributions to Marxist theory and practice. It is a subject on which there was, so far as I am aware, no guidance to be found in Marx or Engels.[2] Yet it was an achievement at once essential to the survival and development of the Soviet Union and of vital importance to the rest of the world.

Outside of Great Britain and the United States, agriculture is still predominantly peasant. The problem of whether such agriculture must go through the British and American stage of relatively large-scale capitalist farming for profit, or can pass straight into a form of socialist development, will confront every other working class when it takes power. Under Stalin's leadership the Russian workers have settled the question by showing that it is possible, although by no means easy, to develop

---

[1] Needless to say, Stalin did not write the First Five Year Plan. We described in Chapter IV how these plans are composed. But it was, above all, Stalin who led the Russian workers in their onslaught upon the problem of building a planned socialist economic system.

[2] Except the prophetic sentence of Engels which we quoted on p. 387. Indeed, although Marx often speaks of " free associations of producers " as being the agents which will carry on production under socialism, and would undoubtedly have hailed collectivization as a vitally important discovery, the precedent for the form of organization adopted for socialist Russian agriculture is to be found in the innumerable attempts to create Producers' Co-operative Societies which have marked working class history. Stalin's great discovery is that in a socialist environment such attempts can succeed.

socialist agriculture directly out of peasant agriculture. Collectivization was the biggest and hardest task which the Soviets have faced. It produced very serious risks and difficulties. Its accomplishment is by far the most important event which has occurred in the world since 1917.

It must not be supposed that these practical achievements of the Soviets under the leadership of Stalin have been made by the simple method of empirical trial and error. Stalin's policy has continually been guided by Marxist theory. It has been essentially dialectical. And Stalin, true to the tradition of every Marxist leader, has explained and defended his policy in a series of books, pamphlets, articles and speeches. These works of Stalin provide the theoretical basis of the present policy of the Soviet Union. In them, and in the resolutions of the Communist party of the Soviet Union, in the drafting of which Stalin has no doubt had a hand, are to be found the contemporary developments and applications of Marxism to the problems of the organization of a socialist economic system. Similarly, in the resolutions of the Communist International and in the speeches, pamphlets, and articles of its leading figures, may be found the application and development of Marxism to the problems of the contemporary struggle of the working class in the capitalist world.

The history of the discoveries of Marx and Engels has been checkered. It is difficult to say whether the new science was more nearly killed by the neglect of the English or the attention of the Germans. The vital, living core of Marxism would hardly have survived unless it had been grasped by Lenin and his immediate associates, and by them transmitted for further and endless development by the working class of the world.

It is interesting to enquire why it was that in Russia alone did Marxism, in the period immediately after the death of its founders, find soil suitable for its development. The explanation is, surely, that Russia during the last years of the nineteenth century and the first two decades of the twentieth century, was passing through that early and difficult stage of capitalist development which occurred in Britain before 1840 and in

Germany before 1870. It was the relatively primitive state of Russian capitalism, still struggling with difficulties which British, German and American capitalism had overcome, which made the Russia of 1890 to 1917 fertile soil for Marxism. It was, above all, the failure of the Russian capitalist class to get rid of the disgusting feudal régime of the Tsar, and establish a modern democratic régime, which helped the Russian Marxists to avoid that emasculation of the science which occurred in Germany. In Germany and Britain it was possible—indeed, to those who could not or would not see that Imperialism was leading to war, it was easy—to believe that capitalism was developing by gradual, easy, democratic stages into socialism. No such illusions were possible in the Russia of the Tsars. The Tsarist police could be relied upon to remind anyone, who was inclined to forget the point, that to be a genuine Marxist was to be a revolutionary.

To-day it is not, or it ought not to be, difficult to see that British, German, and, to some extent, American capitalism overcame those early difficulties amidst which Russian capitalism succumbed by means of imperialist expansion alone. The price of adopting the imperialist pseudo-solution for the inherently insoluble problems of capitalism has been the subjection of the larger part of the human race to merciless, if largely invisible, exploitation; the partition of the whole world between the great empires, and, finally, ever renewed inter-imperialist war. The contemporary world of unemployment, exploitation, crisis and war, and no peaceful ascent to socialism, has been the result of a repudiation of the revolutionary essence of Marxism, and of acquiescence in imperialism, on the part of the leaders of the working class movements of the West.

But at last Marx's and Engels' basic work is being rediscovered in Western Europe and America. For now it is hardly possible to avoid realizing that Marxism has proved to be an essentially correct account of the world in which we live, or of acknowledging that the political action proposed by Marxists offers the sole way of preserving Western civilization.

Chapter XXXIV

The Way to Socialism

THE first purpose of this book has been to describe the objective of the working class movement—to say exactly what socialism and communism are. Its second purpose has been to outline the theory and practice of the struggle for socialism as they have been evolved in the course of the development of the working class movement. There remains the vital question of what is the proper policy for the international working class movement to-day: the question of what is to be done *now* in order to achieve socialism in the five-sixths of the world which are still capitalist.

It is evident that this book cannot attempt to prescribe to the international working class movement any particular policy which will ensure the defeat of capitalism and the coming of socialism. Political policies must vary widely both from time to time and from place to place. The struggle of the workers is world wide, many sided, complex. It is being fought out in London streets, in the mountains of Western China, under the sun of Andalusia and amidst Chicago blizzards. Moreover, it is being fought out not only in every part of the world but also in every kind of social and economic environment. Very different methods of struggle, ranging from the organized strike action of one of the major British Trade Unions to the desperate armed struggle which is at the moment of writing (August 1936) raging throughout Spain, reflect these varying social and economic circumstances. In India and China the workers' struggle is indissolubly connected with a struggle for national self-consciousness and independence. In Britain it contends with the oldest and greatest of imperialisms. In France (as in Britain) it fuses for a time with the struggle to preserve hard-won and historic liberties from the new capitalist tyranny. In Germany, Italy and the other Fascist states it fights to keep alive the secret flame of workers' revolt in the midst of terror and torture greater than the world had hitherto imagined.

No one tactic of working class struggle can be applicable to the huge diversity of the world scene in the twentieth century.

The workers of every country, of colony and of empire, of democratic republic and of Fascist tyranny, have to apply the general principles of the international movement to the various circumstances of their own countries. But they can and do compare their experiences, analyse the causes of their victories and their defeats, learn from each other and so cut short the terribly costly process of trial and error. Moreover, the workers can everywhere (and for their very lives' sake they must) use to the full that ten times tested body of knowledge which we have called the science of social change. For nowhere and never have workers' movements succeeded unless they have mastered and applied the scientific discoveries of Marx, Engels and Lenin. This is by far the most important lesson to be learnt from the history of the last century of working class struggle. It is a conclusion which emerges with especial force from a study of the history of the revived British working class movement which came into existence some fifty years ago.

Before the liberating ideas of Marx and Engels had become effectively accessible to the British workers, British capitalism entered on its highest, imperialist, stage of development. Since Britain was the first in the field, the success of her imperialist adventures was very great. Concessions could, as we saw, be made to the skilled workers sufficient to divide, and so paralyse, the hitherto formidable struggle of the British workers. In the preceding half-century that struggle had failed principally because it had been unable to develop a sufficient comprehension of the social process. Now that the nature of that process had been discovered the struggle itself seemed to have almost disappeared.

In England for thirty years it was almost as if the discoveries of Marx and Engels had never been made. It is probably little exaggeration to say that no one in England between 1850 and 1880 understood what Marx and Engels were doing.[1] After 1880

---

[1] There is a passage in one of Marx's letters which suggests that Ernest Jones the Chartist leader, in the tragic latter part of his life achieved some comprehension of Marxism. But it must have been limited. Again, William Morris showed in many of his writings (such as the *Dream of John Ball*), that he was a serious and able student of Marxism. But Morris was not, and never claimed to be, a

both a school of British Marxists and a revived movement of working class struggle appeared. But the degree of real comprehension which these early British Marxists achieved was limited. Their appearance proved almost as much a barrier as a bridge to any general comprehension of Marxism.

These earliest British readers of Marx and Engels formed a political party called the Social Democratic Federation. Partly because of the disastrous personal failings of its leader, Hyndman, but principally because neither he nor any of his followers ever achieved an adequate comprehension of Marxism, the Social Democratic Federation never became more than a sect. It never succeeded in inspiring and moulding the revived working class movement, which was, from 1889 onwards, coming into being all around it. The failure of the British Social Democrats to master Marxism as a whole meant that they were never able to become more than a propagandist movement. But from the eighties of the last century onwards, they carried on a courageous and persistent, if not always very skilful, propaganda for Marxism in the British Labour movement. In the end, however, the Social Democratic Federation divided. A part broke off, and broke up, into several small revolutionary Marxist parties. Another part forgot its Marxism and became an extremely conservative section of the Labour party. But before this happened an important work of Marxist education had been done amongst the British workers. The post-war development of Marxism in Britain would have been impossible unless this basis had been laid.

In another aspect of their work these early British Marxists failed completely; but this was by no means entirely their fault. They failed entirely to convert to Marxism a number of talented men and women of the middle class who, in the eighteen-eighties, were attracted to socialism and the working class cause. There now arose a considerable school of English socialist thinkers, organised in the Fabian Society. They included serious and sincere social investigators such as Mr. and Mrs. Webb and

political leader. Hence, though his contribution to British socialism is immortal and invaluable, it could only make its effect in the long run. Again, very few people in England understood the practical political work which Marx and Engels were constantly doing, or attempting, in influencing the British Trade Union movement as it slowly moved towards political consciousness.

dazzlingly gifted writers such as Mr. Bernard Shaw. But they none of them attained to any comprehension of Marxism. It was not that they examined Marxism and concluded that it was erroneous. On the contrary, they passionately rejected Marxism while remaining in substantial ignorance of its real nature.[1]

This was the more remarkable in that Engels was living and actively working in London. Engels, however, put his finger on the true explanation of the extraordinary attitude of the Fabians to Marxism in the following passage :

" The Fabians," he wrote, " have enough understanding to see the inevitability of social revolution, but find it impossible to entrust the raw proletariat alone with this tremendous work, and therefore have a partiality for putting themselves at the head. Fear of revolution is their fundamental principle. . . . With great industry they have provided, among all sorts of rubbish, some good pieces of propaganda, in fact the best that the English have provided in this connection. But as soon as they come on their specific tactic, to hush up the class struggle, it gets rotten. Hence also their fanatical hatred of Marx and all of us—because of the class struggle."[2]

Psychologists will have no difficulty in agreeing with Engels that it was essentially their terror of revolution which paralysed the Fabians' intellectual faculties when they heard of Marxism. It was well known that Marxism led to a revolutionary conclusion. Hence, the Fabians unconsciously felt, on no account must it be examined—precisely because if it were examined it might be found to be true.

Thus British socialist thought, from the moment of its rebirth, was split up into Fabianism and the Marxism of the Social Democratic Federation. It was split, that is to say, into a primitive and narrow form of Marxism, which was, in spite of the sincerity of many of its spokesmen, little more than a

[1] The historian of the Fabian Society tells us that its essential accomplishment was that it rescued the newly reborn British Labour movement from Marxist influences. This shows how considerable, in spite of everything, was the influence of the Social Democratic Federation at that time.

An excellent account of the evolution of the working class movement and of socialist thought in the eighties is to be found in Mr. Allen Hutt's aforementioned work *This Final Crisis*.

[2] In a letter to Sorge, January 18th, 1893.

caricature of the ideas of Marx and Engels, and the serious, able, but basically pre-scientific thinking of the Fabians. For Fabian thought, for all its apparent care and thoroughness, never went deep enough or saw widely enough to achieve an adequate comprehension of reality. It never grasped the essential fact that the capture of the power of the state by the working class, and its allies, is a pre-requisite for any substantial advance towards socialism. And this unscientific, Fabian, type of socialist thinking was adopted, in dilute solution, by the new leaders, guides, spokesmen and teachers of the revived working class movement.

This failure of the revived British working class movement to make use of the basic discoveries in sociological science which had been made by Marx and Engels during its thirty years' sleep between 1850 and 1880 is a major historical tragedy. It is outside the scope of this book to attempt to give any account of the history of the British working class movement from its reawakening in the eighteen-eighties to the present day. But no one who makes any serious study of that history will be able to resist the conclusion that the British movement's neglect of the science of social change has again and again brought it to disaster.

But this neglect was itself a reflection of the economic and social conditions in which the British workers movement was developing. Their environment of apparently triumphant imperialism prevented any keen or deep realization of the nature of capitalism, or of their place in capitalist society, from taking hold of the minds of the British workers. Such a realization could only be born of the experiences, trials and errors (especially the errors) of the more intense phase of the class struggle which was forced upon the British workers by the turn of the economic tide which occurred (see p. 318 above) exactly in 1900.

The leadership which the new movement threw up was in its turn a reflection of the partial character of the political awakening of the British workers. The predominant leaders of the movement (who were, almost from its inception until 1931, Mr. MacDonald, Mr. Snowden, Mr. Henderson, and Mr. Thomas) were practical politicians of considerable ability. But their interest in any attempt to define either the goal towards which a working class movement should strive, or the means by which it should attempt to reach that goal, was very limited. They moved, not without skill and tact, on the British political stage, expressing those sentiments and performing those actions which, they sensed, were on the whole expected of them. They knew intimately the type of political consciousness of the growing mass of more or less organized British workers who supported them. They realized, and indeed emphasized, the fact that many even of those British workers who had come to feel that they needed a political party of their own were far from having freed themselves from all their former prejudices. Nor did the labour leaders seek to take them further. Indeed they themselves became, to a considerable degree, transmitting mechanisms, by which the general point of view of capitalism could still be pumped into the minds of those workers who had broken with the old political parties.

It was inevitable that such leaders should, either consciously or unconsciously, collaborate more and more closely with the powerful forces of the ruling capitalist class. They had nothing to restrain them from such collaboration. For they were as devoid as their least awakened supporters of any insight into the history, causes, or objects of the conflict which had called their movement and themselves into existence. They were content to swim upon the tide of events, neither knowing nor caring why or whither that tide was running, so long as it supported them.

Inevitably the tide carried them into the haven of increasingly assiduous co-operation with the masters of Britain; so that year by year they became more and more the mere agents amongst the working class of their real masters, the capitalists. Then they used the hold, which they themselves had done everything to perpetuate, of capitalist ideas over the minds of the workers, as their excuse for never leading their followers in any real struggle against capitalism. Such men, naturally, had no use whatever for the science of social change. They felt that a belief in the actual possibility of establishing a new economic system was a dangerous delusion. For the first three decades of the existence of the revived British working class movement a leadership was maintained which was at least as intent upon keeping the movement from challenging any of the essential conditions of the existence of British capitalism, as of pressing the workers' claims for tolerable conditions of life.

But meanwhile the ever growing pressure which must inevitably be exerted upon the workers of even the richest capitalist empires, as soon as their capitalisms cease rapidly to expand, was driving the British workers, with or without their leaders' consent, to create a more and more powerful, and more and more militant, movement. Solid, numerous and wealthy Trade Union organizations were built up, and considerable improvements in hours, wages and conditions of work were obtained. Moreover (as we saw in Chapter XXVI), the governing class was sufficiently alarmed itself to enact, through the agency of the Liberal Party, an elaborate system of social services. The British workers also succeeded in creating, in the shape of the Labour Representation Committee, which later became the Parliamentary Labour Party, the embryo of a working class political party. But the Labour Party, in its type of organization, its policy, its political philosophy and its leadership, was very far from being the kind of party which, as we have tried to show, it is necessary for a working class to create, if it is to succeed in abolishing capitalism and establishing socialism.

During the immediate pre-war years the British workers became profoundly dissatisfied with the Parliamentary Labour Party. The prestige of its leaders fell to a very low point and, in spite of the rapid growth of the working class movement as as whole, the Parliamentary Party failed to grow. But this dissatisfaction did not result in any serious attempt to transform the Parliamentary Labour Party into the new kind of political organization which we defined in Chapter XV; into a highly organized party, capable of every kind of political activity. It resulted instead in a swing away from political activity altogether; in a swing towards the erroneous conception of achieving the abolition of capitalism along the lines advocated by the Syndicalists: the lines of exclusively industrial and Trade Union activity.

After the war both the British Labour movement as a whole and the Parliamentary Labour Party grew with quite unprecedented rapidity. They grew so rapidly that the Labour Party began to form administrations, and the Trade Union movement began to be faced with the incompatibility of the claims of its members and the necessities of a now declining capitalism. It was then that the full consequences of the fact that the British workers had not yet developed a movement with an adequate understanding of the nature and necessities of their struggle against capitalism, began to make themselves felt. Such an understanding had to be developed by further years of struggle, of set-backs, and of experience. Until that experience had been won the movement could still be influenced, deflected, and to a tragically large extent controlled, by men who had thought out none of the basic problems of a movement driven forward by aspirations incompatible with capitalism. For the failure of the post-war leaders of the British Labour movement, to understand the nature of the epoch in which they lived, lay at the root of the policy of co-operation with the ruling class for which these men fought with all their strength and skill. Mr. MacDonald, Mr. Snowden, Mr. Thomas and Mr. Henderson were all profoundly convinced that British capitalist imperialism had many decades, if not centuries, of expanding development before it. Such a future would provide both the opportunity and the necessity of co-operation with the capitalists by the working class movement. For if British imperialism had another whole epoch of triumphant expansion before it, then it was going to be too strong to be overthrown and strong enough to grant substantial concessions. This wholly erroneous view of the possible future of capitalism, based on sheer ignorance, quite as much as their more obvious personal weaknesses, such as their desire for office, wealth, the applause of the capitalist world, and the simpler forms of personal success, induced the leaders of the British Labour Party to pursue a policy of accommodation to capitalism. And it eventually led three of them into the National Government.

That this optimistic view of the future of British capitalism was mistaken, events were to show. In spite of its victory in 1918, British imperialism never re-entered a period of sustained expansion after the war. Accordingly it was never able to make the series of concessions upon which the labour leaders ha l counted. On the contrary, the now far larger and more powerful working class political and industrial movement was brought up against the basic incompatibility of its demands with the necessities of British capitalism. A period of severe class struggles began. The results of these struggles were fluctuating. At one time (as in the immediate post-war crisis, or at the end of 1925) the strength of working class pressure, or a temporary improvement in the position of British capitalism, resulted in substantial concessions to the workers. At another, a relaxation of the workers' pressure by their leaders, or a worsening of the economic situation of British capitalism, resulted (as in 1926) in the imposition, after tough struggles, of severe cuts. But the final balance of effect has indubitably been markedly unfavourable to the workers. The British Labour movement, still under its original leaders, suffered between 1920 and 1931, a series of severe defeats. Nor could any other result be expected. The movement was still dominated by the disastrously false view that it was living in a period of expanding, ascendant capitalism. It had not yet realized what disasters could be caused by leaders who did everything in their power to damp down and to stifle the struggle of their supporters against the consequences of an actually declining system. In a word there did not yet exist in the British Labour movement any adequate realization, on the one hand, of the necessity of abolishing capitalism, if any substantial benefits were to be secured, and, on the other, of the immensity of that task. Hence no adequate effort was made to forge a political instrument capable of doing the job. No lasting victory could be won until experience had altered all this.

Throughout the whole history of the revived British working class movement another tendency has been slowly but surely making itself felt. From the first, groups of the most militant and class conscious workers felt the need of a transformation of the aims, methods, and forms of organization of their movement. The frightful object lesson as to the real nature and consequences of capitalist imperialism provided by the war gave this, the revolutionary tendency within the British Labour movement, a strong impetus. Moreover, the last phase of the war saw the outbreak of working class revolutions in half the countries of Europe, and the success of one of these revolutions. From the end of the war onwards an ever growing number of British workers came to realize that they were living in a new world of capitalist decline, in which not only the success of their movement, but its very survival, depended upon its revolutionizing itself. In 1920 these workers, who had hitherto been split up into numerous small socialist societies and groups, succeeded, in a large measure, in uniting their forces. The Communist Party of Great Britain was founded and has ever since represented this alternative policy within the British working class movement.

In Britain such a transformation of the working class movement must, inevitably, be a long and difficult process. The whole tradition of British public life, which is itself merely a reflection of the uniquely favoured position of British imperialism, is profoundly inimical to that new kind of political thinking and acting which can alone achieve decisive social change. Hence it was a formidable task to create even the nucleus of those organizations, and means of propaganda and education, without which no working class can carry on a serious struggle against capitalism. That nucleus has been created, but only by means of a stubborn and persistent struggle against what to many seemed insuperable difficulties.

Moreover, the practical political capacity of the few trained Marxists who existed in Britain could only be developed by actual political struggles; it could only be developed by a process of trial and error. Not only had the whole anti-Marxist tradition of the main body of the British Labour movement to be overcome, but the fatally warped and stunted Marxism of the original British Marxist sects had to be transcended. For Marxism is a mantle which can crush as well as clothe. Marxists, for example, have sometimes hastily supposed that their (often partial) knowledge of the science of social change is in itself enough to qualify them for effective political work. But this is not the case. On the contrary, the experience of the British Labour movement demonstrates that although the absence of this knowledge can bring nothing but disaster, this knowledge by itself is no substitute for patience, shrewdness, sensitiveness and general political ability. If a working class movement is to succeed in the vast, subtle, and complex task of effecting social change in an advanced capitalist democracy, it must create organizations whose leading members have *both* qualities; who have fused first-rate political abilities of the traditional sort with a mastery of the science of social change.

In the face of these difficulties, and overcoming them one by one, the struggle of the most clear-sighted and courageous British workers to change the whole character of their movement has gone forward. They have striven to create a movement which would be enabled by its forms of organization, its methods, and its leadership, to pursue a policy of consistent and persistent challenge, instead of accommodation, to the need of British capitalist imperialism.

The culminating disaster of the anti-Marxist, and in effect pro-capitalist, type of policy, organization and leadership of the British Labour movement was reached in 1931 when the second Labour Government collapsed, its three principal members deserted to head the succeeding capitalist administration, and the Parliamentary Labour Party was reduced to the size at which it had stood a quarter of a century before. The shock which these events administered to the whole movement was very great. There was a widespread realization that there must have been something wrong with the policies, principles and methods which had produced this catastrophe. The movement has never since felt faith or confidence in its traditional political philosophy and practice. But there has been, as yet, no general realization of what is the alternative. The movement as a whole has not yet swung over to the only alternative to a policy of adaptation to the needs of a decaying capitalism, namely, a policy of conscious, persistent and cumulative struggle against capitalism. The years between 1931 and 1936 have been a sort of interregnum. The political and industrial strength of the movement has been steadily accumulating again after its dissipation in 1926 and 1931. But in the decisive respect of finding a new policy to replace the old, discredited, but not discarded, policy of accommodation to capitalism, the movement, as a whole, has marked time.

This indecisive, inconclusive condition of the movement has been reflected in the new leadership which succeeded to the posts left vacant by the three deserters, and by the death of Mr. Arthur Henderson. This new leadership has a provisional appearance. It differs from the old, it is true, in certain respects. These differences have made many people in the ranks of the Labour Party hope that in a crisis analogous to that of 1931 the new leadership would not take the same course as the old. Unfortunately, however, such speculations as to the " sincerity " or " insincerity " of particular leaders are not of much value, for we can never possess any substantial evidence upon which to base them. Let us hope that this expectation is well founded. The present leaders of the Labour Party and Trade Union movement are, however, just as ignorant of, and hostile to, the science of social change as were their predecessors. Hence it is difficult to see what could restrain them from following, in critical circumstances, the incomparably easier path of national solidarity. For unless men have understood the historical process as a whole, as Marx called it; unless they can see the whole picture of determinate capitalist decline to war and tyranny; unless they have become convinced of the impossibility of a new epoch of progress except upon the basis of a socialist economic system, they will have no reasons for resisting the enormous pressure " to take the patriotic course," which must always be exercised upon labour leaders in moments of crisis. Moreover, lacking any conviction that the possibilities of capitalism really are exhausted, and that the time of its abolition has come, such leaders always fear nothing so much as being given the opportunity to abolish capitalism. They fear power, and consciously or unconsciously try to avoid it, instead of trying, as every convinced Marxist must do, to acquire power for the working class by the most resolute and energetic action. For, experience has shown, theoretically qualified leaders alone possess that basis of self-confidence which enables a man to be genuinely practical in those profound crises in which nothing less than the issue of class power is in question.

The world situation which confronts the British working class movement is very different from that of ten years ago.

We have now entered on an epoch of which the leading, dominating characteristic is an accentuated and extreme unevenness between the point of economic and political development reached by different parts of the world: an epoch in which great capitalist empires, in every stage of decay and desperation, or of relative revival and self-satisfaction, are struggling with each other for the remaining pre-capitalist areas; and in which for the first time in history there exists a formidable socialist state. The application of the science of social change to this newest world situation, which is unlike anything ever experienced before, is to-day the vital task of the international working class movement. It will probably become clear that the essential principles of working class policy in this world situation were established at the Seventh Congress of the Communist International in August 1935.

That Congress was able to survey the whole world scene. In large parts of the capitalist world the old controversy as to whether the existing political machinery of democratic capitalism could be used by the workers for the purpose of the transition to socialism, could no longer give rise to division in the ranks of the workers' movement. For that democratic machinery no longer existed. In other parts of the world, such as France and Spain, the efforts of the capitalists to abolish democracy and set up their unlimited and ill-disguised dictatorship was, and is, so undeniable that the necessity for the re-union of the working class movement in sheer self-preservation had become so clear that it was being accomplished. Hence over a large part of the world a situation, in which for the first time the Marxist parties affiliated to the Communist International find themselves able to re-animate, to join in a working alliance, and ultimately to fuse, the other working class parties of their countries, has been brought about by the sheer pressure of circumstances.

This swirling stream of world events is now beginning to have its effect in Great Britain. In less than a year it has set up a remarkably strong current of opinion in favour of the accomplishment of the unity of the British working class movement by the acceptance of the British Communist Party's recent application for affiliation to the Labour Party. As the situation develops, this current of opinion will flow more and more strongly. And it will extend itself to America. Events themselves will convince the workers of Britain and America that peace, liberty, and a relatively tolerable standard of life are becoming more and more incompatible with the existence of capitalism; that, consequently, the sole remaining alternatives are to preserve and immensely improve those advantages by the abolition of capitalism, or to see them perish as they have perished in the greater part of continental Europe.

For the difficulties of British and American capitalism must, in the long run, grow greater and greater. There may well be periods of relative recovery. But Britain and America cannot isolate themselves from the general and world-wide decline of the system. And as capitalism declines, it must attack those three elementary interests of the vast majority of the British and American people, namely, peace, democratic liberty and a relatively high[1] standard of life. This new necessity of capitalism gives the working class movements of Britain and America the opportunity to unite. For those who know that the defence of these simple, vital interests cannot be finally successful unless it results in the abolition of capitalism can unite wholeheartedly in the practical work of defending them with those who believe that the present régime of democratic capitalism can be permanently preserved. For this latter illusion must necessarily be shattered by the development of events.

This, then, is the essential task of those who intend to work for the establishment of socialism in Britain and America. Our duty is to join in the work of raising the activity, militancy and political consciousness of the British and American working class movements to an entirely new level. As and when this task is accomplished everything else will follow. Until it is accomplished, no permanent success can be achieved. All our problems of policy, organization and leadership will become soluble as and when the workers themselves, in sufficient

---

[1] It may seem incredible that the standard of life of the British workers, which we described from official documents in Chapter XXVI (and the American standard is now no higher), is relatively high. But so abominable are the conditions of life of the peoples of the other capitalist states that this is the case.

Ps

numbers, and with sufficient clarity, embark upon a policy of serious and persistent struggle against every aspect of capitalism.

In Britain to-day (1936) new forces assure us that it will be increasingly impossible to prevent the British workers from realizing the nature of the task which faces them. A totally unprecedented number of young workers, of students in the universities, and, for that matter, of men and women of every age, and from every class, are making a serious study of the science of social change. And at the same time the organized Trade Union movement, and the Labour Party, are again pressing forward the eternal demand of workers under capitalism—the demand for life, liberty and the pursuit of happiness—that demand which British capitalism has never met, and never can meet. What is above all necessary is that this renewed, spontaneous and inevitable movement of resistance to capitalism should be infused with a more scientific, and, for that very reason, far more militant, political consciousness than has ever been the case before.

It would be foolish to pretend that we can exactly foresee the particular methods by which this transformation of the British working class movement, so that it may become genuinely capable of establishing socialism in Britain, can be accomplished. We can, however, forsee the broad lines upon which we must work. Both common sense and the reverberating experience of all Europe inform us that nothing effective can be done until the working class forces regain their unity. So long as the leaders of the Labour Party and Trade Union movement exclude the Communist Party, and all organizations connected with it, from full participation in every side of working class activity no decisive advance can be made. In the first place the Communist Party, although still small in numbers, to-day contains, or groups round it, the majority of those devoted, tireless, impassioned men and women who always form the living heart of every working class movement. So long as they are excluded the movement as a whole exists rather than lives. Such a divided movement is necessarily preoccupied with its internal dispute. Its leaders are predominantly engaged in fighting, not the capitalists, but those who could be the greatest strength of the movement. Moreover, the Communist Party

is the embodiment of that new conception of working class
politics which we have striven to explain in these pages. The
Communist Party is the only organized body of persons who
possess a knowledge of the science of social change. So long as it
is excluded from full participation in the life of the movement,
the British workers, as a class, remain in the pre-scientific,
more or less unconscious, stage of their political development.
The necessarily small group of persons who have fought their
way through to a conciousness of the whole historical movement
are cut off from the vast body of the working class, which can
alone actually move. The re-union of the working class with its
most active and advanced members is the pre-requisite of everything else.

Upon this basis of working class unity, experience demonstrates, it is possible to build a wide and powerful movement
of all those whose interests are to-day menaced (whether they
realize it or not) by capitalist imperialism. For capitalist imperialism is to-day unable to avoid war, the drastic curtailment of
liberty and democracy, and a cumulative deterioration in the
standard of life of the whole non-capitalist population. This
triple attack (which capitalism cannot prevent itself from
making) upon the vital interests of at least 90 per cent of the
population inevitably drives millions of men and women, for
the first time, into the struggle against capitalism. But they
do not know, and cannot be quickly taught, that, in working
to preserve such simple necessities as peace, liberty and their
livelihoods, they are fighting capitalism. The necessity for such
formations as those of the People's Front movements arises
from these facts. The second specific task in Britain is the creation of such a movement. (It may, however, be that the achievement of workers' unity and the creation of a People's Front will
in Britain be simultaneous events.)

The creation of movements such as these, whether they are
called, as in Europe, People's Fronts, or as in America, Farmer-
Labour Parties, by means of which the whole non-capitalist
population is able to gather round the nucleus of a united
working class movement, is the need of the hour. By their
creation alone can the Western democracies be saved from
fascism and war. But such movements cannot in themselves

carry through the gigantic task of taking the means of production from the capitalist class and building up a socialist system of production. For they contain large contingents from parties and groups which have not yet realized the necessity of this decisive social transformation. There remains, therefore, an imperative need for a single, united highly organized, highly politically conscious working class party of the specific type defined in these pages. The continuous development of such a party remains the most necessary of all tasks. For capitalism will never be abolished so long as the workers only possess a party of the older type; so long as their party is essentially a loose association, the primary function of which is to secure the return of particular candidates at parliamentary and municipal elections.

A working class party which means business must be a much more closely knit, more active and many-functioned association. It must be capable of leading and inspiring every aspect of the working class struggle against capitalism, of which parliamentary elections are only one particular, though often very important, phase. Such a party must be actively engaged in the inspiration and guidance of the Trade Union struggle, in the development, upon genuinely working class lines, of the co-operative movement, and, last but not least, in the political education of the whole working class. Stalin has summed up the function of such an organization by saying that such political parties must perform for the working class the function which a general staff performs for an army. The phrase is illuminating in that it suggests at once that a working class which persists in possessing *two* or more general staffs, which may issue contradictory orders in the face of the enemy, is not likely to enjoy much success.

In a word, the ultimate object of everyone who, in earnest, desires to work for the abolition of capitalism must be to promote the creation of one unified working class party of the new type. This objective is not in any degree contradictory to the other two. It is but a higher development of an alliance between the working class parties, or, as is proposed in Britain, the affiliation of the smaller ones within the federal structure of a Labour Party. (Indeed negotiations for the fusion of the French Socialist and Communist Parties are taking place while this chapter is being written. And before it was finally passed for the press the fusion of all the Marxist parties of Catalonia, in the fires of the Spanish Civil War, was announced.)

The creation of a single, closely united, and highly organized working class party marks a high stage in the development of a working class movement. Neither the British nor (still less) the American movements have reached this stage. For the creation of such a party to become possible, the whole of the working class movement must have become convinced of the necessity of unflinching struggle against capitalism as the only way to victory and, for that matter, to self-preservation. Such a conviction involves the acceptance and comprehension of that whole new political philosophy, programme and form of organization which we have contrasted with the existing character of the Western working class movements; it involves a thorough-going transformation of these movements.

These, then, so far as they can be discerned to-day, are the next steps to the establishment of socialism in Britain and America. The ending of the present fatal divisions in the ranks of the working class; the attraction to a solid, united, working class movement of all the democratic forces of the country; and finally the evolution of a single, unified working class party of the new type,—these are the three great tasks which we can see immediately before us. We shall make no attempt at any discussion of the complex political problems involved in their accomplishment, both because that is not the function of this book and also because only the general direction which the working class movement must take for the next stage of advance to socialism can be foreseen. Indeed, a hundred new and unexpected events may, and probably will, modify even the line of development suggested here. Still these objectives, namely, working class unity, working class leadership for all the progressive forces of the community, and the development of a single unified working class party of the new type, are almost certainly three pre-requisites for the achievement of socialism in Britain and America.[1]

Even when these objectives have been reached, the walls of

[1] In America the first task is, of course, the drawing into politics of the working class—the creation on the only possible basis, namely of that of mass Trades Unionism, of the simplest form of working class political party. (But see below.)

British and American capitalism will not fall as at a trumpet blast. The process of social change in Britain and America is, on the contrary, certain to be long and arduous. Nor does a knowledge of the science of social change enable us to foretell the exact character of the process; to foretell to what extent it may be violent, or at what point in it our existing, capitalist, political institutions will have to be remodelled. The British and American working class movements will strive with all their might to minimize the degree of violence which will accompany the abolition of capitalism. But they will not do so at the cost of choosing the incomparably greater violence which is certain to accompany the continued existence of British and American capitalist imperialism; nor will they suffer from the peculiar illusion that the violence of the process of social change can be minimized by informing the capitalist class that it has only to resort to force in order to assure its own victory.

I cannot, naturally, discuss the task before the emergent American working class movement with even that degree of fullness attempted in the case of the British movement. A British Marxist may perhaps be permitted to say that its prospects seem to him to compare most favourably with those of the British movement. Just because the American working class movement is still in its embryonic, formative period; just because it has not yet crystallized into a Labour party; just because the trade unions are only now emerging as the essential, indispensable agents of the daily struggle of the American workers for tolerable conditions of life,—American Marxists have an incomparable opportunity to avoid the half-century of errors, divisions, tragedies, and betrayals which in Britain have marked the painful growth of a modern working class movement. The American working class movement is in a stage of development strikingly analogous to that reached by the British movement in the eighteen-eighties. Within the American trades unions a battle is being fought out between the non-political, pro-capitalist craft unionism of the skilled workers, and the inevitably political, and potentially anti-capitalist, industrial unionism of the main mass of the working class. At the time of writing (1936) the craft unions still hold their dominance. The 1935 Convention of the A.F. of L. rejected the programme of industrial unionism and reasserted the power of the leadership of the " old unionism," as it was called in Britain.¹ (The 1889 Congress of the British Trade Union movement held at Dundee had exactly the same result.) It seems certain, however, that in the near future the " New Unionism " of the relatively unskilled American workers, organized on an industrial basis, will become dominant. (In Britain this happened at the Liverpool Congress of the Trade Union movement in 1890.)

Again, it seems certain that, just as in Britain the dominance of the industrial unions led, in about ten years, to the formation of a working class political party, so, and probably a good deal more quickly, the placing of the American trades union movement on a mass, industrial basis will create a Farmer-Labour party based on the Farmer's organizations and the Trades Unions. Such a party, it is to be hoped, will have a broad and federal structure. Thus all working class bodies and organizations will have the opportunity of affiliation to it; in a word, it may perform for America the function which the Labour Party was created to perform in Britain. Such a broad and necessarily loosely organized type of party cannot of course be any substitute for that single, highly organized, fully politically conscious party of the working class which is everywhere indispensable to the victory of the workers and the achievement of socialism. Such a distinctive working class party should take (and in the case of the Communist party of the United States is taking) an active part in the creation of the broader, coalition type of organization, and should grow to maturity as a part of the wider body. In this lies the American opportunity to break away from the British precedent. American Marxists will not commit the horrible errors of the Social Democratic Federation. The American Communist party has always demanded the creation of a Farmer-Labour party. And since 1935 it has made this demand a leading feature of its propaganda. This, as we have

¹ Just before this book was passed for the press, news was received of the expulsion by the A.F. of L. of all those unions intending to operate upon an industrial basis. This monstrous decision will no doubt complicate, and may perhaps even delay, the evolution of the American Labour movement. But it cannot prevent it.

seen, is precisely what the British Marxists of the last century disastrously refused to do. Hence there seems to be a good prospect of the appearance of an American working class movement of which the Marxists will be from the outset an integral part. And if (but only if) American Marxists and communists prove themselves the most practical, most far seeing, most courageous, and most efficient members of the American working class movement, they will gain the right to lead it.

It is no easy task to steer exactly the right course between a sterile sectarianism and the gradual emasculation of the essential principles of the science of social change. Yet this is what Marxists must learn to do. The adoption by the Seventh Congress of the Communist International of a policy of attempting by every possible means to bring about the unity of the working-class movements of the world redoubles the need of American and British Marxists for an unremitting study of the basic principles of their science. Just in so far as their practice becomes more flexible, more sensitive, more realistic, so their need for an unshakable mastery of scientific theory becomes more imperative. Indeed, the exiguous nature of the theoretical equipment of many British and American Marxists was itself one of the principal reasons why they were at one time somewhat inflexible. For only those who are sure that they will not break can dare to bend. It is only as and when British and American Marxists raise their qualifications as political scientists to a high level that they begin to succeed in their enormous, complex and prolonged task.

The science of social change, by revealing the determinate curve of capitalist development, on a world scale and over the centuries, gives us an assurance that in the end socialism will be established throughout the globe. For the only alternative to socialism now before the human race is a decline into a new epoch of barbarism, involving the physical destruction of by far the larger part of the population of such advanced, highly integrated, capitalist civilizations as those of Britain and America. And the British and American people will not allow of their own immolation without ever-growing, and in the end successful, resistance. Thus it is true that the stars in their courses fight for socialism. But we cannot rely upon the stars. It may be that if, confident in our own predictions of inevitability, we did nothing, new generations would arise to accomplish our neglected work. In the long run, it may be, no negligence could prevent the coming of socialism. But, as a liberal *savant* has truly remarked, the one thing certain about the long run is that in the long run we shall all be dead. Hence the starry inevitability of the coming of a socialist civilization is no possible reason for inaction on our part. For only by the most determined action shall we achieve socialism in time to save our lives.

An important object of this book has been to show that a knowledge of the science of social change is indispensable to those who wish to work for the abolition of capitalism and the establishment of socialism. But these pages have striven to recognize the essential paradox at the heart of things; to acknowledge the dialectical converse of every proposition under discussion. Thus, for the accomplishment of social change, knowledge is indispensable, but not enough. It is by the courageous, persistent *action* of those who know, that the world can be remade. By wisdom and courage, by patience and audacity, or not at all, we shall conquer.

BIBLIOGRAPHICAL APPENDIX

" If people could only read . . . ! "—KARL MARX

THE neglect on the part of the British working class movement of the discoveries of Marx and Engels enabled the British governing class almost perfectly to suppress the very knowledge of their existence.

This was one of the most remarkable intellectual boycotts in the history of human thought. For example, for fifty years after their discovery no ray of comprehension of even the simpler Marxist conceptions ever penetrated a British university. During a period when Marxist controversy was shaking the whole intellectual life of Germany and Austria; when the chief task of many continental economists, such as Werner Sombart, was so to dilute Marxism as to reconcile it with capitalist economic thinking; when, on the other hand, the foremost capitalist economist in the world, Böhm-Bawerk, undertook as an urgent task the refutation of the third volume of *Capital* as soon as it appeared; when in the European socialist movement what were, in fact, the anti-Marxist, pro-capitalist forces did not dare openly to reject Marxism, but had to fight to " revise " it,—the British universities remained, in this matter at any rate, as sunk in thoughtless meditation as they had been in the days of Edward Gibbon. Nor, although the world resounds with the deeds and the ideas of Marxists, has that reverie been seriously interrupted even now. During the last few years a few brochures on Marxism, patronising or polemical according to their authors' mood, have appeared from the pens of British professors of economics or philosophy, brochures which have demonstrated, merely, their authors' profound conviction that it was unnecessary to acquaint themselves with the elements of the subject under discussion.[1]

Such indifference to the dominating intellectual controversy of our epoch has something almost heroic about it. It is as if the official representatives of British capitalist culture, feeling their world to crumble about them, had determined to remain true

[1] See, for example, Professor Lindsay's *Marx's Capital* or Professor Joseph's *Karl Marx's Theory of Value*.

to one unchanging precept—come what may we will not think. But even such diehards in the cause of ignorance have not been able to prevent, in the last five years, the infiltration of Marxism into one part of the British universities. The older professors[1] can afford to ignore the one body of knowledge which gives some recognizable account and explanation of the world as it has become beyond the boundaries of court or quadrangle. But the students cannot, for they must soon go out into that world. Hence a considerable number of the students in British universities are now demanding an instruction in Marxism which their professors and lecturers cannot, with the best will in the world, provide. (However, the students often find their own way to a discovery of what Marxism is about.)

The history of Marxist thought in America has been somewhat different. In the latter decades of the last century there was a considerable volume of Marxist thinking in America. But it was not American Marxist thinking. It was essentially the thinking of German immigrants who had brought their Marxism with them. Chicago, because it was the centre of German-Americanism, became the centre of this thinking. To this day several of the basic works of Marxism (including the second and third volumes of *Capital*) are available in English in editions published in Chicago alone. Moreover, it was in Chicago that eight German-American Marxists were murdered by due process of Cook county law for the crime (and it is still a crime in many parts of America) of agitating for better conditions for the working class. And these eight defendants in the great Haymarket trial were, as we may know from their superb speeches from the dock, not only men of unflinching courage unto death, but also instructed Marxists.

With the coming of the golden age of American capitalism in the early decades of the twentieth century this species of exotic, acclimatized Marxism faded away. Marxist thinking reappeared in the war and post-war crises in America, and was kept alive by a devoted but small band of men and women

[1] Some of the younger professors and lecturers at British universities show a very different attitude to Marxism, and may soon acquaint themselves with its principles.

during the nineteen-twenties. With 1929, however, a sudden and startling wave of Marxist thinking, speaking, and writing struck the American intellectual world. With a speed and force impossible anywhere else, Marxism has swept through thinking America. It has already struck roots that can never be pulled up.

Thus in both English-speaking countries the boycott of Marxism has been broken. It is no longer possible for the spokesmen of capitalism to ignore Marxism. They are compelled to fight it. And for them, that is the beginning of the end. The approach to Marxism is still a relatively unfrequented path, however. Hence a few directing posts, set up by someone who, like myself, has had to force his way through many a thicket of prejudice and preconception, may possibly serve a useful purpose.

Marx once remarked that the value of commodities was like Mistress Quickly, " of whom Falstaff said ' a man knows not where to have her.' " Much the same problem confronts the student of the science of social change. His difficulty is where to begin.

True, the principles of the science are embodied in the works of Marx, Engels, Lenin, and Stalin, plus the various statements, resolutions, and programmes of the Communist International. But neither Marx, Engels, Lenin, nor Stalin ever undertook a formal, textbook, presentation of the science. This omission was deliberate. For not only were they themselves working out the basic principles of the science of social change, but this science was not, they always maintained, of such a kind as to make possible any form of textbook presentation. To attempt any such thing would be to ossify, and so misrepresent, their whole point of view. The way to present the science, they considered, was by its continual application to, and exemplification by, the political and economic problems which confronted the working class.

The nearest thing to a popular introduction to the science was given us by that supreme master of lucid exposition, Friedrich Engels. For his sustained polemic against Dühring almost amounts to this. But the *Anti-Dühring* begins with fifty odd pages of abstruse and abstract philosophical controversy.

Hence it will hardly serve, especially for British and American readers, as a general introduction to the subject.[1] Serviceable introductions to Marxism do not, then, exist. It is necessary for the student to tackle at once the individual works of Marx and Engels, each of which deals with a particular aspect of the science.

Where, then, should one start ? It is not, I think, possible to answer this question in the same way for every reader. A man's initial point of contact with Marxism must depend on his experience of life, his education and his interests. Thus, an undergraduate of a university will certainly be drawn to one point of contact with Marxism, while an experienced Trade Unionist working at the bench will be drawn to another. The former will probably go to the historical aspects of the science, the latter to Marx's basic elucidation of the economics of the capitalist process of production.

We must make suggestions for both types of readers. For the middle-class reader, then, if he or she has a working knowledge of European history in the nineteenth century, I make this recommendation—*begin with the historical pamphlets*. In particular, the following four pamphlets by Marx are brilliantly written, exciting and illuminating. They form one of the very best introductions to Marxism.

The Class Struggle in France (1848–50). (Lawrence & Wishart. 1934. 3s. 6d.)

Engels began an introduction to a new edition of this pamphlet, published in the nineties, with these words: " This newly republished work was Marx's first attempt, with the aid of his materialist conception, to explain a section of contemporary history from the given economic situation." This pamphlet is the first scientific analysis of a revolution. It tells the story of the French revolution of 1848 in the one way that can make the succession of events comprehensible. Moreover, the pamphlet is witty, vigorous, dashing, brilliant. Marxism here goes into action with all its colours flying.

The afore-mentioned introduction by Engels is a document of

[1] There exists a shorter version of this book, under the title of *Socialism, Utopian and Scientific*, which is in many ways a good point of departure. (See p. 469 below.)

great importance. In the first place, it shows admirably how the working class struggle must be adapted, *within certain strict limits*, to the conditions of time and place: it shows how Marx and Engels were fully aware of the necessity of periods of consolidation and political and industrial organization. More, it shows that Engels hoped passionately that the transit of society from a capitalist to a socialist basis would be effected in the most peaceful manner that was possible. In the second place, it shows, not so much in itself as in its history, how the little men who took charge of the German working class movement at the end of the last century transformed this precept of Engels into the rejection of all methods of struggle other than the ballot-box. For the meaning of this introduction was deliberately distorted when it was published by them in the nineties by the omission of all those sentences in which Engels was careful to point out that, much as the workers would like to take power by peaceful means, there was no recorded example of the capitalist class allowing itself to be superseded without resorting to unrestrained violence in an effort to maintain or restore its position.

Hence with this work the reader is plunged, not only into the Marxist interpretation of events, but also into the interpretation of Marxism. He is enabled to see the lengths to which men have been willing to go to take the revolutionary sting out of the science of social change.

The 18th Brumaire of Louis Napoleon. (Allen & Unwin. 1926. 2*s.* 6*d.*)

This is an account of the *coup d'état* by which Napoleon III made himself dictator of France in 1851. It gives a close analysis of the interplay of class forces which enabled him to do so. It overlaps with *The Class Struggle in France*, but takes the story forward another two years. It is especially striking to-day because it was the first Marxist analysis of a movement which, while it was not Fascist in the modern sense of that word, was analogous to Fascism in that it was a temporarily successful attempt of the governing class to suppress a workers' revolution by a combination of ruthless violence and reckless social demagogy and deceit.

The Civil War in France, by Marx. (Lawrence & Wishart. 1*s*. and 2*s*. 6*d*.)

Here Marx takes up French history again at the moment of its next great crisis. He gives a devastating account of the rule of the reaction in France between 1852 and 1870, under the crowned dictator Napoleon III. Then with burning passion (he was writing within two days of the fall of the Commune) he describes the revolt of the working class of Paris and the establishment of the Commune, after the *débâcle* of the Empire in the Franco-Prussian war. Marx's essential conclusion is that here for the first time in history a modern working class held power, although only for a few weeks. Hence it was for the first time possible to make the deduction that the workers cannot simply take over the existing capitalist state apparatus: that they must abolish that apparatus and create a new one of their own.

The Communist Manifesto, by Marx and Engels. (Lawrence & Wishart. 3*d*. and 6*d*.)

This first summary of Marxism was discussed above (Chapter XXXI). But the *Communist Manifesto* is also a great historical pamphlet; together with the other three it gives the reader a picture of Marx's and Engels' outlook on the events of their youth and early manhood.

After reading the historical pamphlets one must tackle the main works in which the basic principles of the science were originally announced. Here is a list of the most important of them, under the three heads of economic, philosophical, and political works.

ECONOMIC WORKS BY MARX AND ENGELS[1]

The Poverty of Philosophy, by Marx. (Lawrence & Wishart. 2*s*. 6*d*.)

A reply to the French socialist, Proudhon, who had written a book called *The Philosophy of Poverty*. It is important in the sense that Marx here for the first time begins the exposition of distinctive economic views. But the polemical approach is confusing, although lively. On the whole a book to come back to

---

[1] These are not complete lists—but they are perhaps enough to go on with

when the main body of Marx's economic thinking has been mastered.

A Contribution to the Critique of Political Economy, by Marx. (Kerr. 6s. Lawrence & Wishart have an edition in preparation.)

This is a sort of first draft of the early chapters of *Capital*; hence many people may feel inclined not to worry with it to begin with. But, especially for those who have been taught capitalist economics, this book is very valuable. For, as its title states, it is a criticism of existing, capitalist, economic science. Hence the reader is able to see how Marx approached economic problems, and to realize how carefully he mastered the whole existing body of economic knowledge before surpassing it. Moreover, it has two other important things in it. First, it contains a more detailed treatment of money than does Vol. I of *Capital,* which those specially interested in money should not neglect. Marx's essential discoveries on money are contained, however, in Vol. III of *Capital,* Part V. No student of money should omit the study of this great and neglected analysis. Second, the *Critique of Political Economy* has as a preface the best-known definition of the Materialist Conception of History. But personally I have always found the passage obscure and unhelpful. I much prefer Engels' account in *Ludwig Feuerbach* and in the *Marx-Engels Correspondence.* (See Chapter XXVIII of this book.)

Wage, Labour and Capital, by Marx. (Lawrence & Wishart. 4d.)
Value, Price and Profit, by Marx. (Allen & Unwin. 1s.)

These two pamphlets are the best introduction to Marxism for workers. They should read them first. For they explain with extreme directness and simplicity just how the capitalist system works to the advantage of the capitalist and to the disadvantage of the worker.

Capital, by Marx, Vol. I. (Kerr. 10s. 6d. Dents, Everyman edition, in two volumes. 4s.) Vols. II and III. (Kerr. 10s. 6d. a volume.)

It is no use pretending that to tackle *Capital* is not a big job.

But it is always worth mastering one of the two or three books which have changed the history of the world. The main difficulty in *Capital* is the first hundred pages of Vol. I, which are really obscure. Readers are sometimes recommended to start at the end with the historical chapter on primary accumulation. But I am not sure that to do so does not create more difficulties than it avoids. Perhaps the best way is to begin at the beginning, but not to let oneself be held up by obscurities. During a first reading of *Capital* one should push resolutely on, like an invading army which leaves behind untaken such enemy strongpoints as do not fall at the first attack, confident that it can turn round and deal with them at leisure when the whole country has been occupied.

The obscurity of Part I of *Capital* has been, however, an historical disaster. It must have deterred many thousands of potential readers. Nor is all of this obscurity due to the inherent difficulty of the subject matter. It is interesting to notice that Engels attributed it to Marx's ill-health at the time he was writing. The unfortunate Marx was suffering from carbuncles, the result, no doubt, of the grinding poverty in which he and his whole family were plunged. Engels was reading the proofs of *Capital* in Manchester and writes to Marx on June 16th, 1867, that the early chapters bear " rather strong marks of the carbuncles, but that cannot be altered now. . . . At most, the points here established dialectically might be demonstrated historically at rather greater length, the test to be made from history, so to speak. . . . In the abstract developments you have committed the great mistake of not making the sequence of thought clear by a larger number of small sections and separate headings. . . . It is a great pity that it should be just the important second sheet which suffers from the carbuncle imprint." In reply Marx says, " . . . at any rate I hope the bourgeoisie will remember my carbuncles all the rest of their lives." But unfortunately it has not been the bourgeoisie, but us, his sweating, toiling readers, who have had cause to remember those carbuncles !

As to Vols. II and III, the only needful recommendation is the simple one to read them—not to suppose that Vol. I completes the work. Vol. III in particular is essential to an understanding of Marx's structure of economic thought. Engels, in

a letter to Adler, written to the latter on his imprisonment
(*Marx-Engels Correspondence*, p. 532), writes: " As you want
to have a grind in prison at *Capital*, Volumes II and III, I will
give you a few hints to make it easier," and proceeds to give
detailed recommendations which one may or may not find
useful.

Theories of Surplus Value.

This is the fourth volume of *Capital*, published, like Vols. II
and III, posthumously, but edited by Kautsky instead of
Engels. Marx described it as " the history of political economy
from the middle of the seventeenth century." I have not read
it, and it has never been translated into English. But I am
informed by Mr. Maurice Dobb that it is of the highest interest
to anyone who really cares for economics.

POLITICAL AND HISTORICAL WORKS BY MARX AND ENGELS

The Origin of the Family, Private Property and the State, by
    Engels. (Kerr. 2s. 6d. Lawrence & Wishart have an edition
    in preparation.)

This is one of the most important, and least read, of all the
Marxist classics. Indeed, it would not be at all a bad book to
start on. It lays down the basic political conceptions of the
science. No one who has not read it can properly understand
the central political idea of Marxism, viz. the conception of the
state.

The Conditions of the Working Class in England, by Engels.
    (Allen & Unwin. 5s.)

Engels' first work. It remains the only thorough and unflinching account of the conditions of the life of the British workers
before the great surge forward of British capitalism from 1850
onwards. It is also the first work to show clearly why the working class must be the chief agent of social change. (Although
Engels, in a preface which he wrote to a new edition at the end
of his life, considered that it did not show the working-class
character of socialism and communism with sufficient clarity.)

The Housing Question, by Engels. (Lawrence & Wishart. 2s. 6d.)
An explanation of why the housing shortage is never abolished
under capitalism.

The Peasant War in Germany, by Engels. (Allen & Unwin. 4s. 6d.)
Engels' chief historical work.

Critique of the Gotha Programme, by Marx. (Lawrence & Wishart.
3s. 6d. and 2s.)
This is an extremely important work, though it is very brief.
It contains the essential passages in which Marx clearly indicated
how he thought socialist distribution would be, and should be,
arranged. (See Chapter IX of this book.) Besides this, it deals
with several other vitally important aspects of the strategy,
tactics, aims, and principles of a working class movement. Contemporary British and American readers must on no account
allow themselves to be confused by the fact that it was written
as a criticism of a now-forgotten programme of the German
Social Democrats.

Then there are many more historical pamphlets, besides the
four which I have suggested as an introduction to the whole
science. Of these the most considerable is:

Germany: Revolution and Counter Revolution, by Engels.
(Lawrence & Wishart. 2s. 6d.)

NOTE.—Books published by Kerr should be obtainable at all
booksellers and are obtainable at all left wing bookshops, such as
the Workers' Bookshop, 16 King Street, London, W.C.2, and
the People's Bookshops now established in most towns.

PHILOSOPHIC WORKS BY MARX AND ENGELS

A Critique of the Hegelian Philosophy of Right,[1] by Marx.
The Holy Family, by Marx and Engels.
German Ideology,[2] by Marx and Engels.
I put these three together because they are all early philosophical works and none of them are available in English. We
may hope to have them soon, however. Some extremely important passages from them are now available in *Dialectics*, by

---

[1] Extracts available in *Marx on the Jewish Question*. (Lawrence & Wishart. 2s. 6d.)
[2] Extracts from this work are contained in *A Handbook of Marxism*. (Gollancz.)

T. A. Jackson (Lawrence & Wishart. 10s. 6d.). (This is itself an invaluable work of exposition.) In these three early works of Marx and Engels can be traced the genesis of the Marxist outlook on the world.

Ludwig Feuerbach, by Engels. (Lawrence & Wishart. 2s. 6d.)

This superb monograph contains the best elucidations of the materialist conception of history. Moreover, it contains as an appendix Marx's famous " Theses on Feuerbach," of which Engels writes: " These are notes hurriedly scribbled down for later elaboration, absolutely not intended for publication, but they are invaluable as the first document in which is deposited the brilliant germ of the new world outlook."

Dialectics of Nature, by Engels. (Lawrence & Wishart have an edition in preparation.)

Not yet available in English and unknown to me. Said to be Engels' most important discussion of the application of dialectical materialism to science.

GENERAL WORKS

Herr Eugen Dühring's Revolution in Science, by Engels. (Lawrence & Wishart. 5s.)

This is the nearest thing to a general, popular introduction to the science of social change which either of its founders ever undertook. And, if the reader can get over the extremely subtle and obscure philosophizing with which it begins, and also the rather knock-about controversy with Dühring (see p. 211 of this book) which runs right through it, he should begin with it. In any event, no student of Marxism can possibly neglect it. On a dozen particular points it contains the best statement of the Marxist view which has ever been made.

Socialism, Utopian and Scientific, by Engels. (Allen & Unwin. 3s. 6d. and 2s. 6d.)

This is the afore-mentioned abbreviated version of the *Anti-Dühring.* The more abstract philosophical parts are left out, and an exceedingly witty preface by Engels is added. This is a third admirable way into Marxism. (The four historical pamphlets, and the two economic pamphlets, being the other two.)

Marx-Engels Correspondence. A Selection with Commentary and Notes. (Lawrence & Wishart. 5s.)

This selection from the innumerable letters which Marx and Engels wrote to each other (with a good many letters to third parties added) is one of the major, fundamental works of Marxism. Marx and Engels kept up a running commentary, both on current public events and on their theoretical work, which will always remain one of the greatest correspondences that have ever been published. Almost all the letters make brilliant and delightful reading. As, of course, they take a good deal for granted, one should not, I think, begin on them. But at some point every student will certainly want to read them.

These, then, are the main works of Marx and Engels in which, taken as a whole, the basic principles of the science of social change are laid down. Now we come to the development of these principles in order to keep them abreast of developing reality, a development predominantly undertaken by Lenin.

The three essential works of Lenin are *Imperialism, The State and Revolution,* and *What is To Be Done ?*

WORKS BY LENIN

Imperialism: The Highest Stage of Capitalism, by Lenin. (Lawrence & Wishart. 1s. 6d.)

It is by no means easy reading. The first half contains many facts and figures on the tendency to monopoly of pre-war German capitalism and the inevitable connection of imperialist expansion and industrial development. Far more striking facts and figures could be now produced from the history of post-war capitalism; hence the reader is apt to become impatient. Gradually, however, the theme of the book emerges, and the reader is convinced of the real economic causes of war. No one who has not mastered this book can understand the world in which he lives.

The State and Revolution, by Lenin. (Lawrence & Wishart. 1s.)

This is the application to contemporary reality of the basic political principles contained in Engels' *Origin of the Family, Private Property and the State.* It is the central refutation of the view of the non-Marxist and pseudo-Marxist spokesmen in the working class movement that it is possible to go from capitalism to socialism in the economic sphere without a corresponding transformation in the political sphere, without, to be precise, ending the rule of the capitalists and establishing the rule of the workers. Moreover, it shows that the workers cannot simply take over the existing apparatus of government as used by the capitalists. They inevitably have to abolish this apparatus and create a new one of their own.

What is To Be Done ? by Lenin. (Lawrence & Wishart. 2*s*.)

The supreme importance of this book is that it contains Lenin's project for a working class party in the new, twentieth-century sense of that term, which we have tried to define in these pages. The problems of the working class movement are not exactly the same as they were when Lenin wrote nearly forty years ago. For the workers do now possess in almost every country the essential core of a working class party of the new type. Hence the need is now for the workers to develop their parties ; while, at the time Lenin wrote, it was only possible to project the creation of such parties. Historically the book is of profound interest in that it contains Lenin's original (and never abandoned) plan of how to overthrow the Tsarist régime. It shows that Lenin thought out exactly what he wanted to do, how he was going to do it, and then did it.

Materialism and Empirio-Criticism. (Lawrence & Wishart. 10*s*. 6*d*.)

This is Lenin's main philosophical work. Downright blunt, effective, its immediate aim was to prevent, as it succeeded in doing, Russian Marxists, discouraged after the suppression of the revolution of 1905, from putting all their emphasis on the dialectical method, derived from idealist philosophy, and forgetting about the materialist basis of dialectical materialism. Its main significance, however, is not Russian but world-wide. It was a heavy blow at that whole tendency towards the revision, in the sense of the emasculation, of Marxism which, as we noticed in Chapter XXXIII, swept over Europe in the pre-war period. As this tendency, especially in the field of philosophy, ever recurrent, it is a book of high and permanent importance. But it is no use tackling it until one has got a good grasp of the philosophical questions at issue.

The Teachings of Karl Marx. (Workers' Bookshop. 2*d.*)

Lenin wrote this essay for an encyclopædia. It contains a short life of Marx, a summary of his teachings and a bibliography. This is the classical summary of Marxism as a science. It is, however, extremely compressed, and I very much doubt if much can be got out of reading it *before* reading Marx's and Engels' own works. (In any case, I know that I could make nothing of it in these circumstances.) But *after* the original works have been read, Lenin's summary becomes invaluable in that it throws every essential point into high relief.

Two pamphlets, both written after Lenin had become head of the Soviet Government, are also of the highest importance.

The Proletarian Revolution and Kautsky the Renegade. (Lawrence & Wishart. 1*s.* 6*d.*)

This is Lenin's reply to an attack on the Soviet Government's alleged suppression of democracy. This attack was made in the years immediately following the Russian Revolution by the leaders of the socialist parties in Western Europe. Kautsky, the leading German Social Democratic thinker, had published a pamphlet called *The Dictatorship of the Proletariat.* Lenin's reply should be read in conjunction with his *State and Revolution,* to which it is in a sense a sequel. It is extremely interesting to read these two pronouncements of the leader of the first successful workers' revolution, the one written immediately before, and the other soon after, power had been won. The argument of the pamphlet is, essentially, that revolutionary experience had confirmed Marx's and Engels' view that, so long as classes exist, one class will be on the top of the other, dictating to it, and that consequently it is idle to talk of an abstract democracy in which capitalists and workers share alike.

Left-Wing Communism: An Infantile Disorder. (Lawrence & Wishart. 1*s.*)

This pamphlet in a sense completes Lenin's life-work in developing Marxism and applying it to the twentieth-century world.

Having fought out the struggle with the various breeds of revisionist and anti-revolutionary Marxists, he had at the end of his life to turn round and combat the opposite tendency. He had to try to prevent those men and women who had remained true to the working class cause, during the years of betrayal, from cutting themselves off from the main working class movements of their respective countries by a sectarian, unselective, ill-considered attitude of " ultra-leftism." For such an attitude, however natural and inevitable it might be as a reaction from the collapse of the official leaders of the working class movements before the prospect of a struggle for power, was evidently disastrous.

These books and pamphlets are but a very small part of Lenin's writings. The bulk of the rest consists of innumerable occasional articles and speeches. To read through these comments of Lenin's on the events of his time; to mark his unfailing power to react powerfully and accurately to almost literally everything that happened in Europe, from a one-day strike in a Russian textile mill, to the outbreak of the world war,—is to receive the maximum degree of political education which one can receive from reading books. Messrs. Lawrence & Wishart have now published a Selected Works in twelve volumes (six volumes only issued as yet) as well as their large Collected Works in thirty volumes of which only eight volumes are as yet available.

STALIN

Leninism. (Vol. I. Allen & Unwin. 12s. 6d. Vol. II. Allen & Unwin. 10s. 6d. Modern Books. 5s.)

This is Stalin's most important and considered pronouncement on political theory. Stalin is intent to show that Lenin did not merely rediscover and reapply Marxism to the problems of the twentieth century, but made " a further development of Marxism." Moreover, this further development is applicable to the whole twentieth-century world and not merely to Russia.

The book also contains a description of the new type of political party which the working class must create if it is to conquer power. Such a party, Stalin writes, must be much more than the loosely knit electoral machine which the socialist

parties of Western Europe had become. It must be, in Stalin's
phrase, " the general staff of the working class."

Marxism and the National and Colonial Question, by Stalin.
(Lawrence & Wishart. 2s. 6d.)

This is Stalin's main pronouncement on a subject which he
had made especially his own, namely the relationship of the
spontaneous struggle of peoples oppressed by one or another of
the great empires (as his own Georgian people had been oppressed by the Tsarist Empire) and the struggle of the working
class against the capitalist class.

The October Revolution. (Lawrence & Wishart. 2s. 6d.)

This work is to-day of especial interest in view of the recent
(1936) trial of the remaining adherents of Trotsky in the Soviet
Union.

The International Situation, August 1927. (The Communist
International, October 1927.)

The most interesting section of this speech is Stalin's discussion of communist tactics in China. (This section is printed in
A Handbook of Marxism; see below.)

Stalin Reports on the Soviet Union. (Lawrence & Wishart. 2d.)

This important statement covers two fields. First, it sums up
the communist estimation of the world-wide crisis of capitalism,
and of the intensification of that *general* crisis which had been
occasioned by the extreme, cyclical, *economic* crisis from which
the capitalist world was in 1934 just emerging. Second, it sums
up the progress made by the Soviet Union in the First Five
Year Plan.

Address to the Graduates from the Red Army Academy. (Available
in book form in *A Handbook of Marxism*.) Delivered May
14th, 1935.

This is the first of a remarkable series of speeches which Stalin
delivered during the year 1935. They mark the conquest of the
early difficulties and dangers which had marked the establishment of a planned system of production for use in the Soviet
Union. They usher in a stage of extremely rapid economic

development, and a shifting of stress from quantity of production to quality of production. Stalin emphasizes that it is now possible and necessary to pay greater attention to the quality of the life which men lead in a socialist society. Stalin delivered two further speeches of great interest during 1935, namely that delivered to the Stakhanovites (quoted in Chapter XI) and that delivered to the Women Collective Farmers.

It remains to draw the reader's attention to *A Handbook of Marxism*, edited by Emile Burns. (Victor Gollancz. 5s.) This book consists of well-chosen extracts from most of the works listed above. Nobody must suppose that a reading of these extracts is a substitute for reading the works themselves. Still, as few people can afford to possess all the Marxist classics themselves, and so must depend on obtaining them from libraries, etc., the *Handbook* is a most useful possession for reference, consultation, and re-reading.

This Bibliography is confined to the works of Marx, Engels, Lenin, and Stalin. For it is quite impossible to enter the enormous field of working class and socialist literature which now exists in English. One may, perhaps, make an exception in favour of Mehring's classical and beautiful biography of Marx, for this book is essential to an understanding of how and when the Marxist classics were written. It is *Karl Marx*: A Biography. (John Lane. 1936. 15s.)

INDEX